ETHICAL REPORTING OF SENSITIVE TOPICS

Ethical Reporting of Sensitive Topics explores the underlying complexities that journalists may face when covering difficult news stories. Reporting on issues such as suicide, sexual abuse, or migration is a skill that is often glossed over in a journalist's education. By combining theory and practice, this collection will correct this oversight and give journalists the expertise and understanding to report on these subjects responsibly and ethically.

Contributors to this volume are an international group of journalists-turned-academics, who share their first-hand experiences and unique professional insight into best ethical journalistic practice for reporting on sensitive topics. Drawing from a range of case studies, contributors discuss the most appropriate approach to, for example, describing a shooter who has killed a group of schoolchildren or interviewing someone who has lost everything in a natural disaster. Readers are invited to consider factors which have the potential to influence the reporting of these sorts of topics, including bias, sensationalism, conflict of interest, grief, vulnerability, and ignorance of one's own privilege.

Ethical Reporting of Sensitive Topics aims to support *all* journalists, from students of journalism and individuals encountering a newsroom for the first time, to those veteran journalists or specialist journalists who seek to better their reporting skills.

Ann Luce is a Principal Academic in Journalism and Communication at Bournemouth University, UK. She worked for nearly ten years in journalism in the United States. She is author of *The Bridgend Suicides: Suicide and the Media* (2016), and editor of *Midwifery, Childbirth and the Media* (2017). She currently sits on the World Media Task Force for the Reporting of Suicide.

ETHICAL REPORTING OF SENSITIVE TOPICS

Edited by Ann Luce

Routledge
Taylor & Francis Group

LONDON AND NEW YORK

First published 2019
by Routledge
2 Park Square, Milton Park, Abingdon, Oxon OX14 4RN

and by Routledge
52 Vanderbilt Avenue, New York, NY 10017

Routledge is an imprint of the Taylor & Francis Group, an informa business

British Library Cataloguing-in-Publication Data
A catalogue record for this book is available from the British Library

Library of Congress Cataloging-in-Publication Data
A catalog record has been requested for this book

ISBN: 978-0-8153-4865-8 (hbk)
ISBN: 978-0-8153-4866-5 (pbk)
ISBN: 978-1-351-16632-4 (ebk)

Typeset in Bembo
by Deanta Global Publishing Services, Chennai, India

Printed and bound in Great Britain by
TJ International Ltd, Padstow, Cornwall

For my greatest teachers:
Kevin Bingham, Dr Berrin Beasley and Dr Robert Bohle

And for Billy,
my greatest champion, support, and editor

CONTENTS

ILLUSTRATIONS

Figure

Tables

CONTRIBUTORS

Lyn Barnes is a senior lecturer at Auckland University of Technology in Auckland, New Zealand. Lyn has worked in all areas of the media, from print and radio, television news and current affairs, to magazines as a writer and editor. While in academia, she has written extensively on covering day-to-day trauma as a domestic journalist and developed role-playing exercises for her students, which involve professional actors playing the role of victims. This gives students the opportunity to practise interviewing people who are grieving. The actors are skilled at giving constructive feedback and all the students find the exercise valuable for their interviewing skills in general. The theory of balance in trauma journalism was the result of her PhD thesis. A chapter – related to journalists and emotions – was published in *Ethical Space* in 2017. The peer reviewer recommended that it should be called Barnes' theory and used in university journalism classrooms to explore what journalists do, how they are expected to behave in newsrooms, and to open up a wide discussion on professionalism. She is hoping it will.

Mathew Charles is a senior lecturer in journalism and documentary at Bournemouth University, UK. He is an award-winning filmmaker, journalist, and author who has worked extensively on urban violence and the so-called drugs war of Latin America. In 2014, his film *The Engineer*, which paints an intimate portrait of El Salvador's only criminologist, was nominated for Best Documentary at the Hotdocs festival in Toronto and was broadcast on television channels across Europe. The interactive version of the film was awarded the New Media Writing Prize "Audience Choice" Award in 2013. Charles's stories from Colombia, where he is now based, include a two-year investigation into modern slavery and other human rights abuses by the country's neo-paramilitaries in the Bajo Cauca region. This was published by *The Guardian* in 2018. Charles has had unprecedented access to the *Urabeños* criminal network as demonstrated by his investigation *Inside Colombia's*

BACRIM. He has also reported for the BBC, *The Globe and Mail* and Agence France Presse from across Latin America. As an academic, Charles investigates urban violence in Mexico and Central America's Northern Triangle (Honduras, Guatemala, and El Salvador), as well as post-conflict Colombia. His PhD thesis examines theories of citizenship in relation to victims, perpetrators, and journalists living and working in what he describes as the "alternative social disorder" of Colombia's "after war".

Chris Frost is emeritus professor of Journalism at Liverpool John Moores University, UK, where he was head of department. He has been a journalist, editor, and journalism educator for more than 45 years working mainly in newspapers before his move into the academy. He is a former chair of the Association for Journalism Education, which represents virtually all HE journalism departments in the UK and Ireland. He is an executive board member of the Institute of Communication Ethics and co-editor of *Journalism Education*. He sits on the editorial boards of *Ethical Space*, the *Australian Journal of Journalism Research*, and *Journalism and Discourse Studies*. He sits on the National Executive Committee of the National Union of Journalists and has been chair of the union's Ethics Council for many years and is also a National Council member of the Campaign for Press and Broadcasting Freedom. He is a former president of the National Union of Journalists and a former member of the UK Press Council. He has written several books about journalism: *Journalism Ethics and Regulation* (fourth edition, 2015); *Designing for Newspapers and Magazines* (second edition, 2011); *Reporting for Journalists* (second edition, 2010); and *Media Ethics and Self-Regulation* (2000), as well as many book chapters and papers on journalism ethics and regulation. He also gave evidence to the Leveson Inquiry for the National Union of Journalists.

Amanda Gearing is an investigative journalist, author, broadcaster, and academic author. She has enjoyed a long and distinguished career as a reporter in Australia and the UK. She has written for News Limited publications in Australia and Britain and has made radio documentaries for *ABC Radio National* in Australia. Her reporting for *The Courier Mail* from 1997–2007 earned several state and national media awards. In 2012 she won Australia's most prestigious media award, a Walkley Award for Best Radio Documentary for her documentary *The Day That Changed Grantham*. Amanda completed her Master of Arts (Research) in 2012 and her Doctor of Philosophy, in 2016, both at Queensland University of Technology in Australia. In 2017 she published a new edition of her 2012 book, *The Torrent: A True Story of Heroism and Survival*. Amanda also writes for *The Guardian* in Britain and Australia.

Glynn Greensmith is a lecturer in journalism at Curtin University in Perth, Western Australia, but is originally from the UK. He is also a broadcaster for ABC Radio, having been a journalist and producer for the Australian public broadcaster since 2005. He is currently researching the reporting of mass shootings for his

PhD thesis. A previous article on the issue has been published in the journal *Ethical Space*, as well as separate journalism articles in *Fairfax*, *Crikey*, and *The Walkley Magazine*. He has presented his work on mass shootings to the World Journalism Education Congress; has hosted a panel on mass shooting coverage at the Journalism Education and Research Association of Australasia, and presented preliminary findings and discussions on ABC television, to The Australian Press Council, and on ABC Editorial Policies. He studied journalism at Nottingham Trent University in England. In his free time, he likes talking about anything but mass shootings.

John Lister has been a journalist for over 40 years, and specialised in reporting on health services for 34 years. John founded and edited 73 issues of *Health Emergency* newspaper and worked extensively with national and local news media, and at local and national level with health trade unions. He completed a PhD on health system reforms at Coventry University, UK, in 2004, before taking on a part-time position teaching journalism there. He went on to develop an MA course in health journalism, and in that capacity became involved with the EU-funded six-country Health Reporter Training project (Project HeaRT), and in Coventry organised two successful international conferences on health journalism. The second of these resulted in a 300-page edited e-book on health journalism, *First Do No Harm*. He is also author of *Health Policy Reform, Driving the Wrong Way* (2005) and *The NHS at 60: for Patients or Profits* (2008), the most up-to-date history of the NHS in the UK; he also won a Medical Journalists Association Award for this work. He is a proud member of the National Union of Journalists, vice president of the International Association of Health Policy in Europe, as well as editor of *Health Campaigns Together* newspaper and website.

Jeremaiah Opiniano is an assistant professor of Journalism at the University of Santo Tomas in Manila, Philippines. He has reported on international migration issues for a Philippine non-profit news service called the Overseas Filipino Workers Journalism Consortium or OFWJC (www.ofwjournalism.org, a group which he co-founded in 2002), with a focus on overseas Filipinos and global migration issues affecting Filipinos. In 2003, the OFW Journalism Consortium published a reporters' guidebook entitled *Philippine Migration Journalism: A Practical Handbook*. Jeremaiah is currently taking a PhD (by research) in Geography at The University of Adelaide in Adelaide, Australia. Jeremaiah is also publisher of a hyperlocal news group, *The Filipino Connection* (www.thefilipinoconnection.net), which writes economic stories for residents for a city south of the Philippine capital Manila, called Lipa City.

Hilary Stepien is a lecturer in Public Relations at Bournemouth University, UK. After obtaining an MSc in Public Relations at the University of Stirling, she gained experience in public affairs and strategic communication while working in Cabinet Office and the Ministry of Transportation for the Government of Ontario in Toronto, Canada. Hilary's teaching and research interests lie mainly in health communication, particularly where there is a social dimension. For example, she is particularly interested in communication around health conditions that are stigmatised and/or taboo. At present, Hilary's research focuses on news and public relations discourses in the context of competing "truth claims" around vaccines.

Shelley Thompson is a senior lecturer in the Faculty of Media and Communication at Bournemouth University, UK. She is a science journalism scholar, specialising in the reporting of emerging and controversial science. Her current research considers the under-representation of women's voices in news debates about STEMM, following her intervention at the UN Conference on Women and Girls in Science and the Role of the Media in February 2017. Shelley is a former US journalist who worked at a variety of publications covering finance and securities regulation in New York City to politics, education, crime, and health at the two-time Pulitzer Prize winning Eagle-Tribune in its New Hampshire bureau.

Alex Wake is a senior lecturer in Melbourne, Australia, at RMIT University, located on the land of the Wurundjeri people of the Kulin nation. In production of the work for this edited collection, Alex acknowledges the Elders of the land, past, present, and emerging. Alex has been a journalism academic for 15 years, focusing on broadcast and innovative journalism technologies. Her research is centred on journalism education in cultures outside advanced liberal democracies. She has developed a number of resources for journalism students working cross-culturally. Alex worked in Ireland, South Africa, and the United Arab Emirates for a number of newspapers and then as a senior journalist and editor with the Australian Broadcasting Corporation. Alex commenced her teaching career training journalists at the South African Broadcasting Corporation after the election of Nelson Mandela in the transition to democracy, and was later employed as a journalism educator at Dubai Women's College in the United Arab Emirates at the time of 9/11. Many of Alex's research and teaching projects are aimed at improving journalists' understanding of how to work with people from other cultures and improving the portrayal of multicultural and Indigenous Australian groups in the media. Her work acknowledges the value to society of journalists reporting upon traumatic events, and is concerned that media professionals are actively encouraged to protect their mental health while working on these stories.

Kim Walsh-Childers is a former newspaper health reporter who has taught at the University of Florida, USA, since August 1990. She received her undergraduate degree from the University of Missouri-Columbia and her master's and PhD from the University of North Carolina-Chapel Hill. Her research focuses on news coverage of health issues and mass media effects on individual health and health policy. In 2004–2005, she served as a Fulbright Scholar in Ireland, teaching journalism ethics at the Dublin Institute of Technology School of Media and conducting research on the influence of news coverage on Irish health policy development. Her work also has been supported by grants from the Kaiser Family Foundation, the Robert Wood Johnson Foundation, the National Cancer Institute and the US Department of Defense. Her 2017 book, *Mass Media and Health: Examining Media Impact on Individuals and the Health Environment*, helps readers understand how media content, whether intentionally or unintentionally, can influence individuals' health beliefs and subsequent behaviours; in addition, it is one of the few texts to carefully document the research on media influences on health policy. At UF, Walsh-Childers has taught undergraduate courses in newswriting, magazine and feature-writing, journalism ethics and solutions journalism; at the graduate level, she has taught journalism and media ethics courses, mass communication theory and a long-running graduate seminar in mass media impacts on health.

Robert Wyss has been a newspaper reporter and editor for 30 years and a journalism professor for 15 years. He is the author of three books and has written more than a hundred articles for such publications as *The New York Times*, *Christian Science Monitor*, *Audubon*, *Yankee*, and the *Huffington Post*. During his tenure as a fulltime newspaper journalist at the *Providence Journal* and professor of journalism at the University of Connecticut, USA, he specialised in the coverage of environmental issues. Two of his books had environmental themes, *The Man Who Built the Sierra Club* (2016), a biography of David Brower, and *Covering the Environment* (2008). The latter is a journalism textbook about how journalists report on the environmental beat that will be published in its second edition in 2018. He also wrote *Brimfield Rush* (2006), a narrative nonfiction book. Besides writing about the environment, Wyss has taught environmental journalism to undergraduate students, including taking students on trips to the Florida Everglades and the Louisiana Gulf coast to produce print and multimedia reports. He also has taught communication skills to graduate science students under a $500,000 US National Science Foundation grant. He is a member of the Society of Environmental Journalists. Wyss retired from the University of Connecticut in July 2017 but continued at the university in the management of the NSA-funded science communication program.

INTRODUCTION

Ann Luce

In 2005, at the age of 23, I was working as a journalist at the *Florida Times-Union* in Jacksonville, Florida. I had been working in journalism for seven years already as an apprentice, picking up night shifts and covering weekends on local newspapers, taking whatever internships and short-term contracts were available to me before landing permanent posts. The stories I wrote were various and varied: from local strawberry festivals to city council meetings; from covering State Senate to interviewing ambassadors and so forth. I covered 9/11 as well, but for some reason that story didn't affect me too much emotionally or psychologically. It didn't seem odd to me that planes would be flown into buildings to make a political statement, having grown up in the Republic of Ireland in the 1980s/90s watching the ongoing "Troubles" in Northern Ireland on the nightly RTE news: cars-as-bombs or planes-as-bombs, at the time, it seemed like a natural progression to me – I just didn't have the historical knowledge to note the ramifications of this geopolitical event at the time.

I was young; I was eager; and I loved journalism. Not so much the writing, but the research, the investigations, the conversations with people and learning about their lives. Journalism wasn't so much a "job" to me as more akin to a "hobby"; not so much a "vocation", as some journalism colleagues proclaim, but more like a utopian mission that I strongly believed in, a key part of my own identity and self-narrative. Journalism was about changing the world.

My career in journalism changed forever when two events occurred just weeks apart in 2005. Hurricane Katrina was the first natural disaster I covered, starting in late August of that year. Hurricanes were nothing new to me – I had been living in Florida for 10 years – but Katrina, a Category 5 hurricane, was different. It started in Central Florida, devastated Gulfport, Mississippi, decimated New Orleans in Louisiana, before petering out in Texas. I mostly focused my coverage of Katrina on Northeast Florida, and west, towards Mississippi.

What I remember of that time, however, was not the sheer devastation of what I witnessed, but the stories coming in over the wire. This was more than likely my first experience with "vicarious trauma", that is to say, the impact of "experiencing repeated or extreme exposure to aversive details of traumatic event(s)" (Dubberley and Grant, 2017, 2). Nowadays, this includes the ubiquity of user-generated social media; but back then, it was the stories I was reading, the images I was seeing from the Associated Press and Reuters wire services that hit hard most of all, causing a hurricane of emotional distress and trauma.

Less than two weeks after Hurricane Katrina made landfall in New Orleans, a close friend, also a journalist, died by suicide. His death turned my life upside down. Because he had taken his life at a public institution, a local university, newsroom policy deemed that his suicide be covered. The story of his death, written by one of my colleagues, ran on the bottom of an inside page, with a photo of his face. His death received much media coverage in both print and broadcast media, but I found myself conflicted when reading and watching the reports. They seemed insensitive, but I was not sure why. Two days after his death, I returned to work, and my first story was the suicide of a local high-school student, putting me directly in the eye of the storm. While I had covered several suicide stories previously in my career – upon reflection, quite badly, I admit (see Chapter 4), I was now writing about suicide from the perspective of someone who had been *bereaved by suicide*. Ethically, this should not have been allowed. I was in no fit state to responsibly report on the death of a local teenager, to talk to grieving family members and friends. However, this story did catapult me into dedicating the last decade of my life to researching media representations of suicide, a factor that I strongly believe was sparked by my own personal trauma rather than my previous utopian romanticism.

The seismic emotional impact of these two events, paralleled by the lack of organisational support for a young journalist dealing with these topics, led me to leave journalism in the summer of 2006 and venture into the world of academia where I could teach journalism in the way that I felt it needed to be taught. Some might scoff that I wasn't resilient enough, tough enough, "man" enough, that at the age of 23, I should have bounced back quicker. But, alas, I didn't. When one is a young, enthusiastic journalist – with limited experience in the working world – you may not fully recognise the ethical precariousness of a situation until after the fact. My goal, and the goals of the contributing authors featured in this volume, is to better prepare journalists for covering sensitive topics in an ethical and responsible manner.

What is a sensitive topic?

Sensitive topics tend to be those subjects that we don't like to talk about too much; they are difficult, challenging, taboo (in some cases), controversial, overwhelming, and complicated. Distressing topics often get inside one's head and become internally toxic and cankerous.

Perhaps more pointedly, such trauma can remain for an extended period of time and fester like a malignancy. Sensitive topics also tend to have greater ethical implications that a journalist would need to consider, ranging from the most appropriate way to describe, say, a shooter who has killed school children (see Chapter 5) or to how to interview someone who has lost everything in a natural disaster (see Chapter 11). This edited collection is not a book about ethics *per se*, but, rather, it is about the ethical practice journalists should employ when reporting difficult, complicated, challenging, and sensitive social topics.

As journalists, we must acknowledge and accept the responsibility that comes with having the power to affect people's lives. Indeed, we have the power to practice responsibly, ethically, and accurately. As Burns emphasises:

> the power is literally within the individual and is demonstrated with every decision he or she makes about what news is, what questions to ask, what to include and omit, and so on. Every one of these decisions has professional, commercial and ethical dimensions that must be brought into balance by the context of the story.
>
> *(Burns, 2013: 13)*

In many ways, journalists are cartographers, creating the maps by which we understand the world beyond our immediate purview. For Keeble (2009)

> the basic roles of the journalist are to promote peace and understanding, to work with honesty, clarity and compassion, to give voice to the voiceless, the desperately poor, the oppressed; to challenge stereotyping and expose corruption and lying – and to respect diversity and difference.
>
> *(2009: IX)*

Ethical Reporting of Sensitive Topics is aimed at students of journalism but, equally, should be of use to individuals who are encountering newsroom environments for the first time, and for those coming to journalism without any formal training. This volume should also prove useful to the veteran journalist or specialist journalist who seeks to better their skills when reporting sensitive topics.

That said, *Ethical Reporting of Sensitive Topics* does not focus on "Specialist Journalism", for those who develop expertise in a particular field such as fashion, music, sport, business, etc., and focus on those beats alone. General assignment reporters – many of whom typically describe themselves as coming from the "university of life", the "school of hard knocks" – are the "Jack & Jill of all trades", and, as Turner and Orange remark (2013: 3) "typically have insufficient time to acquire more than a basic grasp of most issues: health, business, education, local government". Editors expect that reporters have been sufficiently trained to cover court cases – but what if this is not always the case? What if all one's schooling and depth of teaching were missed out for breadth of teaching? This gap, particularly when journalists cover sensitive topics, is what we hope to fill with this volume, because – specialist or not – at some time or another, any journalist may find themselves covering sensitive topics, whatever they may be.

Take, for example, the issue of suicide. Suicide does not just happen on a crime beat. In 2010, fashion designer Alexander McQueen took his own life. In 2018, Kate Spade, famous for her stylish handbags, also rocked the fashion world when she died by suicide. Both of these stories needed to be covered by both specialist and non-specialist journalists alike. In 2011, ex-Wales football manager Gary Speed died by suicide, a story that was covered heavily by sports journalists. In 2014, actor Robin Williams died by suicide, shocking the celebrity world. Williams' death was covered on both entertainment and news pages the world over. In 2017, Chester Bennington, lead singer for Linkin Park, shocked music fans when he killed himself. More recently, in 2018 celebrity chef Anthony Bourdain also died by suicide, a story that was carried on food pages, news pages, and in magazines around the world.

Celebrity suicides will naturally be covered by specialist and non-specialist journalists alike. But what of the day-to-day coverage of suicide? How does a journalist ethically and responsibly cover the story of the disabled man who killed himself because his benefits were cut (Chakelian, 2015)? How does one report responsibly when research has been published that "exam stress is linked to teen suicide" (NHS Choices, 2016); or how does one provide context when an elderly couple carried out a suicide pact because they didn't want to lose their independence by entering a care home (Smith, 2016)? These questions will be the focus of Chapter 4, "Reporting suicide".

This edited collection is about supporting *all* journalists, with the aim being to provide advice and substantive guidance on covering sensitive topics in a responsible and ethical manner. The chapters here should serve as a practical guide, while merging together theory and practice. Each chapter is grounded in research, so readers can understand the most up-to-date thinking about these sensitive topics in respective and cogent academic fields. There is a selection of topics likely to be of interest to the aspiring reporter – although by no means exhaustive. The book explores the underlying issues journalists may face in contemporary news reporting: bias, sensationalism, conflict of interest, grief, vulnerability, and ignorance of one's own privilege. The various authors discuss common themes and issues that may emerge while reporting on sensitive topics and we consider the ethical and practical dilemmas facing journalists by showing both positive and negative aspects of news reporting through the lens of multiple case studies.

The authors herein are an international group of journalists-turned-academics, meaning we have worked in the field as practising journalists, and now teach thousands of journalism students around the world each year. Each of the contributors in *Ethical Reporting of Sensitive Topics* actively teaches students what we wish we had known when we were starting out. This collection aims to support and guide aspiring and established journalists in relation to sensitive topics. We begin with the collective assumption that readers know how to write and that one has a level of ability in being "able" to do the job, "applying conceptual knowledge and understanding to new and unfamiliar situations" (Burns, 2013: 13). In the various chapters and case studies to follow, we have each sought to offer clear guidance and instructions regarding the way in which one should report on these issues accurately. We have each raised ethical issues that readers will need to ponder and provide explicit guidelines about lines which should not be crossed *in any circumstances*. We have each offered advice on the best ways and practices to interact with vulnerable people, and where to go for the most up-to-date statistics and information on controversial science, health and environment issues. In the final chapter of this book, you will find a handy guide of further hints and tips that journalists should know when faced with reporting on a sensitive topic.

Structure of the book

Ethical Reporting of Sensitive Topics is structured into six parts, the first of which is entitled "Ethics, Responsibility and Self Care". This section is broken down into two chapters, the first of which is written by Prof. Chris Frost, an emeritus professor of Journalism at Liverpool John Moores University in the UK. He is former chair of the Association for Journalism Education UK/Ireland, and a board member of the National Union of Journalists in the UK. Frost's chapter focuses upon "Journalism standards on the job" (Chapter 1), in which he provides guidance and support for readers on journalism ethics, ethics in the workplace, codes of practice, speaking truth to power in the newsroom, and standing up for ethical practice.

The second chapter in this section is by Dr Lyn Barnes, a senior lecturer at Auckland University of Technology in New Zealand. Lyn has written extensively on covering day-to-day trauma as a domestic journalist, and in Chapter 2 she advises readers on how to cope with the tough times. Barnes explores research that indicates traumatic experiences that happen early on in a young journalist's career can have detrimental and substantial effects across many years. She discusses the "macho approach" in newsrooms, whereby openly talking about heady emotions is discouraged, while also offering sage advice on how to engage in self-preparation and self-care so that journalists can become more empathetic and resilient.

Dr Amanda Gearing kicks off "Part II: Reporting Sensitive Topics", with Chapter 3 on reporting child sexual abuse. Gearing, a journalist working for *The Guardian* in the UK and Australia, has investigated some of the most controversial and challenging stories around child sexual abuse in Australia and the UK to date. In this chapter, Gearing explains the cycles of trauma and recovery, as well as an interview method that has been shown to facilitate interviews with trauma victims. She also discusses at length the ethical implications of interviewing someone who was sexually abused as a child. Through case studies, Gearing demonstrates the way in which schools, churches, cultural and sporting organisations that have knowingly harboured abusive employees are being called to account by victims and the public.

Dr Ann Luce has been reporting, researching and writing about suicide for more than a decade. She sits on the International Association of Suicide Prevention World Media Task Force and has contributed to multiple sets of media reporting guidelines on suicide, most notably, guidelines for the World Health Organisation. In Chapter 4 on reporting suicide, Luce discusses the ethical frameworks journalists should follow when reporting on suicide, and explores "The Bridgend Suicides" in Wales in 2008, the suicide of Jacintha Saldanha – the nurse of Duchess of Cambridge, Kate Middleton, when she was pregnant with Prince George in 2012 – and the recent controversy around Netflix's *13 Reasons Why*.

"Part III: Reporting Violence" begins with Chapter 5 on mass shootings by Glynn Greensmith, a lecturer in journalism at Curtin University in Perth, Australia. In his chapter, Greensmith charts the evolution of the random mass shooting, starting in August 1966, and discusses the scripts that are followed by journalists when covering such events. Greensmith offers suggestions on how to change reporting norms and discusses ethical implications if we do not.

Dr Mathew Charles, a senior lecturer in journalism and documentary at Bournemouth University, UK and also an award-winning filmmaker, explores the reporting of urban violence and gangs in Colombia, El Salvador and the UK in Chapter 6. He notes that urban violence has become a central preoccupation of policy-makers, planners, and development practitioners, while journalists have an obsession with "gang warfare". Charles argues that a lack of understanding of the multifaceted nature of violence can lead to sensationalist reporting, thus further fuelling the problem and doing little to enhance contemporary understandings of the phenomenon.

In "Part IV: Reporting Health", Dr John Lister, a journalist for over 40 years who has specialised in reporting on the UK National Health Service, explores critical health journalism in Chapter 7, focusing specifically on the protection against the dissemination of fake, inadequate, or misleading health news. He discusses the commercial and market pressures that impact on specialist health journals, querying the rigour of the peer review process and critical scrutiny of papers and studies published.

Closing out our section on reporting health is Dr Kim Walsh-Childers, a former newspaper health reporter who has been teaching journalism at the University of Florida in Gainesville, Florida since 1990. The National Cancer Institute and the US Department of Defense have supported Walsh-Childers' work. In Chapter 8, "Reporting on drugs, diets, devices, and other health interventions", she argues that consumers face an increasing need for closer involvement in decision-making about their own healthcare and the care of their loved ones. Walsh-Childers argues that journalists who cover health must understand how to make their stories not only understandable and compelling, but also complete.

"Part V: Reporting Science and the Environment" includes three chapters. In Chapter 9, Dr Shelley Thompson and Hilary Stepien explore reporting on controversial science, specifically guiding readers on the questions one needs to ask oneself as one develops stories about science. Thompson and Stepien challenge us to ponder which are the most reputable sources to ensure accurate, accessible, and ethical news, especially when reporting on nanotechnology.

Robert Wyss discusses Climate Change in Chapter 10. Robert is considered a leader on environmental issues in the United States where he recently retired from the University of Connecticut. Recipient of a National Science Foundation grant, and member of the Society of Environmental Journalists, Robert demonstrates the challenges that faced the Paris climate change treaty, which was ultimately an international political, environmental, economic, and regulatory issue. He explains how climate change will likely wreak a range of challenges from rising sea levels, famine, violent storms, and other environmental calamities, exploring the role of journalists in helping readers to understand the complexity of this issue.

Dr Amanda Gearing offers the second essay in this collection in Chapter 11, "Reporting natural disasters in the digital age". Natural disasters, Gearing argues, have high newsworthiness because of their potential impact on large numbers of people. She, too, discusses the impact that climate change is bound to have on the frequency and severity of droughts, storms, floods, fires, cyclones and tornadoes. Gearing provides information for new journalists on how best to prepare to report on natural disasters and, moreover, explores the use of social media in staying connected with a community.

In our last section in this volume, "Part VI: Reporting Cultural, Ethnic and Geographical Difference", Dr Alex Wake, a senior lecturer at RMIT University in Melbourne, Australia, writes about "Reporting on 'other' cultures" in Chapter 12, providing guidance on how to keep one's privilege in check. She asks readers to acknowledge their own cultural and ideological biases, while advising on how to improve coverage of diverse ethnic communities and ensuring better treatment of people from within those communities. Wake outlines some best practice guidelines for reporting in a diverse world as national borders disappear into an increasingly globalised world.

Dr Jeremaiah Opiniano closes out this section with Chapter 13, "Reporting on international migration". Opiniano, an assistant professor of journalism at the University of Santo Tomas in Manila, Philippines, has reported on international migration issues for a Philippine non-profit news service called the Overseas Filipino Workers Journalism Consortium (OFWJC), which he co-founded in 2002. In this chapter, Opiniano guides readers on how to seek sources, especially from overseas migrants, in order to present a balanced picture of the gains and pains of modern-day international human mobility.

Rounding out this volume is a concluding chapter that provides a handy guide to further hints and tips around reporting on these sensitive topics.

What each contributor hopes readers discover and learn in *Ethical Reporting of Sensitive Topics* is that journalism matters; and *how one reports on sensitive topics* in journalism matters a great deal as well. Journalists and reporters *must* report on sensitive topics accurately, ethically, and responsibly. We each hope that the following chapters will provide guidance, information and, in some ways, inspiration. Indeed, journalism matters, but, also, *journalists matter. Ethical Reporting of Sensitive Topics* is dedicated to those who risk themselves out in the field, be it physiologically or psychologically, to bring our daily news from around the world in multifaceted ways, each hoping to make a difference. To return to where I started. Journalism *can* change the world, and I am glad I have not yet lost that particular utopian idealism. But perhaps more than that, journalists can change the world. And that means you!

References

Burns, L.S. (2013). *Understanding Journalism*. London: Sage.

Chakelian, A. (2015). "Disabled man killed himself over benefit cut, coroner rules", *New Statesman*. Available online: [https://www.newstatesman.com/politics/welfare/2015/09/disabled-man-killed-himself-over-benefit-cut-coroner-rules]

Dubberley, S. and Grant, M. (2017). *Journalism and Vicarious Trauma: A Guide for Journalists, Editors and News Organisations*. First Draft News. Available online: [https://firstdraftnews.org/wp-content/uploads/2017/04/vicarioustrauma.pdf]

Keeble, R. (2009). *Ethics for Journalists*. London: Routledge.

NHS. "Exam stress is linked to teen suicide", *NHS Choices*. Available online: [https://www.nhs.uk/news/mental-health/exam-stress-linked-to-teen-suicide/]

Smith, L. (2016). "Couple's heartbreaking suicide pact because they didn't want to go into a care home" *The Mirror*. Available online: [https://www.mirror.co.uk/news/uk-news/elderly-couples-heartbreaking-suicide-pact-8340311]

Turner, B. and Orange, R. (2013). *Specialist Journalism*. London: Routledge.

PART I

Ethics, responsibility and self-care

1

JOURNALISM STANDARDS ON THE JOB

Chris Frost

Out into the world

All journalists start somewhere and the routes into the industry are many and varied, but the most usual route these days, certainly in most first world regions such as the UK, Western Europe, or the US, is to take a college course and then apply for a job.

It is not the intention of this chapter to examine the types of first job many journalists achieve, as these are as wide and as varied as the media industry itself. The chapter intends to look at the problems and challenges new entrants into the industry face in their first job, wherever that may be, and identify how to build and maintain your credibility and integrity as you progress in your career.

Introduction – why me

I have worked as a journalist and journalism educator for more than 45 years – years that have seen enormous change both in the way we work and the type of media we work in and for. All my working life I have tried to ensure the highest ethical standards in publications I have worked for or edited. With the National Union of Journalists, I have helped frame the union's stance on media freedom and journalistic standards; standards that we have campaigned to have applied throughout the industry, giving evidence to parliamentary select committees, NGOs, and the Leveson Inquiry, and instigating other campaigns to persuade members to aspire to the highest journalistic standards. In my academic career, my work has centred on journalistic ethics, regulation, and standards. Many of my research papers examine standards and the ability (or inability) of regulators to uphold them. Part of my work with the NUJ's Ethics Council and the Institute for Communication Ethics has involved discussing difficult ethical problems with various journalists as well as running an ethics hotline for NUJ members – somewhere they can speak in confidence and discuss their concerns without pressure to make a decision one way or the other. All journalists must come to their own decisions about ethical matters taking guidance from codes of practice such as the NUJ's code, or some other code such as UK broadcasting's Ofcom code or the Independent Press Standards Organisation's (IPSO's) for newspaper journalists. It is not the place of this chapter to go into detail about those codes or the regulators who police them but more information can be found in Frost (2016).

A career in journalism

The first job for a new journalist is an exciting adventure, but one that brings difficult decisions as the new entrant learns how to find that winning story, how to stand it up, and how to write it up. These are important skills but a good journalist is also an ethical journalist. For many new journalists, ethics is about the big decisions they've seen on the movies: a decision that only needs to be taken once or twice in a career. In reality though, ethics are the everyday decisions that help you make your journalism the best you can. Many codes of practice around the world start with the concept of doing no harm, but soon run into the problem that many of the really important stories are those that harm somebody: the politician caught out in a sex scandal, the businessman using illegal techniques, the teacher abusing his or her position to have sex with students. All will suffer if their wrongdoing is exposed, but these are all stories in the public interest.

As a new or inexperienced journalist you need to be aware of your relationship with and duty to three different groups:

Your colleagues, including your supervisors and editor;
Your sources and contacts;
Your audience – the public for whom you are writing.

Any good journalism student should have a sound grasp of the media law in their country and will be aware of the codes of practice that might affect them in their working lives. Most codes of practice for journalists around the world cover the following issues:

- Accuracy, truth and a right to reply;
- Privacy and intrusion;
- Harassment and undue pressure;
- Protecting children;
- Discrimination and protecting vulnerable groups;
- Using straightforward means of gathering information;
- Ensuring justice is done through fair trails and presumption of innocence.

But knowing them and putting them into practice on a daily basis is difficult and requires experience. Nor can the new reporter always rely on more senior staff or managers to offer advice. The pressures on editors to get stories that will sell newspapers is often passed on through senior staff to build a culture in the newsroom that encourages poor practice and unethical journalism as happened at the *News of the World* in the UK leading to the Leveson Inquiry in 2011. Journalists seeking to behave ethically need to learn how to resist such pressures.

This chapter will look at problem areas for the new journalist and advise how to spot them and what to do about them. It will also offer advice on how to discuss approaches with managers without damaging your career. It will use case studies from around the world to identify the kinds of ethical traps it is easy to fall into and how to handle them.

Media freedom

Journalists always need to remember that they have a duty to uphold and defend media freedom. This freedom, developed from the human right of free speech, conscience, and opinion, and the right to receive information and the opinions of others, is the freedom to publish in the public interest. However, media freedom is not an absolute right – no publisher or broadcaster has the right to publish anything they want. Individual human rights, constitutional or legal restrictions and audience acceptance all limit what can be published or broadcast. Whilst the media has the right to publish or broadcast views and opinions even if they offend (because the right to publish only inoffensive things is no right at all), in most countries there are limits identified in the laws of defamation, obscenity and fair trial about what can be published and broadcast. In addition, in many jurisdictions, broadcasters are required by law to treat people fairly and are obliged not to broadcast material that might harm or offend people, particularly minors, in the areas of nudity, sex, violence, and death.

An audience's acceptance of certain material may also limit what a particular publication or broadcast can do. If people find what is being published unacceptable, they'll stop reading or watching that publication reducing its impact and obliging it to reconsider its publication choices.

Other individual human rights are also often protected either by a country's constitution, its laws, or by codes of practice. These rights include a right to privacy, a right not to be discriminated against, a right to be presumed innocent until found guilty by a legitimate court, the protection of minors, and the prevention of harassment.

When pursuing a story, journalists need to balance these rights and duties against the right of people to be informed. This involves the public interest: essentially, is the collective public right to be informed more important in this particular story than the individual's right to privacy or protection?

The public interest is not the same as interesting the public (although there can be occasions when interesting the public can be in the public interest – see

Frost 2016). The public interest is about holding those in power or those who benefit from higher social status accountable for that power or social status.

It should also be remembered that many news publications or broadcasters are businesses, there to make profits to enrich shareholders. This often puts pressure on journalists to pursue stories that will draw audiences at the expenses of an individual's right to privacy. Publishers are entitled to use media freedom to make their businesses more profitable but journalists need to be wary about subverting the public interest to publish scandal about the lives of celebrities purely in the pursuit of high readership for their own personal gain and profit or the gain of their publisher.

Ethics

Do you want to be a good journalist, or one that merely gets by? And what does one mean by "a good journalist"? A good journalist is certainly one who is competent at the craft of journalism – those things learned in college about finding stories, researching them and writing them in a commanding fashion. However, a good journalist is surely also someone who believes in what they are doing and is determined to do it in an ethical way. Things can go wrong, though. The pressure to produce stories that are very attractive to readers often overwhelms the ethical concerns about how those stories are gathered or used. A toxic culture can easily develop in newsrooms where a cynical approach to the central part of the journalist's job can lead a reporter to ignore ethics in order to become the biggest "badass" on the desk. It's a macho style of journalism that can often develop in an early career as a young inexperienced journalist attempts to show they are up to the job, but often all it shows is a lack of maturity. It is something all new starters need to guard against.

The new or inexperienced journalist should be fully aware that there is a difference between functionality and ethics. To be a good journalist all need to be functionally good, able to find stories, take fast, accurate notes and write the story up in a stylish way. But they also need to be ethically good, something that is much more personally driven. Editors and others will soon notice if their reporters do not find interesting stories. They will soon complain if they are not supported by accurate details and too many visits from subs re-writing your poorly written copy will soon lead to a poor reputation. However, it might be a long time before you are discovered making up quotes, or inventing stories, or carrying out other forms of unethical behaviour. One should not behave ethically simply for fear of being caught out (although it might be a sensible precaution) but because providing consumers with accurate, interesting, well-written stories is what we do and why people buy newspapers and to provide them with anything else is to cheat them and, worse still, devalue media freedom and the readers' right to be informed. It is the journalist's duty to readers and to their wider rights that insist there should be professional ethics.

Ethics on the job

Many journalists around the world go to college first before becoming practitioners. It is often here that you learn about journalism ethics and media law on such issues as defamation, privacy, court reporting, and privacy. In some jurisdictions a journalist also needs to know the risks of desacato (insulting those in positions of authority). Students often find these topics to be the duller parts of a journalism course but they are essential in teaching how to avoid making a mistake that could land one in jail, or worse still, land one's editor in jail. Because they are duller they are also the parts of the course that the less diligent student is most likely to avoid. This can cause problems when the student finally gets a staff job with a newspaper or broadcaster. Lack of knowledge of the law, ethics, and codes of conduct can lead to serious errors that can lead to dismissal. An examination of complaints to the UK press regulators The Press Complaints Commission and the Independent Press Standards Organisation by the author in 2016 showed that one of the main problems faced by the regional and local press in terms of complaints was a lack of experience or training often compounded by limited supervision.

Having left university, often with only a shaky grasp of law and ethics, new and inexperienced journalists find that there are very different expectations on the job. Time is a serious resource and one often has very little of it to complete a story. The temptation is often to cut corners on research and failing to contact sources or seek a second voice. Press releases are published with very little checking and very limited change. The time to contact an oppositional voice is rare.

You face very different expectations from supervisors and editors. You are expected to follow orders and you are expected to do it quickly, even if that sometimes means you don't do it well or thoroughly. This is difficult to manage. Editors are under pressure and all fear that one day the newspaper will be published or the broadcast transmitted with spaces where stories failed to materialize. Consequently, they are pressing you to ensure you deliver. Because of this, an editor can occasionally instruct you to do something you believe to be unethical. You may consider you are doing something that you believe your editor would want in producing stories that will attract readers and raise circulation. However, it is up to you to challenge an editor if you believe you are doing something unethical. Of course, there are various ways to do this. Whilst time is precious in the newsroom, telling your editor briefly why you are concerned and, even better if you can, explaining how you see a way to get around it will often be taken on board and develop your editor's respect for you as a professional. Often taking a slightly different angle on the story or seeking another source will allow the editor to run the story while you will be able to gather the information in a more ethical way. Never assume that your editor or news editor would be unwilling to discuss the risk of breaching the relevant code of practice by behaving unethically. Of course, if the editor instructs you to go ahead anyway, then you have a dilemma. There are very few options left to you as a new member of staff if the editor instructs you continue harassing a grieving widow or pursuing a celebrity. In the UK, if you are a member of the National Union of Journalists you can ring its Ethics Hotline (0845 450 0864) and seek advice. You can also speak to your father or mother of chapel (office union organiser) who will be able to give advice, approach the editor to pursue the matter or alert the chapel. Any UK press journalist can ring the regulator's whistleblowing hotline (0800 032 0243, or fill in the online form at www.ipso.co.uk/contact-ipso/journalists-whistleblowing-hotline) to seek advice. At the end of the day, though, you may have to decide whether to accept the instruction, resign or risk dismissal. The story of Richard Peppiat, a young man, employed by the *Daily Star* for two years working as a general reporter, is instructive here. He quit the paper with a letter to the then owner, Richard Desmond, that tells of some of the tricks and stunts he was ordered to pull in order to get a story:

> as a young hack keen to prove his worth I threw myself into working at the Daily Star with gusto. On order I dressed up as a John Lennon, a vampire, a Mexican, Noel Gallagher, Saint George (twice), Santa Claus, Aleksandr the Meerkat, the Stig, and a transvestite Alex Reid.
>
> I've been spray tanned, waxed, and in a kilt clutching roses, trawled a Glasgow council estate trying to propose to Susan Boyle (I did. She said no).
>
> *(Guardian, 16 June 2018)*

He talks about being obliged to make stories up; a story about Kelly Brook that was rubbish according to the celebrity earned him a £150 bonus. Finally, he found it too much and quit. His letter spells out the pressures ambitious young journalists can sometimes face:

> Many a morning I've hit my speed dial button to Muslim rent-a-rant Anjem Choudary to see if he fancied pulling together a few lines about whipping drunks or stoning homosexuals.
>
> Our caustic 'us and them' narrative needs nailing home every day or two, and when asked to wield the hammer I was too scared for my career, and my bank account, to refuse.
>
> 'If you won't write it, we'll get someone who will,' was the sneer du jour, my eyes directed toward a teetering pile of CVs.
>
> *(ibid.)*

Ethical challenges in codes

Ethical codes are designed to give guidance to editors and reporters. You should read the codes carefully and ensure you understand them, but there are several clauses that are particularly important and journalists face a lot of pressure to breach them in order to make better stories and raise circulation. Broadcasters in the UK need to read the Ofcom broadcasting code whilst BBC journalists also need to know about the BBC's editorial guidelines (although these are excellent advice for all journalists). Press journalists need to follow the IPSO code whilst all journalists will find the NUJ code useful.

Accuracy, truth, and a right to reply

The temptation to sensationalise a story is often difficult to ignore. This temptation is driven by the realisation that your career could benefit from you being seen as someone who "gets the story". Perhaps the most spectacular example was Jayson Blair, a *New York Times* reporter who was forced to resign as his paper published a 7,239-word front-page article headed "Times reporter who resigned leaves long trail of deception" (nytimes.com) – probably the longest retraction and correction ever published in the world. After a long investigation, the *NYT* found that Blair had often invented sources and their quotes, pretended to have visited places – even claiming expenses while staying at home.

Whilst Blair became a compulsive liar in order to bolster his stories, he was not the first and won't be the last reporter to add a little fictional spice to his reports. However, as he continued to get away with his inventions, he became gradually bolder until eventually his web of lies spun out of control and he was exposed, damaging the credibility of his paper, leading to his editor's resignation and his own. Blair is now a byword for professional immorality.

Whilst fabricating stories, quotes, and sources is clearly wrong, journalists have a stronger duty to accuracy than that. Even if the source is genuine and the quote is accurate, the good reporter still has an obligation to check the accuracy of the quote and find a counter source if necessary. During the Brexit debate in the UK – a referendum to decide if Britain should leave the EU – those seeking to leave, including Boris Johnson, then UK Foreign Secretary, claimed that leaving would save Britain £350 million a week. This was a significant issue in the debate but was later found to be "potentially misleading" by the UK Office for National Statistics as it was a gross figure, not net, and its usage was open to question (www.ons.gov.uk). Johnson was challenged on this figure by several journalists during the campaign but refused to accept that he was relying on a false statistic.

Quotes are tricky things as they are important building blocks of a good story giving evidence from the original, named sources and providing an example of the tone of the story. Quotes should be used as they are given and not edited to suit the story. However, there are times when a little judgment is required. Occasionally even the best public speaker misspeaks. One example I faced as a very young reporter was when a councillor accidentally said something "should not be" when he clearly meant it "should be". I faithfully reported his words, but not surprisingly he wasn't happy next time I saw him. Should I have deleted the word "not" even though he had said it? Probably. I certainly should have spoken to him after the speech or phoned him later to confirm what he meant.

Journalists also need to be careful about using quotes in chronological order. This isn't always possible or sensible, but juggling around with when people said things, especially for broadcast, can interfere with the sense of what they are saying and care needs to be taken to ensure they are not being misrepresented. If their sentences become mangled when speaking to you, then consider putting those quotes in indirect speech so that you can publish the sense of what they were trying to say without making them look like bumbling, inarticulate fools.

As well as checking the accuracy of quotes and testing their veracity where possible, there are other checks journalists should make. Archives and research materials are often problematic. Websites, articles, cuttings libraries, and the like always require double checking. Wikipedia is a great place to learn about the basics of some new topic or person but should never be considered as completely accurate; it is great for background, but double check for publication or broadcast. If you spot any errors in your own publication's web pages, these should be tagged with a correction.

Privacy

A "good" story might sell papers but harm or invade privacy. Some years ago *The Sun* ran a tale about "Randy Mandy", who, together with a male friend, had sex in the business class cabin of an intercontinental flight. Ignoring the *Sun's* obvious misogyny in concentrating heavily on Mandy when it takes two to tango, the story must have been extremely embarrassing for them and their life partners. Was this an invasion of privacy? Well, yes. But was it a justified intrusion? It took place in a public place (an airline cabin in front of a couple of dozen passengers) on a public flight. The story was of interest to the public and probably increased sales on the back of that and was in the public interest in that it allowed a debate about the appropriateness of explicit sexual conduct in public. Some journalists – the UK *Daily Mail's* editor Paul Dacre is one – believe that they are entitled to act as a public guardian of morals, detailing elements of legal, sexual acts carried out in private. In a speech to editors in 2008, he said that Judge Eady "has, again and again, under the privacy clause of the Human Rights Act, found against newspapers and their age-old freedom to expose the moral shortcomings of those in high places"(dailymail.co.uk).

A quick read of the *Daily Mail* also makes it clear that Dacre is quite happy to expose the moral shortcomings of people in low places as well.

Privacy can be breached at several stages of a story, but the key one for the reporter is during its development. Intruding onto private property and harassing people to get information are potential breaches of journalistic codes. Whilst determination is often required to access sources, a direct refusal to speak, whether in person or by phone or e-message, should be accepted and other routes used to try to get the information. Equally, care should be taken with confidential information. Reading letters left openly on a desk is one thing, rifling through someone's drawers whilst they get you a coffee is an invasion of privacy.

Phone hacking was a hot topic during the Leveson inquiry and most journalists now realise that hacking into someone's private voicemail is both a breach of journalistic codes and the law, as is accessing their emails. Facebook and other social media have proved to be useful sources for pictures and personal details. If someone has left their privacy settings at public then it may well be acceptable to access the site (although remember that pictures will be copyrighted). The problem is that not everyone is careful with their privacy settings as they don't expect to become of interest to the public.

The privacy of children is usually taken even more seriously than that of adults in journalistic codes. The expectation is that they should be able to complete their schooling in privacy. This sets the bar even higher in terms of justifying publishing a story. The UK tabloids published a story about a 12-year-old boy (AP) who claimed to be the father of his 15-year-old girlfriend's baby (CS). Several long stories were published giving details and naming them both. Several days later more stories were published telling that DNA testing had proved AP was not the father and that CS had slept with several other boys, one of whom was the father. This unedifying tale was condemned by the Press Complaints Commission as an unnecessary invasion of privacy. In another case, *the Daily Mail* was ordered to pay rock star Paul Weller's children £10,000 for intruding into their privacy after it published pictures of his children on a shopping trip in California.

Source confidentiality

Normally, as well as checking the accuracy of sources, journalists should always identify a source as it adds veracity and authority to the story. We need to know that it was the prime minister that said this or that it was the leader of the local council who said that. Occasionally though, to name a source could put them at risk. A tip-off about criminal behaviour or a whistleblower telling tales of illegality in a company are the kinds of sources who could be at risk if their identity is revealed and journalists often promise such sources confidentiality. The key here is that it is your promise. You are the one who has agreed with the source that in return for information you will keep their identity secret. This is not always feasible though if you are obliged by your contract of employment or by newsroom practice to tell your news editor or producer the identity (the BBC insists on this). This adds difficulties because a journalist can't guarantee to keep an identity secret if someone else knows the information. The journalist would have to inform the whistleblower about the editor's involvement from the start. Pressure may be brought to bear from editors but it is always wisest to keep the information to yourself – you are the one making the promise – provided you can properly justify keeping the source anonymous. If we promise a source confidentiality, we should keep that promise and should not publish their identity or reveal it later to anyone – including a court. Because this is such a binding promise with the possible risk of dismissal or jail, any journalist giving such a promise needs to be sure it is worth the risk. Never promise to keep an identity secret unless you have some idea of what the story is about. A journalist called Nick Martin-Clark interviewed prisoners in Northern Ireland after giving a promise of confidentiality. One of the prisoners, Clifford McKeown, allegedly confessed to the murder of taxi driver Michael McGoldrick. This left Martin-Clarke with the problem of whether he published the confession and went to the police with his information or abiding by the NUJ's Code of Conduct and sticking by his promise. This was a difficult choice – McGoldrick was a high-profile murder and gaining a confession was a great story. Martin-Clark could hardly publish it without revealing his source, nor could he go to the police. Martin-Clark decided to publish the story and breach the Press Complaints Commission code and the National Union of Journalists code. The NUJ later decided that Martin-Clark was not a fit and proper person to join the union – he had resigned after publication of the story.

This is a deontological absolutist dilemma. The codes outline the reporter's duty and give no option but to uphold the promise, yet that would mean Martin-Clark would not be able to publish the story as he would not have been able to name McKeown. The whole point of the interview, and the point of the protection of sources clause in the codes, was to get stories of that kind. However, if he did publish the story he would have breached the code and put himself and his family at risk of reprisals. Many people believe he should have maintained his promise even though that would have meant no publication and no justice for McGoldrick's family as this is the correct deontological position, some others feel his loyalty to the law and the need to publish should over-ride that and that he should have measured his ethical action by the consequences that would flow from his actions. The need for confidentiality of sources is often allied with that of the doctor or lawyer but both these professions are legally and professionally obliged to keep a confidence in that as counsellors their interests should be identical and indivisible to the subject. That is not true of journalists:

> In the case of reporters and source, by contrast, there are non-fiduciary and even adversarial elements in the relationship, with the reporter angling to learn more than the source want to tell and the source trying to promote a particular views, and, of course, from the standpoint of the journalist, the public's interest, not the source's, should be paramount.
>
> *(Klaidman and Beauchamp, 1987: 163)*

We also need to remember that an important job of the reporter is to support stories; to find suitable evidence and name sources with their credentials to alert readers to the story's credibility. As Michael Foley, now an emeritus professor at Dublin Institute of Technology put it:

> How can the public, those who are to be informed by journalism so that they can make the decision necessary in a democracy, trust journalists who offer so

much information without any meaningful indication where it came from? In many, possibly most, cases the anonymous source is not a fearless whistle-blower, but a manipulating spin doctor, working for the rich and powerful and hiding behind a journalist's promise of anonymity. And if that is the case, who gains most by the journalists' willingness to go to prison rather than reveal a source, the source or the public? As the philosopher, Onora O'Neill (2002: 98), commented in her BBC Reith Lecture: "I am still looking for ways to ensure that journalists do not publish stories for which there is no source at all, while pretending that there is a source to be protected."

(Foley 2004: 3)

Whatever your belief, one thing is clear: Martin-Clark's inexperience led him to make promises when he had no idea about what he was agreeing. Had he been aware that McKeown was going to confess to a serious crime, then it would have been foolish to promise not to reveal his source. Anonymous sources can lead us to great stories, but only if we can use the information to stand the story up from other sources. Anonymous evidence risks being no evidence at all.

There may be occasions when the need for anonymity is implied. Bill Goodwin was a young journalist working for a magazine. He was contacted by a reliable source who revealed details of a confidential financial plan for a major software company. Whilst seeking confirmatory information, the company became aware of his knowledge and sought and gained an injunction to prevent publication and sought to get the courts to instruct Goodwin to reveal his source. This was a legitimate use of confidentiality and Goodwin contacted his union, the NUJ, and with its support and the support of his company refused to reveal his source to the court. The case ended up in the European Court of Human Rights, which ruled that attempting to force a journalist to reveal his sources violated Article 105 of the European Convention on Human Rights. Shield law, as it is known, exists in a number of jurisdictions protecting journalists from revealing confidential sources.

In a case in Canada, Ken Peters of the *Hamilton Spectator* wrote an article about abuses in a local nursing home and supported his allegations with documents leaked to him by an anonymous source. Peters was later fined $31,600 by the Canadian Supreme Court for contempt of court after consistently refusing to name his source.

Reporters should also guard against sheer carelessness. In a complaint to the PCC in the UK, a woman from Newcastle, who worked for the Rural Payments Agency, complained that the Newcastle *Evening Chronicle* did not respect her confidentiality after she contacted the newspaper by email to share some of her experiences of the agency but asked to remain anonymous. A reporter from the newspaper forwarded the email to the RPA for comment without removing the complainant's details. The PCC upheld the complaint as "a serious and thoughtless error".

Occasionally you might work on a story that involves a deeper than normal relationship over a long period of time – a running campaign perhaps. You need to be aware that we owe some loyalty to the sources in those kinds of stories and that you may often learn things through that deeper relationship that the source would prefer were not published. You need to ensure full transparency, discussing these things with the source so that you do not betray the trust that has built up over the weeks, possibly months.

Hoaxes, rumours, and false news

Be careful of stories from sources, especially on social media, that could be hoaxes or so-called "false news". False news covers several categories. For US President Donald Trump it seems to mean any news that portrays him in a bad light. Whilst Trump has his own reasons for discrediting stories, we should remember that news reports can often portray facts in a way that can make them sound untrue or portray distorted facts or a collection of facts that make them sound true. Stories are often published in a way that supports the agenda of the publisher or which plays to the prejudices of its readers, making it more attractive for them to buy. Hoaxes are false stories that might be started for one of several reasons: mischief-making, campaigning, or for making money. Rumours often sound like really good stories well worth publishing. It is often suggested that publishing a story along the lines of the "Rumours have been denied that ..." allows the publication to have its cake and eat it, but in fact this is just another way of putting the rumour out there without checking it and could lead to a defamation suit. A Mr Edward Clark complained to the UK's PCC in 2010 that articles in the *Canterbury Times* and the *Herne Bay Times* reported an allegation, sent in an anonymous email to the newspapers, that the complainant – who had been awarded the lead role in his local operatic society's latest production – was an "ex-heroin user". The complainant said that this was incorrect: he had never used heroin in his life. He had made clear his absolute denial of the claim to the newspaper before publication and this had been included in the article. He said that the newspaper should not have published the story based on the unsubstantiated claims of a single anonymous source. The PCC rightly agreed and upheld the complaint. It seems likely that the anonymous email was simply mischief making from a rival for the lead role and should never have been taken seriously.

In another complaint, a Mr Ash Choudry complained to the PCC about an online article in the *Daily Mail* which reported on a Facebook campaign urging Saudi men to whip women who planned to defy a ban on women driving. The complainant believed that the Facebook campaign was in fact a hoax. While the newspaper did not accept that its article was in breach of the Editors' Code, the matter was resolved when it agreed to remove the piece from its website.

Personal lives

Can a journalist have a private life? Many journalists, particularly in the US, believe that journalists should play no part in public life, following their own personal interests in order to keep objective. However, it is unlikely this ever works – journalists have views and private lives. They have children who go to local schools, they can vote, they often meet local politicians and have views about them. They may be involved in local clubs and societies, trade unions or activist groups. It's important to let your news editor know if your hobbies, beliefs, or pastimes risk coming into conflict with your work. For instance, if you are on the local parent–teacher association (PTA) or board of school governors then it might not be wise to become education correspondent for the local paper.

Social networking can also lead to difficulties. Make sure you always Tweet or write in social networking as a person, not a reporter. Using a nickname can be a way around this. You need to ensure that your social media interactions as you are not confused with the reporter. Tony Grossi, who had covered the Cleveland Browns at *The Plain Dealer* in the US for roughly two decades, was removed from the beat by editor Debra Adams Simmons after an ill-considered Tweet went unintentionally viral. Grossi had typed a message, which he termed "a smart-(aleck) remark to a colleague", that called Browns owner Randy Lerner "a pathetic figure, the most irrelevant billionaire in the world". Many companies now have internal policies on social media. The personal use of the internet by BBC staff, for instance, must be tempered by an awareness of the potential conflicts that may arise. The BBC makes clear there should be a clear division between "BBC" pages and "personal" pages and that information disclosed should not bring the BBC into disrepute.

Bribery

Being a journalist can tempt some people to abuse their position by attempting to gain favours or free entry to such things as sports grounds and shows even when you aren't covering the event. Attempting to pressurise people because of your position or making threats to write a damaging story if you don't get your way is clearly unethical and journalists should not take advantage of their position. The same applies to making promises to give a good write up if certain favours are granted.

On occasion, you might be threatened about writing a particular story. Court cases, for instance, have led people to threaten the reporter in court with violence if something is published. It's also possible (although less likely in my experience) that you would be offered a gift with the implied request for a positive write up. In either case, you should tell your editor in order to ensure that any decision taken is based on the complete facts.

Freebies

Whilst taking a bribe to either publish or not publish is clearly unethical and may well be illegal in a number of jurisdictions, there are some potential gifts that are difficult to refuse. Reviews of books, records, films, video games and technology are all difficult without listening to them or trying them out but very few publications are willing to spend a lot of money buying the products and it is normal for companies to send copies for review in order to inform the public and ensure sales. Holidays and car loans are other "freebie" perks that occasionally come to journalists. This is a difficult decision to make. At the end of the day, most journalists take the view that whilst they might be influenced by getting something for free, since it's all free they are able to make balanced comparisons. However, we do always need to be aware that it is free.

Conclusion

Journalism is an important job and can be a rewarding career, but it is not without its challenges especially for someone starting out in the industry. Having struggled to get your first job, it is often tempting to take things quietly and do as you are told, but editors are looking for reporters who are keen and committed and most importantly can bring them good stories. The best way to progress in your career and at the same time be able to hold your head up high by behaving ethically is to get out there and find your own stories.

The sooner editors realise they get more out of you by letting you get on with it than by ordering you to do things you would find distasteful, the sooner you will feel you are getting somewhere.

Whether you start on a local paper, specialist website, or a broadcast station look to your target audience. What kind of stories do they want and who can give them to you? Who do you need to get to know to get good stories? Who in the community you are serving gets to talk to a lot of people? Visit them, talk to them, build a level of working trust with them so that they contact you or you can contact them. Once when on a visit to a distant relative of my wife's before the days of mobile phones a contact tracked me down 200 miles away to tell me the local mayor had died. I was able to get straight on to the story.

The better and wider the range of your contacts, the better the stories. You also need imagination about how you can use these contacts. Every little piece of information you can come across can be looked at to expand into a story, using the right contacts and a good imagination. The weather brings heavy rainfall? Who is badly hit and who benefits? A horrible smell in the air? Where's it coming from, why, and who is concerned about it? A group of people are on the street having an animated conversation. What's going on?

Getting the story does not mean behaving unethically, but it may mean working a little harder. It will leave you proud of what you do and no money can buy that feeling.

References

Article 19 (1998) *Briefing Paper on Protection of Journalists' Sources.* https://www.article19. org/data/files/pdfs/publications/right-to-protect-sources.pdf

Foley, Michael (2004) *Absolutism and the Confidentiality Debate: Confidentiality and Journalists Sources*, Dublin Institute of Technology. http://arrow.dit.ie/cgi/viewcontent.cgi?article=1040&context=aaschmedart

Frost, Chris (2016) *Journalism Ethics and Regulation* 4th edn. London: Routledge

Klaidman, Stephen and Beauchamp, Tom (1987) *The Virtuous Journalist* New York: Oxford University Press

Websites

www.nytimes.com/2003/05/11/national/times-reporter-who-resigned-leaves-long-trail-of-deception.html

www.ons.gov.uk/aboutus/transparencyandgovernance/freedomofinformationfoi/leavecampaignclaimsduringbrexitdebate

www.dailymail.co.uk/news/article-1084453/Paul-Dacres-speech-full.html

https://www.ofcom.org.uk/tv-radio-and-on-demand/broadcast-codes

http://www.bbc.co.uk/editorialguidelines/

www.ipso.co.uk

2

LEARNING TO COPE WITH THE TOUGH TIMES

Lyn Barnes

Introduction

Duncan and Newton (2010) have argued that the death-knock interview is "arguably one of the most challenging tasks a journalist will perform in their career", yet novice journalists are often dispatched to carry them out, without any preparation or support afterwards. Currently, many journalists who have no formal understanding of grief and trauma are routinely sent to knock on the doors of the bereaved (Rees, 2013), and often the only preparation they have is the time it takes to reach the scene (Simpson and Coté, 2006). Covering court can be equally as challenging. This area of study related to domestic journalists had previously been neglected, although research into trauma and war correspondents has been well documented. Unfortunately, the effect of any type of trauma work can have a drip-by-drip effect – and journalists cannot always be emotionless, detached observers (Massé, 2011).

So, what is traumatic stress and how can it affect journalists? Firstly, there are two types of traumatic stress. Direct trauma is the result of experiencing something traumatic directly, for example, witnessing a fatal car accident or a brutal attack on someone. Secondary trauma is just as real but it is second-hand, that is, as a result of listening to someone's tragic story or gruesome details exposed in court.

It's important to realise that trauma has many guises and it can affect people differently, or not at all. For example, you may feel overwhelmed, irritable, suffering from broken sleep or unexpectedly angry. If such reactions continue for more than three months, you may be suffering from post-traumatic stress disorder (PTSD) and it is advisable to seek help to deal with the ongoing symptoms. But, even if the effects are short-term, talking to a friend, colleague or family member helps to unload the burden and change the way traumatic memories are stored in the brain (Hight and Smyth, 2009).

This chapter explores the "theory of balance" to ensure you maintain equilibrium, understand how newsrooms operate and why news is changing, as well as presenting case studies of best and worst practice.

The research

Journalists are at risk of traumatic stress or PTSD because they are on the "front-line" just like police or fire-fighters, yet they are seldom debriefed or offered counselling. Sometimes there's an accompanying feeling of guilt, that journalists are not there to do a "real" job. Whereas police who work on child abuse teams must undergo regular counselling, a journalist may sit through a number of child abuse cases and have to listen to horrific details without counselling afterwards. Police culture has improved over the past 30 years, to the point where counsellors now consider how home life and personal issues may impinge on one's ability to work. Unfortunately, newsroom culture still has a long way to go. It is best to be aware that your work can affect your home life and vice versa. One journalist I interviewed said he would fly off the handle unexpectedly with his children and he didn't know why until he was diagnosed with PTSD.

Interviewing people who are grieving, or reporting stories about animal abuse, can build up over time and be just as traumatic as covering a major earthquake. Research shows that people cope better with natural disasters than man-made tragedies.

Death and near-death stories are more likely to make front page news because of a number of factors, including changes in societal attitudes to death that has moved it from being a private matter to becoming a matter of public interest (Barnes and Edmonds, 2015). Emotions have also become a significant factor in the news process because they have the capacity to engage the audience (Beckett, 2016; Pantti, 2010). The human interest story – that is, a story that focuses on a person in an emotional way to evoke sympathy – is now a staple in the media. These stories are easily sourced through regular contact with emergency services or attending court. They are also easier and cheaper to produce and ultimately more lucrative than quality, in-depth, investigative features that take time and cost money. As budgets tighten in newsrooms around the world, news managers often have to give preference to news stories that will attract larger audiences, and thereby increase profits (McManus, 2009). Today's analytics (or clicks on electronic news stories, or the number of stories forwarded through social media) reveal how well read human interest stories are. If they were not popular, they would no longer feature so frequently (Schaudt and Carpenter, 2009). In fact, some publications are rewarding – and punishing – journalists for click rates (*The Times*, 2015).

In my research into journalist trauma, journalists used the term "discomfort" on a regular basis to describe the feeling of imbalance. As a result, my theory focused on the concept of balance and three levels became apparent in relation to covering trauma: Attaining balance, Maintaining balance and Losing balance. For some journalists, the three stages or phases can be a trajectory.

As with any aspect of life, balance implies a level of movement. For journalists, constant movement or pressure comes from the push–pull phenomenon that keeps them perpetually on edge: the *push* is extrinsic, from editors and other external forces; the *pull* is intrinsic, from the desire to do a good job and work within ethical bounds.

First, journalists have to learn how to attain balance when dealing with trauma. Three sub-categories have emerged as the necessary steps to Attaining balance: *Being "professional"*, *Confronting emotions* and *Learning the rules* of the newsroom. If young journalists achieved all three steps, usually by adopting various coping strategies, they moved on to the next phase or sub-category, Maintaining balance. This is where they were regularly covering trauma-based stories and felt a sense of satisfaction in *Getting the get*, that is, pursuing people for interviews and imagery, and enjoying the challenge. They learned to "play the game" by *Reading the newsroom*: figuring out whether they should share any concerns about their work or keep them to themselves; what the accepted behaviours were; and how to work around them, if necessary. This phase was also dependent on learning how to *Control emotions*.

If their passion for the job began to wane, often from covering too many traumatic events and not acknowledging or knowing how to deal with the stress in a positive manner, some journalists were at risk of Losing balance. At this point, some journalists did not feel they were functioning properly and were *Lacking control* over the outcome of their stories while constantly *Juggling emotions*. This stage could be exhausting, and in time, lead to burn-out or *Hitting the limit*, where they could not face any further work without a negative mental and physical reaction. As a result, they would usually resign because they could not detach emotionally.

Stability or equilibrium at each stage of the theory of balance is dependent on three underlying conditions: preparation, support, and cogitation. Cogitation is a form of self-talk and reflection (Schön, 1983), which some journalists use to psyche themselves up before carrying out a difficult interview.

Preparation refers to the level of knowledge the journalist has about the situation – and how much trauma training they have received. Whether it is carrying out a death-knock interview, or covering a court case, journalists interviewed in my research appeared to maintain balance more readily if they knew as much as possible about the victim, or were familiar with the court procedures. The level of knowledge could affect their response, which in turn could affect their comfort or discomfort levels. If the practical aspects of the court were understood, that could help with *Managing emotions*, for example, when listening to vivid details in an horrific child abuse case. The response indicates how important it is for senior staff to brief someone and share information when assigning a job and that guidance should be given. Support can be physical or mental. Whereas preparation and support are external factors, cogitation is internal. Cogitation can act as a form of self-protection, as these two journalists explain:

> If I'm feeling vulnerable and I don't want to knock on this door … but [I say to myself] "it's your job, you've got to do it" … it's so much about getting the story.

… rather than just reporting on stuff straight, reporting about an incident, I like to try and think how you can create change or something from that incident … Like meaningful, doing meaningful reporting rather than just titillating your audience or telling what's happened, trying to think why am I reporting on this, why do I want to emphasise this? What's the effect of this going to be?

On the job, cogitation can include justifying, or even thinking pragmatically. It is a self-monitoring and self-aligning process and can be affected by the levels of stress hormones in a person's system, adrenaline and cortisol. After an event, it is more of a reflective process, whereby the journalist reconciles what went well and what did not, as well as rationalises to avoid any subsequent unpleasant consequences. It can be punitive but also self-congratulatory, as a way of moving on to the next assignment (Figure 2.1).

Guidance for novice journalists on how to carry out a death-knock interview or cover court cases is usually oral rather than written, as the research from the biggest newsrooms in New Zealand revealed (Barnes, 2016). Many journalists were shocked at the level of detail revealed in child murder cases for example; others felt guilty about invading someone's grief. Most of them tried to control their emotions; they intrinsically knew this was expected of them. That is most likely because the traditional journalist is socialised to remain unflappable

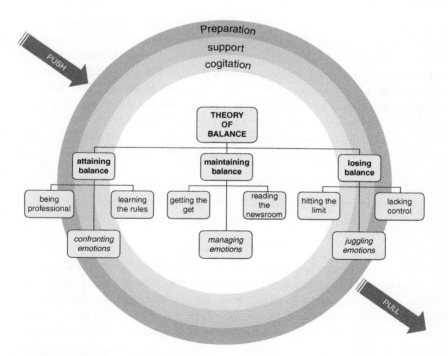

FIGURE 2.1   Barnes' theory of balance in trauma journalism. In all three phases, the level of balance is dependent on preparation, support, and cogitation.

and suppress emotions (Underwood, 2011). However, research suggests that suppressing emotions is neither healthy nor normal. The 2015 study by Hopper and Huxford found there were ongoing risks to emotional suppression or control, and that by deferring emotions journalists might suffer long-term repercussions. They found several of their respondents were still suffering some years later from long-term guilt and self-hatred, a form of post-traumatic stress disorder (American Psychiatric Association, 2015).

My research was inspired by a former student who had been working on a weekend newspaper for two years after graduating. The 23-year-old came to see me about a year after the Christchurch earthquake in New Zealand in February 2011 that killed 185 people. We were talking about her fellow graduates who had covered the earthquake, as several did within weeks of their graduation. But what she said haunted me for some time afterwards: "I feel for those journalists who covered Christchurch, but what about the run-of-the-mill trauma we deal with every day?" She sounded cynical and disillusioned and she began to question her career choice. About six months later she resigned and this is what she wrote in response to reading my work:

> "It's funny how people call PR 'the dark side' when journalists are doing much, much darker stuff on a day-to-day basis. Switching to PR was like taking a walk in the sunshine for the first time in years".

As a trained news journalist myself, we were often accompanied by a senior journalist when we were sent to cover our first fatalities, or at least there was a photographer on hand who often had more experience with trauma than the journalists. Going out on an assignment alone, as many young journalists do now – where they are also expected to take their own photos or video footage – can be tough going, especially if they have to process and reflect on the experience by themselves afterwards. Sometimes they make decisions they regret.

The increasingly intense commercial pressure to be first with the news puts journalists under extreme pressure, as Richards (1998: 150) notes:

> "As ratings and circulation follow the content of the story rather than the manner in which it is prepared, there has been considerable pressure on individual journalists to 'bend the rules' to get the story with the most audience impact".

Not only do journalists experience unexpected emotions with trauma work, but so can people they are sent to interview: traumatised people often react unexpectedly, for example, shouting or swearing abuse. That is usually because they may still be in shock and therefore do not act normally. This is because the amygdala in the brain is doing what it has been programmed to do – to protect that person. The amygdala is responsible for detecting fear and preparing for emergencies. It is an innate mechanism that is responsible for the flight or fight response, and it cannot be altered. If a friend or relative has died suddenly, they will be in shock and they may not be thinking rationally. So, you will have to think carefully about which questions to ask – and how to respond. Rather than rush someone who is distressed, it is usually beneficial to be upfront and honest. For example, take a few minutes to build up some rapport, then be honest and admit you have only ten minutes. Keep your questions open-ended but precise, such as, "Can you tell me what happened?" This is better than something vague and inappropriate, such as "How do you feel?". In fact, avoid this question when-ever possible, because it is usually obvious how a traumatised person feels. Then, listen. Let the person speak, don't interrupt and show genuine empathy by using non-verbal gestures such as nods.

It was easier when journalists were expected to collect only facts and objec-tivity was encouraged. But that's not what readers want now. Wahl-Jorgensen (2013b) argues that subjectivity is necessary to engage an audience. People want facts – and feelings, or emotionality. And that can be hard when you have not been trained to capture emotional quotes. Balancing objectivity and emotionality can affect the journalist's response in any trauma situation, and can in turn affect the consequence or outcome.

Early journalism did not distinguish between fact and opinion but by the end of the nineteenth century publishers and editors had erased the subjective view-point (Wahl-Jorgensen, 2013b). Objectivity implied that journalists should not be affected by their work (Hedges, 2010). Although the process of objectivity was gradual, it reached the point of "near-obsession" (Allan 2004: 23). The ideal of objective, non-biased reporting became institutionalised within American and British journalism culture throughout the 1920s. Journalists were discour-aged from displaying any emotions, mainly because the culture of newsrooms was traditionally stoic and run by men.

Part of the drive towards objectivity was profit driven "to avoid confront-ing unpleasant truths or angering a power structure on which news organisa-tions depend for access and profits" (Hedges, 2010). As the nature of the media industry and its public service role changed, so did the content, which was toned down. As part of the socialisation process, journalists were expected to be staunch. Socialisation, the internalisation of "appropriate" behaviours, is a sub-tle process. It happens by osmosis in newsrooms (Breed, 1955). "Journalists are socialized not just to feel part of a particular group but also to do things in a par-ticular way and to consider that way as natural and desirable" (Singer 2004: 841). To understand this process, it is important to understand how newsrooms func-tion and how newsroom culture develops.

Newsroom culture

Newsroom culture is "enforced" by norms, rules, routines, and shared values of journalists and editors. Willis suggested norms and ethics are learned through "journalistic inbreeding" (2010: 15): journalists learn what is acceptable and unacceptable behaviour from other journalists, who learned it from other journalists. This implies that sometimes spoken rules may be bypassed by unspoken "rules", for example, bending the rules to get a story.

Norms are social expectations that guide behaviour: they guide what journalists should do, ought to do, and are expected to do under certain situations. Most norms in newsrooms are unspoken (Allan, 2004). Schudson (2001) referred to norms in newsrooms as obligations.

Rules are learned and understood as "things that journalists do" rather than as explicit rules of behaviour (Ryfe 2009: 209). Over a period of time, journalists learn to *do the right thing* when covering trauma stories. For example, learning to accept any job being assigned (that is, not saying no) and to be tenacious.

One journalist interviewed for my study into reporting trauma in New Zealand was proud of the fact that she had never refused to carry out a death-knock assignment. She considered giving up on getting someone to talk as failing, and admitted she "did some damage along the way". Interactions at work made her realise that getting the scoop or *"getting the get"* was a priority, no matter the response from victims:

> Saying no is also considered being a failure, especially if the opposition got the scoop. If you say no … but then you've got this thing in your head, what if the XXXXX [newspaper] get it today and you were putting it off. So, it's a bit of a vicious circle.

Routines are used to help journalists recognise, produce, and justify their selection and treatment of news stories (Cottle, 2007). As Cottle points out, routines are often unconscious and may help to account for the relatively standardised form of news produced across news outlets (2007: 3). Routines create consistency. "Although journalists, much like other professionals in the media industries, like to think of themselves as autonomous and creative individuals, in fact, most of the work at news outlets is based on a set of routine, standardised activities" (Deuze, 2008: 14). **Values** are shared assumptions of the group. Wilkins (2014) considered values to be a necessary building block of journalistic ethical choice. Although each country has its own code of ethics for journalists, there are many similarities.

Norms, rules, routines, and values repeated over time constitute a group's ideology. Tacit understanding of professional ideology comes from group interactions over time and is socially learned through everyday life on the job (Zelizer, 2004). Professional ideology is a process by which other ideas and views are excluded or marginalised, therefore, many journalists find it is better to conform to the group. Many endeavour to attain "professional ideals" by acquiring "a thick skin" to become insensitive (Richards and Rees, 2011: 858) to sources through interactions with other journalists. But that is not always a healthy response as there can be "ongoing affective and psychological damage when journalists suppress impulses of sympathy, pity, and guilt to avoid being overwhelmed by their feelings" (Hopper and Huxford, 2015: 26).

Journalists' professional discourse drives the discussion of everyday work and experiences, which creates and maintains their "community" (Zelizer, 1997). Such discourse maintains and teaches journalists what to do and what not to do. To share graphic details of a traumatic story or a gruesome court case, or display some form of bravado, is therefore considered more appropriate than sharing their emotional responses. "The shared past through which journalists discursively set up and negotiate preferred standards of actions hinges on the recycling of stories about certain key events" (Zelizer, 1997: 404).

So, what goes on in the newsroom can become a game of winning rewards and avoiding punishment. Bourdieu (2011) used the metaphor of a game in a *field* to explain how all the players need to accept the rules of the game to win. A *field* is a structured social space, for example, newsrooms are structured hierarchically. Constant, permanent relationships of inequality operate inside this space. The players are "people who dominate and others who are dominated" (Bourdieu, 2011: 40). To advance their position in the *field*, journalists have to earn *capital*. Bourdieu (1992) described three different forms of capital: *economic, cultural*, or *symbolic*. Whereas economic capital refers to material wealth in the form of money or property, cultural capital can include knowledge, skills, and other cultural achievements such as education. Symbolic capital can be accumulated power or status. For example, winning awards for articles may be considered as a symbolic reward. Using Bourdieu's field theory (1998), trauma stories have become *currency,* and securing interviews with people who are grieving can earn journalists more symbolic capital over a period of time.

For a journalist, "playing the game" can mean persevering to get an interview for an emotional story, no matter what the outcome. As one of the participants in my study says:

> … there's been a couple where I've taken it upon myself probably, past the point of being rational, because you get it in your head that you have failed and you want to get this thing … And I kind of just got worked up about it and ended up going out there with a photographer and, you know, they told me to fuck off and shut the door in my face.

A reward system can reinforce professional ideals. Along with rewards and punishments, which may include positive feedback or admonishments from editors, comes a growing awareness in the minds of journalists as to what constitutes a *good* story (Willis, 2010). Young journalists listen to stories from senior staff, reinforcing how *good* journalists should behave. Award-winning journalists talk about "how I got that story" or "how I wrote that story and why". Willis (2010), who studied journalistic decision-making, argued that this was a very real form of indoctrination.

An example from my study of where the reward–punishment system worked was to ensure no one in the office spoke up if they had upset people they were interviewing. This situation could increase the push–pull tension, whereby one journalist wanted the recognition for her efforts, but was aware of the incongruity of the situation and felt guilty about pressuring distressed people to speak:

> You're still that hero in the office, you got the story, you got "the collect", you got the name, so you couldn't then start crying and saying "but it was really hard and they were grief stricken" …

Objectivity did offer advantages at times. Tuchman envisaged it as a strategic ritual that journalists could use as a survival mechanism and to save time. It helped them "accomplish their deadlines, maintain their standing in the eyes of their superiors, and affected the ability of the news organisation to make a profit" (Tuchman, 1972: 664). For example, there was a rule that sources did not see the final story before it went to print. The reason was that it would hold up the publishing process. Schudson considered the ritual to be a "means of social control and social identity" (2001: 165).

Subjective journalism is a direct challenge to the paradigm of objectivity. The ideal of objectivity implies that journalists are impartial observers, who are "entirely neutral" (Wahl-Jorgensen, 2013a). But Wahl-Jorgensen argues this ideal of objectivity is impossible because the reporter's voice, or subjectivity, comes through with their choice of words (2013b: 302). She argues that social values and bias can be detected anyway.

Richards and Rees agree. They described objectivity as "a lurking legacy of the 19th-century positivism for journalists" (2011: 863). Hedges (2010) blames the objectivity paradigm for turning journalists into neutral observers who were "permitted to watch but not to feel or to speak their own voices". Instead, they have been expected to function as "professionals" and "see themselves as dispassionate and disinterested social scientists", because objectivity was synonymous with journalists remaining detached.

> At its ideal, the emotional work of the journalist is aimed at the erasement [sic] of the individual news-worker through the suppression of emotion – the idea that for objectivity, the "I" is repressed for the journalist to function as a "transparent conduit" for information that will enrich society.
>
> *(Hopper and Huxford, 2015: 29)*

Trauma reporting

What to do

Trauma reporting can affect a number of people within a society. It is not simply covering an incident, such as an accident or murder, that makes the news, but the subsequent follow-up stories related to the original incident that can cause conflict. Some people see this as an intrusion into privacy. And it doesn't help that most codes of ethics are vague when it comes to the actual details of intrusion. Words such as *respect* and *privacy* are not clear, as Richards (1998) noted. He also raises the dilemma: "... how does an individual exercise the right 'to resist compulsion to intrude' when a chief of staff, for example, is insisting upon it?" (1998: 155). It is important to remember that everyday people are not used to dealing with the media, unlike politicians, and they may feel feel threatened by your approach. So how can this be addressed so that it is a positive experience for journalist and interviewees?

How to do it

Best practice: changing the power dynamics

It is becoming more commonplace to show the completed story to people interviewed so they can fact-check it before publication. Several journalists I interviewed choose to do this now. Here is how one journalist explained why she felt better about "giving the power back" to her sources.

> I think when I first started reporting, I think this is the thing that young reporters don't do, it's kind of like laying a trap for your interviewee to get them to say the best thing, or to get them to do this, but I think as I've grown as a reporter I've learnt to collaborate with my subjects and say this is what we're looking to do, how do you feel about that? This is what I've got you saying. Do you want to say anything about this? You've said this sentence, you know, and just let them really make sure that what they've said is how they want to sound. Without compromising how they do sound and just making sure that you've not misinterpreted anything.

Collaborating with sources, which has always been frowned upon in the past, is this journalist's way of giving herself "insurance"; it is a self-protective strategy to ensure the facts are correct plus it helps to alleviate any possible feelings of guilt if there is a mistake in the article. By carrying out this process, the journalist acknowledges that people can be fragile when they are grieving, which this journalist learned through past bad experiences.

> ... you've just got to be careful especially when you know, when you are talking about these times, they are really stressful and emotional times for people on the phone. That you've caught them and [it's] just nice to be able to feel like you've got it right and I think that goes a long way to protecting yourself from like I was saying, the guilt or whatever.

This response acknowledges also that traumatised people are not always reliable witnesses because they can be confused about things (Muller, 2010), and therefore checking back with them is ethically advisable.

Worst practice: hiding behind a mask

All journalists practise *emotional labour* at times. This is when we put on a mask as such: for example, a "professional" mask during an interview. This is known as emotional labour. Think of the extreme cheerfulness of Disneyland staff. It becomes a process of managing one's true feelings in order to do the job (Hochschild, 1979). All relationships and communication involve some level of emotional labour; however, the nature of journalists' work requires constantly engaging in emotional labour. Journalists often need "to suppress, fake or enhance emotions during interactions based on the particular display rules advocated by their organisation" (Hopper and Huxford, 2015: 25). But it is not healthy to fake emotions for too long. Hochschild (1983) linked emotional labour to *emotional dissonance*, the strain caused when someone was faking how they felt – and what they were truly feeling. For example, trying to interview someone when you are obviously not coping, as this young woman explained:

> Whereas now I've gone from at the beginning of the job absolutely loving that adrenaline, all that sort of stuff that I used to enjoy and now having a panic attack every time there is a big story. Getting the shakes, feeling sick, vomiting on the side of the road, proper panic attack.

Festinger's (1957) theory assumes that people have an overarching need for cognitive balance or consistency. If the dissonance cannot be resolved, the outcome can be stress, burn-out, or an "estrangement from self" (Hochschild, 1983; Bakker and Heuven, 2006). If a person is completely outside their comfort zone, they could display physiological responses, such as an increased heart rate and psychological reactions, such as a feeling of panic.

Hopper and Huxford's research encouraged them to alert those entering journalism of the need to be aware of the pressure emotional labour can bring "and the long-term toll that process can exact" (2015: 39). Burn-out can affect job performance, job satisfaction as well as work and family relationships, which in turn can lead to diminished productivity and employee turnover (Reinhardy, 2011).

Why do it?

Having covered how to cover a trauma story, we need to consider what you can do as a journalist to ensure you do the best job possible for everyone involved, especially yourself. The better prepared you are, the more likely you are to get a better story. If you are distracted by unexpected emotions or inappropriate questions which result in having a door slammed in your face, you not only jeopardise the outcome, but also put yourself at risk. So you need to protect yourself, and that means before, during, and after a traumatic encounter.

What can a journalist do?

Self-care is critical if you are covering emotional stories on a regular basis, to prevent them taking their toll. Simple steps include deep breathing exercises, which have been shown to be important for the brain, and recognising any signs of stress you are feeling: for example, a twitchy eye or broken sleep. This includes being aware of your basic needs – for example, eating properly, drinking enough water, getting enough sleep – and also taking steps to relieve any stress. It is vital to take the time for a walk or treat yourself to a massage. Or be prepared to tell your managers when issues arise. This is not easy, so it may be wise to alert colleagues first for support, or someone more senior whom you respect, before you go to management. Often managers are unaware of the symptoms of stress or are too busy to notice. That's why it's up to you to take charge with self-care. If you feel you can't approach your editor, contact HR for counselling. The media, as an industry, is evolving and recognising that journalists suffer symptoms of traumatic stress similar to other professions who work on the front-line. Most companies provide at least three confidential sessions free of charge. Some journalists are reluctant to speak up or prefer to seek support independently but this can be an expensive option. "Fear of losing a job, or of being perceived as weak and incapable of taking on big assignments, may prevent some journalists from seeking help, but that doesn't mean help isn't available" (Jones, 2014).

Part of the problem has been that editors are seldom trained to recognise signs of stress or how to prepare staff for covering trauma. It has not been a priority because of "staunch" newsroom culture, although that is slowly changing. Jones (2014) found only one in three media managers in her study reported having had training in how to intervene when employees show signs of depression. Even when they did notice, only 55 per cent of supervisors stepped in. She suggested that in organisations where workers felt uncomfortable about disclosing any mental health issues, employees might be reluctant to seek help and as a consequence, their condition could deteriorate. Novak and Davidson (2013) advocate workshops to promote resourcefulness and to discuss ways of managing experiences to provide opportunities for reflection. The researchers suggested these workshops might also reduce newsroom stoicism. "Promoting the importance of social networks and the role they play in mediating levels of distress should be considered within awareness-raising programmes for both journalists themselves and the organisations they work for" (Novak and Davidson, 2013: 320).

CASE STUDY 1: COURT REPORTING

What can start off as an exciting part of your career, such as covering court stories, can wear people down if they do the same work for too long.

Worst practice

Initially, Jarred says he "got a buzz" out of going to court. But after covering court stories for several years with very little time off, he admits it became overwhelming. Yet he began to feel "territorial" when he was offered other rounds. Some newsrooms make such changes compulsory and there's good reason for that. Being a court reporter is a bit like being a photographer or videographer, it entails repeatedly and constantly seeing the unpleasant side of life. A court reporter also needs to act as a censor and select only certain details for publication that will have been exposed in the courtroom. But it is not always so easy to blank out the rest. So how did Jarred cope? Unfortunately, he shut down his emotions.

> I guess it's a lot easier in that sort of situation to sort of divorce yourself from the facts of what's going on and at first I think when I was court reporting it really got me down. Like hearing about all the details and people's lives falling apart. Not just the victim's but the offender's as well, but now it's almost scarily easy to disassociate myself from that and kind of be desensitised to all that kind of stuff and just ride it.
>
> I think it's getting easier to deal with cases more coldly but I don't want to. It's not something I'm intentionally trying to do because I want to be in touch with the potential emotions of people that go through it. But it does feel increasingly easy to sort of close myself off from the wider sort of emotional approach.

Jarred would be the first to admit emotional dissonance set in and evidence of this was most likely obvious to others in the newsroom. Ideally, he should have been made to take some time off, as that is one of the best ways of coping, but that is not always a possibility. And he didn't want someone else doing his job, so even when he was offered time off, he seldom took it. Yet he knew something was wrong.

> Yeah, but even though you're kind of aware of it metacognitively or whatever they say, it's still hard to stop doing it or to know that you're actively doing it or anything. It's one thing to know you're doing it but it's another to either try and stop or to do something else. Yeah, it just happens and it becomes routine I guess.

Best practice

One young journalist, Courteney, had no idea how to cope after going to court and hearing details of torture. It was her first court case; she had graduated three weeks beforehand:

> You know, your boss calls you up in the morning and says, okay, you're off to the sentencing today. Mother, child abuse, yep, just go for it. Here's a bit of background and on those few instructions [off you go]. You never get any idea of how much detail .... about what the children suffered. Like the fact that there are going to be Victim Impact Statements read out and just that level of detail that they were going to go into and you would have to then make judgments as a journalist about what do I print? ... [This particular case] has been called New Zealand's worse case of child abuse where the kids haven't died.

Knowing there were other young journalists in the courtroom listening as well helped Courteney. She said she found that "comforting". "At least you are not there by yourself". So she sought them out during the court recess (not something that is condoned in the profession because of competition between rival media companies).

> "We were just like, whoa, what happened? And we all kind of had a quick chat about it".

Courteney found a positive strategy to help her get her through. She used cogitation and approached the task in stages.

> I think how I sort of cover, for example, a child abuse murder case is completely different to how I probably did it, probably a year ago. Now it's like, okay, focus on the story, just get your lead, get the basics in. A few more details and then at the break you can stop and be like, okay, that's what's happened. Sweet, what am I going to do next? Just kind of deal with it in chunks in a way.
>
> At the end of the day you can be like, okay number one, look how many stories I've achieved or how like I've actually done a really good job covering this, and in a way I've started to feel like it's a bit of a noble cause kind of like covering child abuse cases because you don't want to be covering another one. So I've actually just got to the point where I feel like it's kind of my duty to ensure this is covered really and so you know, that doesn't happen to another two-year-old kind of thing.

CASE STUDY 2: WORKING ALONE

Staff numbers in newsrooms have decreased considerably over the past decade. Sometimes journalists work remotely, for example, so they don't have colleagues to return to at the end of the day. For example, being a sole regional reporter, constantly on call, is demanding, as Monique found.

Worst practice

> Every day, 24/7, weekends, nights, anything. And when I spoke to the counsellor about it she said she did not know of any profession which is like that. She thought it was totally ridiculous. I mean, even doctors, midwives, have time off, they have some shifts when they are never on call. Whereas that's not the case with us, the only time I ever felt truly relaxed in this job was when I was on annual leave and overseas.

The lack of downtime with being the sole reporter made Monique feel undervalued and she became resentful. She regularly missed meals and sometimes found it difficult to find time to go to the toilet when covering major events. In the end, her husband stepped in and she eventually spoke up. She was relieved to find unexpected support from her boss. She also sought counselling, but she had left it too late. She resigned within six months.

Best practice

Emails to fellow journalists have been a saving grace for Jessie, along with online chats. She found that if she could chat to a friend or write down her feelings in an email it would help to calm her down after a stressful job. Rather than face-to-face conversations that were so important for de-stressing in the past – which usually involved excessive alcohol consumption as well (Underwood, 2011) – young journalists are finding the internet provides some sense of relief. It's important to talk – or blog – about your experiences if your work is emotionally challenging. This goes against traditional thinking that journalists should not have a personal opinion about an event or issue in the news (Fedler, 2004). But the more open journalists are, the sooner attitudes will change. For example, Beck Eleven (2013), a journalist who covered the 2011 Christchurch earthquake, wrote this column for a national newspaper:

> All too often the journalist is at a traumatic scene: In the past few weeks I have spoken to two women affected by domestic violence. One told me her story, calmly and patiently over five hours. The other could not tell me her story because she had died at the hands of her abuser, so her mother told me the story. Again, over five hours.

As a result, there was overwhelming support and concern from other journalists throughout the country and acknowledgement that it was time to talk about the issue. What was obvious from the comments was the psychological damage that some journalists had sustained from covering even mundane crimes. Richards has suggested that when journalists "go public" with self-revelatory articles it is not only indicating to their audience that they are deeply affected by events, but that they need the opportunity to talk to appropriate people and that they may be denied the opportunity because of the "absence of [a] 'sympathetic ear' in the newsroom" (2003: 166).

CASE STUDY 3: MONITOR YOUR BALANCE

It's important to regularly check in where you sit on the scale of balance explained earlier in this chapter. The "theory of balance" is a quick way to assess your equilibrium. And be alert to symptoms of Losing balance: if you feel that you are experiencing unexpected emotions, for example, or you feel depressed or are having recurrent dreams.

Worst practice

Penny covered so many trauma-related stories that she started having nightmares or couldn't sleep. She would snap at colleagues and couldn't relax.

> … House fires and stuff, I always get paranoid about the dishwasher. Dishwashers were always causing house fires and I never really looked into why but there were lots of them and even we had someone come around to do a quote for our insulation and talked about the down lights. Then I'm like, "Oh, my God, the house is going to burn down because the down lights can cause fires with insulation over the top". And how many house fires have I been to where the houses had taken the smoke alarm battery out because they were beeping? So many.
>
> If I was to describe it, I really feel like my body was in that hyper state of just really being completely wired all the time. I remember wanting to just get up and punch someone who was constantly sniffing. It was just so, so aggravating! … I was just constantly on edge and jittery.

Best practice

Sophie accepted her editor's recommendation that she take a break after covering earthquake stories for six months. She had become the go-to person for people all over the country and had interviewed so many widows and children affected by the quakes. So she packed up and went up north to work for another news outlet. Being on solid ground helped her to reground again and two months later she was refreshed and ready to return. She now knows her limits and one of the signs is broken sleep. Some colleagues chose not to take a break but she said she could observe signs in them that they needed time out.

Conclusion

This chapter has attempted to provide guidance about what you can do with any stress involved in your work as a journalist, especially repetitive traumatic stress. Until you know/understand yourself and how you may react, you can't respond appropriately to people, for example, who are grieving. It also involves understanding how newsrooms operate and appreciating the important work that journalists do. It's a culture in transition. You may not have to handle the dead bodies, but your work on the front-line is just as vital in sharing information that may save lives or prevent child abuse. So,

- Expect the unexpected.
- Don't fake it till you make it.
- Listen to your body.
- Self-care is essential.

References

American Psychiatric Association, 2015. *What is posttraumatic stress disorder?*. Available from: http://www.psychiatry.org/patients-families/ptsd/what-is-ptsd [Accessed 21 August 2015].

Backholm, K. and Idås, T., 2015. Ethical dilemmas, work-related guilt and posttraumatic stress reactions of news journalists covering the terror attack in Norway in 2011. *Journal of Traumatic Stress*, 28, 142–148.

Bakker, A.B. and Heuven, E., 2006. Emotional dissonance, burnout and in-role performance among nurses and police officers. *International Journal of Stress Management*, 13 (4), 423–440.

Barnes, L., 2016. *Journalism and everyday trauma: A grounded theory of the impact from death-knocks and court reporting* http://aut.researchgateway.ac.nz/handle/10292/10228 Thesis (PhD), Auckland University of Technology.

Barnes, L. and Edmonds, E., 2015. If it bleeds, it leads?: Changing death coverage. *The New Zealand Herald. Pacific Journalism Review,* 21 (2), 162–172. Available from: https://pjreview.aut.ac.nz/articles/if-it-bleeds-it-leads-changing-death-coverage-new-zealand-herald-1055 [Accessed 3 August 2015].

Beckett, C., 2016. *Navigating a complex media landscape* [Blog post 3 February 2016]. The London School of Economics and Political Science. Available from: http://blogs.lse.ac.uk/communications/2016/02/03/navigating-a-complex-media-landscape/ [Accessed 3 July 2015].

Bourdieu, P., 1992. *Language and symbolic power.* Cambridge, England: Polity.

Bourdieu, P., 2011. *On television and journalism.* London, England: Pluto Press.

Breed, W., 1955. Social control in the newsroom: A functional analysis. *Social Forces,* 33 (4), 326–335.

Cottle, S., 2007. Ethnography and news production: New(s) production in the field. *Sociology Compass,* 1 (1) 1–16. doi:10.1111/j.1751-9020.2007.00002

Deuze, M., 2008. Understanding journalism as newswork: How it changes and how it remains the same. *Westminister Papers in Communication and Culture,* 5 (2), 4–23. Available from: https://www.westminster.ac.uk/camri/publications [Accessed 5 August 2015].

Duncan, S. and Newton, J., 2010. How do you feel? Preparing novice reporters for the death knock. *Journalism Practice,* 4 (4), 439–453. doi:10.1080/17512780903482059

Eleven, B., 2013. Behind the headlines a story is told. *The Press.* 13 March 2013. Available from: http://www.stuff.co.nz/the-press/opinion/columnists/beck-eleven/8914235/Behind-the-headlines-a-story-is-told [Accessed 3 July 2014].

Fedler, F., 2004. Insiders' stories. Coping with newsroom stress: An historical perspective. *American Journalism,* 23 (3), 77–106.

Festinger, L., 1957. *A theory of cognitive dissonance.* Evanston, IL: Row Peterson.

Hedges, C., 2010. *The creed of objectivity killed the news.* 10 February 2010. https://www.truthdig.com/articles/the-creed-of-objectivity-killed-the-news/ [Accessed 15 April 2015].

Hight, J. and Smyth, F., 2009. *Tragedies and journalists.* Dart Center for Journalism and Trauma, from https://dartcenter.org/sites/default/files/en_tnj_0.pdf [Accessed 15 August 2015].

Hochschild, A.R., 1979. Emotion work, feelings, rules and social structure. *American Journal of Sociology,* 85 (3), 551–575.

Hochschild, A.R., 1983. *The Managed Heart: Commercialisation of Human Feeling.* Berkeley, CA: University of California Press.

Hopper, K.M. and Huxford, J.E., 2015. Gathering emotion: Examining newspaper journalists' engagement in emotional labour: *Journal of Media Practice,* 16 (1), 25–41. doi:10.1080/14682753.2015.1015799

Jones, M., 2014. Mental health: Why journalists don't get help in the workplace. 9 December 2014. *Ryerson Review of Journalism.* Available from http://rrj.ca/mental-health-why-journalists-dont-get-help-in-the-workplace/ [Accessed 6 October 2015].

Massé, M., 2011. *Trauma journalism: On deadline in harm's way.* New York, NY: Bloomsbury Publishing.

McManus, J.H., 2009. The commercialisation of news. *In:* Wahl-Jorgensen, K. and Hanitzsch, T., eds. *The Handbook of Journalism Studies.* New York, NY: Routledge, 218–235.

Muller, D., 2010. Ethics and trauma: Lessons from media coverage of Black Saturday. *Australian Journal of Rural Health,* 18, 5–10. doi:10.1111/j.1440-1584.2009.01117.x

Novak, R.J. and Davidson, S., 2013. Journalists reporting on hazardous events: Constructing protective factors within the professional role. *Traumatology*, 19 (4), 313–322. doi:10.1177/1534765613481854

Pantti, M., 2010. The value of emotion: An examination of television journalists' notions on emotionality. *European Journal of Communication*, 25 (2), 168–181. doi:10.1177/0267323110363653

Rees, G., 2013. The trauma factor: Reporting on violence and tragedy. In Fowler, K. and S. Allan. eds, *Journalism: New Challenges* Centre for Journalism and Communications Research Bournemouth University, England. 409–434. Available from: https://microsites.bournemouth.ac.uk/cjcr/files/2013/10/JNC-2013-Chapter-25-Rees.pdf [Accessed 23 February 2014].

Reinhardy, S., 2011. Newspaper journalism in crisis: Burnout on the rise, eroding young journalists' career commitment. *Journalism* 12 (1), 33–50. doi:10.1177/1464884910385188

Richards, I., 1998. Ethics: Journalists and victims. *In:* Breen, M., ed. *Journalism: Theory and practice.* Sydney, Australia: Macleay Press, 141–158.

Richards, I., 2003. When journalists reveal emotions. *Australian Studies in Journalism*, 12, 162–172. Available from: search.informit.com.au [Accessed July 3 2014].

Richards, B. and Rees, G., 2011. The management of emotion in British journalism. *Media, Culture and Society*, 33 (6), 851–867.

Ryfe, D. M., 2009. Broader and deeper: A study of newsroom culture in a time of change. *Journalism*, 10 (2), 197–216. doi:10.1177/1464884908100601

Schaudt, S. and Carpenter, S., 2009. The news that's fit to click: An analysis of online news values and preferences present in the most-viewed stories on azcentral.com. *Southwestern Mass Communication Journal*, 24 (2), 17–26.

Schön, D., 1983. *The reflective practitioner.* New York, NY: Basic Books.

Schudson, M., 2001. The objectivity norm in American journalism. *Journalism*, 2 (2), 149–170.

Simpson, R. and Coté, W., 2006. *Covering violence: A guide to ethical reporting about victims and trauma* (2nd ed.). New York, NY: Columbia University Press.

Singer, J., 2004. More than ink-stained wretches: The resocialisation of print journalist in converged newsrooms. *Mass Communication Quarterly*, 81 (4), 838–856. doi:10.1177/107769900408100408

The Times. 2015. Chase clicks not local news, reporters told. 10 June 2015 Available from http://www.thetimes.co.uk/tto/news/medianews/article4465453.ece [Accessed 16 June 2015].

Tuchman, G., 1972. Objectivity as strategic ritual: An examination of newsmen's notions of objectivity. *American Journal of Sociology*, 77 (4), 660–679.

Underwood, D., (2011). *Chronicling trauma: Journalists and writers on violence and loss.* Champaign, IL: University of Illinois Press.

Wahl-Jorgensen, K., 2013a. The strategic ritual of emotionality: A case study of Pulitzer Prize-winning articles. *Journalism*, 14 (1), 129–145. doi:10.1177/1464884912448918

Wahl-Jorgensen, K., 2013b. Subjectivity and story-telling in journalism. *Journalism Studies*, 14 (3), 305–320. doi:10.1080/1461670X.2012.713738

Wilkins, L., 2014. The newsroom made me do it: The impact of organisational climate on ethical decision-making. *In:* Wyatt, W.N., ed. *The ethics of journalism: Individual, institutional and cultural differences.* Reuters Institute for the Studies of Journalism, University of Oxford: IB Tauris, 33–54.

Willis, J., 2010. *The mind of a journalist*. Los Angeles, CA: Sage Publications.

Zelizer, B., 1997. Journalists as interpretive communities. *In:* Berkowitz, D., ed. *Social meanings of news*. Thousand Oaks, CA: Sage Publications, 401–419.

Zelizer, B. 2004. *Taking journalism seriously: News and the academy*. Thousand Oaks, CA: Sage Publications.

PART II

Reporting sensitive topics

3

REPORTING CHILD SEXUAL ABUSE

Amanda Gearing

The social issue

The sexual abuse of children is a serious crime that can have severe and lifelong consequences for victims (Glaser, 1997; Finkelhor, 1984). Society has become increasingly aware that institutions and families have in the past protected alleged and known offenders and have often disbelieved children who made disclosures about offences committed against them (Royal Commission, 2013; Middleton et al., 2014). Increased community awareness of the incidence of the sexual assault of children is beginning to change the way people and institutions interview suspected victims and respond to disclosures by children (Pipe, 2007).

Child sexual abuse occurs when an adult or adolescent invites or forces a child to observe or participate in sexual acts. Definitions and laws relating to child sexual assault vary from country to country and often from state to state. Child sexual assault is primarily a crime of power and control by a larger, stronger adult over a child who cannot give informed consent and does not fully comprehend the meaning of the acts. Criminal codes define a range of crimes from the lower end of seriousness such as grooming and exposure offences, to the higher end of the spectrum of seriousness involving touching and penetration offences such as indecent dealing with a minor, digital penetration, and rape. Child sexual abuse crimes committed using computers are increasingly common, including possession of child abuse images, trafficking child abuse images and making child abuse images.

Sexual abuse of infants, children, and adolescents occurs in all societies and cultures. Although rates vary, the medical and psychological damage caused can be severe and, at times, fatal (Carlton, 2016). The media has played a central role in hearing, testing, and publicising accounts from survivors of abuse, increasing public awareness of the problem and focusing political pressure for improved child protection policies and laws (Powell and Scanlon, 2015). Media coverage has exposed widespread sexual abuse of children in institutional contexts by trusted adults such as teachers, priests, sporting coaches, celebrities, judicial officers, and child care workers. In addition, media exposure of the culture of these once-trusted institutions, such as churches, schools, sporting, and cultural organisations, knowingly protecting offenders is beginning to lead to legislative change. Recent prevalence studies have shown that about one in three girls and one in six boys experience child sexual abuse (Wright and Keevers, 2014; Jay, 2014). However, children and young people may never disclose the abuse, or may delay their disclosure for many years (Allnock and Miller, 2013).

Reporting on child sexual abuse can be complicated by legal considerations. In many jurisdictions it is illegal to identify a victim of child sexual offences even when they reach adulthood. However, victims may choose to waive their right to anonymity (Morris and Gearing, 2017b). News sources who are victims of abuse are frequently still suffering physical and psychological injuries from the abuse even when the abuse occurred decades earlier. Medical science is only now beginning to quantify the traumatic physical damage to the immature brain of child victims of abuse. Streeck-Fischer and Kolk (2000: 903) found that "exposure to intrafamilial violence and other chronic trauma results in pervasive psychological and biological deficits". Treatment aims to compensate for developmental deficits caused by the traumatic memories (Streeck-Fischer and Kolk, 2000). Busy reporters who invest a lot of time documenting and verifying a story may find their news source's courage evaporate on the eve of publication due to rising fears connected with their trauma. A reporter's expertise in working with survivors can reduce this risk. Well-informed reporting that is trauma-informed can enable the survivor to experience their interaction with the media as therapeutic, in the sense of being liberated from their silence, validated by being believed and regaining personal agency. These positive outcomes are possible even when court processes have been difficult or unsuccessful.

Covering child sexual abuse trials, inquiries, incidents, and law reform are all challenging in various ways. Prolonged exposure of reporters to inhumanity and criminality towards children is confronting. Repeated or intensive exposure can leave reporters overwhelmed by sadness, depression, anger, and a range of other negative emotions. However, taking a break can lead to reporters feeling guilty, feeling like they have let their news sources down. Self-care by reporters to protect their own health and well-being as a priority is essential. Reporters may also be subjected to threats or intimidation by offenders and institutions that apply pressure for the reporter to abandon a story or investigation.

The key competencies required for this work are:

1. To know the criminal code regarding child sexual abuse in your jurisdiction;
2. To know the media law regarding defamation and the right of alleged offenders to protection of their identity;

3. To ensure facts are thoroughly checked and allegations are verified using all available documentation and witnesses;
4. To give fair right of reply to alleged offenders or institutions; and
5. To be prepared to defend your work.

Societies have a collective responsibility for the safety of children. Fair and accurate reporting of the scourge of child sexual abuse is necessary because "societal silence on this hidden crime protects perpetrators and enables abuse to continue" (Wright and Keevers, 2014).

Introduction

My experience in writing about child sexual assault began with reporting on a district court trial in a regional city in Australia in 1997. I saw evidence revealed in the court that the biological father of a child had sexually assaulted his own son. The son, by then an adult, was severely affected, and no longer trusted other people. The impact of the offences on the victim was profound: he was living in an isolated place on a property with high fences and guard dogs and kept a cache of weapons for protection. In later trials I saw similar chronic or lifelong effects on victims of abuse due to the betrayal of their trust as children.

The three case studies in this chapter are all cases I covered in Australia in 2001, in England in 2012, and in Wales in 2017. The first case was a rare civil trial in which a young woman sued an Anglican Diocese for personal injury caused by sexual abuse by a senior boarding master in a primary boarding school. The Diocese was found vicariously liable for the abuse and the Diocese was ordered to pay her a record damages award of $834,000. Of this amount, $400,000 was an award for exemplary damages for the Diocese's disregard of the plaintiff's rights after the Diocese knew about the abuse but which they denied for 11 years until making an admission in court. That case trained a spotlight on church institutions protecting child sex offenders in Australia because the archbishop, Peter Hollingworth, was head of the Diocese that was found guilty of negligence. By the time the case was being heard, Hollingworth had been appointed the governor-general of Australia. The case sparked media and political calls for a Royal Commission into child sexual abuse. The Royal Commission did not eventuate then but it was eventually established in 2012. In 2017, the Commission released a 17-volume report sharing the findings of the world's most thorough and extensive inquiry into child sexual abuse to date (Royal Commission into Institutional Responses to Child Sexual Abuse, 2017a).

In 2012, another victim of abuse, this time in England, contacted me alleging abuse by a former Anglican Dean of Manchester. I researched the story using digital technologies to locate other victims in Australia, the UK, and New Zealand and to document the facts. I was able to verify from documents that the church in England and Australia had protected a known offender from the 1950s until his death in 2009. To publish the story, I collaborated with two reporters, one in the UK and one in Australia, who were both working for national news-papers. Media coverage led to an independent inquiry and a police investigation in the UK into a senior member of the clergy.

In 2017, another international investigation began when a lawyer in England contacted me about a class action against a monastic order that had failed to protect children from a known paedophile on one of Britain's Holy Isles, Caldey Island in Wales. The story was published in *The Guardian* and on BBC Wales in November 2017. More than a dozen whistle-blowers then contacted me, alleging abuse by the same offender on Caldey Island from 1956–1992.

This chapter will outline the information that I wish I had been taught when I stepped into that first trial in 1997, as well as useful information that I have gathered since then. The take home messages of this chapter are:

1. To learn how to interview traumatised news sources;
2. To learn how to verify allegations using documentary evidence and cor-roborating witnesses; and
3. To learn how to avoid legal difficulties.

The research

Research is making society more aware of the incidence of child abuse and of the severe and lifelong consequences for victims (Glaser, 1997). However, it is often a secret crime (Davies, 1998). Secret criminality remains secret unless the crimes are made public by some mechanism that activates authorities to protect the vulnerable and to punish offenders. The role of the media in discovering, unveiling and making private crimes public cannot be underestimated in the formation of public action and policy (Goddard and Saunders, 2000; Nelson, 1984). The deaths of children from sexual abuse, for example, have led directly to new policies such as mandatory reporting of suspected abuse (Goddard and Liddell, 1993).

Given the secret nature of paedophilia, society relies upon victims to iden-tify offenders to the authorities – yet this may be fraught with danger and fear for victims. Research continues to indicate that 60–80 per cent of children and youths who have been subjected to sex offences withhold disclosure until adult-hood (Alaggia, 2010). Even in cases where children do report, their disclosures are not always acted upon (Allnock and Miller, 2013; Ullman, 2002). Disclosure is difficult and it may take victims many years to be willing or able to report the abuse, depending upon the age and development of the child, the relationship of the child to the perpetrator, the severity of the abuse and the availability of support (Salter, 2015).

Some victims of child sexual abuse continue to be victimised by their per-petrators as adults over many years because the offender may physically or psy-chologically retain control over the victim (Middleton, 2013; Connolly, 2009).

Salter describes the paradox that "in order to detect sexual abuse, we depend on abused children to speak out, but they are often in environments in which they can't rely on support or understanding" (2015). Salter suggests that, rather than ask victims why they didn't report sooner, it would be more appropriate to ask *why* the victims had to wait so long to be heard (Salter, 2015). The concealment of abuse by victims, perpetrators, and institutions leaves them silenced and their symptoms untreated, sometimes for many years. This frequently results in worsening physical and psychological damage of the victim and results in offenders remaining at large and able to prey on other children.

Child sexual abuse has long been recognised as a crime but public aversion to the concept of harm to children mitigated against disclosure in public forums such as the media. Crimes involving the murder of young children have been reported in newspapers since the 1800s (Miller, 2013). However, it was not until the 1960s that Kempe "discovered" what we now call child abuse when he described what became known as the "battered child syndrome". He told fellow physicians that the syndrome should be considered as a possible explanation for "any child exhibiting evidence of fracture of any bone, subdural hematoma, failure to thrive, soft tissue swellings or skin bruising, in any child who dies suddenly, or where the degree and type of injury is at variance with the history given regarding the occurrence of the trauma" (Kempe et al., 1962).

Greater understanding of the dynamics of child sexual abuse by the medical profession, child protection professionals and researchers has precipitated media coverage that has led to improved community awareness of the complex dynamics of sexual predation of children. However, until the 1970s, disclosure of child sexual abuse was frequently met with disbelief and victims were sometimes punished for fabricating "tales". Children might be accused of lying, fantasising or being seductive (Goddard and Mudaly, 2011). However, false allegations of sexual abuse are, in fact, very rare, representing only about 1.5 per cent of disclosures (Oates et al., 2000).

During the 1980s, research into child sexual abuse became more prominent in the scientific research literature. David Finkelhor's ground-breaking research announced that child sexual abuse was a newly identified problem that "is a new one and a challenging one" with "a very sobering message for those of us who work with children" (Finkelhor, 1984). However, Finkelhor noted the failure of professionals to identify the problem, lamenting that "we have ignored such a fundamental reality as this, that most of our scientists, physicians and educators failed to see how much sexual abuse was occurring and how profound its consequences were" (Finkelhor, 1984: 114). An important finding of his study was that people in positions of authority represented a significant threat to children:

> A second large category of abuse worth distinguishing is abuse at the hand of non-family caretakers, such as child-care workers, teachers, clergy, music teachers and sport coaches. These cases generally provoke a great

deal of public controversy, since they often involve individuals who have been trusted and respected by the general community.

(Finkelhor, 1984: 104)

Research on journalistic coverage of child sexual abuse has been framed in the past, as part of a wider gender debate. In male-dominated newsrooms, stories about child abuse were considered to be "soft news" and were assigned to female journalists (Skidmore, 1998). The issue became front page news in the UK in June 1987 when a contentious case of suspected widespread abuse emerged in Cleveland, a poor area in north-east England. Suspected abuse of 200 children was reported after social services removed victims of suspected abuse from their parents. The issue became public when social services could not cope with the number of children taken into care. The coverage was framed in terms of a "moral panic" in which medical and legal experts did not agree on an appropriate social response to the revelations. The sudden spike in suspected abuse cases in just a few months was suspicious because only 30 children had been removed in the previous year. Angry parents demanded second opinions claiming the medical assessment techniques used by two paediatricians were faulty (Nava, 1988).

During the 1990s media coverage of child sexual abuse cases became much more common because offenders in positions of power and authority were charged and jailed. By the late 1990s the dire consequences of child sexual abuse on children throughout their childhood and adulthood were documented by several researchers (Glaser, 1997; Briggs and Hawkins, 1997; Briggs and McVeity, 2000). At the same time, the potential of the internet as a means for paedophiles to groom and offend against children was being realised, and organisations and governments began a task of helping adults to protect children from cyber criminals who target children online (Stanley, 2001). By the mid-1990s, the scandal of child sexual abuse itself was overshadowed by controversy over whether reports by children of abuse were reliable.

> Almost as soon as the existence of widespread abuse within "ordinary" homes became public knowledge, this was over-shadowed by a series of high-profiled "scandals", such as Cleveland, Rochdale and Orkney. The focus turned to questions of misdiagnosis, inappropriate intervention and the supposed coaching of children to make false accusations. More recently "false memory syndrome" has hit the headlines suggesting that some adults' accounts of abuse can also be discredited. The news coverage often gives the impression that the main risks are not to *children*, but to parents, particularly fathers.
>
> *(Kitzinger, 1996)*

However, other instances of mass child abuse continued to attract coverage in the US, UK, Australia, and other countries. In London, journalist Eileen Fairweather began investigating allegations of child sexual abuse in Islington's

Children's Homes. The stories were at first branded as "gutter journalism" but the coverage eventually precipitated 13 government inquiries that forced resignations and reforms (Fairweather, 1998: 19). The exposure of the "paedophiles, pornographers and pimps" who had controlled the Islington Children's Homes was ultimately due to a whistle-blower who had painstakingly gathered the evidence (Fairweather, 1998: 20).

In the early 2000s media coverage of deaths from torture and abuse of babies and young children in state care and the systemic corruption of institutions to protect offenders from prosecution in the mainstream churches brought the issue to prominence in the public arena and onto the political agenda in many countries (Goddard and Saunders, 2001). In the US, the *Boston Globe*'s coverage of the scandal of Catholic church officials protecting paedophile priests became a global story and later a movie "Spotlight" (*Boston Globe* Investigative Staff, 2002). A team of reporters from the *Globe* began researching one paedophile priest John Geoghan and expanded their research, eventually proving that Cardinal Bernard Law was aware of the abuse but did nothing to stop it. The final count was about 90 paedophile priests in the Diocese who had been systematically protected from prosecution.

Meanwhile in Australia, a civil action in Toowoomba reached court and the Diocese of Brisbane was found negligent for failing to protect a boarder girl from a paedophile boarding master. Even though the offender died by suicide, the Diocese was found to be vicariously liable for the offending and the court awarded her record damages of AUD$834,000 including an award of AUD$400,000 in exemplary damages for its behaviour towards her after it knew about the abuse. This behaviour included refusing to pay for counselling for at least two abused children, appearing to blame the victims for the offender's death by suicide, and denying the offences for 11 years until capitulating and admitting the offences on the first day of trial. Calls for a Royal Commission into child sexual abuse were rejected by the government but a later prime minister, Julia Gillard, established a Royal Commission into institutional responses to the sexual abuse of children in 2012.

By the 2010s national inquiries, established in various countries, including Ireland, Germany, the USA and Australia found longstanding systemic abuse in churches and other civil institutions that cared for children. British celebrity entertainer and philanthropist Sir Jimmy Savile was exposed as a serial paedophile in 2012 a year after his death. An ITV documentary triggered a news media "feeding frenzy" that exposed the former national treasure to be, in fact, a prolific predator who had been "hiding in plain sight" and who had abused up to 450 teenage girls (Greer and McLaughlin, 2013). The BBC's initial denials of any responsibility for covering up Savile's offending incensed victims who came forward and spoke to the media and police. Police established Operation Yewtree to investigate Jimmy Savile and expanded the operation to include other celebrities (Gallagher, 2014). By 2015 Operation Yewtree had made 19 arrests. Seven people were convicted, including Australian entertainer Rolf Harris. Operation

Yewtree precipitated two subsequent police actions, Operation Hydrant which also investigated celebrities and institutional offenders and Operation Ravine which investigated Walton Hop disco. Critics of Operation Yewtree claimed it degenerated into a media "witch hunt".

Despite growing public understanding of the impact of abuse on victims, there is still a significant power imbalance between adult sex offenders and their victims that means offenders are still rarely prosecuted, convicted, or adequately punished. In addition, offenders have promulgated a series of myths about the dynamics of child sexual abuse that are self-serving. These include claims that children fantasise abuse, that a child "initiated" the abuse, that the child was "coached" to make allegations, that biological parents would not abuse their own children, or that children lie about abuse. If the abuse cannot be denied, the myths take a different form: that abuse is not harmful or that the perpetrator offended because they had been subjected to offences as a child themselves. Studies have shown this last excuse is rarely the case and polygraph testing of offenders has shown the claims are unreliable (Hindman and Peters, 2001). In fact, the opposite is far more likely to be true: victims are likely to be very protective of children and are very unlikely to offend themselves (Mallett, 2015). Victimisation is more likely to be a protective factor against a person later becoming an offender (Lambie and Johnston, 2016). The Lambie and Johnston study of 47 survivors reported that adult survivors said their reason for not offending was directly related to their own experience of sexual abuse victimisation. They were able to name four protective factors that prevented them from offending: empathy, morals, lack of sexual desire, or a combination of the previous three (Lambie and Johnston, 2016).

Public debate about incestuous, or intrafamilial abuse, now centres upon disagreement about whether adults should believe children who disclose abuse by a parent. Intrafamilial child abuse is highly contested by alleged offenders, especially in Family Courts, where offenders frequently advocate for their right to a continued parentchild relationship with the alleged victim or victims of abuse. Protective parents frequently report that civil authorities such as police and Family Courts are reticent to prosecute incestuous offenders and may disbelieve the child's disclosures, leading to victims being subjected to court-ordered contact with the offender (Wilson, 2001). Adult victims of domestic violence, who are nevertheless reluctant to believe a former partner capable of committing sex offences against their own child or children, may be reluctant to report alleged offences for fear of violent reprisal against themselves or their children (Diemer, 2014). Protective parents are routinely accused of fabricating allegations; coaching the child to make false allegations; attempting to alienate the child from the other parent; or emotionally "harming" the child by facilitating medical care or disclosure to authorities. However, research has shown that there is evidentiary value in drawings by young children for identifying child abuse (Briggs, 2015). Failures of authorities to believe and protect children who disclose abuse are beginning to be reported (Berkovic and Gearing, 2015).

Public debate is focusing on the risks to children posed by the seal of the confessional espoused by some mainstream churches. In Australia, the Royal Commission found that clergy and other offenders had "used the confessional to exculpate themselves of guilt" (Salter, 2017). One offender, Michael McArdle, admitted in an affidavit that he had confessed to molesting children 1,500 times over 25 years to 30 priests (Foster, 2017). The Royal Commission recommended that the failure by clergy to report knowledge about child sexual abuse gained in the confessional should be a criminal offence and called for the creation of a new offence of failing to report sexual abuse in institutions (Royal Commission into Institutional Responses to Child Sexual Abuse, 2017b). The offence would apply "to any adult who owns or manages or who is a staff member or volunteer of a relevant institution, or who otherwise requires a Working with Children Check clearance for their role" (Royal Commission into Institutional Responses to Child Sexual Abuse, 2017b).

Victim impact

The impact of abuse on victims can be serious, including physical and psychological conditions that may be prolonged and continuous or chronic over their lifetime. Victims have a higher risk of disabling behaviours such as drug and alcohol abuse, dysfunctional relationships, inability to trust authorities, inability to access medical or psychological help, and inability to engage with education (Glaser, 1997; Briggs and Hawkins, 1997). These symptoms impact on the ability of victims of abuse to secure and maintain stable employment that reflects their intellectual potential. Survivors may experience a range of psychiatric symptoms including suicidality, post-traumatic stress disorder and dissociative identity disorder (Middleton, 2007; Middleton, Sachs and Dorahy, 2017).

Covering child sexual abuse

Best practice in this field requires the reporter to learn specialist knowledge about this field of criminality, to adopt trauma-informed interviewing methods, and to learn and develop sound research techniques. Adopting the principle of "first, do no harm" in relation to victims of child sexual assault coverage is a useful guiding principle. The health and welfare of victims should be a higher-level consideration than the urgency of news deadlines or other pressures imposed by media managers.

Interviewing and research techniques

Before agreeing to interview a victim of abuse, I ask the potential news source what their intention is in approaching me. For example, they may want the offender criminally or civilly prosecuted, or they may want to publicly expose systemic corruption. I ask if the victim has family support and a medical support network.

This will give an indication of how robust they will be to cope with an investigation and news coverage. I am careful not to overpromise. I clearly tell the news source what I cannot do. I also ask if the abuse has been reported to police. If not, I discuss with the person the pros and cons of pausing the story until the victim reports to police and any other relevant authorities. I then do some preliminary research about the offender and the institution concerned before the interview. This preliminary discussion may help the news source to clarify their wishes and may result in the victim deciding to take legal action rather than seeking media coverage. Although this may result in no story at the time, it also avoids having to spend time working on an investigation that has to be abandoned later if the victim decides to take legal action before speaking publicly.

On the interview day, I arrange to meet in person if possible. If this is not possible, I use a communication method such as Skype or Facetime so I can see the interviewee and so they can see me. I use the trauma interview method I devised in 2011 while covering the South East Queensland flood disaster, as described in Chapter 11 of this volume. This method involves asking the interviewee to explain what happened and listening to their whole narrative before asking questions. This honours the interviewee and assures them they are being fully heard. The interviewer needs to be aware that victims may jump over the actual particularisation of the sexual assaults in their narrative – just as trauma victims jump over the details of witnessing a death or serious injury. This enables them to regulate their emotional arousal and cope with giving their narrative.

Assembling their narrative enables the interviewee to connect disparate scattered trauma memories such as what they saw, heard, smelled, tasted, or felt, into a cohesive narrative. This narrative technique replicates the method of interviewing that psychologists use with traumatised patients (Norman, 2000; Crossley, 2000). Psychologists theorise that because trauma disrupts routine assumptions about our life, the work done in the brain to assemble a narrative, begins the process of making sense of what happened, or finding meaning in the events (Crossley, 2000). As I listen to the narrative, I record the interview and make eye contact with the interviewee. I do not write notes as this would be distracting but I mentally note parts of the story that I will ask about in more detail. At the end of the narrative I ask my questions. These may include whether the victim knows of other victims of the same offender, or whether they know of additional offenders. In my experience, there is usually more than one offence and there is usually more than one victim of an offender. It is useful therefore to ask the interviewee if they have any evidence of other victims or offenders who are connected with the main offender. It is also useful to explore whether the crimes were reported to other people such as parents, siblings, close friends, or possibly a teacher, priest or other adult.

After the interview there will usually be quite a lot of verification to undertake that will take some time. The news source is asked to provide any documents and photographs and contact details for people who might be able to assist with verification of every fact that can be verified, including names, dates, places, events and associations between people and organisations. Any relevant photographs or videos are gathered. The next task is to reflect upon whether crimes have been committed based on the relevant criminal code in the relevant jurisdiction. Historic offences may need further research to find older versions of the criminal code on the relevant parliamentary website to check that alleged offences were in the code at the time and that they still are in the code.

The information gathered can be placed in a timeline that provides a useful reference for the mounting dossier of information. A network of association between the victims, offenders, and others involved will also help to conceptualise the story. The next phase is to consider how viable it will be to publish the story. If the offender is alive, defamation issues regarding the offender will constrain and might prevent publication. The offender's identity may need to be protected. Allegations may need to be qualified as being "alleged" offences. Also consider whether the offender has been convicted before. If they have, potential defamation problems may be lessened. If the offender has died, defamation may no long be a problem. This may provide more safety in publication but the story might not be as strong from a news impact point of view.

Framing

It is constructive to frame child sexual abuse stories into the contemporary sociopolitical narrative rather than to present them as isolated and potentially gratuitous stories of childhood trauma. Establishing the reason for the interviewee seeking media attention can help to focus the story on a timely public debate. Victims frequently seek media coverage because their intention in speaking publicly is to educate the community to understand a particular aspect of the dynamic of child sexual abuse that might help to prevent the abuse of other children in future. This sense of doing something positive can have a powerful and cathartic effect on the victim in the absence of criminal or civil legal proceedings or even if civil and legal proceedings have occurred. Media reporting of historic and current cases of abuse benefit society in several ways: firstly, by alerting the public and legislators to the need for improved child protection strategies and laws; secondly, by raising community awareness of the seriousness and prevalence of child sexual abuse; and thirdly, by providing victims with acknowledgement of their experience.

Language

Adopting language that is clear and direct rather than euphemistic is appropriate for these types of stories. Care should be taken not to minimise or euphemise the criminality of child sexual abuse because these dehumanise and demean the dignity of the child victims (Goddard and Saunders, 2000). For example, a textual study of UK and Australian media coverage of child abuse found that reports sometimes objectified children as "it" even when their gender was known

(Goddard and Saunders, 2000). The analysis also found that the choice of words used to describe the assaults of children minimised the perception of harm done to the child; for example, the repeated rape of a ten-year-old girl by her step-father was described in terms of a consensual adult relationship. The reporter wrote of "an affair" in which the "relationship" developed and that "the couple" denied having sex. The offences were discovered when the girl was found to be pregnant (Goddard and Saunders, 2000). The most appropriate words for particularising offences are those used in the relevant criminal code.

Anonymity

In many jurisdictions, it is illegal to identify child victims of sex offences, even when the victims reach adulthood. The identity of these victims is protected because they are victims of a sexual crime. However, some victims who speak to the media may wish to waive their right to anonymity (Morris and Gearing, 2017b). News editors will prefer for victims of abuse to be named; however, victims cannot be required to waive their anonymity. In case study 1, the adult plaintiff, Lyndal, maintained her anonymity throughout the trial and in the following years. She identified herself only by her first name when she became the subject of a movie in 2017 that portrayed the court room drama. The victims in case study 2 were willing to be identified in the media. In this case the main news source had a strong resolve to have his name and photograph as a child and as an adult published because he knew the offender had later victims and he knew they would have seen his childhood photograph in the offender's study, in the Diocese of Manchester. His plan worked. The later victim did recognise his photograph in the newspaper and made contact with me as a result. If a news source agrees to waive their right to anonymity, it is worthwhile having the interviewee sign a statement to that effect before publishing the story. The first group of victims in case study 3 were all anonymous.

Reporters should also carefully consider whether a victim of abuse might be adversely affected by being publicly named. If a victim makes allegations via the media, the story would need to be factually very strong and the alleged offender must be given right of reply. Even so, legal advice should be sought before the story is published.

The identity of a person alleged to have committed a sexual offence on a child is also protected by law, at least until they have been committed for trial. In some jurisdictions the identity of an alleged offender may be protected until they are convicted of an offence or plead guilty. A name of the perpetrator of an incestuous offence cannot be published even after conviction because this would identify the victim. Victims who choose to waive their anonymity should be asked to sign a statement to that effect. Editors will have these stories checked by their lawyers but reporters need a working knowledge of the law regarding anonymity of victims and alleged offenders. In some jurisdictions the penalty for identifying a victim may include jail terms. Identifying someone wrongly as a child sex offender could result in a costly defamation action for the media outlet and/or the reporter.

CASE STUDY 1

Lyndal vs. The Corporation of the Synod of the Diocese of Brisbane

This story began for me with a phone call from the chief of staff in November 2001 asking me to cover a civil trial in Toowoomba Supreme Court. The trial could not begin that day because the jury panel had accidentally been sent home. I was asked therefore to go to the court registry, obtain the statements of claim and defence, and write a preview story for the following day's edition. The story was published on day one of the trial (Gearing, 2001b). My story unwittingly threatened to unravel the defence strategy.

Institutions that care for children such as schools, churches and other organisations routinely hold personal injury insurance policies which indemnify them in case they are sued by a victim of abuse. Insurers usually reserve the right to have carriage of any legal action brought by a plaintiff. In this case, the defence barrister was representing the Diocese's insurance company. She had prepared a strategy to mitigate their potential liability and damages by making a surprise admission that the abuse had, in fact, occurred. The admission was made reluctantly but the tactic of making the admission was the only way the defence could hope to have a crucial piece of evidence excluded from the case by no longer being probative. The offender had written a suicide note naming the plaintiff and another 18 girls, as well as referring to other children at another school, as girls he "loved". The defence wanted this evidence excluded because it proved the Diocese knew that other children had also been abused by the offender.

The barrister brought a copy of the newspaper into court, held it up, and shook it, and argued that mention of the suicide note in the article meant the Diocese could not obtain a fair trial. She asked for the case to be dismissed. Fortunately, that bid failed but the attempt put reporters covering the case on notice that our reporting of the case would need to be absolutely accurate.

Once the suicide note was excluded from the evidence, witnesses needed to practice not mentioning the document. Evidence from several witnesses was therefore heard by a process called "voir dire", without the jury present, to ensure the witnesses did not accidentally mention the disallowed suicide note. Other victims of the same offender who read the news coverage were incensed that the church was defending the case and came forward to become witnesses in the case. The negligence of the Diocese was highlighted when the plaintiff gave evidence that her boarding master had told her to meet him after lights out in a student common room to which he held the only key (Gearing, 2001a). Several days into the case, the governor-general of Australia, Peter Hollingworth, who had been the archbishop of the

Diocese at the time the abuse was discovered, was mentioned in evidence. He had told a psychologist who sought help for the victims and their families that he could not do anything to help because he was tired and needed a holiday. The story shot from state to national news and from being a regional court report to a national political story. The case ran for more than three weeks, building in prominence as the scandal was exposed and more news outlets began to cover the story.

The jury found the church and the school had been negligent and that they were vicariously liable for the assaults. The jury awarded the plaintiff exemplary damages against the Diocese (Gearing, 2001c). The verdict was the first time an Australian school was held vicariously liable for the actions of a teacher – even though the actions were criminal (Gearing, 2001d). In a record award of damages to that date, Lyndal was awarded $415,000 in compensatory damages for the abuse, another $400,000 in punitive damages for the Diocese's disregard of her plight after it knew about the abuse, and $19,000 interest (Gearing, 2001c).

Once the court case was over, there were many loose ends that still needed investigating. My first task was to try to obtain a copy of the controversial suicide note. On the weekend after the verdict, I did manage to obtain a copy which was published the next day. The political fallout was swift. Child safety organisations condemned the failure of the archbishop to care for the victims of abuse. Victims of abuse at other Diocesan schools came forward to the media. Child safety organisations called for a Royal Commission but this was refused by the Federal Government. The new archbishop of the Diocese established an Inquiry (O'Callaghan and Briggs, 2003). Once the findings were released in mid-2003, the governor-general resigned.

A subsequent case of child sexual assault at the same Toowoomba school some years later precipitated the lawyer who had represented Lyndal to make a movie to highlight the scourge of child abuse in our society. Australian "A" list actors joined the cast of the movie *Don't Tell* which won several film awards. In 2012, Australia's prime minister, Julia Gillard, established a Royal Commission into Institutional Responses to Child Sexual Abuse. The Commission was triggered after investigative journalist Joanne McCarthy's reporting in another regional city, Newcastle in New South Wales, led to claims by police that Catholic church figures had shut down police investigations into child sex crimes committed by Catholic priests. More than 7,500 people spoke to the Royal Commission in private sessions and 2,340 alleged offenders were referred to authorities, including police. The Royal Commission made adverse findings against the former governor-general but even so, he continued to receive about $500,000 a year in wages and entitlements due to his former appointment as governor-general (Thomas, 2017).

CASE STUDY 2

Eli Ward vs. The Diocese of Manchester, UK

In 2012, BBC personality Jimmy Savile was exposed by a former detective turned journalist Mark Williams-Thomas in an ITV documentary as one of Britain's most prolific sex offenders (Greer and McLaughlin, 2013). Williams-Thomas used a methodical analogue investigation and passed intelligence to police (Halliday, 2013). Police launched Operation Yewtree to deal with a flood of complaints about other celebrities that has been dubbed the "Yewtree effect" (Gallagher, 2014). By 2015, 19 people had been arrested. Seven of the arrests led to convictions.

A victim of abuse who saw the news coverage realised for the first time that what he had thought was "friendship" with the former dean of Manchester, Robert Waddington, had been in fact criminal behaviour. The victim, Eli Ward approached a local newspaper and a national newspaper. Neither would publish his story. Ward began to search the internet for more information. Here he came across an article about a school in north Queensland where Waddington had been headmaster in the 1960s. Ward's online searches revealed an article that I had written in 2009. The article was about a subsequent headmaster of the same school, St Barnabas in Ravenshoe who was jailed for child sex offences (Gearing, 2009). Eli Ward contacted me by email through the contact page on my website and attached a letter he had written to the archbishop of Canterbury disclosing the abuse. Luckily, when I received the email, I was in Europe. I arranged to meet Mr Ward in Cambridge a few weeks later.

At this meeting I interviewed Eli Ward. He was struggling to trust anyone but the fact that I had come from outside the UK seemed to help him to trust me. I explained that if there was one victim, there would be many. The challenge was to find the others. Eli knew there were more as Waddington had many photos of boys in his study in the deanery. Eli had been introduced by Waddington to another victim but this man had apparently died by suicide. I met Eli several times in that week and gradually pieced together Waddington's offending career in London in the 1950s, Australia in the 1960s, Carlisle in the 1970s, Manchester in the 1980s, and York in the 1990s and 2000s.

Ward reported to police, even though the offender was dead. Manchester Police searched the Manchester Diocese and unearthed a single page document – a child safety report that provided important evidence (Manchester Cathedral, 2013). The report documented that the Diocese had received an "Australian complaint" but gave no name or contact details. These two words, however, were the clue that led to unravelling half a century of cover-up of a known sex offender by the church in Britain and Australia. Before the internet age, it would have been almost impossible to find a specific victim of crime by a specific offender without having a name. However, ordinary English keyword searches of the internet can be used to find needle-in-a-haystack evidence. I used key words about the offender, the school and "pedophile" (using the Australian spelling) in a series of Google searches. After about two hours I found a social media post by an Australian man, on a New Zealand social media webpage. In the post, the man, Bim Atkinson, named Waddington as a paedophile and named another teacher at his school as a "Waddington-induced paedophile" who had been jailed. Here was a victim and a lead to a criminal record that I could verify through court records – which was validated. Eli was not the only victim – as predicted – but we did not know if Bim Atkinson was still alive. I promised to search for him upon my return to Australia. Once back in Australia, I used an online telephone directory, found Mr Atkinson and told him about the investigation to that point. He was willing to help. The institutions that in the past knew they had the power to withhold information, were no longer able do so. The internet enabled silenced victims on both sides of the globe to find other victims, pool their evidence and prove institutional knowledge of offending.

Bim Atkinson had had a 14-year legal battle for justice and had a large cache of letters, photos, and other documents that proved he had informed the Dioceses of Manchester, York and North Queensland about Waddington's offences. He had reported Waddington's crimes to the church in England in 1999 and had warned them not to allow Waddington to have access to children. Bim also reported Waddington's crimes to Australian police in 2004 but they did not extradite Waddington to Australia. Waddington died in 2009 without a conviction. After interviewing Bim I was able to introduce him to Eli in a skype conference call. Eli asked Bim if he had been in a school play called *Peer Gynt* that Waddington had directed. Bim had the photographs. Eli recognised the children in the photos from Waddington's study. To facilitate communication, I created a secret Facebook group for Eli, Bim, and myself which enabled us to communicate easily despite the time zone difference of ten hours.

Within a couple of weeks, I drafted the main feature story. I then invited two reporters to collaborate, one in Australia and one in Britain. Even though *The Times* and *The Australian* are News Limited publications they had not collaborated on an investigation before so it took some days for the reporters and their managers to agree on how to publish a front page story simultaneously across time zones in print and online. The agreement was for *The Australian* to print in hard copy and online at the same time as *The Times* published online (O'Neill, McKenna, and Gearing, 2013; McKenna, Gearing, and O'Neill, 2013). Once the story landed, more victims came forward (McKenna and Gearing, 2013). The Diocese of York established an Inquiry that validated the claims of the victims (Cahill, 2014). The Inquiry's findings of systemic failures precipitated the resignation of the former archbishop of York, Lord David Hope of Thornes (Bingham, 2014).

CASE STUDY 3

TSV, RSJ, AMK, CCK, EPS, and YOR vs.
The Abbot of Caldey Abbey

A Catholic Benedictine monastery, Scourmont in Chemay, Belgium, was thriving in the 1920s. Needing room to expand, it bought Caldey Island off the coast of Wales and assigned monks to the monastery at Caldey Abbey. One of the monks, Thaddeus Kotik arrived on Caldey Island in 1947, studied in Chemay, and was ordained in 1956. Kotik sexually assaulted many children who lived on Caldey Island or who visited the island with their parents on religious retreat holidays or as day trippers. One of the girls left the UK with her parents and moved to Australia in the mid-1980s. She and her sister reported the abuse to their school in Australia. The school did not forward their report disclosures to police or even to the parents. "Charlotte" launched a civil action that was defeated because the action was statute barred by the Statute of Limitations. The Abbey claimed they were not liable for the abuse and refused even to apologise. "Charlotte" wanted to expose the abuse in the media. Her lawyer, who happened to be the same lawyer who had represented Eli Ward, contacted me and asked if I would report the story. I interviewed "Charlotte", obtained the legal documents, and interviewed the other plaintiffs in the UK. The story was commissioned by *The Guardian* UK and was followed by *BBC Wales* (Gearing, 2017). The newspaper's lawyers were nervous about the story because of the small population of about 40 people on the island. This meant it might be possible that the victims could be identifiable even though their names were changed and identifying details were omitted. The impasse was solved by asking each of the plaintiffs to sign a letter saying they understood some people may be able to identify them.

Two days later the abbot admitted the abuse, admitted the abbey's failure to report the offender to police and issued a public apology on Facebook (Morris and Gearing, 2017a). *The Guardian* included my email address in the coverage so that other victims could contact me. More than a dozen victims made contact with me, reporting Kotik and other offenders on Caldey Island (Gearing and Sherwood, 2017; Gearing and Morris, 2017) and the presence on the island of at least one fugitive sex offender.

Conclusion

Media coverage of child sexual abuse is continuing to illuminate society's understanding of the complexity of these sinister crimes against children. Embarking on this type of reporting is challenging but also potentially rewarding. Reporters working on these stories should prepare by doing the following tasks:

1. learning how to interview traumatised news sources;
2. learning how to verify allegations using documentary evidence and corroborating witnesses; and
3. learning how to avoid legal difficulties.

References

Alaggia, Ramona. 2010. "An Ecological Analysis of Child Sexual Abuse Disclosure: Considerations for Child and Adolescent Mental Health". *Journal of the Canadian Academy of Child and Adolescent Psychiatry* 19 (1): 32–39.

Allnock, Debra and Pam Miller. 2013. "No one noticed, no one heard: a study of disclosures of childhood abuse". NSPCC.

Berkovic, Nicola and Amanda Gearing. 2015. "The Family Court's dilemma in cases of child sexual abuse". *The Australian*. 11 July.

Bingham, John. 2014. "Ex-Archbishop quits over Church of England child sex abuse revelations". *The Telegraph*.

Boston Globe Investigative Staff. 2002. *Betrayal: The crisis in the Catholic church*. Boston, MA: Little, Brown.

Briggs, Freda. 2015. *Issues in child protection*. University of South Australia.

Briggs, Freda and Russel Hawkins. 1997. *Child Protection: A Guide for Teachers and Child Care Professionals*. NSW: Allen and Unwin.

Briggs, Freda and Michael McVeity. 2000. "Teaching Children to Protect Themselves". Sydney: Allen and Unwin.

Cahill, Sally. 2014. *Inquiry into the Church of England's response to child abuse allegations*. UK.

Carlton, Alexandra. 2016. "Abbey committed suicide after years of alleged sexual abuse". *news.com.au*. 16 October 2016.

Connolly, Kate. 2009. "Josef Fritzl trial: 'She spent the first five years entirely alone. He hardly ever spoke to her'". *The Guardian*. 19 March.

Crossley, Michele. 2000. *Introducing narrative psychology: Self, trauma and the construction of meaning*. Buckinghamshire: Open University Press.

Davies, Nick. 1998. "The most secret crime: The epidemic in our midst that went unnoticed". *The Guardian*. 2 June.

Diemer, Kristin. 2014. "Trivialising and excusing violence against women". In *The Drum*. Australia: ABC News.

Fairweather, Eileen. 1998. "Exposing the Islington children's homes scandal: A journalist's view". In *Whistleblowing in the social services: Public accountability and professional practice*, edited by G Hunt, London: Arnold, 19–40.

Finkelhor, David. 1984. "Child sexual abuse: Challenges facing child protection and mental health professionals". In *Childhood trauma: Separation, abuse, war*, edited by Elisabeth Ullmann and Werner Hilweg. Hants, England: Ashgate.

Foster, Chrissie. 2017. "Evil hid behind handy seal of confession". *The Australian*. 18 August.

Gallagher, Bernard 2014. "Rolf Harris guilty: but what has Operation Yewtree really taught us about sexual abuse?". In *The Conversation*. London: The Conversation.

Gearing, Amanda. 2001a. "Court told of trysts at night". *The Courier-Mail*. 14 November.

Gearing, Amanda. 2001b. "Former pupil sues church over 'abuse'". *The Courier-Mail*. 13 November.

Gearing, Amanda. 2001c. "Record payout for sex abuse". *The Courier-Mail*. 8 December.

Gearing, Amanda. 2001d. "Suffer the children". *The Courier-Mail*. 15 December.

Gearing, Amanda. 2009. "Archbishop's Chaplain behind bars at last". *Online Opinion.* 29 April.

Gearing, Amanda. 2017. "Revealed: monk who abused children on 'crime free' Caldey Island for decades". *The Guardian.* 17 November.

Gearing, Amanda and Steven Morris. 2017. "Sex offender hid in Caldey Island abbey for seven years". *The Guardian.* 24 November.

Gearing, Amanda and Harriet Sherwood. 2017. "Three more women allege abuse by Caldey Island monk". *The Guardian 21 November..*

Glaser, Bill. 1997. "Paedophilia: The public health problem of the decade". *Paedophilia Policy and Prevention* (12): 4–13.

Goddard, Chris and Max Liddell. 1993. "Child abuse and the media: Victoria introduces mandatory reporting after an intensive media campaign". *Children Australia* 18 (3): 23–27.

Goddard, Chris and Neerosh Mudaly. 2011. "Crimes cloaked in euphemisms". *The Australian.* 25 August.

Goddard, Chris and Bernadette J Saunders. 2000. "The gender neglect and textual abuse of children in the print media". *Child Abuse Review* 9: 37–48.

Goddard, Chris and Bernadette J. Saunders. 2001. "Child abuse and the media". *Child Abuse Prevention Issues* 14 (Winter 2001).

Greer, Chris and Eugene McLaughlin. 2013. "The Sir Jimmy Savile scandal: Child sexual abuse and institutional denial at the BBC". *Crime, Media, Culture* 9 (3): 243–263.

Halliday, Josh. 2013. "Mark Williams-Thomas: I ran the Savile film like a criminal investigation" *The Guardian, 24 February..*

Hindman, Jan and James Peters. 2001. "Polygraph testing leads to better understanding adult and juvenile sex offenders". *Federal probation* 65 (3): 8–15.

Jay, Alexis. 2014. *Independent inquiry into child sexual exploitation in Rotherham: 1997–2013.* Yorkshire: Rotherham Metropolitan Borough Council.

Kempe, C.H., F.N. Silverman, W. Droegemuller, and H.K. Silver. 1962. "The battered child syndrome". *Journal of the American Medical Association* 18 (1): 17–24.

Kitzinger, Jenny. 1996. "Media representations of sexual abuse risks". *Child abuse review* 5 (5): 319–333.

Lambie, I. and E. Johnston. 2016. "'I couldn't do it to a kid knowing what it did to me": The narratives of male sexual abuse victims' resiliency to sexually offending". *Int J Offender Ther Comp Criminol* 60 (8): 897–918.

Mallett, Xanthe 2015. "Child sex abuse doesn't create paedophiles". In *The Conversation.* Australia: The Conversation Media Group.

Manchester Cathedral. 2013. "Statement regarding former Dean Waddington".http://www.manchestercathedral.org/news/208/statement-regarding-former-dean-waddington.

McKenna, Michael and Amanda Gearing. 2013. "Robert Waddington's cycle of abuse stretches beyond 50 years". *The Australian.* June 1. http://www.theaustralian.com.au/news/nation/robert-waddingtons-cycle-of-abuse-stretches-beyond-50-years/story-e6frg6nf-1226654874606.

McKenna, Michael, Amanda Gearing, and Sean O'Neill. 2013. "Child sex scandal in two countries rocks Anglican church". *The Australian.* 10 May http://www.theaustralian.com.au/news/nation/child-sex-scandal-in-two-countries-rocks-anglican-church/story-e6frg6nf-1226639078714.

Middleton, Warwick. 2007. "Reconstructing the past: trauma, memory and therapy": Background paper for the seminars "Trauma, dissociation and psychosis: Metaphor, strategy and reality", convened by the Delphi Centre in collaboration with The Cannan Institute and the Trauma & Dissociation Unit, Belmont Hospital, Sydney 4–5 May 2007, Westmead Hospital & Brisbane 18–19 May 2007, The Bardon Centre.

Middleton, Warwick. 2013. "Ongoing incestuous abuse during adulthood". *Journal of Trauma & Dissociation* 14 (3): 251–272.

Middleton, Warwick, Adah Sachs and Martin J. Dorahy. 2017. "The abused and the abuser: Victim–perpetrator dynamics". *Journal of Trauma & Dissociation* 18 (3): 249–258.

Middleton, Warwick, Pam Stavropoulos, Martin J Dorahy, Christa Krüger, Roberto Lewis-Fernández, Alfonso Martínez-Taboas, Vedat Sar and Bethany Brand. 2014. "The Australian Royal Commission into Institutional Responses to Child Sexual Abuse". *Australian & New Zealand Journal of Psychiatry* 48 (1): 17–21.

Miller, Daniel. 2013. "Britain's worst ever serial killer: The Victorian 'Angel Maker' who murdered 400 babies". *The Daily Mail*. 23 February.

Morris, Steven and Amanda Gearing. 2017a. "Caldey Island abbot apologises over failure to report abuse claims". *The Guardian*. 23 November.

Morris, Steven and Amanda Gearing. 2017b. "Woman abused as a child by Caldey Island monk waives right to anonymity". *The Guardian*. 22 December.

Nava, Mica. 1988. "Cleveland and the press: Outrage and anxiety in the reporting of child sexual abuse" *Feminist Review* (28 Family Secrets: Child Sexual Abuse (Spring, 1988)): 103–121.

Nelson, B.J. 1984. *Making an issue of child abuse: Political agenda-setting for social problems*. Chicago: University of Chicago Press.

Norman, Judith. 2000. "Constructive narrative in arresting the impact of post-traumatic stress disorder". *Clinical Social Work Journal* 28 (3): 303–319.

O'Callaghan, Peter and Freda Briggs. 2003. *Report of the Board of Inquiry into past handling of complains of sexual abuse in the Anglican Church Diocese of Brisbane*. Brisbane.

O'Neill, Sean, Michael McKenna and Amanda Gearing. 2013. "Former Archbishop of York 'covered up' sex abuse scandal". *The Times*. May 10. http://www.thetimes.co.uk/tto/faith/article3760816.ece.

Oates, R. Kim, David P.H. Jones, David Denson, Andrew Sirotnak, Nancy Gary and Richard D. Krugman. 2000. "Erroneous concerns about child sexual abuse". *Child Abuse & Neglect* 24 (1): 149–157.

Pipe, M.E. 2007. *Child sexual abuse: Disclosure, delay, and denial*. 1st ed. New York: Routledge.

Powell, Fred and Margaret Scanlon. 2015. *Dark secrets of childhood: Media power, child abuse and public scandals*. 1st ed: Policy Press at the University of Bristol.

Royal Commission. 2013. "The Royal Commission into Institutional Responses to Child Sexual Abuse": Australian Government.

Royal Commission into Institutional Responses to Child Sexual Abuse. 2017a. *Criminal justice report*. Sydney: Australian Government.

Royal Commission into Institutional Responses to Child Sexual Abuse. 2017b. *Criminal Justice report: Failure to report offence*. Sydney.

Salter, Michael. 2015. "Why does it take victims of child sex abuse so long to speak up?". In *The Conversation*. Australia: The Conversation Media Group.

Salter, Michael. 2017. "Royal commission provides a vital blueprint for justice for sex abuse victims – now it's time to act". Australia: The Conversation Media Group.

Skidmore, Paula. 1998. "Gender and the agenda: News reporting of child sexual abuse". In *News, gender and power*, edited by Cynthia Carter, Gill Branston, and Stuart Allan. London: Routledge.

Stanley, Janet. 2001. "Child abuse and the Internet". *Child abuse prevention* 15 (Summer 2001): 1–18.

Streeck-Fischer, Annette and Bessel A. van der Kolk. 2000. "Down will come baby, cradle and all: Diagnostic and therapeutic implications of chronic trauma on child development". *Australian and New Zealand Journal of Psychiatry* 34 (6): 903–918.

Thomas, Hedley. 2017. "Turning a blind eye". *The Australian*. 3 August.

Ullman, Sarah E. 2002. "Social reactions to child sexual abuse disclosures: a critical review". *Journal of Child Sexual Abuse* 12 (1): 89–121. http://dx.doi.org/10.1300/J070v12n01_05. doi:10.1300/J070v12n01_05

Wilson, Robert Fretwell. 2001. "Children at risk: The sexual exploitation of female children after divorce". *Cornell Law Review* 86 (2 January 2001): 253–327.

Wright, Amy Conley and Lynne Keevers. 2014. "We all have a role in protecting children: End the silence on abuse". In *The Conversation*. Australia: The Conversation Media Group.

4

REPORTING SUICIDE

Ann Luce

The social issue

Historically, suicide is perhaps *the* sensitive topic par excellence, especially the ways in which it is discussed in Western societies and cultures – or, more pointedly, *not* discussed, as the case may be. It is certainly a taboo issue, steeped in stigma – religious, moral, political, social, and cultural. Globally, more than 800,000 people die by suicide on an annual basis; suicide claims more lives than war, murder, and natural disasters combined (WHO, 2017a; AFSP, 2015). Suicide is a global issue that accounts for 1.4 per cent of all deaths worldwide, making it the 17th leading cause of death in 2015 (the most recent statistics available).

Research shows that for every person who dies by suicide, between six and 135 people are significantly impacted (Cerel et al., 2018; CALM, 2016). For every individual who kills her/himself, at least 20 more will attempt to take their own life (WHO, 2017a). Every 40 seconds a person dies by suicide, yet the World Health Organisation estimates that this will increase to one death every 20 seconds by 2020 (Befrienders, 2017; WHO 2017b).

Arguably, a suicide story has the potential to cause harm, but if reported responsibly, sensitively, ethically, and with care (read: non-sensational[1]), then such harm can be mitigated.

The nature of a suicide story means that death is at the heart of it, and death remains one of the great taboos to openly discuss. However, death by suicide is not like natural death, be it from old age or illness. Death by suicide can often be sudden, unexpected and violent, which can substantially lead to trauma for the bereaved, especially those in close proximity.

Those bereaved by suicide, often called "suicide survivors", often struggle to fully understand what has happened. Coupled with the suddenness of a suicidal death, suicide survivors can also experience extreme emotional and physical reactions, including: post-traumatic stress (PTSD); stigma; and isolation. There is also a lack of privacy; police investigations; practical concerns; family; friends and community tensions. There are also the survivors' questions: Why did this happen? What could I have done? (SobsUK, 2017). To complicate matters further, the available evidence demonstrates that a suicidal death places those bereaved at a significantly higher risk for depression, admission to psychiatric care, and suicide themselves (Cerel et al., 2016; Pitman et al., 2014).

When suicide prevention experts call for better reporting of suicide, they are trying to support not only those people who may be vulnerable and contemplating suicide, but also those who have already been bereaved by suicide. As a journalist, one has an ethical duty to ensure that one's reporting does not cause harm (Keeble, 2009). In many countries, professional codes of practice exist to guide and assist in the reporting of suicide, yet more often, suicide is covered off under a general heading of "minimize risk, do no harm".

In the UK, The Editor's Code of Practice, regulated by the Independent Press Standards Organisation (IPSO) (2018) states in Clause 5: "When reporting suicide, to prevent simulative acts care should be taken to avoid excessive detail about the method used." In OFCOM (2017) guidelines, the communications regulator in the UK that oversees TV, radio, and video-on-demand, advice states that "methods of suicide and self-harm must not be included in programmes except where they are editorially justified and are also justified by the context".

In the United States, the Society for Professional Journalists (2018), in its section on minimising harm, states: "Balance the public's need for information against potential harm or discomfort. Pursuit of the news is not a license for arrogance or undue intrusiveness".

In New Zealand, journalists must follow guidelines provided by the Ministry of Health (NZMoH) and also the Coroner's Act of 2006, which stipulates that method of, location of, or description of death by suicide cannot be reported. A journalist may describe the death as a suicide "if the coroner has completed a certificate of findings". Additionally, all media outlets have codes of practice that should be followed unequivocally.

Australia stands out as the leader in ethical and responsible reporting of suicide, although suicide prevention experts in that country would still argue there is much work still to be done. Australia's Department of Health and Aging supports Mindframe (2014), a national media initiative on responsible and ethical reporting of mental illness and suicide, organised and facilitated by EveryMind (formerly the Hunter Institute of Mental Health). There are five key areas the national media initiative addresses within its ambit: media professionals; the mental health and suicide prevention sector; journalism and public relations education (working in universities); stage and screen; and police. Mindframe works with journalists directly on ethical and responsible reporting of suicide stories and also monitors stories and provides feedback on best – and worst – practice.

In addition to country-specific professional codes of practice for journalists, there are also multiple sets of guidelines that journalists can draw from in order to report responsibly, including, for example: the World Health Organisation; Samaritans (UK/Ireland); Save.org; Mindframe; National Union of Journalists; American Foundation for Suicide Prevention; American Association of Suicidology; Canadian Psychiatric Association, Canadian Association for Suicide Prevention; MediaWise; Papyrus; Irish Association of Suicidology; New Zealand Ministry of Health; and the Mental Health Foundation of New Zealand.

The majority of these guidelines advise similar caution, but for the purpose of this chapter, I will focus specifically on those offered by the World Health Organisation (WHO) as these are non-country specific and can be used by any journalist in the world. The WHO guidelines have been recently updated in 2017 (WHO/IASP, 2017).

Introduction

My first suicide-related story was about a suicide support group in Jacksonville, Florida, where I was working as a journalist at the time. I was to report on the suicide of a local young man and discuss how the support group was helping his mother. I approached the story as a non-critically reflective journalist would: do some background, find some sources, get some quotes, write it and move on. When speaking to this bereaved mother on the telephone, I was empathetic, but certainly not prepared to listen to her cry for 90 minutes. I was taken aback by the depth of her grief and, as a 21-year-old with little experience of death, I was completely unprepared, and certainly lacked the knowledge and emotional intelligence necessary to support a source who was suffering enormously.

Fast forward two years and I became a member of that very same support group. Just months previously, a very dear and close friend took his own life (recounted in the introduction to this volume). I am not sure if I will ever fully recover from the emotional trauma that I experienced in the aftermath. Richard chose to kill himself at a local university and newsroom policy at the time stipulated that suicides in public places were both newsworthy and in the public interest. Thus, Richard's suicide was covered by my newspaper, written by a colleague who sat near to me. Richard's death received much coverage in both print and broadcast media, but I found myself conflicted when reading and watching the reports. They seemed insensitive, but I was not sure why.

With the benefit of hindsight and self-reflexivity, the suicide stories I wrote early on in my career were definitely problematic. My stories were, unfortunately, stigmatising, sensational, and did not take into account how the bereaved might feel when reading my stories: I did not provide any hotline support phone numbers or websites; I did not even consider the types of phrases and wording that I chose. Admittedly, I was ignorant, even though guidelines existed and I had the capability of acquiring the knowledge. Sadly, I just did not make the effort.

Following Richard's suicide, the responsible and ethical reporting of suicide became a personal crusade. I changed how I reported and wrote about suicide.

Through my journalism, I campaigned for the creation of the Office of Suicide Prevention and Drug Control in the State of Florida and the Florida Suicide Prevention Strategy Paper, which finally came into existence in 2007. I also received a "Responsible Reporting of Suicide" award from then-Governor Jeb Bush in 2006 for a series of editorials which examined suicide in Florida from religious, moral, social, and cultural perspectives. I now sit on the International Association of Suicide Prevention World Media Task Force. I have co-written two sets of WHO Reporting Guidelines on Suicide, as well as contributed to guidelines for bloggers and new guidelines for young people about how they can communicate safely about suicide in online territories.

By the end of this chapter, I would like journalists to:

- Use WHO guidelines to report suicide
- Seriously consider the impact that reporting has on those bereaved by suicide
- Carefully choose tone, tenor and language
- Report ethically and responsibly
- Educate your audience about suicide

The research

In simple terms, suicide is the taking of one's own life. Understanding suicide, however, is complex and by no means simple. French sociologist, Emile Durkheim (1897/1951), is often credited with establishing the sociological framework for how we currently understand suicide. Durkheim argues that suicide is the result of society's strength or weakness of control over an individual (Berman and Jobes, 1991), identifying four categories that a completed suicide would fit into based on the individual's connection to society. For Durkheim, these categories are egoistic, altruistic, anomic, and fatalistic.

According to Durkheim, egoistic suicides are not connected with, or dependent upon, community. In journalistic terms, this could be a story about a person who is detached from society as a result of mental illness. In contrast, altruistic suicides are related to a person's integration into a group; this person feels no sacrifice is too great for the good of the larger group. For example, these might be stories about suicide bombers.

Anomic suicides occur when the individual is not capable of dealing with a crisis rationally, or when their relationship with society is suddenly changed. As I have written elsewhere, "Suicide is the solution to a problem in this form" (Luce, 2016: 86). This may be a story about a banker who has died-by-suicide as a result of losing a great deal of money following a crash in the stock market. The last category, according to Durkheim's framework, is that of the "fatalistic suicide", perhaps caused by excessive societal regulation such as restricting an individual's freedom. These types of stories may feature suicides in countries such as Belarus or North Korea, where the form of government is dictatorship and the rates of suicide are extremely high (WHO, 2014).

While Durkheim articulated the framework for how we understand suicide, it was American suicidologist Edwin Shneidman (1969) who furthered the field regarding our understanding of the particulars of suicide: what might be the main causes, the reasons why, the type of person, common methods, and strategies of prevention. Shneidman first formulated his theory of "psychache" – put simply, a mental pain that leads to suicide – in the mid-late 1960s. In Shneidman's account, in order to prevent and address the issue of suicide, it is best to ask about a person's emotions, rather than engage in the study of the structure of the brain, social statistics or mental diseases. When presented with the suicidal individual, argued Shneidman, we should ask two questions: "Where do you hurt?" and "How can I help you?" (1996: 6):

> In almost every case, suicide is caused by pain, a certain kind of pain – psychological pain, which I call psychache. Furthermore, this psychache stems from thwarted or distorted psychological needs. In other words, suicide is chiefly a drama of the mind. Even though I know that each suicidal death is a multi-faceted event – that biological, biochemical, cultural, sociological, interpersonal, intrapsychic, logical, philosophical, conscious and unconscious elements are always present – I retain the belief that, in the proper distillation of the event, its essential nature is psychological. That is, each suicide drama occurs in the mind of a unique individual.
>
> *(Shneidman, 1996: 4–5)*

As I have written elsewhere, "the essential fact to keep in mind when dealing with suicide is that it never happens to someone who is happy or joyous. Instead, it is the result of negative emotions and anguish" (Luce, 2016: 87).

The "why" of suicide

At the foundation of every journalism story are the 5W's: who, what, when, where, and WHY? The number one issue facing a journalist when covering a suicide is the fact that they cannot answer the "why" question: the only person who can tell a journalist why the suicide happened is dead.

Precipitating factors, of course, can be identified to try and explain or provide context for a suicide, but these are multiple and are only best guesses (Jourard, 1969; Douglas, 1969; Shneidman, 1985; Barker et al., 1994; Bird and Faulkner, 2000; Kerkhof and Arensman, 2001; Shahtahmasebi, 2015) . Some examples are:

- Willing of self-destruction
- Motivation to be dead
- Suffering ill health
- Relationships
- Losing one's fortune
- Humiliation/shame/defeat/disgrace/anger/rage/hostility

- Living conditions: unstable or living alone
- Physical, sexual and mental maltreatment in childhood
- Substance abuse: drugs, alcohol
- Mental health: depression, hopelessness, powerlessness, personality disorders, previous psychiatric treatment, trauma
- History of broken homes/family violence
- Weather

Historically, suffering with depression has been the single reliable indicator of suicide. According to Depression Alliance, a person suffering with depression tends to experience feelings of low mood that are acute, lasting weeks, months, and even years.

> The feelings are intense and tend to exhibit both psychological and physical signs: persistent sadness, helplessness, hopelessness, sleeplessness, loss of energy, loss of self-confidence, loss of self-esteem, difficult concentrating, loss of appetite, avoidance and isolation.
>
> *(Depression Alliance, 2018)*

That said, Shahtahmasebi (2015) airs his frustrations about the politicisation of suicide prevention policy development, which has been classified globally under the heading of mental health. He laments that the list of risk factors for suicide is so long:

> Such a list of risk factors would mean that the whole population is at risk of suicide. The suicide population is very diverse and no one factor is statistically significant as a leading factor. The only common factor between suicide cases in each group is the outcome of suicide.
>
> *(Shahtahmasebi, 2015: 1148)*

Here, Shahtahmasebi complicates the reporting of suicide. One of the main issues with suicide is that it seems to deflect all efforts to categorise or define it. Suicide can happen at any age; it can happen in any geographic location; it happens to both sexes (though men are more likely to kill themselves, while women attempt suicide more often). There is a wide range of reasons that *could* cause a suicide, but the fact of the matter remains: *we just do not know why someone chooses to take their own life.* As a journalist, this makes the job particularly difficult – explaining "why" something happens is one of the foundational tenets of journalism.

The "how" of suicide

If answering "why" is the number one problem facing a journalist when reporting a suicide, then the second issue is centred on "how" the suicide occurred.

The most common methods used in suicides are: poisoning and pesticides (including car exhaust fumes), hanging and suffocation, drowning, firearms, jumping, cutting and piercing, and overdoses (WHO, 2008; Bird and Faulkner, 2000). Different countries will have different methods of choice, such as firearms in the US, charcoal burning in China, pesticides in India, hanging and suffocation in the UK.

Most professional codes of practice, and all media guidelines, as discussed earlier in this chapter, state that suicidal method should not be reported in any journalism story "because this will increase the likelihood that a vulnerable person will copy the act" (WHO/IASP, 2017). Stories such as, "Spade was found hanged by a [red] scarf she allegedly tied to a doorknob" (Levenson and Gingras, 2018) or *The Sydney Morning Herald*'s (2008) reporting on a UK man who killed himself by tying a "chainsaw to the leg of a snooker table and plugged it into a timer" are found to be contravening guidelines and codes of practice worldwide because of the specificity of the method.

The challenge journalists face is recognising what to report and what to exclude. As Roy Greenslade wrote in the aftermath of Robin William's suicide in 2014 in *The Guardian*:

> To report that a person hanged himself is fact. To report where it took place is a fact. To report other details … was wrong … Making such decisions about what should and should not be reported has never been so difficult.
> *(Greenslade, 2014)*

Within the field of suicidology, the "Werther Effect", or suicide copycat theory, is a theory that states media reporting is a direct cause for "copycat" or "imitative" suicides. Simply stated, the more a journalist reports suicide, the more suicides will occur. Coined by David Phillips in 1974 in the USA, he named the theory from Goethe's 1774 book, *The Sorrows of Young Werther*, when several suicides allegedly occurred following the publication of the book (although this has not been verified beyond hearsay). Those who died-by-suicide allegedly dressed in a similar fashion to Young Werther and also adopted his method of killing himself. Since the 1970s, there have been more than 100 other investigations into imitative suicides, and members of the International Association of Suicide Prevention and the WHO believe that "collectively, these studies have strengthened the body of evidence in a number of ways" (2017: 11). What these groups of international scholars consistently fail to mention, however, is that not all of these studies can adequately replicate the Werther Effect.

I take issue with "Werther Effect" research because few, if any, of these studies actually engage with audiences. The "hypodermic needle approach" to media research (Werther Effect research, mostly quantitative research) assumes that all media audiences passively accept media "messages" and this is simply not the case (Barker and Petley, 2001; Jamieson et al., 2003; Hittner, 2005; Temple, 2008). What this body of work suggests is that media audiences will be encouraged to see suicide as an option to solve their problems based purely on the fact that a suicide is reported in the media. Simon Cross, a media academic in the UK, sums it up best:

> Let me ask a straightforward question: how do we know that some who commit suicide may have been influenced by either the suicide of someone else or the depiction of suicide, factual or fictional? Unfortunately, I have no hope of furnishing you with a conclusive answer to this question since (as I see it) we can never know because the only people who can confirm that they have been influenced by a depiction of suicide are *dead*. It may appear as though I am being pithy with a sensitive issue. This is not my intention since it remains an inconvenient truth that "copycat suicides" are *by definition* dead and unable to shed light into how "insensitive" reporting led to their suicide. This simple, but decisive point pulls the rug from under the common sense view that some suicides must be copycats because they have chosen to kill themselves in a manner akin to someone whose suicide has been reported. However, correlation does not equal causality i.e. because events occur in near time does not mean that one *causes* the other. To surmise that a depiction of suicide influenced someone to take their own life obfuscates the myriad psychological and social complexities engulfing individuals and which contribute to their decision to end their life.
>
> *(Cross, 2007: 20)*

Markey and Ferguson (2017) call these illusory correlations, which "create the false sense that events are connected, when they are, in fact, not related at all" (2017: 77). A good example of this is the Bridgend Suicides in Wales in 2008 where media reporting was blamed for the continuation and increase in suicides that year (neither is true). The first death attributed to this spate of suicides occurred in September 2006, when Dale Crole went missing and, later, his body was found in January 2007. Just six weeks later, his friend David Dilling killed himself, followed by another friend, Thomas Davies a week later (Smith, 2008). It was not until a year later that the coverage of the suicides in Bridgend began, and journalists were blamed for the deaths. Reporting of suicide and the suicides in Bridgend were not related; in fact, the suicide rates in Bridgend have stayed at similar rates for the last decade, while media coverage has been practically non-existent (Luce, 2016).

Yet, thinking about media reporting of suicide is slowly beginning to change within the field of suicidology. Niederkrothenthaler et al. (2010) articulated a new frame of reference called the "Papageno Effect", which focuses on the *protective* factors of reporting. They state:

> In Mozart's Opera [*The Magic Flute*], Papageno becomes suicidal upon fearing the loss of his beloved Papagena; however, he refrains from

suicide because of three boys who draw his attention to alternative coping strategies.

(2010: 234)

What the "Papageno Effect" has done is to empirically show that the media can
have a "protective effect ... on positive coping in adverse circumstances" (241).
To achieve that protective factor, however, journalists must first report on suicide responsibly. Following my research into the Bridgend suicides, I created a
framework to identify how and where in their reporting journalists are reporting
irresponsibly (Johns et al., 2014; Luce, 2016; Johns et al., 2017). I identified five
main categories of description that journalists use to sensationalise and stigmatise
suicide:

- Reaction to death by those left behind *(when answering what?/why?)*;
- Reason for the death *(when answering why?/how?/where?)*;
- Description of the deceased *(when answering who?/when?/where? how?)*;
- Infantilisation *(when answering what?/why? how?)*; and
- Blaming internet/social media *(when answering what?/where?/why?/how?)*.

These categories are summarily framed by questions around why suicide occurs
and ideologies of childhood. My research showed that the most prevalent discourses that surround suicide in media reporting are that, firstly, it should never
happen and, secondly, that people should die naturally, preferably in old age. To
reinforce that discourse, journalists tend to deem all adult suicides to be child-
ish acts and "other" those that die into a category of the "deviant non-child".
It appears, then, that an overarching assumption underpinning media reporting
of suicide is that it is an immoral destabilising force, a wrecking ball in a liberal
democratic society. As such, journalists play a significant role in maintaining balance and replicating acceptable discourses around the issue of suicide in society.

There are four simple rules journalists can follow to assure responsible reporting of suicide; I have linked these to the categories listed above so you are clear
where this tends to happen.

Journalists should not:

- Sensationalise *(reaction to death by those left behind; blaming internet/social media)*
- Stigmatise *(infantilisation; reason for death; description of deceased)*
- Glorify *(describing deceased; reason for death)*
- Gratuitously report on suicide *(reason for death [method]; description of the deceased)*

(helpful mnemonic device: SSGG)

Journalists have the power to report suicide responsibly and ethically, but keep
in mind that the person who has killed himself or herself has exercised autonomy over their own life and has chosen to die. A journalist's responsibility lies

with regularly reflecting on the impact one's stories might have on the bereaved. Journalists also play a significant role in educating audiences about suicide, which can include the warning signs and the effect suicide can leave in its wake.

Covering suicide

At the start of *The Myth of Sisyphus* (1942), French philosopher Albert Camus wrote: "There is but one truly serious philosophical problem and that is suicide. Judging whether life is or is not worth living amounts to answering the fundamental question of philosophy". For journalists, when someone dies by suicide, there are many more questions that must be answered.

The first question that must be asked in any newsroom is: why are we running this story? Is it "in the public interest", or is it of "interest to the public" (in a voyeuristic sense)? I would hope that the reason would serve the greater good – that is, there are more benefits to society at large in sharing the story than not.

There will be times when a suicide story needs to be reported on the grounds that it is newsworthy. Ethical discussions will need to take place. Time, care, and attention are required, and as the journalist writing about this sensitive topic, it is up to the reporter to get it right.

Reporting on suicide

When reporting on a suicide one must focus on the *types* of story you are writing and also one's sources of information: people, statistics, and social media.

Types of stories

When writing about grief, Duncan (2012) has identified five narrative themes, formats, or types of stories that journalists follow when reporting.

(1) *Event-driven story*
     This is the first story that acknowledges someone has died. The story leads with the death, its unusualness, or some form of public involvement, such as the discovery of the body for example (Duncan, 2012). When covering a suicide, journalists need to be careful not to sensationalise, stigmatise, glorify, or glamorise the death.
(2) *Tribute driven story*
     This type of story tends to come a few days after the death has been reported. The focus tends to shift to the bereaved family's devastation by the loss. When the death is a suicide, extra care must be given when interviewing bereaved family members and friends (see below).
(3) *Post-judicial story*
     This story happens after the conclusion of a court case or inquest, when the bereaved give media outlets their reaction to the verdict. Suicides, like all

unnatural deaths, warrant a legal investigation by coroners in order to rule out foul play. The law in the UK requires that the intention of a suicide victim – to die – must be known without any doubt. By hiding verdicts, or leaving them "open", a coroner can be seen to save a family from shame, embarrassment, and stigma (Luce, 2016: 101).

(4) *Anniversary story*

The anniversary tends to appear 12 months after the date of the death, but can also occur at five years, ten years or any significant anniversary date. When covering the anniversary of a suicide, think about whether or not this is appropriate. Think about those bereaved, and think about the impact to the local community (if any).

(5) *Action-as memorial story*

This tends to be the more positive of the grief stories, focusing more on remembering the person who has died. When it comes to suicide, this could include activities such as candlelight walks, raising funds for mental health charities, or setting up a trust in memory of the person who has died.

Sources of information

People

A "death knock" is a term used in the newsroom to describe the widespread practice of interviewing recently bereaved relatives. The goal is to ask about the deceased's life, their character, and the events leading up to the death and about the family's loss (Duncan, 2012). Caution should be taken when interviewing someone bereaved by suicide as they could be in a crisis situation themselves. People bereaved by suicide are at an increased risk of suicide or self-harm while they are dealing with their grief (SOBS, 2017). Respect for their privacy should take precedence. That being said, those bereaved by suicide can serve as useful sources when trying to educate communities about suicide, but these *must* be volunteers, rather than door-stepped.

If interviewing someone bereaved by suicide, whether it is in the hours following a death or a year later, journalists should be aware that talking about past suicide experiences may trigger painful memories and emotions (WHO/IASP, 2017). When arranging an appointment for an interview, let the bereaved person choose the location. Sometimes this will be at the family home, other times it could be a coffee shop, the location of the suicide, or a grave. It is important for the bereaved to feel that they are in control of the interview.

It is also best practice to provide some support information that can be left with the bereaved following the interview. One should recognise that speaking about suicide in close proximity could place a bereaved person in crisis, so do not leave them to struggle alone. A leaflet for a hotline or support group will be adequate here. Be aware that through investigation, one may gain more in-depth information about the suicide or the deceased that the bereaved do not have. Publishing this material could be quite harmful, as pointed out by extant WHO and IASP guidelines:

> Reporters also need to carefully consider the accuracy of any information received from the bereaved during an interview because their recall of specific memories, statements or behaviours of the suicide may be clouded in acute grief.
>
> *(WHO/IASP, 2017)*

Statistics

It is preferable to lead a suicide story with facts to provide context. Make sure that statistics do not inflate or conflate numbers. Suicide statistics should come from credible sources, such as WHO, Office of National Statistics (UK); Centres for Disease Control and Prevention (USA); Mindframe (Australia); Ministry of Health (New Zealand); Eurostat (EU).

Social media

Social media posts from a deceased individual should not be published or quoted from because they tend to glamorise and glorify suicide. It is also advisable to refrain from publishing suicide notes, final text messages, and emails from the deceased individual. Little context can be provided as to the meaning behind these types of messages (WHO/IASP, 2017). One should show caution and restraint when engaging in online memorial sites. Relating to this, journalists should not freely quote from memorial sites unless explicit consent has been obtained from the person who has posted the information, so as not to inadvertently cause undue stress and harm to those who have been bereaved.

Writing a suicide story

There are some guidelines journalists should follow when writing a suicide story to ensure ethical and responsible reporting.

Headlines

It is not an option to go for the cheap headline or the quick pun. For a suicide story, headlines should not include the method of death, the location of death, or even the word suicide (WHO/IASP, 2017). Most media organisations that fail to follow these guidelines are often found to be sensationalising suicide or are gratuitously reporting on the method of death, thus potentially causing harm to those bereaved.

Phraseology/Language

Language is crucial. Every single word and phrase in the story needs to be scrutinised to ensure that one is not inadvertently articulating stigma and sensation. Journalists need to think about phrases such as "commit suicide" – an unacceptable phrase that is steeped in historical conceptions of criminality (Luce, 2016). Most editorial guidelines in newsrooms will also advise to not use this particular phrase (BBC, 2018; *The Guardian*, 2015). Instead, "died by suicide", or "took her life", or killed himself". Phrases such as "successful" and "unsuccessful" suicide should also not be used as that implies triumph or failure. Do not talk about "suicide epidemics", which sensationalises suicide. Instead, "increasing suicide rates" should be used (or equivocal terms). Suicide is a public health problem and, as such, one has a responsibility to share risk factors, combined with messages about the prevention of suicide. This element can help educate the public about the importance of suicide prevention.

Method

This has already been discussed at length in this chapter, but here again, "detailed description and/or discussion of the method should be avoided because this will increase the likelihood that a vulnerable person will copy the act" (WHO/ IASP, 2017: 6). Journalists should also avoid indicating that a suicide method is rare or novel.

Location

What do the Golden Gate Bridge (USA), Aokigahara forest (Japan), Clifton Suspension Bridge (UK), and The Gap (Australia) all have in common? They are common suicide hotspots, or sites.

> Particular care should be taken by media professionals not to promote such locations as suicide sites by, for instance, using sensationalist language to describe them or overplaying the number of incidents occurring at that location.
>
> *(WHO/IASP, 2017: 7)*

Production of a suicide story

Now that the reporting and writing of a story are complete, attention needs to turn to ethical and responsible portrayal in newspapers, broadcast, and online.

Fact boxes/information boxes/sidebars

One of the most important pieces of information that you *must* include with your suicide story is a fact box, information box or sidebar, clearly stipulating where audiences can seek further support and information, such as The Samaritans (UK/Ireland), Lifeline/Veteran's Crisis Line/The Trevor Project (USA), Lifeline/Kids Helpline/Beyond Blue (Australia), Lifeline/Suicide Crisis Hotline (New Zealand). According to the WHO and IASP (2017), providing a long list can be counter-productive, so choose one phone number and one website to accompany the story.

Placement

Suicide stories should not be placed prominently for fear of sensationalising and glamorising the death. Undue repetition of suicide stories is also problematic (WHO/IASP, 2017). As a guide, in a newspaper, stories should be on inside pages, preferably on the bottom left. In broadcast, stories should be after the second or third break in the broadcast, while online posts should be further down a page, or even several clicks into the website. This also applies to celebrity suicides.

Online and multi-media

Search engine optimisation

SEO, or search engine optimisation, is about making stories stand out in search engine listings (Hill and Lashmar, 2014). While media organisations are keen to have their stories situated at the apex, the ethical reporter will make sure responsible reporting is maintained. SEO should not provide hyperlinks to suicidal method or location. Instead, hyperlinking should lead to support organisations such as the WHO, or other local suicide prevention organisations.

Photos, video, and slideshows

No matter the medium, stories need "art". These could take the form of photos or video, or combined together as interactive slideshows. I would urge caution here. While it might be newsroom policy to pull photos or video from Facebook, Weibo, QZone, Google Images, YouTube, Instagram, or Snapchat for a "regular" story, in the case of a suicide, explicit permission should be obtained from family members, as publication of these items can cause great distress and further propagate a crisis for those bereaved.

Video and audio

Use extreme caution before running audio or video footage of emergency calls – remember, these should not indicate method or location in any way (WHO/IASP, 2017: 9). If pulling audio from podcasts, SoundCloud, or AudioBoo, be sure to obtain permission from family members who may not wish to hear their deceased loved one on the air or on a news website.

Infographics

Before turning to infographics to visualise suicide information, please take time to consider the reason and rationale. If trying to visualise suicide statistics, be sure to use facts from reliable sources (see statistics section above).

While it might be appealing to visually represent suicide through the use of a map, this should be avoided. Using a map indicates the location of a suicide, which in turn could sensationalise or glorify this particular type of death in an area or community.

A "word cloud" may not be relevant while discussing an individual death, but if a journalist is trying to educate about suicide, perhaps a collection of tweets from Twitter could be represented in this way – again, journalists need to think about their ethical responsibility to their audience and use good judgement on whether a "wordle" fits the tone of the story.

Cartoons should be avoided to represent suicide – they are generally not in good taste and tend to overly glorify and glamorise the act of suicide.

Covering a celebrity suicide

Specialist and non-specialist journalists alike will naturally cover celebrity suicides due to the popularity of the person who has died and what they have culturally contributed to society. All celebrity suicides should be covered accurately, ethically and responsibly – just because a famous person has died-by-suicide *does not mean* that irresponsible reporting is permitted. Celebrity suicides should not be glamorised and the method of death should not be described in detail as was the case with Kate Spade (2018) and Robin Williams (2014).

> A focus on the celebrity's life, how he or she contributed to society and how their death negatively affects others is preferable to reporting details of the suicidal act or providing simplistic reasons for why the suicide occurred.
>
> *(WHO/IASP, 2017: 4)*

An information box, fact box or sidebar should always accompany any suicide story regarding a celebrity death.

Suicide reporting guidelines

As mentioned earlier in this chapter, there are multiple sets of guidelines on reporting suicide. The WHO guidelines are international and can be used and applied by any journalist in any country across the world:

http://www.who.int/mental_health/suicide-prevention/resource_booklet_
    2017/en/

This section has aimed to provide guidance on how to cover suicide in a responsible and ethical manner looking at how you report, write, and portray suicide stories. The next section will look at three case studies to provide further guidance on best and worst practices when reporting a suicide.

CASE STUDY 1

The Bridgend Suicides, Wales, 2008

The spate of suicides that occurred in Wales in 2008 is a prime example of what *not to do* when covering a suicide story. Between January 2008 and June 2008, the former mining town of Bridgend had 20 suicides amongst people aged 15–29. These suicides drew attention from local, national, and international media organisations, sparked by a sensational piece of copy provided by the wire service for Wales, Wales News Service, to all tabloids and broadsheets within the UK. The story constructed Bridgend as "Britain's suicide capital", "death town", and described the suicides as part of a "suicide craze", and attributed them to a "suicide cult". *None of this was true.*

The Mirror ran a headline:

> "Suicide Town: Parent's anguish as seven young friends all hang themselves in the space of one year".

The Daily Mail:

> "The internet suicide cult: chilling links between seven youngsters found hanged in the same town. They lived and died online".

The Guardian was not much better:

> "Police suspect internet link to suicides: seven young people found dead in last 12 months. Mother urges parents to monitor computer use".

The Sun: "Bebo mates in suicide chain".

All stories at the time referred to a link between the internet and the suicides (which also was not true). Thus, a moral panic was discursively constructed by news media.

A moral panic is a widespread fear that indicates that someone, or something, is a threat to the moral fabric of a society (Cohen, 2002). In the case of Bridgend, the "folk devil" was the Internet or, more specifically, social networking sites. One needs to remember that in 2008, the social network website Bebo was extremely popular in the UK and Ireland. MySpace was on its last legs, and a little-known company named Facebook was poised to take over the world. YouTube had only been around since mid-2006 and was slowly growing a following, while it would be a full year before Twitter fully emerged in 2009. The act of suicide is viewed as a noxious threat to society, but coupled with fear of unregulated social networking sites and the internet playing a significant role in a perceived immoral way to die, and a moral panic was born (Luce, 2016).

Throughout the coverage, journalists pointed to the internet and social networking sites as the primary culprit for why the Bridgend suicides continued to happen. All of those who died were members of social networking sites such as Facebook, Bebo and MySpace. As many of them were "friends" with each other on these sites, journalists jumped to the conclusion that the deaths must have been linked, despite evidence to the contrary. It can be seen, then, that journalists often did not report the suicides in a responsible, non-panic inducing way by centring attention onto the affordances of new media – a common enough occurrence in historical terms – as scapegoat.

In addition to the moral panic that was discursively constructed, those who died-by-suicide in Bridgend were demonised and infantilised by journalists, described in terms relating to childhood. Contemporary conceptions of childhood in society deem that children are weak, innocent, gullible beings in need of protection – so too are those who die by suicide or attempt suicide, it seems, even when they are adults. This infantalising is much easier to implement when the story features young adults – neither children nor grown-up. Moreover, since Western notions of childhood tend to construct children as either being "normal" or "deviant" to coincide with certain expectations around childhood as a time of life of innocence and naivety, those who kill themselves were labelled as "deviant". As suicide is even less acceptable in childhood, those children and young adults who killed themselves in Bridgend were very easily slotted into the discursive category of "deviant child".

In writing a suicide story, journalists have the power to replicate stigmatising discourses or to shift perceptions on how people should think and react to suicide. Journalists need to be aware of underlying fears that could emerge during the reporting of a suicide story, and they also need to take care in how they describe those who have died-by-suicide; that is to say, one should take care not to demonise or infantilise. A person has decided to take their own life – that decision should, at the very least, be respected as a choice.

CASE STUDY 2

Suicide of Jacintha Saldanha vs. Australian DJs, 2012

In December 2012, two Australian DJs from Austereo's 2DayFM radio show in Sydney, Mel Grieg and Michael Christian, attained the phone number for the King Edward VII hospital in London, where Duchess of Cambridge Kate Middleton was being treated for morning sickness during her pregnancy with Prince George. The DJs planned to prank call the hospital to try and get information about Middleton, which they successfully accomplished.

When Grieg and Christian rang the hospital, they were immediately put through by nurse Jacintha Saldanha (unknown at that time) to the ward where Middleton was being treated. In a two-minute, 17-second phone conversation, the charge nurse shared personal details about Middleton, with whom she believed to be Queen Elizabeth II of England.

The prank phone call was considered to be hysterically funny by the DJs. Several times during the segment, Grieg and Christian stated they could not believe they had been put through. "If this has worked, this is the easiest prank we've ever made", Christian declared on the air. The joke was well received around the world, with the recording making it to Twitter and onto YouTube. Media outlets around the world picked up the story and everyone had a laugh at the Royal Family's expense. While the hospital was apologising to Prince William and to the Duchess of Cambridge for breaching confidentiality, there were neither threats of fines, sackings, legal action nor any death threats.

This all changed when Jacintha Saldanha killed herself three days later. What followed can only be described as worldwide outrage and uproar about the death of Saldanha. Both DJs were blamed for her death, both were placed on leave, and both suffered significant mental health distress as a result of Saldanha's death.

This story raised ethical issues in Australia and legal issues in the UK. While British prosecutors did not bring any charges against the two DJs, in Australia, the national media watchdog, Australian Communications and Media Authority (ACMA), ruled that 2Day FM had breached clause 6.1 of the *Commercial Radio Australia Codes of Practice and Guidelines 2011* which "prohibits the broadcast of statements by identifiable persons without their consent", and clause 9.1 of the code, which "prohibits participants in live-hosted entertainment programmes from being treated in a highly demeaning or highly exploitative manner". The investigation did, however, state that 2Day FM "did not breach clauses that contained information regarding decency or privacy obligations". In essence, the two DJs, were cleared of any responsibility for Saldanha's suicide. Perhaps more controversially, this was the correct decision.

Jacintha Saldanha was 46 years old at the time of her death. She was born in India and had been living with her husband and two children in the UK since 2002. She was found hanged in the nurses' quarters attached to King Edward VII hospital. Saldanha had a history of mental illness, having previously attempted suicide twice a year earlier (Luce, 2016). She faced no disciplinary charges at the hospital for her minor role in the prank (transferring the call). Suicidologists would agree that Saldanha, at some point, was going to die-by-suicide, due to the fact that she had attempted several times previously and also had a serious history of mental health difficulties (Hawton and van Heeringen, 2009; Mesoudi, 2009; Shahtahmasebi, 2015).

Journalists were quick to blame when it came to explaining why Saldanha died-by-suicide. The "why?" of suicide, as explained earlier in this chapter is complex at the best of times; there is never a simple explanation as to why someone decides to take their own life, and the triggers for such deaths can be multiple. During the coverage, journalists also continuously "othered" the act of suicide, focusing on the fact that Saldanha was from India, indicating that someone who was British would not have carried out such an act, something that was also seen during the Bridgend suicides (those suicides were a Welsh problem, not an English one) (Luce, 2016).

Journalists also stigmatised mental health – they didn't explore her history of suicide attempts and history of mental health challenges. Instead, reporters sensationalised how she died, why she died and did not provide any context as to how previous mental health challenges could have affected her decision to die during this time (Luce, 2016). The poor reporting during this story had an impact not only on Saldanha's bereaved family and friends, but also on the two DJs whose lives changed significantly as a result of her death.

Journalists need to not sensationalise when covering suicide stories such as these. Considerable thought, critical thinking, and investigative journalism are needed. Journalists had an opportunity here to educate citizens about suicide and the impact it can have on those left behind. Instead, journalists went for the cheap shots, blamed the DJs, and reinforced stigma – not an example of responsible or ethical reporting.

CASE STUDY 3

13 Reasons Why, 2017–ongoing

On March 31, 2017, Netflix released its teen drama series *13 Reasons Why*, based on the book of the same name published a decade earlier. The series revolves around the suicide of 17-year-old Hannah Baker and her friend Clay Jensen, who is trying to cope in the aftermath of her death. Hannah leaves a box of cassette tapes that detail the "13 reasons why" she killed herself. While the series initially received positive reviews from critics and audiences, it was the representation of rape and suicide that prompted mental health professionals to call for censorship, trigger warnings, and a use of media reporting guidelines for fear of copycat suicides.

The issue here is that journalists did not critically engage or question what mental health professionals demanded. Journalists fear of reporting suicide is an anecdotal opinion from years of talking to journalists and media professionals. Journalists fear being linked to the notion that journalism may cause suicide, but the one thing that gets lost in this is a journalist's role in questioning societal norms and holding power to account, and that means mental health profession- als, too. Media academic William Proctor (2017) explained in *The Conversation*:

> It is not the media, in whatever form, that should be causing anxiety, but substantial cuts in mental health funding as well as the continuing discrim- ination and stigma attached to such conditions. As clinical psychologist David Swanson argues, *13 Reasons Why* will not cause people to take their own lives. It is anxiety, depression and major stress that are the triggers.

Yet in the weeks following the release of the programme, mental health pro- fessionals framed the narrative around fear and worry of copycat suicides. Journalists did not critique the fact that audiences interpret, evaluate, and use media in a variety of different ways (Proctor, 2017). Journalists did not ques- tion the sensationalist cautionary letters sent to parents by schools about the series. Journalists did not query the banning of the book from schools, a book that had been sitting on school library bookshelves and had been taught in English classes around the world for the previous decade. Journalists did not take the opportunity to further investigate the issue of suicide in their local communities, nor did they educate citizens about the warning signs of sui- cide. Journalists did not explore the political ramifications of cutting mental health funding, nor did they critically self-reflect on how the coverage they were creating further added to the stigma of suicide. Instead, journalists were duped into participating and replicating a moral panic about the representa- tion of suicide in *13 Reasons Why* and the fear that this programme would bring about even more suicides.

The scene of the suicide in *13 Reasons Why* made me cry. It was horrific, disturbing, and uncomfortable. It made me want to look away and it also brought up feelings and memories about my own bereavement 11 years earlier. But I supported the decision to represent the suicide, however brutal it was. In mainstream media, it is quite rare to see suicide represented on television or in film, or at least, not an accurate representation. This particular depiction showed that suicide is not a painless death, and that there is struggle, angst, and pain – plenty of pain. Fictional representations of suicide also never show what a suicide does to those left behind. This series is tackling the issue of suicide bereavement, a prime opportunity to write a series of stories about what suicide does to those who have been bereaved.

Instead, mental health professionals called for censorship for fear that copycat suicides would happen (they did not, despite sensationalised media reports). When Netflix refused to take down the programme, the second-most viewed Netflix season in the first 30 days after it premiered (Spangler, 2017), mental health professionals, including the International Association of Suicide Prevention, of which I am a member, called for media reporting guidelines to be used by Netflix.

Media reporting guidelines have been created for journalists, *not* fictional representations of suicide. The only guidelines, to my knowledge, that have been created for stage and screen are from Mindframe in Australia and the Samaritans in the UK, which have a factsheet for drama portrayal in television and film. When mental health professionals called for censorship (similar to the call for cessation of reporting by police and mental health charities during the Bridgend suicides in 2008), the use of guidelines and trigger warnings to be placed at the start of the programme and before the episodes that represent difficult subject matter, all they did was fuel the fire more. Proctor (2017) stated: "As we now surely know, from countless moral campaigns of this kind, scapegoating media as forbidden only challenges people to seek it out to learn what all the fuss is about."

As you can see in this case study, we are not talking about the reporting of an individual's suicide, or the impact a suicide can have on those bereaved. This case study is about when a journalist has to cover "a non-suicide" suicide story. Responsible reporting *must* be of the utmost importance. Journalists need to carry out their duty as watchdog, even when the story is about suicide. Critically engage with the information presented to you, ask questions, and look at the research. Do not let a vocal lobbying group lead the story. The mantra should be: investigate, investigate, and investigate.

Conclusion

Suicide stories must be reported responsibly, sensitively, ethically, and without sensation. In this chapter, I have provided four simple rules, which should help to assure responsible reporting. Journalists should not:

- Sensationalise
- Stigmatise
- Glorify
- Gratuitously report details about method of suicide

I also discussed at length how journalists should approach reporting a story, such as choosing the right story type; interviewing the bereaved; finding reliable suicide statistics; and using quotes from social media. I also discussed the writing of a suicide story where a journalist should think about non-sensational headlines, phraseology, and language, and not gratuitously provide details about method or the location of a suicide. I expanded further when discussing how to produce a suicide story, urging journalists to incorporate fact boxes, information boxes and sidebars with helpful information. I discussed the placement of stories, both in print and online, and discussed at length how to use search engine optimisation, photos, video, audio, slideshows, and infographics in a responsible manner. I advised on best practices when reporting on celebrity suicide, and also advised journalists to consult WHO media reporting guidelines when working on a suicide story. What I hope you now understand having read this chapter is that you *must*:

- Use WHO guidelines to report suicide
- Seriously consider the impact your reporting has on those bereaved by suicide
- Report ethically and responsibly
- Educate your audience about suicide

Note

1 When I discuss sensational reporting in this chapter, I am referring to the practice of presenting a story or information within a story that is intended to provoke public interest or excitement at the expense of accuracy.

References

American Foundation for Suicide Prevention. 2015. *Suicide claims more lives than war, murder and natural disasters combined.* [online]. USA. Available from: https://afsp.donordrive.com/index.cfm?fuseaction=cms.page&id=1226&eventID=5545 [Accessed 3 August 2018].

Australian Communications and Media Authority. 2015. [online]. Australia. Available from: www.acma.gov.au. [Accessed 3 August 2018].

Barker, M. and Petley, J. 2001. *Ill Effects: The Media/Violence Debate*. London: Routledge.

Barker, A., Hawton, K., Fagg, J., and Jennison, C. 1994. Seasonal weather factors in parasuicide. *British Journal of Psychiatry*, 165(3), 375–380.

BBC Editorial Guidelines. 2018. *Section 5: Harm and Offence*. [online]. UK. Available from: https://www.bbc.co.uk/editorialguidelines/guidelines/harm-and-offence/suicide [Accessed 3 August 2018].

Befrienders Worldwide. 2017. *Suicide Statistics*. [online]. UK. Available from: https://www.befrienders.org/suicide-statistics [Accessed: August 3 2018].

Berman, A.L., and Jobes, D.A. 1991. *Adolescent suicide assessment and intervention*. Washington, D.C.: The American Psychological Association.

Bird, L. and Faulkner, A. 2000. *Suicide and Self-Harm*. London: The Mental Health Foundation.

Campaign Against Living Miserably (CALM). 2016. *UK's biggest survey on impact of suicide*. [online]. UK. Available from: https://www.thecalmzone.net/2017/11/uks-biggest-survey-impact-suicide/ [Accessed 3 August 2018].

Camus, A. 1942. *The myth of Sisyphus*. Paris: Editions Gallimard.

Cerel, J., Brown, M.M., Maple, M., Singleton, M., and van de Venne, J. 2018. How many people are exposed to suicide? Not six. *Suicide and Life Threatening Behaviour*. [online]. Available from: https://onlinelibrary.wiley.com/doi/full/10.1111/sltb.12450

Cerel, J., Maple, M., van de Venne, J., Moore, M.M., Flaherty, C., and Brown, M. (2016). Suicide exposure in the community: Prevalence and correlates in one US state. *Public Health Reports*, 131(1), 100–107.

Cohen, S. 2002. *Folk devils and moral panics: The creation of the Mods and Rockers*. London: Routledge.

Cross, S. 2007. Why the copycat theory on suicide coverage is a conceptual red herring. *Ethical Space: The International Journal of Communication Ethics*, 4(4), 19–21.

Depression Alliance, 2018. Available from: www.depressionalliance.org [Accessed August 3 2018].

Douglas, J.D. 1969. The absurd in suicide. In E. Shneidman (ed.) *On the nature of suicide* (pp. 111–119). San Francisco: Jossey-Bass, Inc., Publishers.

Duncan, S. 2012. Sadly missed: The death knock news story as a personal narrative of grief. *Journalism*. 13(5), 589–603.

Durkheim, E. 1897, 1951. *Suicide*. New York: The Free Press, A Corporation.

Greenslade, R. 2014. Reporting Robin Williams's death – the good, the bad and the ugly. *The Guardian*. [online]. UK. Available from: https://www.theguardian.com/media/greenslade/2014/aug/13/robin-williams-national-newspapers [Accessed 3 August 2018].

The Guardian's Editorial Code. 2015. [online]. UK. *Available from:* https://www.theguardian.com/info/2015/aug/05/the-guardians-editorial-code [Accessed August 3 2018].

Hawton, K. and van Heeringen, K. 2009. Suicide. *Lancet*, 373(9672), 1372–1381.

Hill, S. and Lashmar, P. 2014. *Online journalism: The essential guide*. London: Sage.

Hittner, J. 2005. How robust is the Werther Effect? A re-examination of the suggestion imitation model of suicide. *Mortality*. 10(3), 193–200.

Independent Press Standards Organisation (IPSO). 2018. *The Editor's Code of Practice*. UK. [online]. Available from: https://www.ipso.co.uk/media/1058/a4-editors-code-2016.pdf [Accessed 3 August 2018].

Jamieson, P., Jamieson, K.H., and Romer, D. 2003. The responsible reporting of suicide in print journalism. *American Behavioural Scientist*, 46(12): 1643–1660.

Johns, A., Hawton, K., Gunnell, D., Lloyd, K., Scourfield, J., Jones, P.A., Luce, A., Marchant, A., Platt, S., Price, S., and Dennis, M.S. 2017. Newspaper reporting on a cluster of suicides in the UK. *Crisis: The Journal of Crisis Intervention and Suicide Prevention*, 38(1), 17–25.

Johns, A., Hawton, K., Lloyd, K., Luce, A., Platt, S., Scourfield, J., Marchant, A.L., Jones, P.A., and Dennie, M.S. 2014. PRINTQUAL – A measure for assessing the quality of newspaper reporting in suicide. *Crisis: The Journal of Crisis of Intervention and Suicide Prevention*, 35(6), 431–435.

Jourard, S.M. 1969. The invitation to die. In E. Shneidman (ed.) *On the nature of suicide* (pp. 129–141). San Francisco: Jossey-Bass, Inc., Publishers.

Keeble, R. 2009. *Ethics for journalists*. Oxon: Routledge.

Kerkhof, A.J.F.M. and Arensman, E. 2001. Pathways to suicide: The epidemiology of the suicidal process. In K. van Heeringen (ed.) *Understanding suicidal behaviour: The suicidal process approach to research, treatment and prevention* (pp. 15–39). Chichester: Wiley.

Levenson, E. and Gingras, B. 2018. Kate Spade, fashion designer, found dead in apparent suicide. *CNN*. [online]. USA. Available from: https://edition-m.cnn.com/2018/06/05/us/kate-spade-dead/index.html [Accessed 3 August 2018].

Luce, A. 2016. *The Bridgend suicides: Suicide and the media*. London: Palgrave MacMillan.

Markey, P.M. and Ferguson, C.J. 2017. *Moral combat*. Dallas: BenBella Books Inc.

Mesoudi, A. 2009. The cultural dynamics of copycat suicide. *PlosOne*, 4(9), 1–9.

Smith, R. 2008. Father of Bridgend suicide teenager says death was linked. *The Mirror*. [online]. UK. Available from: https://www.mirror.co.uk/news/uk-news/father-of-bridgend-suicide-teenager-says-294433 [Accessed 3 August 2018].

Mindframe. Australian Government under the National Suicide Prevention Program. 2014. [online] Available from: http://www.mindframe-media.info [Accessed 3 August 2018].

New Zealand Coroner's Act of 2006. [online]. New Zealand. Available from: http://www.legislation.govt.nz/act/public/2006/0038/latest/DLM377809.html [Accessed 3 August 2018].

Niederkrothenthaler, T., Voracek, M., Herberth, A., Till, B., Strauss, M., Etzersdorfer, E., Eisenwort, B., and Sonneck, G. 2010. Role of Media reports in completed and prevented suicide: Werther v. Papegeno effects, *British Journal of Psychiatry*, 197(3), 234–243.

OFCOM. 2017. *Section Two: Harm and Offence*. [online]. UK. Available from: https://www.ofcom.org.uk/tv-radio-and-on-demand/broadcast-codes/broadcast-code/section-two-harm-offence [Accessed 3 August 2018].

Phillips, D.P. 1974. The influence of suggestion on Suicide: Substantive and theoretical implications of the Werther Effect. *American Sociological Review*, 39(3), 340–354.

Pitman, A., Osborn, D., King, M., and Erlangsen, A. 2014. Effects of suicide bereavement on mental health and suicide risk. *The Lancet Psychiatry*, 1(1), 86–94.

Proctor, W. 2017. Why psychologists have got it wrong on 13 Reasons Why. *The Conversation*. [online]. UK. Available from: http://theconversation.com/why-psychologists-have-got-it-wrong-on-13-reasons-why-79806 [Accessed 3 August 2018].

Shahtahmasebi, S. 2015. Suicide research: Problems with interpreting results. *British Journal of Medicine and Medical Research*, 5(9), 1147–1157.

Shneidman, E. 1969. Discussion. In E. Shneidman (ed.) *On the nature of suicide*. San Francisco: Jossey-Bass, Inc., Publishers.

Shneidman, E. 1985. *Definition of suicide*. New York: John Wiley and Sons, Inc.

Shneidman, E. 1996. *The suicidal mind*. New York: Oxford University Press.

Survivors of Bereavement by Suicide. 2017. [online]. UK. Available from: https://uksobs.org/ [Accessed 3 August 2018].

Society for Professional Journalists. 2018. *SPJ Ethics Code.* [online]. USA. Available from: https://www.spj.org/ethicscode.asp [Accessed 3 August 2018].

Spangler, T. 2017. Netflix's 'Marvel's The Defenders' poised for binge-viewing pop, data indicates. *Variety.* [online]. USA. Available from: https://variety.com/2017/digital/news/netflix-marvel-the-defenders-binge-viewing-data-ratings-1202532453/ [Accessed 3 August 2018].

The Sydney Morning Herald. 2008. [online]. Australia. *UK man kills himself with chainsaw.* Available from: https://www.smh.com.au/world/uk-man-kills-himself-with-chainsaw-20081120-6bq4.html [Accessed 3 August 2018].

Temple, M. 2008. *The British Press.* Maidenhead: Open University Press.

World Health Organisation. 2008. *Methods of Suicide: International suicide patterns derived from the WHO mortality database.* [online]. Available from: http://www.who.int/bulletin/volumes/86/9/07-043489/en/ [Accessed 3 August 2018].

World Health Organisation. 2014. *Preventing Suicide: A Global Imperative.* [online]. Available from: http://www.who.int/mental_health/suicide-prevention/world_report_2014/en/ [Accessed 3 August 2018].

World Health Organisation. 2017a. *Suicide Data.* [online]. Available from: http://www.who.int/mental_health/prevention/suicide/suicideprevent/en/ [Accessed 3 August 2018].

World Health Organisation. 2017b. *Release of Mental Health Atlas 2017.* [online]. Available from: http://www.who.int/mental_health/en/ [Accessed 3 August 2018].

World Health Organisation and International Association of Suicide Prevention. 2017. *Preventing Suicide: a resource for media professionals-update 2017.* [online]. Available from: http://www.who.int/mental_health/suicide-prevention/resource_booklet_2017/en/ [Accessed 3 August 2018].

PART III

Reporting violence

5

REPORTING MASS SHOOTINGS

Glynn Greensmith

The social issue

This chapter will examine one of the strangest and (seemingly) most prevalent crimes of the last 60 years: the mass random shooting. Through charting the evolution of the crime itself, alongside the evolving nature of the reportage it generates, I will use a multi-disciplinary approach to develop our collective understanding of the consequence of certain types of coverage – the "script", to be outlined shortly – and journalistic/editorial decision-making.

Before 1966, the mass random shooting was extremely rare. The first was recorded as perpetrated by Ernst Wagner, in Germany, in 1913, followed by shootings in Melbourne in 1923 and New York in 1949 (Mullen, 2004). During the period 1913–1966 there were very few mass shootings of random individuals, but the cases involving the shooting of random people generated more news coverage than those involving family murders, even though family murders were much higher in number (Duwe, 2000; Mullen, 2004; Cantor, Mullen, and Alpers, 2000).

This chapter will detail what happened on 1 August 1966, at the University of Texas, USA and why it ranks as the "first" modern mass shooting. I will explore the script that was written by the media coverage that day, and how the crime itself then went from being rare to around 15 major occurrences a year, almost immediately.

I'll use three case studies to explore this topic:

- The coverage of the Dunblane and Port Arthur massacres in *The Mercury* newspaper (Tasmania) in 1996
- The coverage of the Umpqua Community College shooting in 2015
- The amok phenomenon

Finally, after identifying and analysing the relevant elements of the current media script in relation to modern mass shootings, this chapter will detail the inter-disciplinary call to change the nature of this coverage, and will offer simple, practical alternatives to existing reporting norms.

What is the mass random shooting?

The term "mass random shooting" itself lacks a single definition, but the description by the United States Congressional Research Service has become widely accepted: a crime in which three or more people selected indiscriminately, not including the perpetrator, are killed (United States Congress, 2012).

This chapter will seek to explore the history of mass shooting coverage, the research into the impact of that coverage, and the increasingly cogent argument that a change in the way this crime is reported could have a dramatic impact on its prevalence.

It is highly likely you are familiar with the crime of the mass random shooting, due to the extremely high level of media coverage it generates. School shootings in particular seem to hold a horrified fascination for both news outlets and their audiences, whether we go back to Dunblane, in Scotland in 1996, or the Columbine High School in 1999, the Sandy Hook Elementary School, also in the United States, in 2012, or more recently, the Marjory Stoneman Douglas High School in Florida in February 2018.

As a newsworthy subject it's an easy sell: these are horrific crimes and traditional news values demand we investigate them and provide our audience with the information they need to know what has happened, and potentially help people understand (or feel like they understand) what could have caused such an unimaginable crime to occur.

The Dunblane massacre (17 killed – 16 of them children) led to significant impacts on gun ownership laws and culture in the UK, and that effect was mirrored in the crime that occurred in the following month: Port Arthur in Australia (35 killed). Port Arthur was the last major shooting in Australia, and also led to sweeping changes in gun ownership legislation and gun culture in general.

Whatever the successes we've seen in some countries, you wouldn't be wrong if you felt the problem was getting worse. The three deadliest public mass random shootings in the US have all occurred since 2007, with the Orlando nightclub shooting in 2016 – which left 49 people dead and 53 wounded, the worst in US history for only just over a year (Lankford, 2016). In October 2017, 58 people were killed, and a staggering 851 injured in a mass shooting in Las Vegas. In February 2018 the murder of 17 people (mostly children) at a school in Parkland, Florida, again generated shock around the world.

Even countries outside the US, and without their infamous gun ownership laws, have not been immune. In July 2011, 77 people were killed by one gunman in Norway.

It wasn't always this way. These numbers have not always been the case. The research in this chapter will point to the "first" of the modern mass shootings, on 1 August 1966; this is where the crime as we know it today first began.

Introduction

On 22 July 2012, while sat at my desk at Curtin University in Perth, Western Australia, I picked up *The West Australian* newspaper. Dominating the front page was a bright bold picture of a man who had walked into a cinema screening of the movie Batman, in Aurora, Colorado, set off tear gas grenades, and began shooting indiscriminately with a range of firearms. Twelve people would die, and 70 more were injured. Among the victims were a 6-year-old girl, who was killed, and her pregnant mother, who survived, but lost the baby.

That unpleasant fact serves to highlight what numbers cannot always do: this was a horrific and cowardly crime, with consequences that will last a lifetime for everyone who was there. Yet alongside the large, bright, bold, photograph on the front page of my newspaper – way over on the other side of the world – was the headline "I'm the Joker', an apparent reference to both the movie being screened and the killer's attire.

On a moral level, I was horrified. A man who committed this type of crime gets his picture on the front page of newspapers all over the world, and even gets a nickname? It seemed wrong. But I had never - in my years of journalistic study, practice and teaching – come across any information on the appropriate and/or ethical implications around the coverage of a mass random shooting.

I resolved to dig further. This chapter will examine the coverage of mass shootings, and will provide detailed analysis of mass shooting case studies, to see if there may be lessons that can be learned.

I hope you will take away:

- A detailed understanding of the background, context, and nature of mass random shooting reportage, and the damage it can do.
- How history offers compelling insights and lessons for modern reporting.
- The increasing appetite for changing the nature of mass random shooting coverage, and how simple such changes can be.
- A broader understanding – alongside all the chapters of this volume – of the imperative upon all of us, as practitioners, students, and teachers of journalism, to understand the power and the consequences of what we do, and the decisions we make.
- A simple guide to how you can report this crime in an ethical way.

The research

The literature relating to this topic, both broadly and specifically, is extensive, but this section will provide you with a snapshot, and give you a sense of just how many different fields of study relate to this subject.

There has been debate and discussion on the nature of media effects (generally, and specifically in relation to violence), since the 1920s. Although journalism exists as a profession rooted in public interest and in the circulation of responsible media, it has always been subject to commercial pressures. As such, it has long been acknowledged that crime is a popular subject for news coverage, because of the view among editors and proprietors, real or perceived, that it boosts circulation figures.

In an effort to make crime news more entertaining, and thus more appealing to consumers, the news media over-represent violent, interpersonal crimes because they are dramatic, tragic, and rare in occurrence. Consequently, few crimes are more newsworthy than mass murder because it is a shocking, infrequently occurring crime; globally, the average is only 26 a year, involving a relatively large number of fatalities (Duwe, 2000).

What is the script?

Prior to the 1960s, there are just a handful of recorded incidents of individuals undertaking the mass murder of random people. Whilst there was news value and interest in the crimes, these early examples did not generate the kind of in-depth coverage we see today.

That changed in 1966, when many scholars identify the coverage assigned to Charles Whitman as marking the "first" of the modern-day mass shootings (Dietz, 1986; Duwe, 2000, 2004; Fox and Levin, 1998; Mullen, 2004; Cantor, Mullen, and Alpers, 2000; Cantor, Sheehan, Alpers, and Mullen, 1999). The analysis of the details of Whitman's crime indicates how the media coverage differed in nature from that given to previous mass shootings. The event was also covered live, as it unfolded, and with significant visual impact via the new medium of television. That new way of covering a mass shooting was adopted by almost all media in every Western country – hence why we call it "the script".

In seeking to construct a news story from any event, the journalist always seeks to answer the questions "Who? What? Where? When? How? Why?" in relation to stories on crime, the "What? Where? When?" questions usually provide the basic factual details of the incident. But it is in seeking to determine, and report on, the "Who? How? Why?" that news outlets have utilised, to varying extents: descriptions of the perpetrator; methodology of how the crime was committed; and speculation or analysis of a (potential) motive. These provide a reason to dive into every aspect of the killer's life: letters; social media/online posts; manifestos. In 1966 the script for covering mass shootings began, and the number of incidents dramatically increased (Cantor, Mullen, and Alpers, 2000: 55).

In 1986, it was Dietz who argued – whilst naming the crime "pseudocommando" – that the role of the media was not just an influence on the motivation of the crime, but inherent to it:

> The predictably high publicity attending these crimes is among the motives of their perpetrators … offenders in each of these categories see headlines

as one of the predictable outcomes of their behaviour, which they pursue in part for this purpose."

(Dietz, 1986: 477)

This implies that coverage of one mass shooting can influence the likelihood of another. It wasn't just the publicity itself, it was the way the story was framed. That is the script: any potential shooter, having seen a specific and consistent way such crimes are reported, can reasonably predict they too would receive such coverage if they committed a similar crime.

Cantor and Sheehan (1996) conducted a media-specific investigation into mass shootings by examining the potential role of the media in the Hungerford massacre in the UK on 19 August 1987, which occurred ten days after a mass shooting in Melbourne, Australia (9 August 1987). They attributed the short time lag effect to be relevant to copycat modelling, and found:

> From [a] high degree of consistency of content … it seems reasonable to conclude [that] reports were similar enough for [the] Hungerford subject to derive a consistent description of the [Melbourne] model with whom he may have identified.

(Cantor and Sheehan, 1996: 262–263)

Further studies by the same scholars, however, find that a short time lag may not be an appropriate reference for a model of media influence on mass shooters; unlike suicides (Pirkis and Blood, 2001a). Importantly, informing an evolution of the understanding of how these crimes and their perpetrators differ from previous modelling, Cantor et al. argue that media effects may operate for periods of ten years or more; and are not confined geographically (Cantor et al., 1999: 287).

Other studies have found mass shootings, and school shootings in particular, do have evident contagion, and a measurable effect is detectable within 13 days of the reported shooting (Sherry et al., 2015: 1).

Cantor, Alpers, and Mullen (2000) examined seven case studies of mass murders, in the UK, New Zealand, and Australia. Their work relates all of their seven case studies to the amok phenomenon, which will be explored in greater depth later in this chapter. Cantor, Alpers, and Mullen (2000) found other commonalities:

- All the murders were an a-typical form of suicide
- Perpetrators all displayed a marked sense of entitlement, but grossly deficient social networks and fragile identities. An element of "achieving" social status was inherent in their motivation for their crimes
- They desired to "upstage" other mass shootings, or achieve a "record" number of fatalities

Whilst the analysis from Forensic Psychiatrist Professor Paul Mullen's research, and previous studies (Cantor et al., 1999; Cantor, Mullen, and Alpers, 2000;

Dietz, 1986), may rule out the crime being committed as a copycat event, due to the variances in time lag and testimony, Mullen crucially notes the inherent link of such acts to other crimes of the same nature, arguing that:

> ... virtually all perpetrators of autogenic massacres [Mullen's term for "pseudocommando" killings] are carrying out a project of murder–suicide in which they intend to kill as many people as possible then to die among their victims and [they are] adopting an existing script for murder suicide that they have acquired from reading about or seeing it in news or dramas. These massacres are acts of mimesis and their perpetrators are imitators.
>
> *(Mullen, 2004)*

Imitators, but not copycats.

Mullen's seminal work is crucial in separating the effects of media coverage on mass shootings from established suicide research and the accepted copycat effect. Mullen emphasises the imagined role that dying was to play in the intended acts of the five surviving killers he interviewed. According to Mullen's analysis of his data, the decision to die by suicide came first; the idea for dying as part of a particular type of crime followed. (Mullen, 2004: 321)

It is critically important to note that the psychiatric research has found that, in the vast majority of the cases studied, the killer was not deemed to be a psychopath:

> Most perpetrators of autogenic massacres do not ... appear to have active psychotic symptoms at the time, and very few even have histories of prior contact with mental health services.
>
> *(Mullen, 2004: 321)*

What Mullen is saying here is that, from a psychiatric perspective, what made these men kill was something other than being psychotic. As we will see when we look at amok, history tells us when we provide someone with a script that says there is a way to make everyone know their name, motivation for murder, even mass murder can extend beyond the clinically insane and psychotic. This is the reason we must look at the role of journalism.

As part of this multi-disciplinary approach, there are now examples of individuals/groups impacted by mass shootings calling for a change in the way they are reported. "Don't Name Them" calls for the focus to be on victims, survivors, and people who tried to help, rather than the shooter – as per the script (Blair et al., 2015). "No Notoriety" was set up after the shooting in Aurora, Colorado, and also pressures media outlets to stop focusing on the killer.

What Dietz (1986) calls "pseudocommando"; what Cantor et al. (1999, 2000) describe as a "civil massacre", and what Mullen (2004) calls the "autogenic massacre" is a crime where the assailant:

- Intends to die
- Intends to kill as many people as possible before that death

- Has inherent in the motivation of the crime a desire for a specific type of news coverage to be received

Multiple research studies show the mass random shooting to be:

- An atypical form of suicide
- Influenced by media reports on previous mass shootings
- Predicated on the same level of coverage being received for a crime of a similar (imitative) nature

The mass random shooter is not a copycat: he (and it is almost always males who carry out these crimes) desires his own level of "fame" and is adopting a script – an understanding of how the crime will be reported, based on previous media reports, to achieve it (Greensmith, 2015: 76).

Covering mass shootings ethically

For further clarity, let's frame the discussion around how we apply the six classic news questions in an ethical manner. Our discussion on "the script" focuses on:

Who?

Extensive details of the perpetrator, not the victims, survivors, or anyone else impacted by the crime.

How?

Detailed description of how the crime was committed, thereby breaking down logistical and emotional boundaries for potential shooters, as well as giving them goals to try and surpass.

Why?

If in seeking to provide an answer as to why anyone would carry out such a horrific act, we explore and publish blog posts, diary/social media entries, home videos, manifestos, and extensive descriptions of the perpetrator to see if it provides clues, we are delivering the benefit that we know many shooters sought when planning/committing the crime. It is these elements that make naming and showing them so problematic.

In simple news terms, when covering a mass shooting a journalist should seek to:

- Report the facts of the crime (What? Where? When?).
- Keep the focus on the victims, survivors, and those impacted, rather than the killer.

- Avoid detailed description of how the crime was committed.
- Avoid speculation of motive and only report official findings, when they are released, from police investigations, psychiatric evaluations, detailed research, court and coroner's reports.

There has long been an ethical tension around news outlets seeking an immediate answer to a question that cannot be answered quickly. When it comes to reporting the motivation for these terrible crimes, the ethical imperative is clear: wait for the evidence; report it accordingly, and don't focus on the killer.

CASE STUDY 1

Dunblane and Port Arthur

On 13 March 1996, a man named Thomas Hamilton walked into a gym class at Dunblane Primary School, near Stirling in Scotland. He pulled out four, legally owned handguns and began firing at the children and teachers. Sixteen children would die, none of them older than six. One teacher was also killed. Hamilton eventually turned a gun on himself.

On 28 April 1996, in the tourist town of Port Arthur on the Tasmanian coast, in Australia, a man called Martin Bryant began a killing spree that would eventually claim the lives of 35 people. Though he later said his intention was to die in the act, Bryant would live.

Forensic Psychiatrist Prof Paul Mullen, who provided the psychiatric report for the trial of the Port Arthur killer, Martin Bryant, directly attributes Bryant's actions to the news coverage of the Dunblane massacre, 46 days previously. He found that Bryant was suicidal, but turned the suicide plan into a mass murder after witnessing the coverage received by Thomas Hamilton (Mullen, 2004: 319).

In my research, I have analysed the scope and nature of the coverage of both Dunblane and Port Arthur, in the main Tasmanian daily newspaper, *The Mercury*, for eight days after the crimes were committed. I also interviewed journalists working in Tasmanian media at the time.

The purpose of these case studies is simple: now that we've identified a consistent framing of coverage around mass shootings – the script – I want to see how or if it applies to these incidents. Mainly I will look at:

- Identification of the killer.
- Description of how the crime was committed.
- Speculation (not evidence based) as to motive, including any notion of insanity.

I am also looking for:

- Any descriptions of the crimes as "records" in terms of fatalities/injuries.

- Whether any discussion was undertaken – within the Port Arthur coverage – of the proximity of the two crimes, and/or any discussion of pertinent theories around the coverage of mass random shootings as a potential motivator for triggering future attacks.

When looking at the Dunblane massacre coverage in *The Mercury*, March 14–21, 1996, Table 5.1 shows how many times these instances occurred (Table 5.1):

TABLE 5.1 Number of times these instances occurred when looking at the Dunblane massacre coverage in *The Mercury*, March 14–21, 1996

Total number of articles	35
Photo of perpetrator	5
Name of perpetrator	24
Details of life/history of perpetrator	9
References to mental health	10
Reference to other potential motivators and/or gun ownership laws etc.	10
Reference to previous massacres – in proximity or motivation	5

Sample headlines, quotes, and stories:

Headline: He might have heard voices in his head

"If there is one thing these people have in common, it is that they tend to look remarkably ordinary. They tend to be reclusive, very private people. They don't have normal social relationships, no girlfriends usually."

Glenn Wilson of the Institute of Psychiatry told Sky television.
"He might have heard voices in his head telling him he had to do this."

Note in this story there is no mention of the research or theories into the nature of media coverage as a possible cause. There an ethical responsibility for journalists to discuss or refer to the research into media coverage of these crimes as a possible motivation.

The use of the word "might" in the headline underlines the speculative nature of the attempt to address mental health as a factor, implying insanity or schizophrenia as a cause without the evidence to support the claim. This is unethical and has been the subject of concern from a wide variety of mental health groups, who worry at the media's equating of mental health conditions and mass murder (Pirkis et al., 2001b). It has also been found to not be part of the typology of all mass shooters (Mullen, 2004; Lankford, 2016; Palermo, 1997; Pirkis et al., 2001b).

Reporting a confirmed diagnosis can be problematic and cause stigma for sufferers of a condition, but to speculate without confirmation is inaccurate and unethical.

Headline: The Scoutmaster from Hell

A large picture of the killer, with the caption "Thomas hamilton (sic): A shabbily dressed loner"

> ... it has emerged Hamilton, 43, wrote to the Queen just five days ago, accusing the Scout Association of mounting a campaign to sully his reputation; was a gun and photography enthusiast whose home is said to have been covered in pictures of semi-naked boys; and was forced to resign as a Scout leader more than 20 years ago after claims of improper behaviour ...

This piece has a strong focus on identifying the killer. As the lines between fame and infamy blur, is it possible for a potential killer to think any coverage is good coverage? Are we giving them what they want when we delve into their life and report it for all to see, with no real way of knowing whether we're uncovering any actual clues as to why they committed this act? (Lankford, 2016: 123)

Headline: Dunblane echoes other mass murders

> Ryan, 27, a fantasising gun fanatic, killed 15 people before taking refuge in John O' Gaunt comprehensive school [Hungerford] where he shot himself in the head with a pistol tied to his wrist with a bootlace.

This article pays particular attention to a previous mass shooting that happened in Hungerford, UK, in 1987. That shooting happened just ten days after a mass shooting in Melbourne, Australia that was widely reported in the UK media, but the article makes no reference to the proximity of the two crimes. Is there an ethical responsibility to note the time proximity of one mass shooting to another?

When looking at the Port Arthur massacre coverage in *The Mercury*, April 29–May 6, 1996, Table 5.2 shows how many times these instances occurred:

TABLE 5.2 Number of times these instances occurred when looking at the Port Arthur massacre coverage in *The Mercury*, April 29–May 6, 1996

Total number of articles	179
Photo of perpetrator	2
Name of perpetrator	8
Details of life/history of perpetrator	7
References to mental health	5
Reference to other potential motivators and/or gun ownership laws etc.	3
Reference to previous massacres – in proximity or motivation	3

Sample headlines, quotes, and stories:

Headline: Gunman was diagnosed as schizophrenic

The 29-year-old gunman who slew 33 people yesterday was recently diagnosed as schizophrenic.

The man, from Clare St, New Town, was last night described as "a nice bloke".

The man who performed the psychiatric assessment of the killer said no such diagnosis of schizophrenia existed.

Headline: Highest toll by a lone gunman

With 33 dead and more than 15 wounded, the Port Arthur disaster writes Australia into a bloody history book.

...

Previously Australia's worst thrill-killing shooting occurred in a crowded Sydney shopping centre in 1991.

As discussed previously, if the killer is not a copycat and are seeking their own fame, does reporting of "records" feed into their motivation, giving them something to try and surpass?

Headline: The troubled mind of Bryant

On one hand he is happy and friendly.
He always has a cheeky grin.
He would not hurt a fly, one neighbour said yesterday.
But Martin Bryant can also intimidate people.

A series of small descriptions by people who knew or were acquainted with Bryant dominate this article. Despite the headline, there is no psychiatric/emotional analysis.

Instead, this article ends:

Another was surprised at mention of Bryant's recent diagnosis as a schizophrenic.
He said he had never been treated by authorities as a mental-health patient.

Headline: Move to jail within a week

The alleged gunman from the Port Arthur massacre will be moved from the Royal Hobart Hospital within a week.

The script changes. After the second day of reporting, Martin Bryant's name all but disappeared from the coverage in *The Mercury*. The saturation coverage continued, but none of it now referred to the alleged killer, instead focusing on the victims/survivors, and fall out. After 30 April there are no more identifiers, and no more speculation as to motive or mental state.

Headline: Value in lessons of Dunblane

> Some of the experience gained by police after the massacre of Scottish schoolchildren at Dunblane will be applied in the aftermath of the Port Arthur massacre.

> Tasmanian Police Commissioner John Johnson said the Chief of Police for Central Scotland had been helpful in advising Tasmanian emergency services what sort of work they could expect in the coming months.

There is no other reference to the proximity of the shooting that happened just the month before. Again, does comprehensive, ethical, reporting demand the close proximity of the two crimes be more clearly identified and reported?

Analysis

- Sixty-eight per cent of the articles covering the Dunblane massacre feature one or more identifiers of the perpetrator.
- Just 14 per cent of articles covering the Port Arthur massacre, in the same newspaper, feature one or more identifiers of the perpetrator.

This stark disparity is partly explained by a conversation between *The Mercury's* editorial team and the-then Tasmanian Director of Public Prosecutions Damian Bugg. Mr Bugg called the paper and warned them about the nature of their reporting of the suspect in custody, as the case would soon be "*sub judice*" (literally "under judgement", when a case is before the courts, materials which may impact the "administration of justice" are not published or broadcast by news outlets).

There was also a community backlash against the way the paper identified/ lionised Bryant on the second day of coverage, but the editorial team told me it was the "*sub judice*" element which dramatically changed the nature of their reporting.

As a local tragedy, it is not surprising that the Port Arthur shootings produced 179 articles, compared to 35 for Dunblane, over eight days. There was strong evidence for the application of the traditional reporting script in the first two days' reporting: (inaccurate) reference to mental illness; reference to the number of fatalities being a "record"; detailed descriptions of the killer – his history, home, personality.

But what is obvious in the comparison of the reporting of these two crimes in the same newspaper is that Dunblane reports focused more on the killer. Thomas Hamilton had his life dissected and discussed in great detail, as the paper sought to answer why this terrible crime had occurred.

Yet there was never any discussion of research into the role media coverage can play. More tellingly, there was no discussion – in any of the 179 articles in *The Mercury* on Port Arthur – of the proximity of the crimes, and how expert analysis exists claiming that such proximity was no coincidence.

The Mercury's coverage of Port Arthur was:

- More sensitive to the emotions of readers
- More strongly focussed on victims' experiences than their coverage of Dunblane
- Less focused on who the killer was, with little speculation as to why he would commit this terrible crime
- Detailed in its descriptions of the response of authorities: emergency services; legal; and political
- Strongly local/community focussed

If *The Mercury* had used a similar reporting focus for the Dunblane massacre, might there not have been a Port Arthur massacre? We may never know.

CASE STUDY 2

Umpqua Community College, USA

On 1 October 2015, Chris Harper-Mercer, a 26-year-old student, walked into the Umpqua Community College in Oregon, USA. He opened fire on staff and students; one Associate Professor and eight students were killed. Harper-Mercer then shot himself in the head.

This is a fascinating case study for us because of the moment local Sheriff John Hanlin delivered a statement at a press conference, where he said:

"I will not name the shooter … I will not give him the credit he probably sought prior to this horrific and cowardly act."

I chose to examine the coverage of this shooting in *The West Australian* newspaper, representing a different geographical area to *The Mercury*, as well as a different parent company. I also wanted to know if the refusal to name the killer, by the sheriff in charge of the investigation, formed any part of the reporting.

If so, was it accompanied by any discussion of the research into mass shootings and media coverage? Twenty years after the shootings in Dunblane and Port Arthur, have there been changes to the script?

Over eight days there were only five articles covering this crime, from Oct 3–8.

Headline: Gunman Hunted for Christians – Another US Massacre (A front-page section with just this headline and a picture of the killer.)
Headline: US Massacre – Christians in killer's gun sights.
Headline: Killer spared life of "lucky" student messenger

Analysis:

- As might be expected, the shooting received less coverage than the Dunblane shooting.
- Only two articles did not name or show the killer.
- There was stronger perpetrator focus than victim focus.
- Several of the articles referenced gun control legislation in the US, and the political fallout from the shooting.
- There was a detailed identification of the killer under the premise of trying to understand why he committed the crime.
- There was not a single mention of the Sheriff's refusal to name the killer.

The Umpqua killings articles stuck to the existing script of mass shooting reporting: cover the perpetrator, include several elements of identification; examine their life to seek to understand why they may have committed the crime.

That the Sheriff leading the case considered the desire for fame/notoriety through media coverage was a potential motive for the killings was not considered newsworthy. Yet it is telling that many news outlets reported something simple and prescient the killer had written online:

"Seems the more people you kill, the more you're in the limelight."

CASE STUDY 3

The Amok phenomenon

We've been talking about the crime of the mass random shooting, specifically. But at this point it is crucial to note that for all the many reasons humans have fought and killed each other over countless millennia, the act of killing random individuals for no apparent reason is not recorded at all in Western culture. There is research into varying forms of mass murder undertaken for a particular purpose, such as the Nordic concept of going "Beserk" (Palermo, 1997), and the Mediterranean "Devotio" (Preti, 2008: 546), but these were usually to achieve military aims.

There is only one historical global record of this crime, and it provides us with a crucial case study in helping us understand the modern mass shooting.

In parts of South East Asia, though most prevalent in the Malay Peninsula, scholars recorded a phenomenon called "amok".

Captain Cook is credited with making the first outside recordings of "amok", after witnessing the phenomena among Malay tribesmen during his voyage in 1770. Spores (1988) labels it as when "an individual unpredictably, and without warning, manifests mass, indiscriminate, homicidal behaviour that is authored with suicidal intent."

Scholars have debated the nature of the suicidal intent, but it is crucial to our understanding of the anticipated outcome of the "amok" attack: death is expected.

Local mythology held that the behaviour was caused by the "hantu belian", an evil tiger spirit that entered a body and caused the actions of "amok". Because of these spiritual beliefs "amok" was actually tolerated, maybe even legitimized, within the culture. (Spores, 1988: 7)

Or to put it another way: a person contemplating committing such a crime had a firm understanding of how the crime would be spoken about (i.e. how it would be proxy reported). A script existed for the narrative of this crime.

Mullen (2004) refers to "amok" in his comparative study of several perpetrators of mass shootings, including Martin Bryant (Port Arthur, 1996), and Julian Knight (Melbourne, 1987). He describes "amok" as:

> ... a mechanism used by young men following some form of public humiliation to regain face and social prestige, the manner of their death being a vindication of their courage and potency.
>
> (Mullen, 2004: 321)

However, during the 1800s at a time of Dutch and British influence in South East Asia, there was a reduction in "amok" attacks in the region. The authorities focused their efforts on capturing the perpetrator, instead of killing him.

This dramatically affected the perception of the outcome in the eyes of potential attackers and the wider community.

To be captured while engaged in "amok" in late nineteenth century Malaya or Indonesia would have meant execution or incarceration in a prison or lunatic asylum, all prospects far removed from the denouement sought by the "amok" runner in wilfully initiating the episode (Spores, 1988).

This strategy reduced the frequency of amok, by removing elements they believed the perpetrators sought:

> ... thereby serving to rob amok of any glamour or heroicism that some might see vested in the practice.
>
> (Spores, 1988: 79)

In essence, colonial authorities changed the script. They altered the way "amok" was talked about, perceived, related – reported – and the behaviour largely ceased. This shows us the difference a positive script, an ethical/public interest-driven way of reporting an event can make compared to the kind of reporting highlighted in the first two case studies.

Conclusion

The script for the coverage of mass shootings was written on 1 August 1966. Once extensive details of the crime dominated media coverage – the identity of the gunman; his method; speculation as to why he would do such a thing; antihero/notoriety status – mass killings exploded in number. The prevalence of the crime is inextricably linked to the way they came to be reported. (Collins, 2008; Dietz, 1986; Mullen, 2004; Cantor et al., 1999). The notion of the script helps us understand that the way mass shootings became covered after 1966 became the norm for all outlets in the majority of countries.

The model of "amok" is a key development in our understanding of the relationship between mass murder and the way the perpetrator is talked about/reported.

There has been a notable shift in attitudes towards the media's identification of the mass shooting perpetrator. Increasingly, news outlets, law enforcement officers, and public officials, have refused to name the shooter (Greensmith, 2015: 79) and this suggests a new appetite for understanding the ramifications of the dominant narrative of coverage of these crimes.

The 2016 mass shooting at the Pulse nightclub in Orlando, Florida, produced a high profile reaction around the naming of the killer. Then-Director of the FBI James Comey said:

> You will notice that I am not using the killer's name and I will try not to do that. Part of what motivates sick people to do this kind of thing is some

twisted notion of fame or glory and I don't want to be part of that for the sake of the victims and their families. And so that other twisted minds don't think this is a path to fame and recognition.

(Gurman, 2016)

On CNN, host Anderson Cooper also refused to name the killer, and turned the focus instead to the victims of the crime:

There's one name you will not hear in the broadcast, one picture of a person you won't see. We will not say the gunman's name or show his photograph. It has been shown far too much already. Over the next two hours ... we want to keep the focus where it belongs, on people whose lives were cut short.

(Wilstein, 2016)

The media coverage is increasingly identified as a causal motivation for mass shooters:

These killers want the publicity, they want to go down in infamy. Achieving the highest body count is one way to do that. The media have not only a right but a responsibility to report the news. The problem is the way the news gets reported. The emphasis is usually not on the victims but on the killer. ... We make celebrities out of monsters.

(Zarembo, 2016)

US academics Lankford and Madfis (2017) have tried to put this issue on the agenda of major US news outlets. Their suggestion of "Don't name them, don't show them, but report everything else" is a pragmatic start to generate momentum for understanding the consequences of this script, and the dramatic impact changing it could have.

References

Blair, J. P., Hendricks, D., Keyes, J.-M. & Smith, R. 2015. Don't Name Them. http://www.dontnamethem.org/.

Cantor, C. H. & Sheehan, P. W. 1996. Violence and media reports—a connection with Hungerford? *Archives of Suicide Research*, 2, 255–266.

Cantor, C. H., Mullen, P. E. & Alpers, P. A. 2000. Mass homicide: the civil massacre. *The Journal of the American Academy of Psychiatry and the Law*, 28, 55–63.

Cantor, C. H., Sheehan, P., Alpers, P. & Mullen, P. 1999. Media and mass homicides. *Archives of Suicide Research*, 5, 285–292.

Collins, R. 2008. Violence: a micro-sociological theory, Princeton: Princeton University Press.

Dietz, P. E. 1986. Mass, serial and sensational homicides. *Bulletin of the New York Academy of Medicine*, 62, 477–491.

Duwe, G. 2000. Body-count journalism: the presentation of mass murder in the news media. *Homicide Studies*, 4, 364–399.

Duwe, G. 2004. The patterns and prevalence of mass murder in twentieth-century America. *Justice Quarterly*, 21, 729–761.

Fox, J. A. & Levin, J. 1998. Multiple homicide: patterns of serial and mass murder. *Crime and Justice*, 23, 407–455.

Greensmith, G. & Green, L. 2015. Reporting mass random shootings: The copycat effect? *Ethical Space*, 12, 73–80.

Gurman, S. 2016. Comey's refusal to name gunman marks change in terror talk. https://www.apnews.com/0c872f1626214812a986879edd53ab71.

Lankford, A. 2016. Fame-seeking rampage shooters: initial findings and empirical predictions. *Aggression and Violent Behavior*, 27, 122–129.

Lankford, A. & Madfis, E. 2017. Don't name them, don't show them, but report everything else: a pragmatic proposal for denying mass shooters the attention they seek and deterring future offenders. *American Behavioral Scientist*, 62, 1–15.

Mullen, P. E. 2004. The autogenic (self-generated) massacre. *Behavioral Sciences & the Law*, 22, 311–323.

Palermo, G. B. 1997. The berserk syndrome: a review of mass murder. *Aggression and Violent Behavior*, 2, 1–8.

Pirkis, J. & Blood R. W. 2001a. Suicide and the media: a critical review, Canberra: Commonwealth Department of Health and Aged Care.

Pirkis, J., Blood, R. W., Francis, C., Putnis, P., Burgess, P., Morley, B., Stewart A. & Payne, T. 2001b. The media monitoring project: a baseline description of how the Australian media report and portray suicide and mental health and illness, Canberra: Commonwealth Department of Health and Aged Care.

Preti, A. 2008. School shooting as a culturally enforced way of expressing suicidal hostile intentions. *Journal of the American Academy of Psychiatry and the Law*, 36, 544–550.

Sherry, T., Andres, G.-L., Maryam, K., Anuj, M. & Carlos, C.-C. 2015. Contagion in mass killings and school shootings. *PLoS ONE*, 10, e0117259.

Spores, J. C. 1988. Running amok: an historical inquiry, Athens, Ohio: Ohio University Press.

United States Congress. 2012. Investigative Assistance for Violent Crimes Act of 2012, Pub. L. No. 112–265, 126 STAT. 2435 (2013).

Wilstein, M. 2016. CNN's Anderson Cooper fights back tears reading Orlando victim names. http://www.thedailybeast.com/cnns-anderson-cooper-fights-back-tears-reading-orlando-victim-names.

Zarembo, A. 2016. Are the media complicit in mass shootings? http://www.latimes.com/nation/la-na-orlando-shooting-media-20160618-snap-story.html.

6

REPORTING URBAN VIOLENCE AND GANGS

Mathew Charles

The social issue

When I was working in El Salvador in 2012, a teenage member of the *Barrio 18* (18 Street) gang told me he was fighting for "the cause". When I asked what that cause was, he simply replied, "To die". It struck me how someone so young could have no respect for human life, not even his own. In 2017, a young Colombian paramilitary would use similar language. "As a soldier, I'm ready for death. All soldiers want to die in battle", I was told.

The permeation of violence into daily life is becoming ever more common in many countries, especially in those we consider to be the "Global South". Even in more developed nations such as the United Kingdom, where knives are the most common cause of death in homicide, and are often associated with gang-related violence, there has been a steady rise in knife crime year-on-year since 2014 (Shaw, 2018). Violence or the fear of violence is, therefore, a daily reality for millions of people around the world.

Some of the highest homicide rates occur in cities that are not actually at war. For example, between 1978 and 2000, more people (49,913) were killed in the slums of Rio de Janeiro than in all of Colombia, a country experiencing civil conflict (Dowdney, 2004). Indeed, Latin America and the Caribbean (LAC) remains the world's most violent region. According to the Mexican NGO, the Citizen Council for Public Security and Criminal Justice (CCSPJP), 43 of the world's most dangerous cities in 2017 were in the LAC region, with the remainder in the USA and South Africa. The world's top ten most murderous cities were all in Mexico, Venezuela, and Brazil (CCSPJP, 2018).

The United Nations Office on Drugs and Crime says that 30 per cent of the homicides in the Americas are attributed to organised crime and gang-related violence. This is compared to less than 1 per cent in Asia, Europe, and Oceania (UNODC, 2013). In Mexico, this figure reportedly rises to 75 per cent (Dittmar, 2018). It should be noted, however, that the presence of a strong underworld does not always translate into high murder rates. In Medellín, Colombia's second city, for example, there has been a remarkable decrease in the number of murders in the past 20 years. This is largely attributed to a truce between the city's criminal gangs (Southwick, 2013).

In attempting to deal with high levels of violence, LAC governments have often adopted policies that add fuel to the fire. The excessive use of the military in what have become known as *mano dura* or "firm hand" policies for domestic security tasks has contributed to generally increasing levels of violence (Wolf, 2017). In Venezuela, for example, security forces were responsible for 20 per cent of all murders in 2017 (Clavel, 2018). Furthermore, some studies have made direct correlations between trust in law enforcement and high levels of crime (see Vilalta Perdomo et al., 2016).

The UNODC (2013) also says that it is the world's poorest communities who suffer most from violence (see also Winton, 2004; Briceño-León and Zubillaga, 2002). However, the Inter-American Development Bank argues that LAC homicide rates are higher than they should be given the income levels of the countries concerned. To suggest that socio-economic factors are the root cause of violence is therefore an over-simplification. Other factors such as weak state institutions, rapid urbanisation, unequal access to public services, and, of course, organised crime, all play a part in the complex web of issues which fuel and maintain violence and the structures, which underpin it (Jaitman, 2017).

Violence is also expensive. The Inter-American Development Bank estimates that LAC countries spend $236 billion annually on violence (Jaitman, 2017: xii). In Guatemala, the direct costs of violence, concentrated primarily in the capital city, were estimated at $2.4 billion or 7.3 per cent of GDP in 2005. This is more than double the damage caused by Hurricane Stan in the same year and more than double the combined budget for the ministries of agriculture, health, and education in 2006 (World Bank, 2011: 3). Similarly, it has been estimated that if Jamaica and Haiti reduced their crime levels to those of Costa Rica, they could increase their annual GDP growth by 5.4 per cent (World Bank, 2011: 3). While spending on education and health appears to be positively correlated with improved outcomes in those sectors, spending on combatting violence has not been associated with improved citizen security and lower crime rates (Jaitman, 2017; World Bank, 2011).

Given all of this, the media's attention to urban violence is perhaps unsurprising. Gang conflict and organised crime have inspired some brilliant journalism and documentaries over the years. For example, the vivid portrayal of life in El Salvador's 18 Street by Cristian Poveda in his film, *La Vida Loca* (2008), exposes a deep social neglect of the communities at risk. Filmed over 16 months in a suburb of San Salvador, it is perhaps the most intimate portrait of gangster life to date. Access is also behind the success of Matthew Heineman's award-winning *Cartel Land* (2016), which blurs comfortable distinctions between good and evil and right and wrong. Vigilantism is used as a vehicle to explore the social complexities of violence and the knotty motivations of those who perpetrate it. Similarly, the immersive journalism of Salvadoran online news portal, *El Faro*, and in particular its award-winning reporter Oscar Martínez and his *Sala Negra* team, has given voice to the marginalised, deconstructing the demonization of gang members. Likewise, the painstakingly forensic investigative methods of Mexican journalist Annabel Hernández have also questioned stereotypes and have exposed lies, cover-ups and corruption in the country's battle with organised crime.

On the contrary, the more "point and shoot" or "parachute", "run and gun" reporting of Sky One's *Ross Kemp On Gangs* series and National Geographic's *The World's Most Dangerous Gang* have been accused of glorifying violence and gang culture and exploiting their sources (see Gunckel, 2007). It is hard to deny that a lack of understanding of the dynamic and multifaceted nature of violence can lead to sensationalist reporting and exploitative programme-making. Critics believe that this, in turn, simply fuels gang violence and does little to enhance our understanding of the issue (see Peetz, 2008 and Penglase, 2007). The conclusion is that irresponsible journalism, characterised by an over-reliance on entertainment values, can overplay the risk associated with urban violence (see Cruz, 2011; Caldeira and Holston, 1999). Such sensationalism promotes fear and mistrust, and does little to bring "us" closer to the distant suffering of "them" or to contribute to our understanding of what has become a truly global phenomenon.

Introduction

For many journalists, living in communities under the control of drug cartels and gangs, what they report on and how they report it can be the difference between life and death. This applies not just to the reporter, but also to the contributors they work with. The ethical challenges involved are immense and should not be underestimated. Journalists covering this issue have a responsibility to ensure their work does not perpetuate violence. They should refrain from making judgements and over-simplifications, which pit victims against perpetrators, and they should explore this social phenomenon through lenses other than those provided by the state and its institutions. As with all issues, journalists have a duty to see beyond and call out bias.

It should be noted that most of the examples in this chapter come from Latin America. The reasons are twofold. First, this is the context of my own experience and research, and second, the theoretical and empirical output of scholars specialising in the study of urban violence is predominantly focussed on this region. However, given the broad approach adopted in this chapter, the debates and issues raised will still be of relevance to journalists and scholars working in other geographical and social contexts.

It is hoped that this chapter can offer advice and guidance to those reporters who both live and work in violent contexts, but also to those who may visit temporarily and "parachute" in. At *El Faro* in El Salvador, they reject journalists who "turn up, interview a few teary mothers and desperately try to persuade a young gangster to wave a gun on camera and talk about the hatred for their rivals". These reporters "arrive with pre-conceived ideas", "lack an in-depth understanding" and "apply formulaic storytelling techniques before they fly home onto the next story", according to one of the online portal's senior editors.

There is of course no doubt that indigenous reporters are closer to the story when it comes to gang conflict because they often live and work within such violence. However, this does not discard what is sometimes excellent reporting by international reporters or filmmakers. It is important to remember that distance can also bring insight. There needs to be a recognition that as journalists we report for a wide range of diverse audiences, each of which has different needs and expectations.

On the other hand, clearly both indigenous and international media can be guilty of sensationalism and misrepresenting urban violence, as we will see below. The aim of this chapter is therefore to draw on my own experiences, but also on those of the many journalists I have interviewed and worked with in the last few years, to provide examples of both best and worst practice. This chapter will establish some core principles, which could apply to both national and international media on either end and across the spectrum of "legacy" and "alternative" news. Therefore, when reporting gangs and urban violence, I would suggest three broad guidelines.

It is important to:

1. Establish an independent narrative, one that is not over-reliant on official sources.
2. Gain access on the ground and reflect the thoughts, needs, and actions of the local community, including those who commit violence.
3. Deconstruct rather than perpetuate the victim-perpetrator dichotomy.

The above is not presented as a rigid framework, rather as advice for those reporters, who may be embarking on this topic for the first time or for veteran correspondents, who perhaps want to produce a more nuanced journalism.

Before we discuss these guidelines in more depth, the next section of this chapter will provide an overview of current research about urban violence and news coverage of gangs and gang conflict. This is followed by an exploration of three case studies based on my own personal experiences and research, before the chapter concludes with an overview and some further suggestions for best practice.

The research

Urban violence is related to complex social, economic, political, and institutional processes. It is much more complex than "war". Reporters wishing to engage with this issue should think carefully about their choice of vocabulary. Journalism about urban violence should acknowledge that the phenomenon is rooted in a variety of exclusions, which range from the macro to the micro (Winton, 2004). At the macro level, the state fails to make citizenship meaningful. There is perhaps a lack of education, for example. As a result, there is increasing social fragmentation and polarisation (Wolf, 2017). Furthermore, youth exclusion has also been related to globalisation. That is to say that through an engagement in crime, gangs offer the prospect of economic sufficiency in the face of a lack of alternative opportunities (Cerbino, 2012; Cruz, 2011, 1999a, 1999b). Similarly, at the micro level, research points to the absence of family cohesion and support. Gang membership can therefore provide a sense of belonging and community (Wolf, 2017; Cerbino, 2012; Rodgers and Muggah, 2009; Rodgers, 2003).

In some countries, especially those of Latin America, it has become increasingly difficult to distinguish violent actors in what has become a "multifarious network" of perpetrators within the urban context (Winton, 2004: 169). However, it is important to make distinctions between drug cartels and street gangs. Although both of these actors may be involved in the drugs trade, the former is organised and part of a transnational network, while the latter is less structured and less hierarchical. Although there is increasing empirical evidence that these actors co-operate or sometimes even merge, still little is known about the nature and extent of such partnerships. Usually, however, the relationship is hinged on the sale and distribution of drugs. As Moser and McIlwaine (2004) identify, drugs are integral to many forms of violence at the local level from gang warfare to robbery, to the murder and social cleansing of addicts and domestic quarrels or assault in the home.

Both cartels and gangs exert institutional dominance and impose their own systems of justice and social norms in the communities that they control. For Dowdney (2003), drug factions have become a recognised socio-political force through which democracy is replaced by "narcocracy". Even in the UK, for example, drug gangs seek to recruit teenagers and children to manage their "county lines", which are distribution networks between ports, the larger cities, and coastal towns. UK gangs have also been known to take over the homes of the vulnerable, which are then converted into distribution centres. This is the process known as "cuckooing".

In communities with a strong presence of gangs, the state often increases its mechanisms of control in an attempt to counteract their growing power and influence. Therefore, as Winton (2004) argues, these communities are subject to manipulation by the state, the drug groups and the elite political sector, and are permanently caught between multiple power systems.

The highly visible nature of gangs and urban violence can result in a phenomenal amount of media attention. Yet media reports can exaggerate the actual occurrence of gang violence and often serve "to obscure far more insidious violence such as that associated with organised crime" (Winton, 2004; Moser and Winton, 2002: 25). As Cruz (2011) has noted, most studies on urban violence tend to focus on organised crime and the "criminalisation of youth" (2011: 21), without considering that the states themselves "foster the conditions for the escalation of violence" (2011: 8). The blatant instrumental "criminalisation" of gangs by the state has become a means of concealing more fundamental social and economic injustices (Cruz, 2011; Cruz et al., 2017; Rodgers and Muggah, 2009).

Most of the academic literature analysing coverage of urban violence, gangs and drug cartels focuses on what we might consider bad practice. In order to meet our ethical responsibilities as journalists, which will be explored later in this chapter, it is essential to learn from this research.

Caldeira and Holston (1999) have argued that urban violence in Brazil generates a "talk of crime" in which the repetition of stories about crime produces feelings of fear. This spiral of fear and violence, Caldeira and Holston argue, has a profoundly negative impact, producing a "disjunctive democracy", where rights such as freedom of expression and assembly are largely honoured, yet rights such as freedom from torture, summary execution, or arbitrary arrest are routinely violated (see also Pinheiro, 2000). Fear, in turn, leads people to restrict their movements and exacerbates violence by encouraging illegal responses to perceived criminality, such as supporting death squads and violent policing (Penglase, 2007; Caldeira, 2000).

Penglase (2007) concludes that gangs and violence are represented by images and metaphors that focus on the danger of "infection", and which advocate the need for "prophylaxis". Steve Macek (2006) has also identified a "discourse of savagery" by which the media vilify urban youth and deploy metaphors of "contagion" and "penetration", often delivering grisly details in a sensationalistic tone. As Reisman (2006) has pointed out, this kind of sensationalistic media coverage, "often displaying images of tattooed young men being arrested or bloody shots of injured victims and corpses", has "contributed to a culture of fear that encourages government suppression, with little public support for a more balanced approach"(2006: 150). Esbensen and Tusinski (2007) assert that this sensationalism is based on a stereotypical representation of gangs. They argue that youth gangs are problematic enough in reality without the media contributing to exaggerations of their attributes.

Similarly, Correa Cabrera (2012) explains how the mass media have created what he calls a "spectacle" of border violence in the US as an offshoot of Mexico's drugs war. This perpetuates an alarmist view, which projects a "spillover" of violence into the United States.

Gunckel (2007) describes how what he calls "gangsploitation" documentaries foster "an exploitative gaze", which depicts gang life as entertainment. This glorification of gang membership and gang culture is sometimes apparent even through the "sobriety" of print and television journalism, he argues (2007: 38). For Gunckel, "gangsploitation" includes the perpetual use of "sensational-istic imagery" and emphasises "intensified enforcement", rather than examin-ing structural causes or proposing a broader range of solutions to the violence (2007: 38). This argument is supported by Poynting et al. (2001), whose study of Middle Eastern gangs in Sydney, Australia concludes that complex class-related social realities are over-simplified, misread, and misrepresented.

Huhn et al. (2006) argue that it has become common to state that criminal violence has superseded political violence in Central America to the extent it has become normalised. There are signs that the problem of juvenile delinquency is emerging as "ordinary violence" in the region. They argue that the leading newspapers in Costa Rica, El Salvador, and Nicaragua tend to neglect critical news related to the deeper roots of criminal violence. That is to say that gangs and organised crime simply become part of the discourse to such an extent it becomes an accepted characteristic of social life.

Rodriguez (2012) and Erbensen and Tusinski (2007) have highlighted an over-reliance on official sources at the expense of experiential testimonies of victims' families. This therefore institutionalises the dominant frames being pro-jected by the state at the expense of victims and their relatives, who are seem-ingly not considered an authoritative news source. In contrast, however, Cote and Simpson (2000) propose that better reporting about trauma can enrich pub-lic awareness and empathy for the suffering of others.

This section has depicted what we might consider bad practice when it comes to reporting urban violence and has presented academic research, which high-lights some of the issues those covering gangs and urban violence might want to consider. In short, an ethical journalism about gangs and does not perpetuate the violence and does not demonise those who perpetrate it.

It must be stressed that not all coverage of this social issue is problematic and further sections of this chapter will serve to highlight some examples of best practice.

Covering urban violence, drug cartels, and gangs

As we saw above, one of the biggest dangers in reporting this social issue is that it is presented as a simple war with opposing factions. The complexity of the structures that underpin urban violence is ignored in favour of simple narratives, which can glorify gang culture, exploit victims, and exacerbate social inequali-ties. In worst cases, journalism propagates the position of the state, which can scapegoat gangs and communities in order to conceal its own failures or politi-cal motivations. Such journalism fails to meet its ethical responsibilities towards the audience and contributors. Journalism, in the context of urban violence, should help viewers, listeners and readers understand what can be a terrifying concept. It should not sustain or promote, but rather identify and challenge, violent structures. It should protect those we interview from further harm and exploitation, and it should hold the powerful to account.

Gangs and cartels are lumped together under the umbrella of organised crime without proper analysis of the dynamics at play between these two actors. As one reporter in Honduras told me, "We react to events. We don't get to the root of the problem". Another danger associated with simply reacting rather than digging deeper, is that urban violence becomes normalised. One editor told me in El Salvador, "If we don't act instead of reacting, nothing will change".

The following case studies are therefore intended to demonstrate the challenges involved in reporting urban violence. They are presented as opportunities for others to learn from in order to shape their own journalistic practice. Though the examples developed below all come from Latin America, many of the general themes will apply to other social and cultural environments. Indeed, regardless of geographical context, an independent narrative on urban violence, which ensures reporters meet their ethical responsibilities would have the following characteristics:

- It covers not only the what and the how, but also the who, where, when and crucially the why.
- It is critical of the established discourse on violence.
- It questions the role of the state and does not legitimise dysfunctional institutions.
- It reports and analyses all sides of the argument.
- It treats all parties as equals – both perpetrators and victims of violence.
- It seeks out new voices to interview (e.g. community leaders, the marginalised, academics).
- It does not rely on official press releases or statements and instead actively questions them.
- It seeks out contact in the "criminal" world.

This list may appear obvious to those who warn against the "churnalism" first reported by Nick Davies (2008), but it is important to remember what can be specific constraints on journalism practice in violent societies. Perhaps more importantly, it is essential to consider the implications and consequences of these constraints. It is no surprise that governments try and control information, often using it for their own gain. In violent contexts, these governments may wish to manipulate the public and journalists into supporting a more hard-line approach or they may wish to use gang violence to cover up their own political failings. Journalism that does not follow an independent narrative in these circumstances is likely to therefore perpetuate violence, rather than enhance our understanding of the phenomenon. In such an environment, these guiding principles of an independent narrative (which are not exhaustive) are therefore suggested as a starting point for ethical practice.

CASE STUDY 1

Filming *The Engineer*: representation, interviewing, and trauma

The Engineer was released in 2013. The documentary examines the fragile and controversial 2012 truce that was brokered between El Salvador's two biggest gangs, MS-13 and 18 Street. As the number of murders fell, disappearances increased. *The Engineer* follows the life of El Salvador's only criminologist, Israel Ticas, as he struggles to unearth hundreds of missing teenagers.

Reality, sensationalism, and glorification

The Engineer was described by *Rolling Stone* magazine as "raw and painful". Indeed, it is not a film for people with a weak stomach. But what is shown in the film is nothing to the horrors we witnessed during our time in El Salvador. Much of the material was simply too graphic to include in the final cut. Still, the violent scenes in our film horrify some people. This was not unexpected. We want to shock. We want to jolt people from their comfort zones. But where is the line with sensationalism? Do such images exploit the suffering of grieving families? Do they disrespect the dead? There are no clear-cut answers to these questions, but this section will outline how we confronted this challenge.

One of the most shocking and even disgusting sights was inside a funeral home. A naked 16-year-old boy was dumped on a concrete slab. A shirtless undertaker cracked open the boy's rib cage to embalm him. I am not sure what upset me most: the body laid so bare, or the brutality of the undertaker, smoking and talking on his hands-free as he tossed the boy around like a pancake. But this is how death is treated in El Salvador. It is routine. It is reality. And this is what my co-director and I wanted to show. So how can we navigate this path between emotional impact and causing offence? This is no easy task. It will depend on many factors, including target audience and cultural context. The BBC's Editorial Guidelines on violence in news and current affairs offer some useful advice.

The essence of our dilemma with *The Engineer* was deciding which images proved the familiarity and routineness of violence (which were therefore central to the story), and which were simply gratuitous or sensationalist and in bad taste. We carefully and painstakingly selected and discussed each image used. We would ask ourselves if we could tell the story with a different image or sequence of images. Therefore, as directors, we engaged in much discussion and debate, both with each other, and with people who were seeing the material for the first time.

Initially we had lost all sense of what would be going too far with these gruesome images. We had seen so many dead bodies that we had no idea of what was shocking or real, and what might be considered "yellow" and in poor taste. Working as freelancers and independently, we do not always have the support systems and checks and processes of major broadcasters to support us. Nonetheless, it is important to engage a second (or even perhaps a third and fourth) pair of eyes, as we did. In short, seeking feedback is essential.

We included shots of the boy on the slab in the end, but we did not show his open chest. We did, however, show the boy's face as the undertaker applied make-up to it. This is because 16-year-old David was more than just a body; he was not just another victim. The story of what happened to David – his struggle to escape the clutches of 18 Street and the impact of his death on his family and his brother, in particular, became one of the main narratives in *The Engineer*. It was therefore important to identify and humanise David. As tragic as his story was, he needed to be more than a name for our audience. We had to show his face.

Perhaps the biggest failure of *The Engineer* is one which we actually had no real control over. It refers to the children involved in the gangs. Legally and ethically, we are obliged to hide the identities of minors. In most civilised democracies, it is illegal to film or interview children without the consent of their parent or guardian. Ethically, it is vital that members of gangs or drug cartels are not identified on camera, in print or otherwise. By showing their faces or giving their real names, it can make your contributors targets for retaliation or even "out" them to friends and family members who may be unaware of their status. Yet this anonymity obscures the complexity of the story. The tragedy of these children, many of whom are forced to kill or be killed, is lost behind the pixilation of their faces. Their crimes and their guilt are countered by their childlike purity and almost virtuous appearance, but this is invisible to viewers of *The Engineer*. To the ear, these children are monsters, but to the eye, they are angels. This is a juxtaposition we fail to show. We are unable to. For me, the viewer not being able to look these children in the eye and – *see* what appears to be innocence – counters the repugnance of what they can *hear* and distorts and simplifies the reality of El Salvador. Indeed, with most documentaries or TV news reports about gangs, it is all too easy to "criminalise" or "demonise" gangsters and perpetrators of violence when their faces have to be hidden. This is the "gangsploitation" and glorification of gang culture we saw defined above.

However, producers have a responsibility to film contributors in a way, which does not simply portray them as evil and project fear. Whatever the underlying reasons, many gang members that will be interviewed will have committed crime, and sometimes potentially quite violent ones at that, but simplified and exaggerated representations do nothing to explore the complexities of urban violence. Adequate time and consideration should therefore be given to thinking about how contributors will be filmed. The visual framing of the interview, the music used and how sequences are constructed are therefore just as important as the content of the interview itself.

Challenging the perpetrators

However hideous their crimes, it is probably not necessary to challenge your contributors. All programmes and broadcasters will have their required styles, but confrontational interviews are unlikely to provide anything worthwhile and may land the interviewer in danger. A reporter does not need to be Jeremy Paxman or Wolf Blitzer to get to the truth, especially in story- and narrative-driven pieces. A reporter is more likely to get something out of their interviewee if they treat them as an equal. It should be a chat, not a formal grilling. Though the *Ross Kemp On Gangs* series has been criticised by some, Kemp's style of interviewing is informal and effective. He manages to ask the questions needed, without putting his interviewees on the spot. He builds a clear rapport with the gangsters he meets, but remains firm in his questioning.

Knowing when to challenge and when to ask straight questions is a useful skill all journalists should develop. Having the confidence to let the interviewee speak and understanding that audiences are intelligent enough to read between the lines, especially if there is sufficient contextualisation for the contribution, often results in a more natural feel. It is important to let audiences find their own way through a narrative, otherwise, the piece can feel too contrived.

I learned this largely because of *The Engineer*. Securing access to the gangs was a vital part of our film. We did not want to speak only to those gangsters in prison, who were relatively easy to access. Instead, we wanted to know what it was like on the streets, but for that, we needed the permission of the leaders.

During the truce in El Salvador, the imprisoned gang leadership was promoting peace at whatever the cost, but the foot soldiers on the ground were telling a different story. The problem was, if we were to confront the leadership about this, access on the ground could be lost. Instead of grilling the leaders of MS-13 about the shambles of a truce, we were forced to ask rather more polite questions about it. At first, this felt like a betrayal of journalism ethics. We were not holding them to account, challenging their lies or exposing their deceit. In order not to jeopardise our chances of getting the access and images we needed, we gave the MS-13 leadership an easy ride. At least that is how it felt at the time. In retrospect, however, we still achieved our journalistic objectives. We showed the fragility of the truce and we exposed it as a smokescreen. We asked the difficult questions, but we did not challenge what we suspected were lies. Instead, the audience was able to make up their own mind. I do not mean there is ambiguity. I mean the answers of MS-13 are challenged by the facts themselves and by the other interviews and stories in the film.

Grieving families

Filmmakers build up a strong bond with the characters in their documentaries. In El Salvador, grieving families let us into their homes. We became part of their lives, even if just for a short time. Many families thought we were the answer to their problems. Of course we weren't. We were actually at risk of exacerbating their grief, and we were honest about that, but we became part of their story.

El Salvador is a very poor country. It is therefore not uncommon for contributors to ask for money. I would not recommend this. It is dangerous territory to offer payment for interviews. It would be considered unethical by most respectable news organisations and broadcasters, and would bring a reporter's credibility into serious question. Instead, it might be wiser to invite contributors to lunch or pay for their travel. There was one occasion in El Salvador when we made a contribution towards the costs of a funeral. This came from our own pocket and not from the budget of the film. Incidentally, it is not a funeral that appears in the documentary, but it still makes me uneasy.

I have worked in some difficult situations as a journalist, but never have I witnessed such trauma and hopelessness as in El Salvador. The grief of so many mothers who have lost their children to the gang conflict was simply heart-breaking. For me, it is not dodging bullets that is the most difficult, it is confronting the weight of the families' grief. A reporter can leave a hostile environment (usually), but what we see and hear will stay with us forever. This undoubtedly makes us better journalists, but it can also cause psychological injury, as explored by Lyn Barnes in Chapter Two of this volume. Reporters working in these circumstances need to understand trauma and be able to recognise the signs of post-traumatic stress in their colleagues.

During one interview with a mother in El Salvador, she began to cry so much she could not speak. I stopped the interview and consoled her with a hug. This is not the best idea. When interviewing someone who is likely to get upset, it is wise to have someone they know on hand, who can step in and take care of the interviewee. It is also a good idea to have at hand numbers and contacts of where further help and support can be obtained, if needed.

Interviewing grieving families is a challenge, but it is one we must rise to if we are to ensure our work has an emotional impact. Of course, that does not mean that these families should be exploited. They need to be approached carefully and the line of questioning needs careful planning. The timing of the interview request is also important. As reporters, we should never intrude on a family's grief.

CASE STUDY 2

Inside Colombia's BACRIM: non-official sources and naming names

Inside Colombia's BACRIM is an investigation published by Insight Crime in 2017. It is the result of two years of immersion in the Bajo Cauca and presents the workings of a local cell of the *Urabeños*, Colombia's biggest criminal network. It highlights human rights abuses, identifies drug trafficking routes, and exposes networks of murder.

The inclusion of non-official and "underworld" sources

Reporters and filmmakers have hitherto tended to cover the ongoing civil conflict and the resurgent drugs gangs in Colombia mainly through contact with official government and military sources. The idea with this investigation was to speak to those who not just suffer violence, but those who perpetrate it. The objective was to understand how an *Urabeños* cell operates at the local level. This chapter argues that urban violence will only be fully understood if we include a wider range of voices in our coverage. More specifically, as journalists, we have a duty to include and represent the marginalized communities in this debate, including the gang members or "criminals" themselves. Only then can we begin to question the information that comes to us through official channels and be able to hold the authorities to account over levels of violence.

In the case of the Bajo Cauca, this provided logistical challenges. Even though I had been given permission to visit gang-dominated territory, it soon became apparent that people there were not able to speak openly about their experiences. I would have to arrange transport and alternative locations for interviews with those who were willing to talk, including community leaders and families affected by the violence. This is perhaps best exemplified by a separate piece I wrote for *The Guardian* in 2018. I had been given a tip-off by a local resident that the gang were keeping locals as slaves. Some 80 families were reportedly being forced to work in cocaine laboratories and in illegal gold mines. Although several sources from within the gang confirmed this was true, I needed to hear first-hand from the "slaves" themselves. It took two years to make contact with them through intermediaries and then arrange for them to be able to leave their village that was controlled by the gang and meet me in a place we could talk openly.

Naming names

Murdered Mexican journalist Javier Valdez Cardenas once explained to me how he covered organised crime, "Well, you cover your ass! That's how," he said. "You have to work out who has the power. Who is killing people in the street? Who distributes the drugs? What accomplices do they have? You need this information in order to know what you're going to publish and more importantly, to know what not to publish."

Over two years in the Bajo Cauca, I was able to depict the structure of more or less an entire local cell. The investigation includes a diagram of this illegal network. The dilemma was whether or not to include names and faces; I felt this made the story more real and humanised it somehow. However, it also exposes gang members to the authorities and even their friends and families, who might not be aware of their involvement. After careful discussion, the decision was made to only publish names if those involved were known to the police.

Then came the dilemma of whether to include the names and images of my sources. If they were omitted, it could be clear to the rest of the gang who had been speaking to me. I decided to leave this decision to each contributor. I explained what the consequences might be and left it to them to decide if they wanted to be included or omitted. Interestingly, most decided to be left off, worried more about legal proceedings than what the gang leadership might do.

It must be stressed that it is incredibly dangerous to name names. Those who live and work in environments with a large gang presence have developed varying degrees of self-censorship. For those of us who just visit, it may be easier to consider naming names, but it must be understood that this will more than likely close down further access. Naming names will also make a reporter a legitimate target.

Most gangsters have an alias, but I would think twice before mentioning real names. I would argue this is really only relevant in specific investigations where the story is documenting particular crimes or human rights abuses and where it becomes necessary to hold certain individuals to account.

CASE STUDY 3

La Niña. A night with a Colombian paramilitary: access and risk

La Niña is a piece of creative non-fiction, which was published in 2017 by Fresher Publishing and BBC Radio 4's "From Our Own Correspondent". It also forms part of a transmedia documentary project, *After War*.

It is the story of a night out with a senior paramilitary, alias *el Soldado* or the Soldier. It recounts an interview in a bar and a subsequent mystery tour of his turf, involving cocaine, prostitutes and guns. *La Niña*, which means "the girl", is how gangs refer to pistols in this part of the world.

Getting access: the "snowball effect"

Gangs and cartels are hidden populations that are incredibly difficult to access. For me, being allowed into this underworld was testimony to the time I spent in the field. I gained the trust of local people, who introduced me to those with connections to the criminal community. In most communities affected by violence, those in direct contact with the gangs and cartels are never very far away. From there, it was simply a case of the "snowball sample" effect, whereby one gang member introduced me to the next, and the next and so on. Reporters should not underestimate the amount of time and effort this can take. I spent two years cultivating the contacts I needed for this story.

Managing risk

Dangerousness in the field can be categorised under two general classifications: danger posed by the gang members and by the social environment. It is important to speak to people who know the region. Are there places to be avoided? Particular behaviours or activities that may draw unwanted attention or pose a specific threat? Which are the safest hotels? Is there a hospital? If this is abroad, it is wise to notify the local embassy of a reporter's presence and consider informing the local authorities too, although in countries with difficult regimes, this may not be advisable. In the Bajo Cauca, I was in regular contact with the police. They would check in regularly to see where I planned to go and what I had been doing. It was only when they started to ask whom I had met and with whom I had been working that I became suspicious. I would also check-in regularly with contacts in the UK. Friends and family were given contact lists of people they could contact should I go missing and they were given instructions on how to raise the alarm.

There are also practical considerations when interviewing criminals or gang members. The reporter must ensure that somebody knows where they are going to conduct the interview and who with. The reporter should also have a plan to let somebody know they have returned safely. I would do this each time and also try to make sure I met gangsters in a public place, though this was not always possible for reasons of confidentiality.

Reporters must constantly be aware of their surroundings. If a reporter is carrying expensive equipment such as a laptop or camera, then he or she needs to be aware of the attention this may draw. There is a small possibility it may also result in theft. At times, in sensitive situations, there may also be a need to "stand back" from the newsgathering – to put away the pen and paper and make only mental notes. I could often be mistaken for a member of the United States Drug Enforcement Agency (DEA). My presence with a notepad or camera could scare people and deter them.

It is probably worth remembering that the more time in the field, the more comfortable one becomes, but this is arguably when a reporter is at most risk. Complacency is dangerous.

Conclusion

This chapter has explored some examples of best and worst practice when covering urban violence and gangs. It has presented three case studies, which have stressed the importance of three broad guidelines established at the beginning of this chapter:

(1) **It is important to establish an independent narrative, one that is not over-reliant on official sources.**
 The objective of an independent narrative is to ensure fair and balanced reporting, which does not scapegoat gangs and communities affected by violence to propagate politicised rhetoric.

(2) **Gain access on the ground and reflect the thoughts, needs, and actions of the local community, including those who commit violence.**
 Urban violence is all too often covered from the "official" perspective. That is to say through government statistics and interviews with the authorities, including the police and military. This does not necessarily produce an accurate or balanced picture of how communities living with violence on the ground may experience gang conflict. Talking to those who perpetrate and those who live with violence may provide stories that question and counter dominant arguments and perhaps even expose state and institutional failures.

(3) **Deconstruct rather than perpetuate the victim–perpetrator dichotomy.**
 It is easy to demonise those who perpetrate crime, but not as easy to question their motives or identify the structures, which may be underpinning the wider issue of urban violence. By deconstructing this dichotomy, reporters

can explore and point to long-term structural issues, which may in turn be highlighted by policy-makers and other key stakeholders, and overall provide a deeper contribution to our understanding of the urban violence and gang phenomenon.

References

Briceño-León, R. and Zubillaga. V. (2002). Violence and Globalisation in Latin America. *Current Sociology*, 50(1), 19–37.

Caldeira, T. (2000). *City of Walls: Crime, Segregation and Citizenship in São Paulo*. Berkeley, CA: University of California Press.

Caldeira, T. and J. Holston. (1999). Democracy and Violence in Brazil. *Comparative Studies in Society and History*, 41(4), 691–729.

Cerbino. M. (2012). El Lugar de la Violencia. Perspectivas Criticas Sobre Pandillerismo Juvenil. Quito: FLACSO.

Citizen Council for Public Security and Criminal Justice (CCSPJP). (2018). Seguridad, Justicia y Paz. Mexico City: CCSPJP. Available at: https://www.seguridadjusticiaypaz.org.mx/biblioteca/prensa/send/6-prensa/242-las-50-ciudades-mas-violentas-del-mundo-2017-metodologia

Clavel, T. (2018). Why Latin America Dominates Global Homicide Rankings. *Insight Crime*, March 12. Available at: https://www.insightcrime.org/news/analysis/why-latin-america-dominates-global-homicide-rankings/

Correa-Cabrera, G. (2012). The Spectacle of Drug Violence: American Public Discourse, Media and Border Enforcement in the Texas-Tamaulipas Border Region During Drug War Times. *Norteamérica*, 7(2), 199–220.

Cote, W. and Simpson, R. (2000). *Covering Violence: A Guide to Ethical Reporting About Victims and Trauma*. New York: Columbia University Press.

Cruz, J.M. (1999a). El Impacto Psicosocial de la Violencia en San Salvador. *Pan American Journal of Public Health: Special Issue on Violence*, 5(4), 295–302.

Cruz, J.M. (1999b). La Victimización por Violencia Urbana: Niveles y Factores Asociados en Ciudades de América Latina y España. *Pan American Journal of Public Health: Special Issue on Violence*, 5(4), 259–267.

Cruz, J.M. (2011). Criminal Violence and Democratisation in Central America: The Survival of the Violent State', *Latin American Politics and Society*, 53(4), 1–33.

Cruz, J.M., Rosen, J.D., Amaya, L.E., and Vorobyeva, Y. (2017). *The New Face of Street Gangs. The Gang Phenomenon in El Salvador*. Miami: Florida International University. Available at: https://www.scribd.com/document/342930507/The-New-Face-of-Street-Gangs-The-Gang-Phenomenon-in-El-Salvador

Davies, N. (2008). *Flat Earth News*. London: Chatto and Windus.

Dowdney, L. (2003). *Children of the Drug Trade: A Case Study of Children in Organised Armed Violence in Rio de Janeiro*. Rio de Janeiro: 7Letras. Available at: http://www.coav.org.br/publique/media/livroluke_eng.pdf

Dowdney, L. (2004). *Neither War nor Peace: International Comparisons of Children and Youth in Organized Armed Violence*. Rio de Janeiro: Viva Rio/Instituto de Estudos da Religiao.

Dittmar, V. (2018). Study: 2017 Was Deadliest Year for Homicides Linked to Organised Crime in Mexico. *Insight Crime*, January 26. Available at: https://www.

insightcrime.org/news/analysis/2017-deadliest-year-organized-crime-related-homicides-mexico/

Esbensen, F.A. and Tusinski, K.E. (2007). Youth Gangs in the Print Media. *Journal of Criminal Justice and Popular Culture*, 14(1), 21–38.

Gunckel, C. (2007). "Gangs Gone Wild": Low Budget Gang Documentaries and the Aesthetics of Exploitation. *The Velvet Light Trap*, 60, 37–46.

Huhn, S., Oettler, A., and Peetz, P. (2006). Exploding Crime? Topic Management in Central American Newspapers. GIGA Working Paper No. 33. Hamburg: The German Institute of Global and Area Studies.

Jaitman, L. (2017). The Costs of Crime and Violence. New Evidence and Insights in Latin America and the Caribbean. Washington DC: The Inter-American Development Bank. Available at: https://publications.iadb.org/bitstream/handle/11319/8133/The-Costs-of-Crime-and-Violence-New-Evidence-and-Insights-in-Latin-America-and-the-Caribbean.pdf?sequence=7&isAllowed=y

Macek, S. (2006). *Urban Nightmares: The Media, the Right, and the Moral Panic over the City*. Minneapolis: University of Minnesota Press.

Moser, C. and McIlwaine, C. (2004). *Encounters with Violence in Latin America: Urban Poor Perceptions from Colombia and Guatemala*. London: Routledge.

Moser, C. and Winton, A. (2002). Violence in the Central American region: towards an integrated framework for violence reduction. ODI Working Paper No. 171. London: Overseas Development Institute.

Penglase, B. (2007). Barbarians on the Beach: Media Narratives of Violence in Rio de Janeiro, Brazil. *Media, Crime and Society*, 3(3), 305–324.

Peetz, P. (2008). Discourse on Violence in Costa Rica, El Salvador and Nicaragua: Youth Crime and the Responses of the State. GIGA Working Paper No. 80. Hamburg: The German Institute of Global and Area Studies.

Pinheiro, P. S. (2000). Democratic Governance, Violence, and the (Un)Rule of Law. *Daedalus*, 129(2), 119–43.

Poynting, S., Noble, G., and Tabar, P. (2001). Middle Eastern Appearances: "Ethnic Gangs", Moral Panic and Media Framing. *Australian and New Zealand Journal of Criminology*, 34(1), 67–90.

Reisman, L. (2006). Breaking the Vicious Cycle: Responding to Central American Youth Gang Violence. *SAIS Review*, 26(2), 147–52.

Rodgers, D. (2003). Youth Gangs in Colombia and Nicaragua – New Forms of Violence, New Theoretical Directions? In: A. Rudqvist. *Breeding Inequality – Reaping Violence. Exploring Linkages and Causality in Colombia and Beyond*. Uppsala: Collegium for Development Studies.

Rodgers, D. and Muggah, R. (2009). Gangs as Non-State Armed Groups: the Central American Case. *Contemporary Security Policy*, 30(2), 301–317.

Rodríguez, S.M. (2012). Reporting on Victims of Violence: Press Coverage of Extrajudicial Killings in Colombia. *Signo y Pensamiento*, 60, 187–208.

Shaw, D. (2018). Nine Charts on the Rise of Knife Crime in England and Wales. BBC News, 25 January. Available at: http://www.bbc.co.uk/news/uk-42749089

Southwick, N. (2013). Medellin homicide rate tumbles after mafia pact. *Insight Crime*, November 13. Available at: https://www.insightcrime.org/news/brief/medellin-homicide-rate-down-60-from-2012/

United Nations Office on Drugs and Crime (UNODC) (2013). Global Study on Homicide. Vienna: UNODC. Available at: https://www.unodc.org/documents/gsh/pdfs/2014_GLOBAL_HOMICIDE_BOOK_web.pdf

Vilalta Perdomo, C.J., Castillo, J.G., and Torres, J.A. (2016). Violent Crime and Latin American Cities. Washington, DC: Inter-American Development Bank. Available at: https://publications.iadb.org/handle/11319/7821

Winton, W. (2004). Urban Violence: A Guide to the Literature. *Environment and Urbanization*, 16(2), 165–184.

Wolf, S. (2017). *Mano Dura. The Politics of Gang Control in El Salvador*. Austin: University of Texas Press.

World Bank (2011). Understanding and Supporting Community Responses to Urban Violence. Washington, DC: The World Bank. Available at: https://www.unicef.org/protection/Violence_in_the_City.pdf

PART IV
Reporting health

7

REPORTING CRITICAL
HEALTH JOURNALISM

John Lister

The social issue

The subject of this chapter is the poor quality of much health journalism, and the inadequate or sometimes misleading information (Belluz, 2016) that is therefore purveyed to the majority of the news-consuming public, with even more serious potential problems for those who receive their information at second hand via conversations or social media (Brooks, 2016) .

Health and healthcare are issues that have a near-universal appeal in every country of the world. Whatever the healthcare system, whatever the location of the country, scarcely a person can be found who is not at some point concerned about their own health and potential access to healthcare, or the health of partners, siblings, parents, children, colleagues, or neighbours. Health issues, therefore, tend to score relatively high on most measures of "news values" – since it potentially has relevance and proximity to most news audiences, and often combines other elements sought after by editors – good news, bad news, timeliness, and controversy (Brighton and Foy, 2007).

The hope is that journalists reading this chapter will develop:

- A keener appreciation of the need for a critical, analytical approach to reporting on health – and the availability of materials that can assist.
- An awareness of the problems of writing a health story from any one source or press release – and of some possible alternative sources for cross-reference or comment.
- An idea of possible ways of checking and seeking balancing, critical comment in articles that can offer the news audience the best chance of properly understanding the issue.

There are many ways health appears in the news: human interest stories tell of those coping with or overcoming illness; endless lifestyle and consumer health stories discuss diet and the latest guidelines of what might be good or bad to eat and what might affect our health; stories on eating disorders, obesity, alcohol, and tobacco consumption and other issues; and an almost infinite range of medical stories – on new treatments, effective and ineffective; new drugs; new diseases; and feared epidemics. There is another whole specialist area reporting the business of the big pharmaceutical companies, the merits and demerits and cost-effectiveness of the various products they develop, the legal challenges brought over failures or side-effects of drugs, the licensing of new drugs, and the need to expand some neglected areas of drug research.

Health and healthcare often also feature on the *political* and parliamentary agenda. As this chapter is written, Theresa May's government is once more under fire for the pressures, delays, bed shortages, under-funding, and problems of the NHS in England – while similar issues are being raised in the news media in Scotland, Wales, and Northern Ireland – although some journalists new to the topic remain barely aware that the systems in the three devolved administrations are now so different from that in England. Every new year also brings another rehash of the inconclusive debate over whether there is a need to revise the very basis of the National Health Service, 70 years old in 2018, or maybe look to one or other of the various alternative (and mostly more expensive) international models, most frequently France, Germany, Netherlands, or Switzerland – all of them insurance-based systems that are much more expensive than England. Every government is eager to pose as having the answer to long-standing problems of resources and their own formula for how healthcare should be organised and delivered.

As a result, the news media also feature political and ideologically charged debates on how government money is to be spent, how health services should be organised, and how far the bodies organising healthcare should be locally and democratically accountable. Contested questions such as the appropriate role (if any) of private-sector for-profit providers, the extent of reliance on public-sector funding, the quality of services, local access to services, and the length of time people wait for non-emergency care are a stock feature of politics, and therefore political news, in every country which has embraced the need for universal healthcare – while a very different debate continues to rage over the uniquely costly, wasteful, and inefficient American system.

Introduction

Although I have been active as a health journalist for 34 years – analysing and seeking to publicise changes in the National Health Service on behalf of pressure group, London Health Emergency, and reliant upon the quality and consistency of my reporting for any wider impact – my interest in the wider issues of health journalism arose from my part-time work as a senior lecturer at Coventry University, UK, from 2004 to 2013, where I developed a one-year MA specialist course in health journalism.

I was invited to join the EU-funded project on Health Reporter Training (Project HeaRT, 2011), which set out to investigate the extent to which health journalists had received any appropriate training in health as a specialist subject, what training courses were available, and develop learning materials to address gaps in training in six member states: Estonia, Finland, Germany, Greece, Romania, UK.

A questionnaire in all six countries revealed a worryingly consistent pattern: health reporters generally were unenthusiastic about the quality of specific areas of health journalism produced by their colleagues, with, at most, 39 per cent regarding coverage of *any* of the main areas of health reporting as either good or excellent. The samples were small, of course, but it should worry any journalist to find that important areas of reporting are not only done badly but perceived by their peers as poor. Almost a third of respondents felt coverage of Health Disparities (the higher levels of ill-health and lower life expectancy among poorer and disadvantaged sections of the community) was poor, with more than a quarter feeling that Medical Research and Science and Health Care Quality and Performance were also poorly reported – two areas where there is a concentration of public relations effort, but an evident lack of critical journalism (Project HeaRT, 2011).

We were conscious at the time that much of the research and development of training that had taken place, and the majority of the current literature on health journalism, was from the USA where the relatively large and influential Association of Health Care Journalists (AHCJ) has been able to secure some charitable funding and sponsorship to hold an annual conference and other activities, although AHCJ confines itself to a limited level of political critique. The equivalent bodies in Britain and Europe are far less developed.

Worse, there seemed a general acceptance by journalists (and their editors) that while specific specialist knowledge in health journalism would be good to have, this is neither required as a basis of securing a job as a health reporter, nor is it seen as an objective for which employers and editors are prepared to offer any support – or even time off for staff to engage in courses. The low levels of staffing in newsrooms and the relatively low salaries of the journalists meant that there was little flexibility for staff to acquire further training in working hours, and little spare money in their pockets to pay for additional courses or allow journalists easily to negotiate additional time off.

To combat this issue, we created an e-book (Lister, 2014) with all its references and suggested sources as live hyperlinks. It is designed to be kept on a laptop and/or desktop computer to enable the suggestions and sources to be accessed quickly and easily while the journalist is at work. The website, offering a wealth of free information and resources, has been online since 2012 and has had more than 350 downloads, a third of them from the UK. You can find the e-book here: www.europeanhealthjournalism.com.

The research

What limited studies and debates there are on health journalism still show a large-scale problem with the quality of health reporting. For example, the pioneering

American website healthnewsreview.org[1] (now endangered once again by a loss of funding), which analyses coverage of news topics by the mainstream press and broadcast media, including some British publications, has drawn attention to a number of problems (Adams, 2017). The website is well aware of the close working relationship between the public relations industry and the mainstream media. Schwitzer (2018) argues that those in public relations are seeking to get free headline coverage, publicity, and in some cases advertising for their clients' services in the media. Journalists, whose job it is to look beyond the carefully selected information in press releases to fill in some of the gaps and ask the questions the PR teams would rather they didn't ask, should be producing news, rather than publicity puff. Healthnewsreview.org has been consistently pressing for higher standards of press releases that present a fuller and more honest picture of the new treatments and drugs that they are promoting.

After 11 years, reviewing more than 2,500 news stories and 500 media press releases on new drugs and treatments, healthnewsreview.org summarised its findings on the five most telling of the ten criteria used to evaluate the quality of reports:

- Sixty-nine per cent of news and 92 per cent of press releases failed adequately to discuss costs associated with new drugs and treatments.
- Sixty-six per cent of news and 73 per cent of press releases failed adequately to assess – how big (or small) – the potential benefits of new drugs and treatments.
- Sixty-three per cent of news and 77 per cent of press releases failed adequately to assess the scope of the potential harms of new drugs and treatments.
- Sixty-one per cent of news and 71 per cent of press releases failed to evaluate the quality of evidence in regards to new drugs and treatments.
- Fifty-four per cent of news and 59 per cent of press releases failed to discuss alternative options in regards to new drugs and treatments (Green, 2017).

The scale of the problem with press releases is, of course, part of the explanation of the large proportion of poor news reports: journalists have wrongly relied on these releases and allowed their exaggerations, omissions, and errors to shape the reporting (Sumner et al., 2014). The biggest problem, especially when journalists have too little knowledge or too little time (Stead, 2016) is that they can wind up uncritically repackaging material handed down in press releases or statements – becoming little more than "stenographers" (Schwitzer, 2014).

But the problem is by no means limited to the US media. It may come as a surprise to many British readers that one of our "quality" newspapers which also has an influential and highly successful website, *The Guardian*, was one of the four news organisations given the lowest average scores by healthnewsreview. org. By comparison *The Guardian* rates fairly well on a broader infographic compiled by the American Council on Science and Health ranking the news media coverage of science topics, in which Britain's *New Scientist* and *Economist* are in the topmost bracket; the *Telegraph* comes out in a middle ranking; and the *Daily Mail* is consigned to a category labelled "ideologically driven or poor reporting", just short of the level of "pure garbage" (Berezow, 2017).

Although there is no equivalent summary of these findings, the valuable British website "Behind the Headlines", from NHS Choices (www.nhs.uk/news/), also maintains a running commentary on some of the current stories and the way they are covered in the media – and is not afraid to name the newspapers which fail to deliver accurate and appropriate information. A study of these comments by health journalists would repay the effort by alerting them to the most common pitfalls and weaknesses in reporting, while also filling in the kind of background information that would make a useful and interesting story: for example, "'No solid evidence' vitamin D keeps the brain healthy" (July 12) contrasts the *Daily Mail* coverage with the original research. Another example "Is sleep apnoea a risk factor for dementia?" (July 6) takes the *Independent* to task for misleading coverage of a small-scale study.

It's also important for journalists new to health reporting not to become too easily impressed by the apparent authenticity and credentials of the previously free to access peer-reviewed journals many of which, such as the BMJ, are now behind paywalls. Questions have been raised over the standards and reliability of even venerable peer-reviewed journals. *Lancet* editor Richard Horton has been among the more forthright in setting out the pressure exerted on editors by the wealthy and powerful pharmaceutical industry among others. In written evidence to a House of Commons Health Committee back in 2004, Horton identified ten ways in which the independence of peer-reviewed journals can be undermined, from the covert through to the overt offer of "kick-back" bribes to editors for publishing specific papers promoting products – and of course some researchers (Horton, 2004; Prasad and Rajkumar, 2016; Joyce, 2017; Neuen, 2018).

The problem is also one of inadequate initial reporting of clinical trials, perhaps shaped by some of the same pressures (Altman, 2015), but any weakness in news reports is likely to be compounded by the further level of simplification by PR staff from the researchers' institution seeking publicity (Sumner et al., 2014). The role of PR is to present the most favourable possible image of a company, an institution, or an individual. Although ethical PR never invents any facts, some PR professionals do seek to find ways to achieve higher-profile news coverage by eliminating nuances and subtleties in some of the research they are publicising, effectively "sexing up" and distorting the carefully crafted research documents to reach a tabloid and TV audience. If this grossly simplified version of a complex report is received by reporters unwilling or unable to check everything and ask awkward questions, seriously misleading stories can emerge. A press release should *never* be more than a starting point for a news story on anything, but least of all on a health topic.

Authors such as Ben Goldacre and many other leading voices have pressed for open access to all data gathered by researchers from clinical trials of any new drug or treatment so as to avoid selective use of favourable data and suppression of less positive or even negative results. Others, such as Ivan Oransky and Retraction Watch, have focused on securing the full retraction of inadequate, misleading, or down-right fraudulent articles and any further references to them, and spreading news of retractions as widely as possible. In its opening blog, Retraction Watch points out:

> Retractions are not often well-publicized. Sure, there are the high-profile cases …. But most retractions live in obscurity in Medline and other databases. That means those who funded the retracted research – often taxpayers – aren't particularly likely to find out about them. Nor are investors always likely to hear about retractions on basic science papers whose findings may have formed the basis for companies into which they pour dollars. So we hope this blog will form an informal repository for the retractions we find …"
>
> *(Oransky and Marcus, 2010)*

One other aspect that is worth noting is that as an unintended consequence of pressure to make more journals free to access for readers, many journals (some even claiming to be "peer-reviewed"), have begun charging sometimes very high fees (averaging £1,727) to academics seeking to publish their work (Durham University, nd). While an elite of "open" access journals are undoubtedly of high quality (and some which do not levy publication charges are of poor quality) (Suber, 2013), some "predatory journals" are little more than scams to raise cash (Kolata, 2013): where these journals bother producing any publications at all, they are unwilling to invest in suitably qualified staff to address even basic errors of spelling and syntax, let alone vet their scientific credibility. Journalists new to health reporting need to keep a critical awareness of the quality of content, integrity and credentials of any journal that is provided "free" on this basis.

"Sting" operations have shown that these fake journals, which masquerade under high-sounding titles, are happy to accept poor quality articles, and even accept bogus academics as editors (Kolata, 2017). Some fraudsters have gone even further and conned desperate academics into signing up for spurious conferences (Burdick, 2017). So it's important for journalists seeking to investigate a topic but lacking the funds to pay per view for paywalled articles from some of the leading journals to be vigilant and critical in assessing the calibre of information in more obscure, less reputable, free access journals. A useful rule of thumb is that if you can spot any error – even spelling – it should be grounds for suspicion.

Covering health and healthcare

While there is wide appeal of "health" as an issue across the world, this means there is also a huge amount of health reporting in the mainstream media.

There are four key factors that make health and healthcare an issue rather more special and challenging for a journalist to cover adequately:

- It tends to appear complex, especially to those unfamiliar with the issues on a day-to-day basis. However efforts to simplify it – whether by PR staff seeking to grab attention for new research or new products, or by journalists and sub-editors with often limited knowledge of the subject themselves – for news editors and a general news audience often result in a distortion.
- Like many other aspects of modern society, in many countries healthcare, and the drugs and techniques it uses, are changing very rapidly. In addition to this, in England the National Health Service itself as a system has been subjected to a virtually non-stop succession of poorly understood "reforms" and reorganisations since the mid-1980s. These changes can easily disorientate journalists who are not both up-to-date and willing to take a critical approach.
- While accuracy and providing full information are important for all sectors of journalism – from travel guides to city news, crime and court reports and environment – the concern with some health reporting is that the spread of inaccurate, inadequate, or misleading information can potentially lead to large numbers of people taking decisions that can impact on their health, or potentially even endanger life (Nature, 2017; Govender, 2017). There are few if any other areas of reporting where this is a danger.
- Yet while conveying appropriate health and healthcare information will be widely recognised as important, only a small minority of journalists producing this information for print, broadcast, or online have any training at all on health issues. Even the majority of specialist health reporters are largely self-taught, with a mere handful able at least to fall back on some form of health professional qualification even when they lack training in health journalism (Project Heart, 2011). Indeed, very few courses offering any education or training in health reporting exist, especially in Europe; even these train only small numbers.

Most of the output of the most expert journalists is consumed by a very small segment of the news audience, while the vast majority of people accessing news on health get it from mainstream media or social media where it tends to be of lower quality. The latest audience figures confirm this long-standing pattern. In Britain, for example the publications of the specialist health press – the *British Medical Journal*, the *Health Service Journal*, the *Nursing Standard*, *Nursing Times*, and other even more specialised titles for GPs and other groups of staff – have a combined print circulation in the UK of fewer than 200,000 weekly (BMJ, 2018); indeed, the *Health Service Journal* printed magazine ceased publication in 2017, and *Nursing Times*, which once sold over 70,000 per week, is now printed only monthly, with most output online. By contrast even after the inroads of the internet, the main daily newspapers have a combined circulation of 4 million per day on weekdays and 5.5 million on Sundays, with a daily readership estimated at almost 17 million (Newsworks, 2018).

For the specialist health press and the mainstream news outlets, the focus is increasingly on online readers through dedicated paywalled websites: the *BMJ* claims 3 million online readers each month, and the websites of *Nursing Times* and the *HSJ* each claim 117,000 "unique users" (although almost all of these will be from a specialist reading audience of health professionals, managers, and academics). Some additional specialist journals, free to access, appear only online, such as *Pulse* and *GP* magazines for GPs, and *Community Care*, the magazine primarily for social care which also reaches health staff. And while the nursing journals and the *BMJ* do carry some limited news coverage and analysis, their main focus and depth of content are on professional and clinical issues rather than more general news stories.

Here, too, the contrast with the wider news media is massive. The national daily newspapers in England have an online readership of over 30 million, reaching 36 million with the widely read *Metro* and *London Evening Standard*. The nationals also have a combined Twitter following of over 21 million and a massive Facebook following (Newsworks, 2018). Regional and local news outlets add even more to the reach. In addition to this, the mainstream broadcast media supplement their on-air audience with an enormous social media following. The specialist health press has a total Twitter audience of less than 500,000 (Newsworks, 2018).

The problem with the vast majority of the public relying on their health news and information from the output of inexpert journalists in under-staffed, under-pressure newsrooms competing for space against "clickbait" trivia and ephemeral showbiz and "celebrity" coverage is a significant one.

CASE STUDY 1

Ill-judged panic: ibuprofen linked to heart failure

Exaggerated reports of dangers or benefits of drugs in the mainstream popular press can encourage a wider news audience either to stop taking drugs they have been prescribed or to seek out a drug which may be harmful to them. Health reporters have an ethical duty to avoid giving such misleading information: "First do no harm".

In 2017 a Danish academic study in the *European Heart Journal* (Sondergaarde et al., 2017) reported concerns that use of non-selective non-steroidal anti-inflammatory drugs (NSAIDs) – most notably ibuprofen and diclofenac – was associated with an increased early risk of out-of-hospital cardiac arrest (OHCA). The paper itself warned that there were limitations to the study and the extent to which it could go beyond associating facts to identifying causes:

> The main limitation of the study is inherent in the observational nature of the analyses. The treatment allocation is not randomized and the study

reports only associations and therefore any conclusion on causality should be made with caution. (Sondergaarde et al., 2017)

Sadly by the time most of the mainstream news media picked this up, any such subtlety had been lost.

The *Daily Mail*, for example, in an article bylined from the Australian Associated Press (2017), used the headline "Nurofen linked to a 31 per cent increased risk of heart attacks". The *Independent* warned: "Ibuprofen should not be sold over the counter, researchers have said after discovering it increases the risk of cardiac arrest by 31 per cent" (Forster, 2017).

The *Daily Express* (Giles Sheldrick) ignored the figure for ibuprofen, and chose instead to highlight the highest increased risk, 50 per cent for diclofenac, in an article that begins: "PAINKILLERS dramatically increase the risk of a fatal heart attack, a study suggests". It quickly warned: "Millions of people in Britain regularly take the pills, including ibuprofen. Researchers warn that users are up to 50 per cent more likely to suffer heart failure" (Sheldrick, 2017). Sheldrick also adds another element that is not mentioned in the report, but only in the press release: "Pain sufferers should take no more than 1,200 mg of ibuprofen a day – equivalent to six small tablets, they say."

The *Guardian* echoed similar warnings: "There have been fresh calls for restrictions on the sale of the painkiller ibuprofen after another study found it heightens the risk of cardiac arrest. Taking the over-the-counter drug was associated with a 31% increased risk, researchers in Denmark found" (Weaver, 2017). The *Guardian*'s story included a link to the original press release (European Society of Cardiology, 2017). This was the source of the quotes used in each of the news reports. While *The Guardian* did not refer to the original paper, it did, at least, give some balancing information (a quote from the Proprietary Association of Great Britain).

Two issues should occur to the journalists in each of these stories, but clearly did not. The first and most obvious is to establish how high is the inherent level of risk of heart attack, which use of these drugs might increase by 31 or 50 per cent? None of these reports addresses this question. But using Google searches and a calculator it doesn't take long to work it out.

According to the British Heart Foundation, there were 158,000 heart attacks in the UK in 2015 (BHF, 2018). Office for National Statistics (ONS) figures show the UK population at that point was 61.5 million, and the adult (16+) population, more vulnerable to heart attack, was around 48 million. This gives an average risk of a UK adult suffering a heart attack of 0.3 per cent – three per 1,000 people. A 31 per cent increase would increase that to four in every 1000, and a 50 per cent increase would raise it to 4.5. Of course there are other risk factors that can increase the odds of individuals having a heart attack, meaning that an average for the population as a whole is not always appropriate, but for journalists the point is that using a vague and unexplained percentage figure in this way does not help an average person understand the actual level of risk or the significance of the increase.

The second issue is that neither the dramatic headline from *The Guardian* coverage ("Calls for ibuprofen sale restrictions after study finds cardiac arrest risk") nor the quotes from the report's author Professor Gunnar H. Gislason of Copenhagen University Hospital, warning of the dangers of the drugs and suggesting they should not be sold over the counter ("I don't think these drugs should be sold in supermarkets or petrol stations where there is no professional advice on how to use them") are taken from the original report. They appear only in the press release.

By contrast, the conclusion of the report itself is relatively bland:

"Our findings support the accumulating evidence of an unfavourable cardiovascular risk profile associated with use of the non-selective NSAIDs. This calls for special awareness in order to balance risks against benefits in treatment with NSAIDs".

One reason for the difference, other than the PR team's eagerness to "sex up" the story and grab some headlines for an otherwise relatively low-key report, is that the report itself is about the use of NSAIDs supplied on prescription, with patients taking them on doctor's orders. The paper makes quite clear that it is NOT a study of use of NSAIDs bought over the counter; indeed "we do not have information on use of over-the-counter drugs".

So while it may be reasonable for Prof Gislason to add in his warnings, they are his views, not the result of the study, the news audience seeing these conclusions will be unaware of this, and more likely to be occasional purchasers of over the counter ibuprofen than receiving them on prescription.

Other points could be made, but it's clear that the problems in most of the media reports centre on the journalists having relied only on the press release and not looking at the original article, and a failure to understand or correctly explain relative risk. Balanced comment and informed critique of the coverage of this and many similar stories can often be found in healthnewsreview.org or on the NHS-supported and searchable "Behind the Headlines" series.

CASE STUDY 2

Misleading claims: "clinically proven" ear plugs; benefits for Gingko Biloba

While some of the media scares and warnings are inappropriate and often wildly exaggerated partial reports, the quest for "good news" features can also end up with unsupported claims, which can also mislead people into buying useless or even potentially dangerous products.

For example, healthnewsreview.org in January 2018 probed beneath the claims that a brand of ear plugs had been "clinically proven" to be effective for migraine sufferers – although why the reviewer chose a story emanating from a 2016 press release, and coverage in the *Wall St Journal* in 2016 is not immediately clear! Reviewer Sue Rochman followed up, asking to see what evidence there was to support the claims for the earplugs: she found that although what research had been done was conducted by Princeton Consumer Research, the "industry experts in claims substantiation studies", it fell well short of any proper scientific test. It was a survey of 40 users' perceptions of improvement when using the product, and "no actual clinical data was recorded about migraine frequency or intensity". There were many other weaknesses. After looking at the study, Adam Cifu, MD, a professor of medicine at the University of Chicago "didn't mince words". In an email comment, he described the study as "utterly worthless" (Rochman, 2018).

In another example, in December 2017, "Behind the Headlines" (2017) unpicked the extravagant claims for the effectiveness of the herb Ginkgo Biloba. It had been promoted by the Mail Online, which quoted a study claiming it could help "boost memory, strength and speech in stroke survivors". "Behind the Headlines" cites a series of weaknesses in the research but also warns that

> long-term outcomes and possible adverse effects weren't examined …
>
> Ginkgo Biloba can interact with several other drugs and is known to have blood-thinning properties. People recovering from stroke shouldn't take GBE without consulting a health professional.

The results of the study were far from conclusive: it found that "people who took GBE alongside aspirin for six months had around a 1-point greater improvement on a 30-point cognitive assessment compared to those who took just aspirin". "Behind the Headlines" (2017) comments: "Whether this difference is significant is another matter".

Journalists need to be aware of spurious and inflated claims for products and the extent to which they have any credible scientific research behind them. If in doubt it is always best to double check with reliable expert opinion, such as "Behind the Headlines" or healthnewsreview.org.

CASE STUDY 3

Accountable care organisations – why major reforms are always "little known"

When it comes to reporting on health policy issues, journalists from the mainstream media and their editors tend to lag behind the unfolding of complex changes, holding back on any attempt to analyse or explain policies and reorganisation of services until they are well advanced or even already in progress. In England, with the rapid pace of change that has prevailed in the NHS for the last 30 years or so, and especially in the last decade, this has been a recurring problem.

The change of government in 2010 was rapidly followed by the publication of a lengthy, complex and detailed White Paper, followed early in 2011 by the Health and Social Care Bill – before most news audiences were even fully aware of the proposals. The Bill was over 400 intricate pages of parliamentary language, which few MPs and fewer outside parliament had troubled to read. When campaigners attempted to generate a public debate over the issues, and challenge details of the Bill, they were fighting an uphill battle seeking any exposure in a mainstream media that was barely even summarising the government case, let alone subjecting it to much criticism or analysis (Lister, 2014: Davis et al., 2015).

Since the Bill was finally forced through the House of Lords in the spring of 2012, and rolled out from April 2013, there have been a series of further changes which have been only belatedly and superficially covered in the mass media. Among these was the development, following a circular from NHS England just before Christmas 2015, of 44 new strategic bodies covering England – each of which during 2016 drew up a Sustainability and Transformation Plan (STP) – in a secretive process excluding health staff, the local public, local politicians and of course the press. Only from the summer of 2016 did it become possible to get any serious attention paid by the mainstream media to what was being decided in these often controversial – and in the main extremely poor quality – plans (Boyle et al., 2017).

There was increasing public awareness of the plans, and readiness to protest about potentially controversial local changes. This, later coupled with the prolonged hiatus of two pre-election "purdah" periods for local elections and the snap general election in 2017, left the STPs trailing far behind their intended timetable for implementation, while the funding squeeze has also meant there is no capital available for any new projects to go ahead (BMA, 2017). From the middle of 2017, the emphasis from NHS England has shifted again, away from STPs and towards what should have been the next step on the road, the establishment of "Accountable Care" organisations and local systems. Although it was mentioned in the *Five Year Forward View* (NHS England, 2014) the concept of accountable care (developed in the USA), remains profoundly ambiguous and poorly understood. Of the 44 STPs, more than 30 make some reference to moving towards an accountable care model, although there are many different interpretations of what that means (Boyle et al., 2017; Lister, 2018).

The problem is that, once again, little information on these new forms of organisation has appeared in the mainstream media, and no real debate: the ACOs are almost universally described as "little known" bodies, in a similar fashion to the STPs before them (Campbell, 2017). Despite the name, it is clear from the way that the eight "vanguard" projects have been conducted that neither the government nor NHS England nor any local leadership has any wish to engage with consultation – with local communities or with councillors and MPs – or genuine accountability. ACOs, again, like the STPs before them, lack any legal status (Khan, 2017; Bate, 2018).

ACOs have emerged out of attempts to work around the fragmented structures and endemic competitive market entrenched by the 2012 Act (Keogh, 2018), and despite hints in the Conservative manifesto for June 2017, it is clear that ministers, since the election, have neither the will nor the parliamentary majority required to push through what would be at best a poorly understood, and at worst an unpopular and controversial change in the law (Lister, 2017: 11).

Plans have been centred on pushing through new regulations to facilitate ACO contracts, since regulations are not subject to the same level of parliamentary scrutiny. While the specialist health service press has to some extent followed these twists and turns, much of the coverage and analysis in the mainstream press has been patchy – and few other than the best-informed journalists, campaigners, and an elite of NHS managers have been able to keep pace with developments (Thomas, 2018).

Campaigners have been trying to tease out clear information on the extent to which the ACO proposals are likely to open up a fresh round of involvement of private sector providers, management consultants, contractors and even insurers. Fears have been amplified by the refusal of ministers or NHS England to give a cast-iron guarantee that there will be no further privatisation through ACOs (Cowburn, 2018), and the publication of a draft contract for ACOs which makes room for the private sector (Vize, 2017). It states clearly that:

> There will be no formal restrictions on who can hold the Contract. Both NHS bodies (e.g. a Foundation Trust) and non-NHS bodies (e.g. a GP Limited Liability Partnership) can bid to provide the ACO. (para 4)
>
> Any organisation can partner with others to bid for the Contract and this includes voluntary organisations. (para 10)
>
> The Public Contracts Regulations (PCR 2015) require that contracts for clinical services with a lifetime cost over the £589,148 threshold must be advertised to the market. [...] commissioners are required to act fairly and transparently and treat all potential providers of the relevant services equally. (from para 4)
>
> (NHS England 2017)

A news audience that has not been offered up-to-date information on these developments is a news audience potentially disenfranchised. A reporter who does not try to bring a critical approach to bear on health policy issues can easily and unwittingly wind up acting effectively as "stenographers" retailing the PR statements of politicians and others pursuing an agenda which could put local services at risk. Without any information on the proposals and their implications, people are unlikely to feel any need to respond.

Major changes with long-term implications could, under those circumstances, be pushed through, exploiting the ignorance of the large majority of the people whose services are potentially at risk. Health journalists worthy of the name should at least be aware of the broad lines of the changes that ministers are seeking to bring about, and some level of analysis of their consequences – or at least be aware of sources of informed and critical comment other than the official press releases and statements gushing out from huge Department of Health and NHS communications teams.

In its 70th year, the NHS needs bold and incisive reporters to challenge its weaknesses and failures, publicise its successes and the achievements and commitment of its staff, and be aware of its value and the underlying risk that its future could be put in jeopardy – by policies that most people neither know of nor understand.

Conclusion

Poor quality health reporting is a disservice that effectively misinforms, or reinforces the ignorance and prejudice of the news audience: giving misleading information on drugs and treatments can encourage people to take unwise, unhealthy, and sometimes even dangerous decisions; in this way it can do harm – and fall short of the ethical standards health journalism should uphold. For example, scaring people away from properly using ibuprofen might result in them resorting to even more dangerous alternatives.

Just as being found out in a lie is poison for any public relations professional, publishing any news which has to be revised, or which is soon discredited, or that inflates claims and hysterical warnings without justification, runs the risk of creating cynicism and distrust of other health coverage: people who cannot access quality health reporting from the mainstream media may turn to even less reliable sources – such as random internet sites or the advice of no-better-informed friends.

Journalists in busy newsrooms often have little grounds for satisfaction in their work, but at least taking the time to double check and investigate the facts behind a press release can offer some reason to feel cheerful at the end of a hard day, especially when a potential error can be found and averted.

This chapter has attempted to set out the need for health reporters to take a critical, analytical approach to reporting on health – and the availability of materials that can assist.

The three case studies underline the dangers of writing a health story from any one source or press release – and suggest a few possible alternative sources for cross-reference or comment.

It's important to find some way of including at least one balancing, critical comment in articles that can offer the news audience the best chance of properly understanding the issue.

Each health journalist who takes the job seriously will want to draw up what could be a growing list of well-informed experts and people able to give responses based on evidence, as well as where necessary a political balance from a political or trade union spokesperson. We don't want every article to say the same thing, but we do need every article to reflect a critical approach that allows the news audience to develop its own understanding.

Note

1 HealthNewsReview will no longer regularly publish from January 2019. The 6000+ articles already published on the site will remain available for three years. Click here to find out more: https://www.healthnewsreview.org/2018/12/5-categories-of-quality-web-content-for-you-to-explore-when-we-cease-daily-publication/

References

Adams, J.U. (2017) 2017 year-ender: What I've learned from reading health news every morning, *healthnewsreview.org* December 21, https://www.healthnewsreview.org/2017/12/2017-year-ender-ive-learned-reading-health-news-every-morning/

Altman, D.G. (2015) Clinical trials: Subgroup analyses in randomized trials—more rigour needed. *Nature Reviews Clinical Oncology* 12, 506–507.

Australian Associated Press (2017) Nurofen linked to a 31 per cent increased risk of heart attacks – leading to calls to restrict over-the-counter sales, *Daily Mail* online, March 16, http://www.dailymail.co.uk/news/article-4321810/Nurofen-linked-increased-risk-heart-attack.html#ixzz55HouidXi, accessed January 2018.

Bate, A. (2018) *Accountable Care Organisations*, Commons Briefing Paper, Number CBP 8190, 9 January, researchbriefings.files.parliament.uk/documents/CBP-8190/CBP-8190.pdf

Behind the Headlines (2014) Ibuprofen unlikely to extend life, NHS, December 19, https://www.nhs.uk/news/medication/ibuprofen-unlikely-to-extend-life/

Behind the Headlines (2017) Ginko may "help boost brain recovery after stroke" researchers report, NHS, December 17 https://www.nhs.uk/news/neurology/ginko-may-help-boost-brain-recovery-after-stroke-researchers-report/, accessed January 2018.

Behind the Headlines (2018) Ibuprofen linked to testosterone problems, NHS, January 9, https://www.nhs.uk/news/medication/ibuprofen-linked-testosterone-problems/

Belluz, J. (2016) Health journalism has a serious evidence problem. Here's a plan to save it, *Vox*, June 21, https://www.vox.com/2016/6/21/11962568/health-journalism-evidence-based-medicine, accessed January 2018.

Berezow, A. (2017) Infographic: The best and worst science news sites, American Council on Science and Health, March 5, https://www.acsh.org/news/2017/03/05/infographic-best-and-worst-science-news-sites-10948

BHF (British Heart Foundation) (2018) Heart statistics, https://www.bhf.org.uk/research/heart-statistics (latest figures), accessed January 2018.

BMA (British Medical Association) (2017) Capital crisis: STP money fails to materialise, February 14, https://www.bma.org.uk/news/2017/february/nhs-needs-9-5-to-transform, accessed January 2018.

BMJ (British Medical Journal) (2018) Media pack, http://www.bmj.com/company/wp-content/uploads/2016/12/2017-BMJ-Media-Pack.pdf, accessed January 2018

Boyle, S., Lister, J., Steer, R. (2017) *Sustainability and Transformation Plans. How Serious Are the Proposals? A Critical Review*, South Bank University, London, available https://healthcampaignstogether.com/pdf/sustainability-and-transformation-plans-critical-review.pdf

Brighton, P., Foy, D. (2007) *News Values*, Sage, London.

Brooks, J. (2016) Does Health Journalism Do More Harm Than Good?, *KQED Science*, https://ww2.kqed.org/futureofyou/2016/05/16/is-health-journalism-doing-more-harm-than-good/, accessed January 2018.

Burdick, A. (2017) "Paging Dr Fraud": The fake publishers that are ruining science, *New Yorker*, March 22, https://www.newyorker.com/tech/elements/paging-dr-fraud-the-fake-publishers-that-are-ruining-science

Campbell, D. (2017) These little-known opaque bodies could run health services. Are they legal? *The Guardian*, November 7, https://www.theguardian.com/society/2017/nov/07/vital-nhs-account-acos-legal-challenge

Cowburn, A. (2018) Senior Conservative MP urges Jeremy Hunt to put the brakes on backdoor NHS privatisation, *The Independent,* January 19 http://www.independent.co.uk/news/uk/politics/jeremy-hunt-sarah-wollaston-nhs-privatisation-health-social-care-accountable-care-organisations-a8168571.html

Davis, J., Lister, J., Wrigley, D. (2015) *NHS for Sale*, Merlin, London.

Durham University (nd) Open Access: FAQs https://www.dur.ac.uk/research.innovation/outputs/openaccess/oafaq/gold/

European Society of Cardiology (2017) "Harmless" painkillers associated with increased risk of cardiac arrest, Press Release, March 15, https://www.escardio.org/The-ESC/Press-Office/Press-releases/harmless-painkillers-associated-with-increased-risk-of-cardiac-arrest?hit=twitter, accessed January 2018.

Forster, K. (2017) Calls for sales restrictions on painkiller due to cardiac arrest risk, *The Independent*, March 15, http://www.independent.co.uk/life-style/health-and-families/health-news/ibuprofen-cardiac-arrest-risk-sales-restriction-painkiller-study-a7631561.html, accessed January 2018.

Govender, S. (2017) Mistakes, Muddles, and Mixed Messages: How disjointed health reporting is confusing the issues and costing lives, Reuters Institute Fellowship Paper, University of Oxford, http://reutersinstitute.politics.ox.ac.uk/sites/default/files/2018-01/Serusha%20Govender%20-%20Mistakes%2C%20Muddles%2C%20and%20Mixed%20Messages.pdf, accessed January 2018.

Green, S. (2017) The Ethics of Science and Health Journalism: A Q&A with Gary Schwitzer, *Discover the Future of Research*, June 8, https://hub.wiley.com/community/exchanges/discover/blog/2017/06/07/the-ethics-of-science-and-health-journalism-a-qa-with-gary-schwitzer, accessed January 2018.

Horton, R. (2004) Memorandum by Richard Horton (PI 108) Minutes of Evidence to Commons Health Committee https://publications.parliament.uk/pa/cm200405/cmselect/cmhealth/42/4121604.htm, accessed January 2018.

HSJ (Health Service Journal) (2018) HSJ Facts and Figures https://www.hsj.co.uk/marketing-solutions/facts-and-figures, accessed January 2018

Inserm (2018) Beware of Sustained Ibuprofen Use in Men, Press release, January 8, http://presse.inserm.fr/en/beware-of-sustained-ibuprofen-use-in-men/30386/, accessed January 2018.

Jaklevic, M.C. (2018) Ibuprofen linked to male infertility? It's pure speculation, January 10, *healthnewsreview.org*, https://www.healthnewsreview.org/2018/01/ibuprofen-infertility/

Joyce, M. (2017) Why we should care that many editors of top medical journals get healthcare industry payments, *healthnewsreview.org*, November 16, https://www.healthnewsreview.org/2017/11/158902/

Keogh, B. (2018) The NHS turns 70 this year, and it's Britain's greatest medical innovation, *The Guardian Comment is Free*, Jan 1, https://www.theguardian.com/commentisfree/2018/jan/01/nhs-70-britain-medical-heath-service-penicillin-ivf

Khan, S. (2017) Jeremy Hunt faces legal action over attempts to "Americanise" the NHS, *The Independent*, November 3, http://www.independent.co.uk/news/uk/politics/jeremy-hunt-health-department-nhs-legal-action-americanise-privatisation-customers-id-pay-a8033986.html

Kolata, G. (2013) Scientific articles accepted (personal checks, too), *The New York Times*, April 7, http://www.nytimes.com/2013/04/08/health/for-scientists-an-exploding-world-of-pseudo-academia.html?pagewanted=1

Kolata, G. (2017) A scholarly sting operation shines a light on "predatory" journals, New York Times, March 22, https://www.nytimes.com/2017/03/22/science/open-access-journals.html

Kristensen, D.M., Lethimonier, C.D., Mackey, A.L., Dalgaarde, M.D., De Masie, F., Munkbøl, C.H., Styrishave, B., Antignac, J.-P., Le Bizec, B., Platel, C., Schmidt, A.H., Jensen, T.K., Lesné, L., Guittot, S.M., Kristiansen K., Brunak S., Kjaer M, Juul A., and Jégou B. (2017) Ibuprofen alters human testicular physiology to produce a state of compensated hypogonadism, *PNAS Early Edition*, December 1, http://www.pnas.org/content/early/2018/01/03/1715035115.full.pdf, accessed January 2018.

Leu, C. (2015) Giving credence: Why is so much reported science wrong, and what can fix that? *California Magazine*, https://alumni.berkeley.edu/california-magazine/winter-2015-breaking-news/giving-credence-why-so-much-reported-science-wrong-and, accessed January 2018.

Lister, J. (ed.) (2014) *First Do No Harm: Reporting on Health and Health Care*, (e-book) Libri, Farringdon, http://www.libripublishing.co.uk/Products/ProdID=113

Lister, J. (2017) *Into the Red Zone*, Health Campaigns Together, https://healthcampaignstogether.com/pdf/NHS%20Into%20the%20Red%20Zone%20final.pdf

Lister, J. (2018) New bodies: not accountable, and don't care, Health Campaigns Together, https://healthcampaignstogether.com/pdf/HCTNo9.pdf

Nature (2017) Science journalism can be evidence-based, compelling—and wrong. Editorial, March 7, https://www.nature.com/news/science-journalism-can-be-evidence-based-compelling-and-wrong-1.21591

Neuen, D. (2018) Peer-review and publication does not guarantee reliable information. *Students 4 Best Evidence.* 2.10 January, https://www.students4bestevidence.net/peer-review-and-publication-does-not-guarantee-reliable-information/

Newsworks (2018) Figures for mainstream press http://www.newsworks.org.uk/Market-Overview

NHS England (2014) Five year forward view, October, https://www.england.nhs.uk/wp-content/uploads/2014/10/5yfv-web.pdf, accessed January 2018.

NHS England (2017) Contract package: questions and answers. New care models August, https://www.england.nhs.uk/wp-content/uploads/2016/12/1693_DraftMCP-9_A.pdf, accessed January 2018.

Oransky, I., Marcus, A. (2010) Why write a blog about retractions? *Retraction Watch*, http://retractionwatch.com/2010/08/03/why-write-a-blog-about-retractions/

Prasad, V., Rajkumar, S.V. (2016) Conflict of interest in academic oncology: moving beyond the blame game and forging a path forward, *Blood Cancer Journal* 6, e489.

Project HeaRT (Health Reporter Training Project) (2011) *WP2 Report | Health Journalism in Europe: situation and needs*, http://www.project-heart.eu/reports/HeaRT_Survey_Report.pdf, accessed January 2018.

Rochman, S. (2018) "Clinically proven" ear plugs for migraines make news headlines, with little evidence they work, *healthnewsreview.org*, January 9, https://www.healthnewsreview.org/2018/01/clinically-proven-ear-plugs-for-migraines-make-news-headlines-with-little-evidence-they-work/

Schwitzer, G. (2017) 2017 Journalism report card, *healthnewsreview.org*, December 19. https://www.healthnewsreview.org/2017/12/2017-journalism-report-card-health newsreview-org/

Schwitzer, G. (2018) Local news hype of robotic surgery doesn't match many hysterectomy patients' experiences, *healthnewsreview.org*, July 17, https://www.healthnewsreview.org/2018/07/local-news-hype-of-robotic-surgery-doesnt-match-many-hysterectomy-patients-experiences/

Sheldrick, G. (2017) Painkillers warning: Common pain pills, including IBUPROFEN, increase risk of heart attack, *Daily Express*, March 15, https://www.express.co.uk/life-style/health/779247/painkillers-increase-risk-heart-attack-ibuprofen

Sondergaard, K.B., Weeke, P., Wissenberg, M., Scherning Olsen, A.-M., Fosbol, E.M., Lippert, F.K., Torp-Pedersen, C., Gislason G.H., Folke, F. (2017) Non-steroidal anti-inflammatory drug use is associated with increased risk of out-of-hospital cardiac arrest: a nationwide case–time–control study, European Heart Journal – Cardiovascular Pharmacotherapy 3, 100–107.

Stead, S. (2016) Public Editor: Rushing a story is the No. 1 cause of errors in journalism, *The Globe and Mail*, March 17, https://www.theglobeandmail.com/community/inside-the-globe/public-editor-rushing-a-story-is-the-no-1-cause-of-errors-in-journalism/article29272343/, accessed January 2018.

Suber, P. (2013) Open access – six myths to put to rest, *The Guardian*, October 21, https://www.theguardian.com/higher-education-network/blog/2013/oct/21/open-access-myths-peter-suber-harvard, accessed January 2018.

Sumner, P., Griffiths, S.V., Boivin, J., Williams, A., Venetis, C.A., Davies, A., Ogden, A., Whelan, L., Hughes, B., Dalton, B., Boy, F., Chambers, C.D. (2014) The association between exaggeration in health related science news and academic press releases: retrospective observational study, *BMJ* 2014;349:g7015.

Thomas, R. (2018) Creation of first ACOs put on pause, *Health Service Journal*, January 23, https://www.hsj.co.uk/service-design/creation-of-first-acos-put-on-pause/7021517.article

Vize, R. (2017) Ministers' under the radar NHS reforms are fuelling public anxiety *The Guardian*, December 15, https://www.theguardian.com/healthcare-network/2017/dec/15/under-radar-nhs-reforms-fuelling-public-anxiety, accessed January 2018.

Weaver, M. (2017) Calls for ibuprofen sale restrictions after study finds cardiac arrest risk, *The Guardian*, March 15, https://www.theguardian.com/society/2017/mar/15/ibuprofen-sale-restrictions-study-increased-cardiac-arrest-risk

8

REPORTING ON DRUGS, DIETS, DEVICES, AND OTHER HEALTH INTERVENTIONS

Kim Walsh-Childers

The social issue

Consumers today face an increasing need for closer involvement in decision-making about their own healthcare and the care of their loved ones, within an environment that is increasingly complex and challenging. Although people prefer to receive health information from healthcare providers, access to health professionals is limited, and these providers often have too little time to answer consumers' questions fully. In some locations, particularly the United States and New Zealand, consumers also are exposed to an increasing barrage of health marketing messages. In this environment, consumers more than ever need high-quality, accurate, and complete information about health products, practices, and services.

For the journalists who serve as the most common source of health information for most consumers, the health beat encompasses a broad range of topics, from news about diets, drugs, tests, and various types of therapy to health policy debates, insurance and even issues such as crime and climate change that have health impacts. However, research suggests that health-related research reported in scientific journals or at medical conferences is one of the most important, if not the most important, influences on health news coverage (Entwistle, 1995; Stryker, 2002). As such, news reports commonly focus on, or at least include, discussions of research related to health interventions, including diet, drugs, medical devices, diagnostic and screening tests, surgical procedures, and other types of therapy. Unfortunately, many journalists acknowledge that limitations in their ability to understand health research make it challenging to cover this research accurately and with sufficient context. In addition, the sheer volume of studies being published means it would be nearly impossible for any journalist, no matter how well versed in understanding research, to keep up with even the most important studies.

For instance, the US National Library of Medicine estimates that, in 2016 alone, it added 869,666 citations for medical research articles to MEDLINE (National Library of Medicine, 2016). The focus of this chapter, then, is to help you think through coverage of such research systematically to make sure your health stories include the information consumers need most.

Introduction

"Need a 'sweeter' way to lose weight? Eat chocolates!" advised *The Times of India* (2015). "Chocolate accelerates weight loss," crowed the United Kingdom *Express*, (Barns, 2015), while the *Daily Star* promised, "Eating chocolate can help you LOSE weight" (Mitchell, 2015). The *Huffington Post* declared, "Excellent news: Chocolate can help you lose weight" (Lombrozo, 2015). Print, broadcast, and online news outlets worldwide carried similar encouraging headlines (Godoy, 2015).

While the headlines and the related stories most likely gladdened the hearts of many who read or watched them, there was one serious problem with the news of chocolate's miraculous weight loss benefits: It was fake. The article on which the stories were based had been published in an "open-access" journal (*International Archives of Medicine*) that doesn't require rigorous peer review, and the study itself had been set up to essentially guarantee statistically significant findings. The lead author, a journalist and PhD with expertise in the molecular biology of bacteria, had worked with a German doctor and two German documentary film-makers to "demonstrate just how easy it is to turn bad science into the big headlines behind diet fads" (Bohannon, 2015, para. 5).

Unfortunately, the "chocolate diet" hoax only illustrated a problem that extends far beyond journalists' reporting on chocolate or weight loss and far beyond the topic of what does or doesn't constitute a healthy diet. The work of health news watch organizations like healthnewsreview.org[1] in the United States and MediaDoctor sites in Australia, Japan, Germany, and elsewhere, along with a significant body of scientific research (including mine), show that news coverage of a wide variety of health interventions, including diet, drugs, surgery, screening tests, etc., often fall far short of providing consumers with the information they need to make health decisions for themselves and their families.

Many health reporters today may have more scientific background and training than I had when I was writing health stories for a daily newspaper. In fact, when I began working as a health reporter, I had had no formal training in health beyond a couple of undergraduate psychology courses. During my brief stint (about three and half years) writing for a newspaper, I learned a fair amount about medical terminology, various diseases and health conditions I covered, and the US healthcare system's strengths and weaknesses. However, the vast majority of that knowledge was gained in the course of my own reporting, meaning my knowledge gains were somewhat haphazard and decidedly incomplete.

Nonetheless, both my research and my informal observations as an occasional story and news release reviewer for healthnewsreview.org confirm that news outlets have made relatively little progress – and in some cases, have regressed – in terms of their coverage of health interventions.

The aim of this chapter, therefore, is to help journalists and journalism students understand more fully why their coverage of health research matters and how to ensure that their reporting on health research is accurate, contextually situated, and complete enough to help their audiences make better health decisions. I would argue that unless health reporting is accurate, complete, and contextually situated, it violates essentially universal requirements for journalism ethics: to seek the truth and report it as fully and accurately as possible and to minimize harm. Even the best, most carefully researched health story can cause unintended harms due to readers' or viewers' misinterpretation. It is the health journalist's duty, however, to ensure that his or her reporting does not make such misinterpretations nearly inevitable because the stories are incomplete, inaccurate, out-of-context, or sensationalized.

This chapter, therefore, uses specific stories (good and bad) published in major news outlets to highlight some of the most common pitfalls journalists encounter in writing about health research. It also offers some tips journalists can use to improve their stories about health and medical interventions – all the actions consumers may take, either with or without professional medical assistance, in their attempts to improve their health, reduce health risks, identify emerging concerns, or respond to existing health problems.

Key takeaways from this chapter include the following:

- Health reporting matters. People use what they learn from news media to make personal and family health decisions.
- Even without formal scientific training, journalists *can* improve their understanding of medical research and their ability to report on that research in ways that help consumers.
- The key to better health research reporting is really much the same as for reporting on any other topic: look for sources who don't have conflicts of interest to help you understand what's important and what is or isn't worth reporting.

The research

In an ideal world, individuals would receive high-quality health education during their elementary and secondary schooling and would obtain all the other health information they need through regular, detailed, and comprehensive conversations with trusted health professionals. Certainly, consumers consistently identify health professionals as their preferred sources for health information (Koch-Weser et al., 2010; Vader et al., 2011). However, the average US citizen visits a health professional four times each year (McCarthy, 2014), and the average health visit lasts between eight and 19 minutes (Chen et al., 2009; Gottschalk and Flocke, 2005; Tai-Seale et al., 2007). In other countries, visits to the doctor may be much more common (9.7 visits per year, on average, in Germany; 13 visits per year, on average, in Japan), but may not last much longer (Konrad et al., 2010). As a result, media sources, including both news reporting and health-related websites, serve as critical providers of health information for substantial percentages of the population (Brodie et al., 2003; Gaglio et al., 2012; Geana et al., 2011; Kakai et al., 2003; Murphy et al., 2010).

While some individuals likely read or watch health news stories simply because they're interesting or entertaining, the research also demonstrates that people use the information they receive through health news to make important health decisions for themselves and their family members. For instance, researchers have identified exposure to news coverage of screening mammography as a key influence on women's use of mammograms (Jones et al., 2006; Yanovitzky and Blitz, 2000). Attention to health news also influences efforts to find additional information about cancer (Niederdeppe et al., 2008), and news coverage of the risks related to trans-fat consumption influenced sales of trans-fat-containing products (Niederdeppe and Frosch, 2009). Among college students, the framing of stories linking vaccination to autism influenced readers' beliefs about vaccine safety and predicted the likelihood of obtaining vaccinations for children they might have in the future (Dixon and Clarke, 2012). Li and colleagues (Li et al., 2008) found that iodized salt sales increased in Australia in response to a brief period of increased newspaper and television coverage of its health benefits.

Unfortunately, the research also has documented that health news is often flawed. Analyses of health stories have shown that they often sensationalize, overplaying both health risks and the potential benefits of various dietary interventions, screening tests and treatment approaches (Bubela and Caulfield, 2004; Moriarty and Stryker, 2008; Reynolds, 2001; Schwartz and Woloshin, 2002; Walsh-Childers et al., 2016). Through an analysis of nearly 2,000 health news stories assessed by healthnewsreview.org, my colleagues and I found that fewer than one-third of the reviewed stories adequately addressed the benefits, potentials risks, or costs of health interventions. At least half of the stories failed to address alternative approaches, and nearly 40 per cent of the stories included no independent sources (those with no connection to the intervention being discussed) and/or failed to provide information about potential financial conflicts of interest among the sources they quoted (Walsh-Childers et al., 2016).

What difference does it make if journalists don't provide all the data people need to make well-informed health decisions? One outcome may be a significant tendency for people to assume that every medical intervention is beneficial, leading to overuse of screening tests and over-diagnosis of "cancers" and other health problems that, left untreated, never would develop to the point of causing significant health problems. In fact, the research shows that many consumers equate more and more expensive treatment with better healthcare (Carman et al., 2010; Kravitz and Callahan, 2000; Schwartz et al., 2004), which may reflect consumption of health news that overplays the benefits and underplays the harms of testing and treatment.

Inadequate reporting also may encourage widespread acceptance of – and even consumer demand for – labelling borderline conditions as a "pre-disease" status (e.g., "pre-diabetes" or "pre-hypertension"). When this labelling encourages consumers to adopt healthier lifestyles, these "pre-disease" diagnoses may be beneficial; however, when the response instead is to initiate drug treatment that may itself produce significant negative side effects, it's debatable whether the patient ends up healthier in the long run (van den Bruel, 2015; Welch et al., 2011; Yudkin and Montori, 2014).

Covering health research and interventions responsibly

To be considered truly ethical in their work, journalists are required to produce accurate *and* complete stories that minimize the likelihood of harm, either to those about whom they are writing or to their audiences. One important practice journalists could adopt to ensure better – and therefore more ethical – coverage of health interventions is to use as a checklist the criteria healthnewsreview.org and the various MediaDoctor sites worldwide have developed for assessing the quality of health stories. Before submitting a story for broadcast, publication, or online posting, journalists should answer the following questions about the story:

1. **Does the story give the audience a sense of how much the intervention costs?**
    Consumers need to know how much they will have to pay for any health intervention they might be considering, whether it is a new drug, a specific type of surgery, or simply a lifestyle change. (Yes, regularly eating high-quality farmed or wild-caught fish is generally good for one's health. In many countries, it's also too expensive for many families.) Obviously, this is most crucial in countries where consumers may have to pay a significant portion of their healthcare bill out-of-pocket, but even when people have comprehensive private insurance or government coverage of healthcare expenses, consumers should know how much their health choices cost. After all, ultimately they will pay those costs directly or indirectly through higher insurance premiums or higher taxes. Ideally, the story also will compare costs for the featured health intervention versus alternatives. For instance, a story describing a new drug to reduce high blood pressure should compare the likely cost of that drug both to older hypertension drugs and to lifestyle changes that could offer the same benefits.
2. **Does the story adequately quantify the benefits consumers could expect to receive from this intervention?**
    Too often, health stories present every new drug, medical device, screening test, surgical technique, or another type of therapy as a dramatic improvement over previous approaches. Quite often, however, the average patient

would benefit only marginally more from the new product, test, or service than from older approaches; "new" does not always mean "better". Consumers need to know whether choosing that new hip implant over the older version will reduce their recovery time by two weeks or by a few hours, or whether the new version of a drug reduces side effects by 75 per cent or by 7 per cent. Certainly, some consumers will choose the intervention that offers any increase in benefits, but they must have concrete information about the level of benefit they might receive to be able to weigh the benefits against any potential increase in costs or negative side effects.

3. **Does the story adequately explain the potential harms associated with use of this intervention?**

    The research on journalists' success in explaining the harms of various health interventions is somewhat mixed. As noted earlier, some research suggests that journalists generally fail to provide adequate information about the potential harms associated with drugs, medical devices, tests, surgery, and other medical procedures, while others have found that journalists tend to overplay the risks associated with various dietary and behavioural habits, diseases, and other potential health threats. In some cases, this over-emphasis on risks stems from the journalist's failure to fully understand the health threat; nonetheless, both failing to provide accurate risk information and sensationalizing health threats conflict with the journalist's ethical duties to report accurately and to minimize harm. What consumers need in every health story is a balanced presentation that offers specific, quantified information about the risks associated with specific health choices. Journalists, therefore, should strive to help audiences understand the types and levels of harm (if any) they might experience through specific health choices. Yes, a new anti-cholesterol drug might reduce one's harmful cholesterol levels by 20 per cent, but how does that translate into reduced risks of suffering a heart attack or stroke *and* to what extent will this new drug increase the individual's risk of liver damage or Type 2 diabetes?

    In discussing both risks and benefits, it's particularly important that journalists understand and convey the difference between relative risk versus absolute risk, a distinction that is often ignored. Let's say, for instance, that a journalist is writing about a hypothetical study linking coffee consumption with stomach cancer. The study results show that, among people who drank no coffee, there was only one case of stomach cancer per thousand participants, whereas among those drinking three or more cups of coffee per day, there were two cases of stomach cancer per thousand. That would mean three-cup-a-day coffee drinkers have *twice* the risk of developing stomach cancer, compared to non-coffee drinkers. That relative risk comparison, all too often, will be the basis of the story.

    However, in this hypothetical example, drinking coffee still is associated with only a two-in-one-thousand likelihood of developing stomach cancer;

that's the absolute risk – and not especially headline-worthy. Because news releases reporting on study results may tend to focus on relative risks or benefits to grab journalists' attention, it's critical that reporters take a sceptical approach, making sure that they understand the absolute risks and benefits of health interventions. Then their stories, in turn, can help audiences understand whether these risks or benefits are substantial enough to consider in their health decision-making.

4. **Does the story adequately describe the quality of the evidence supporting use of the intervention?**

    All scientific research is not created equal, nor are all peer-reviewed journal articles created equal. A study showing that treatment with a new drug improved cognitive function in 30 lab rats with Alzheimer's-like symptoms might be interesting, but it tells us next-to-nothing about the likelihood that the drug in question would benefit people with Alzheimer's disease. Before writing stories about the latest research, journalists should consider a number of issues, including:

    - Were the research participants humans or animals? If the study involved lab rats, the results are, at best, years away from offering any true benefit to humans.

    - Which humans were involved? If all of the study participants were middle-aged white men, the findings won't necessarily apply to women, men of other races, or even men in other age groups. So be cautious about how you describe who should pay most attention to the findings.

    - What was the sample size? In general, a larger sample size should give you more confidence in the study's findings.

    - What kind of study was it? Studies linking dietary or behavioural habits to health outcomes often rely on correlational data, rather than experimental data. But only in a controlled experiment can researchers truly draw conclusions about causation.

    - Do the study's findings agree or conflict with what other researchers studying the same question have found? Context is always important, and journalists should make certain they tell readers whether previous studies provide support for or call into question the conclusions of the research they're reporting.

Numerous other pitfalls can trap well-meaning journalists into giving bad research more attention than it deserves. Fortunately, even journalists who know little about how research is done can learn a lot about how to judge the quality of a study through free resources online. Some of the best include the story reviews, blog posts, and toolkit offerings from healthnewsreview.

org. Other outstanding sources of high-quality information include the Association of Health Care Journalists' website (healthjournalism.org)[2], Journalist's Resource (journalistsresource.org), maintained by Harvard University's Shorenstein Center on Media, Politics and Public Policy, and the University of Southern California's Center for Health Journalism (centerforhealthjournalism.org). In addition, the Cochrane Library provides "systematic reviews of primary research in human health care and health policy ... internationally recognized as the highest standard in evidence-based health care resources" (Cochrane, 2017, para. 1).

5. **Does the story commit disease mongering?**

Journalists are guilty of unethical disease mongering when they overstate the extent or the seriousness of a health issue. Disease mongering also includes narrowing the boundaries of what's considered medically normal for conditions such as blood pressure, diabetes, sexual function, and moodiness so that people who previously would have been considered healthy can be diagnosed as sick – and therefore in need of (often expensive) treatment. Journalists can avoid disease-mongering and the harms it can produce for their audiences by making certain their stories clearly define who is – and who is not – at real risk for particular diseases or conditions, focusing on the average person's experience rather than extreme cases, and refusing to treat normal conditions of life (like aging, menopause, pregnancy, etc.) as diseases. In particular, this means viewing news release claims about the scope of a disease or condition with significant scepticism, especially when the news release or other information comes from a company or organization that stands to benefit from inflated public concern about the disease (Heisel, 2012a, 2012b).

6. **Does the story use independent sources and identify conflicts of interest?**

We would all like to believe that health professionals and health researchers offer health information based solely on the scientific evidence and, perhaps, their own personal experience in treating patients. However, both doctors and researchers are human, and the research shows they can be influenced by business relationships as well as ideology. That doesn't mean journalists should never use as sources health professionals or researchers who might have financial interests in drugs, devices, products, or services about which they're speaking. It does mean, however, that journalists should always do the necessary research to know what those potential conflicts of interest might be, to explain any conflicts to their audiences, and to seek comments from experts familiar with the research issue who do not have any financial, organizational, or ideological conflicts of interest. As the Association of Health Care Journalists' Statement of Principles states: the ethical health journalist must be "vigilant in selecting sources, asking about, weighing and disclosing relevant financial, advocacy, personal or other interests of those we interview" and "report possible links between sources of information (studies or experts) and those (such as the manufacturers) who promote a new idea or therapy" ("Statement of Principles," n.d., para. 7–8).

The US Center for Medicare and Medicaid Services' Open Payments database (https://openpaymentsdata.cms.gov/) allows anyone to look up individual doctors and teaching hospitals to see how much they have received, and from whom, for services unrelated to patient care. In the United Kingdom, the Association of the British Pharmaceutical Industry maintains a similar database, Disclosure UK (http://www.abpi.org.uk/our-work/disclosure/Pages/DocumentLibrary.aspx), which lists payments the pharmaceutical industry has made to doctors, nurses, and other health professionals and health organizations.

7. **Does the story compare the new approach with existing alternatives?**
   "New", of course, is an important part of news, so it's understandable that journalists want to inform their audiences about the newest developments in health. However, in medicine, newer does not always equal better. Stories about new medical products, services, or treatment approaches, therefore, should include a comparison of the new intervention to existing alternatives, which – by definition – have more extensive track records. In fact, some critics of the healthcare system note that 90 per cent of new drugs approved by the US Food and Drug Administration do not offer any significant benefit over older drugs (Light et al., 2013); about 20 per cent of new prescription drugs are found to cause serious negative side effects after they are approved (Light, 2014). Others argue that "advances" in medical screening tests often lead to over-diagnoses that cause more harm than good (Moynihan et al., 2012; Welch et al., 2011). Journalists can help their audiences resist the allure of the new by systematically comparing any new medical intervention to existing options (including lifestyle changes) in terms of costs, benefits, and potential side effects.

8. **Does the story establish the availability of the treatment/test/ product/procedure?**
   Without a doubt, health researchers make some amazing discoveries through studies involving cells grown in petri dishes and animal models. But only a fraction of these discoveries lead to improvements in human health. For instance, researchers estimate that only 8 per cent of cancer drugs that work in animal models prove effective for humans (Mak et al., 2014). This high failure rate means journalists must exercise extreme caution in writing about the results of research using animals rather than humans. In addition, even when a new drug, device, or test has been approved for use in one country or region, it might not be approved for

use in other countries. In other cases, approved health interventions may be available only through clinical trials or to individuals who can pay exorbitant fees out-of-pocket because health insurance companies do not view the intervention as cost-effective. Journalists writing about new treatments, tests, products, and procedures should make clear in the story how widely available the intervention is, how likely it is that insurance providers will cover it, and how long it might be until health professionals have the appropriate training to use that intervention successfully (Schwitzer, n.d.).

9. **Does the story establish the true novelty of the approach?**

The US FDA considers drugs that have not previously been approved for use in the United States to be "new" drugs – no matter how long the drug has been in use in Europe or even in Canada. That fact, along with US regulations intended to encourage drug companies to develop drugs for rare diseases, has allowed some pharmaceutical companies to get FDA approval – and enormous profits – from buying manufacturing rights to drugs that had previously been available as generics outside the United States. Medical devices, too, might have received approval in one country or for treatment of a specific medical issue but then be repurposed by manufacturers hoping to expand the market for the device. Journalists should be sceptical of claims that any medical intervention is truly new. When the intervention *has* been used before, even for different diagnoses or different population groups, journalists owe their audiences a discussion of consumers' and health professionals' previous experience with the intervention.

10. **Does the story rely solely or largely on a news release?**

Shrinking staffs, tighter budgets, and the explosion of public relations efforts aimed at increasing coverage of health products, health providers, and even health researchers have made it tougher than ever for journalists to avoid letting the steady flow of news releases influence the decisions they make about what health stories to cover. Even so, it should go without saying that journalists should never publish a story based on a news release without at least incorporating additional material drawn from independent reporting. Studies of the quality of health-related news releases have shown that they often omit important information about the research or the interventions they discuss or make inappropriate claims about the implications of the research (e.g., claims about human health based on lab animal research) (Kuriya et al., 2008; Woloshin et al., 2009). Journalists who rely too heavily on news releases are likely to commit these same errors, leaving their audiences without the information they need to decide how, or if, the story is relevant to their own lives.

CASE STUDY 1

The Guardian reports on study about statins and heart disease risk

In September 2016, researchers from Imperial College London and the University of Glasgow published a paper in the journal *Circulation* describing results from 20 years of follow-up data on a subgroup of Scottish men who had originally participated in a five-year randomized trial comparing heart disease among men who took a widely used anti-cholesterol drug versus a placebo. The researchers concluded that taking statins had both short- and long-term benefits.

The Guardian, in reporting on this study, used only the relative benefit data from the study, which showed that there were 28 per cent fewer heart disease deaths among men who had taken statins compared with those who took the placebo. However, the story left out the *absolute* risk comparison, which showed that 9.03 per cent of men who had taken a placebo in the original study died of heart disease, compared to 6.69 per cent of men who had taken a statin – a far less impressive difference. The story also failed to discuss the potential side effects of taking statins over long periods of time; most commonly, these side effects include muscle pain, weakness, and damage. Statin use also has been linked, less definitively, to liver damage, an increased risk of Type 2 diabetes and memory loss or confusion (Mosher et al., 2017).

Another problematic feature of the story was that it failed to mention that Sanofi, which manufactures and sells statins, funded the entire study. In addition, five of the *Circulation* paper's eight authors had financial ties to Sanofi, either in the past or at the time the paper was published. The story included only two sources – the study's lead author and the medical director of the British Heart Foundation. However, the direct quotes used in the story precisely matched those included in an Imperial College news release about the publication, suggesting that *The Guardian* reporter did no independent reporting for the story. healthnewsreview.org concluded that the use of identical quotes strongly suggested that *The Guardian* story was simply a rewrite of a news release (Mosher et al., 2017).

Yet another problem with the story was that it provided no information about the limitations of the study, which included the fact that the researchers had no information about whether the men they were studying had used statins or any other drugs during the 15 years since the end of the original randomized study. The study's authors note that "it cannot be assumed that the outcomes are only modulated by statin use or non-use," but *The Guardian*'s story did not mention this. It also does not mention the possible confounding effects of substantial declines in smoking over the 20 years since the original study began. Although the headline, lead, and some of the quotes noted that the study involved only men, the story also included quotes implying that women should assume the results apply to them as well, although no women participated in the study. For instance, a paraphrase attributed to the study's lead author argues that "people with lower levels of cholesterol ... who otherwise appear healthy, should also be treated with statins" ("Statins cut," 2017, p. 9), even though the study involved only men who began the study with very high LDL ("bad" cholesterol) levels.

Overall, *The Guardian*'s story omitted nearly all of the information readers would need to make informed decisions about the use of statins, particularly for people who currently do not have heart disease. Although healthnewsreview.org found the story "not guilty" of committing disease-mongering, it noted that there's great potential for overtreatment when healthy people are encouraged to take any prescription drug; in addition, the story failed to discuss the costs of the drug, which can add up to nearly $1,500 annually for a name-brand statin in the United States (Mosher et al., 2017).

CASE STUDY 2

Reuters reports on long-term follow-up of the Women's Health Initiative hormone study

One of the more widely publicized health research stories of the past two decades was the decision to end the Women's Health Initiative (WHI) trials, which were examining the use of hormone replacement therapy among post-menopausal women. The original study, funded by the US government, was discontinued in 2002 after initial data suggested that women taking man-made estrogen and progestin had increased risks of heart attacks and strokes, along with breast cancer. After news of the study's cancellation broke, the use of hormone replacement therapy (HRT) declined significantly among all age and racial groups in the United States and even among women abroad (Hillman et al., 2004; Parente et al., 2008; Silverman and Kokia, 2009).

Because many doctors have been reluctant to prescribe HRT and many women have been hesitant about using it since the end of the original WHI, the 12 September 2017 publication of a long-term follow-up study showing no increased risk of death among HRT users was an important health story. Reuters Health covered the story the same day the follow-up study article was published in *JAMA*, the journal of the American Medical Association, under a headline declaring "Menopause hormone therapy not linked to premature death". The story noted that the new study involved 27,347 post-menopausal women who had enrolled in the original study between 1993 and 1998; the new study followed these women, who had taken either hormones or a placebo for five to seven years, through 2014 – as much as 21 years altogether (Rapaport, 2017).

Unlike the original WHI, which was meant to test whether taking hormones reduced women's risk of developing heart disease, the follow-up study did not examine benefits; instead, it focused on whether women who took hormones were more likely to die than those who did not. The overall results showed no significant differences in mortality for women who did or did not take hormones during the study period, although death rates were 30 per cent lower for women who began taking HRT at age 50–59. Over the long term, however, Reuters reported that "women's age when they joined the study no longer appeared to significantly influence death rates" (Rapaport, 2017, para. 12).

In contrast to *The Guardian*'s story about statin use and heart disease, the Reuters story about the long-term outcomes of the Women's Health Initiative met nearly every relevant criterion, other than discussing the cost of hormone replacement therapy. As noted earlier, the study didn't investigate the benefits of taking HRT; it focused on potential harms, and the story discussed that potential in ways that neither overplayed the potential harm nor suggested that HRT was safe for all women to take. In fact, the story closed with a quote from Dr Melissa McNeil, a women's health researcher not affiliated with the WHI study, who noted that before the original WHI study, doctors believed hormone replacement therapy was safe for all women; after the trials were discontinued, the consensus was that HRT was *unsafe* for all women. McNeil – an independent source – concluded that "(t)he take-home message now is that for the right patient, hormone therapy is safe and effective" (Rapaport, 2017, para. 16).

In assessing the story, healthnewsreview.org pointed out that the story makes clear that any woman considering the use of HRT should talk with her healthcare professional about the risks and benefits. Nonetheless, the Reuters story provided important information, including discussing the limitations of the study, describing what's new about the study's results and avoiding disease-mongering. Although the study clearly compared the alternatives of taking vs. not taking hormones, the writer also might have offered information about other steps women can take to reduce or cope with menopause symptoms. The only criteria not met at all was a discussion of costs, a bit of information that would have been easy enough for the reporter to add through calls to local pharmacies and/or insurance providers. With that addition, the story could have offered an example of best practices in covering health research.

CASE STUDY 3

Sydney Morning Herald story promises hair test for breast cancer

Breast cancer consistently ranks among women's greatest health fears. It's also safe to say, however, that no woman ever looks forward to having a mammogram for a variety of reasons, including cost, the discomfort involved, and the need to visit a lab with specialized equipment and staff training. In addition, given recent evidence suggesting that one-third of all the breast cancers identified through mammography represent over-diagnosis (Jørgensen et al., 2017), leading to unnecessary treatment, scepticism about the "life-saving" value of mammograms is growing. Given that background, research suggesting that doctors could screen for breast cancer by analysing women's hair would naturally be a huge story. That may explain why the Sydney Morning Herald was so enthusiastic about the potential for this technology in its January 2012 story "Hair test for breast cancer on the horizon".

As surprising as that idea is, some research has supported the idea that there are detectable differences in the hair of women with and without breast cancer even before treatment begins (Corino et al., 2009; Corino and French, 2008; James, 2006). The Morning Herald story, however, did not appear to address any of this published research. Rather, it reported that an Australian company, SBC Research, was embarking on "an 80-patient trial to test its hypothesis that women with breast cancer have higher levels of phospholipids in their bloodstream that can be detected in hair" (Hagan, 2012, para. 2).

The story, unfortunately, seems to have failed on every criterion used by MediaDoctorAustralia, healthnewsreview.org and other health journalism reviews. First, the story provides no mention of cost, nor does it make any attempt to quantify the benefits this new test might offer over existing screening tests, including mammography and clinical breast exams. Obviously, a non-invasive test that requires none of the discomfort of mammography would indeed offer significant benefits – but only if the test was both sensitive and specific, meaning that it accurately detected breast abnormalities likely to cause significant health problems and correctly identified women who did not have breast cancer. For many, if not most, medical tests, these two characteristics are somewhat in conflict, with more sensitive tests producing higher rates of false-positive results and more specific tests more likely to return false-negative results. Thus, any story about a new test that would be administered to apparently healthy women should discuss the evidence that this test would be better than existing alternatives in terms of accurately identifying women with breast abnormalities likely to lead to life-threatening disease.

Another important flaw in the story is that it provided no discussion of the potential harms of the test, which could include both failure to alert women to breast cancer requiring treatment and – perhaps more likely – the risk of over-diagnosis leading to unnecessary treatment. Given that, as noted earlier, researchers now estimate that one of every three breast cancers identified through mammography represents over-diagnosis, the danger that a screening test might result in healthy women being subjected to debilitating and potentially disfiguring overtreatment is an important harm, one journalists should be careful to address.

In writing about health interventions, health journalism experts also recommend that stories should help their audiences understand the quality of the evidence supporting use of the intervention. On this criterion, too, the *Morning Herald* story fell short. In this case, the study meant to determine whether the promoted test would be useful had not even been conducted yet, and even if it had been, the study being discussed would involve only 80 patients – far too small a sample to give most researchers any confidence in the study results. Despite that lack of solid evidence, the story's headline described the hair screening test as "on the horizon", and the cutline/caption under an accompanying photograph stated that "(m)ammograms may become a thing of the past" (Hagan, 2012).

The headline and photo cutline/caption also contributed to the story's failure on another criterion, which is whether the story helps audiences understand the availability of the test. In this case, the headline and cutline/caption suggested that, in the near future, breast cancer screening would involve women submitting a few strands of hair rather than having their breasts painfully squashed and subjected to radiation. Because the research was so preliminary, developing a hair screening test likely would be years in the future even if the study mentioned in the story produced overwhelmingly positive results.

In addition, in noting that SBC Research planned to commercialize the test and make it "available to women of all ages", the story came dangerously close to disease-mongering, in that it suggested that healthy women of all ages should be getting screened for breast cancer. That recommendation contradicts the current medical consensus, which is that most women with no family history of breast cancer should wait until age 50 to begin breast cancer screening. And even that advice has come under fire from some experts who argue that breast cancer screening, especially among younger women, contributes more to overdiagnosis and overtreatment than to saving lives (van den Ende et al., 2017; Welch et al., 2016).

As noted earlier, some published research has suggested that hair analysis could be used to screen for breast cancer. The *Morning Herald* reporter could have reached out to researchers involved in any of these previous studies for comment on the SBC screening test's approach and potential. It appears she did not because the only two sources quoted in the story were an SBC researcher and the company's chief scientist; obviously, both had significant conflicts of interest. Comment from independent sources also might have helped the journalist on another criterion, establishing the true novelty of the approach. Those independent sources might have mentioned that earlier studies attempting to screen for breast cancer through analysis of hair structures had failed (Laaziri et al., 2002) or that other researchers were examining the possibility of using analysis of trace elements in women's hair to identify breast cancer (Gholizadeh et al., 2013).

The fact that the *Morning Herald* story failed on the first nine criteria strongly suggests that it may also have failed on the tenth – avoiding relying entirely on a news release in writing the story. I was not able to find such a news release online, so it may be that the story (which also ran in the *Brisbane Times*, with the same author) was not based on a news release. Regardless of its source, however, the story offered substantially more in the way of promotion of SBC Research than it offered to women seeking information about effective alternatives to mammography.

Conclusion

As the three case studies – and indeed, the entire chapter – illustrate, providing complete, accurate, useful, and responsible coverage of health interventions is a challenging task. Most health journalists today are deluged with news releases and other communications from scientists, universities, journals, and commercial organizations seeking to use news stories to promote their latest research and their products to the public. The public, in turn, seems quite interested in the latest health news. In the United States, *Prevention* and *Women's Health* magazines were among the four magazines that increased their newsstand sales in 2014 (Sebastian, 2014), and both magazines remain among the most widely circulated health and fitness magazines in the United States ("Most popular," 2016). Four of the five science stories listed among the *New York Times'* most widely read stories of 2016 dealt with health topics (Bevacqua et al., 2016). In addition, searching for health information is one of the most common online activities for people in the United States, the United Kingdom and many other countries worldwide (Fox and Duggan, 2013; McCaw et al., 2014; Powell and Clarke, 2006).

But the research also indicates that people don't consume health news simply to be informed or entertained; people use what they learn from health news stories to make decisions about their own health behaviours. Journalists' reporting on health can influence everything from the foods people choose to whether they have their children vaccinated to how they interact with their physicians and other health providers. That reality means journalists have a tremendous responsibility to strive to provide people with the best possible information about health interventions – the diets, drugs, devices, tests, and therapies that can affect not only consumers' health and quality of life but in some cases their survival.

While the idea that one's stories could have life-and-death implications may be daunting, journalists need not have formal medical science training to provide excellent coverage of health research and interventions. However, they do need to develop a systematic approach to reporting and writing health stories to make sure that every story provides the information people would need to make rational decisions. Many consumers, of course, will consult a health professional before making major health decisions, and in some cases, the health professional's opinion (e.g. for a specific drug, medical device, or surgical approach) may carry greater weight than the patient's in determining the treatment the individual receives. Nonetheless, even when a doctor makes the final call, journalists can equip consumers to participate more effectively in health decision-making by providing complete information about the costs, benefits, and harms of an intervention, alternative approaches, the evidence supporting use of each approach, etc.

As is arguably true in every other type of journalism, one of the most important steps the journalist can take is to vet the claims primary sources make about a health intervention with independent sources with nothing to gain or lose from the success or failure of that approach. These independent sources can help the reporter to understand – and to be able to explain to his/her audience – what is and isn't true, and what is and isn't important in the information provided by those who do have a stake in consumers' decisions about health interventions. In effect, the journalist can help to provide consumers with a critical second or third opinion about the value of a specific health intervention. At the least, this should help the consumer ask better questions when discussing testing, treatment, and lifestyle options with his or her health providers.

Note

1 HealthNewsReview will no longer regularly publish from January 2019. The 6000+ articles already published on the site will remain available for three years. Click here to find out more: https://www.healthnewsreview.org/2018/12/5-categories-of-quality-web-content-for-you-to-explore-when-we-cease-daily-publication/
2 Some resources on the AHCJ website are accessible only to members.

References

Barns, S., 2015. Chocolate accelerates weight loss: Research claims it lowers cholesterol and aids sleep. *The Daily Express* [online]. Available from: http://www.express.co.uk/life-style/health/567211/Chocolate-weight-loss-lowers-blood-cholesterol-aids-better-sleep [Accessed 9 September 2017].

Bevacqua, A.I., Bhaskar, S., and Debelius, D., 2016. The most-read stories of 2016. *The New York Times* [online]. Available from: https://www.nytimes.com/interactive/2016/12/19/business/media/top-stories.html [Accessed 20 October 2017].

Bohannon, J., 2015. I fooled millions into thinking chocolate helps weight loss. Here's how. *io9*. Available from: http://io9.gizmodo.com/i-fooled-millions-into-thinking-chocolate-helps-weight-1707251800 [Accessed 9 September 2017].

Brodie, M., Hamel, E.C., Altman, D.E., Blendon, R.J., and Benson, J.M., 2003. Health news and the American public, 1996–2002. *Journal of Health Politics, Policy and Law*, 28, 927–950.

Bubela, T.M., and Caulfield, T.A., 2004. Do the print media "hype" genetic research? A comparison of newspaper stories and peer-reviewed research papers. *Canadian Medical Association Journal*, 170, 1399–1407. doi:10.1503/cmaj.1030762.

Carman, K.L., Maurer, M., Yegian, J.M., Dardess, P., McGee, J., Evers, M., and Marlo, K.O., 2010. Evidence that consumers are skeptical about evidence-based health care. *Health Affairs*, 29, 1400–1406. doi:10.1377/hlthaff.2009.0296.

Chen, L.M., Farwell, W.R., and Jha, A.K., 2009. Primary care visit duration and quality: Does good care take longer? *Archives of Internal Medicine*, 169, 1866–1872.

Cochrane, 2017. What is Cochrane evidence and how can it help you. Available from: http://www.cochrane.org/what-is-cochrane-evidence [Accessed 12 October 2017].

Corino, G.L., and French, P.W., 2008. Diagnosis of breast cancer by X-ray diffraction of hair. *International Journal of Cancer*, 122, 847–856. doi:10.1002/ijc.23085.

Corino, G.L., French, P.W., Lee, M., Ajaj, M.M., Haklani, J., Mistry, D.A.H., Phan, K., and Yuile, P.G., 2009. Characterization of a test for invasive breast cancer using X-ray diffraction of hair: Results of a clinical trial. *Breast Cancer: Basic and Clinical Research*, 3, 83–90.

Dixon, G., and Clarke, C., 2012. The effect of falsely balanced reporting of the autism-vaccine controversy on vaccine safety perceptions and behavioral intentions. *Health Education Research*, 28, 352–359. doi:10.1093/her/cys110.

Entwistle, V., 1995. Reporting research in medical journals and newspapers. *BMJ*, 310, 920. doi:http://dx.doi.org/10.1136/bmj.310.6984.920.

Fox, S., and Duggan, M., 2013. Health Online 2013. Pew Research Center Internet and American Life Project. Available from: http://www.pewinternet.org/2013/01/15/health-online-2013/ [Accessed 20 October 2017].

Gaglio, B., Glasgow, R.E., and Bull, S.S., 2012. Do patient preferences for health information vary by health literacy or numeracy? A qualitative assessment. *Journal of Health Communication*, 17 Supplement 3, 109–121. doi:10.1080/10810730.2012.712616.

Geana, M.V., Kimminau, K.S., and Greiner, K.A., 2011. Sources of health information in a multiethnic, underserved, urban community: Does ethnicity matter? *Journal of Health Communication*, 16, 583–594. doi:10.1080/10810730.2011.551992.

Gholizadeh, N., Kabiri, Z., Kakuee, O., Saleh-Kotahi, M., Changizi, V., Fathollahi, V., Oliaiy, P., and Omranipour, R., 2013. Feasibility of breast cancer screening by PIXE analysis of hair. *Biological Trace Element Research*, 153, 105–110. doi:10.1007/s12011-013-9671-2.

Godoy, M., 2015. Why a journalist scammed the media into spreading bad chocolate science. *NPR*. Available from: http://www.npr.org/sections/thesalt/2015/05/28/410313446/why-a-journalist-scammed-the-media-into-spreading-bad-chocolate-science [Accessed 9 September 2017].

Gottschalk, A., and Flocke, S.A., 2005. Time spent in face-to-face patient care and work outside the examination room. *Annals of Family Medicine*, 3, 488–493. doi:10.1370/afm.404

Hagan, K., 2012. Hair test for breast cancer on the horizon. *Sydney Morning Herald* [online]. Available from: http://www.smh.com.au/national/health/hair-test-for-breast-cancer-on-the-horizon-20120126-1qjt4.html [Accessed 13 October 2017].

Heisel, W., 2012a. Complete health reporting: Avoid extremes to avoid disease mongering. Center for Health Journalism. Available from: https://www.centerforhealthjournalism.org/2012/06/13/complete-health-reporting-avoid-extremes-avoid-disease-mongering [Accessed 7 October 2017].

Heisel, W., 2012b. Complete health reporting: Steer clear of disease-mongering quicksand. Center for Health Journalism. Available from: https://www.centerfor

healthjournalism.org/blogs/2012/06/06/complete-health-reporting-steer-clear-disease-mongering-quicksand [Accessed 7 October 2017].

Hillman, J.J., Zuckerman, I.H., and Lee, E., 2004. The impact of the Women's Health Initiative on hormone replacement therapy in a Medicaid program. *Journal of Women's Health*, 13, 986–992. doi:10.1089/jwh.2004.13.986.

James, V.J., 2006. A place for fiber diffraction in the detection of breast cancer? *Cancer Detection and Prevention*, 30, 233–238. doi:10.1016/j.cdp.2006.04.001.

Jones, K.O., Denham, B.E., and Springston, J.K., 2006. Effects of mass and interpersonal communication on breast cancer screening: Advancing agenda-setting theory in health contexts. *Journal of Applied Communication Research*, 34, 94–113.

Jørgensen, K.J., Gøtzsche, P.C., Kalager, M., and Zahl, P.-H., 2017. Breast cancer screening in Denmark: A cohort study of tumor size and overdiagnosis. *Annals of Internal Medicine*, 166, 313–323. doi:10.7326/M16-0270.

Kakai, H., Maskarinec, G., Shumay, D.M., Tatsumura, Y., and Tasaki, K., 2003. Ethnic differences in choices of health information by cancer patients using complementary and alternative medicine: An exploratory study with correspondence analysis. *Social Science and Medicine*, 56, 851–862.

Koch-Weser, S., Bradshaw, Y.S., Gualtieri, L., and Gallagher, S.S., 2010. The Internet as a health information source: Findings from the 2007 Health Information National Trends Survey and implications for health communication. *Journal of Health Communication*, 15, 279–293. doi:10.1080/10810730.2010.522700.

Konrad, T.R., Link, C.L., Shackelton, R.J., Marceau, L.D., von dem Knesebeck, O., Siegrist, J., Arber, S., Adams, A., and McKinlay, J.B., 2010. It's about time: Physicians' perceptions of time constraints in primary care medical practice in three national healthcare systems. *Medical Care*, 48, 95–100. doi:10.1097/MLR.0b013e3181c12e6a.

Kravitz, R.L., and Callahan, E.J., 2000. Patients' perceptions of omitted examinations and tests. *Journal of General Internal Medicine*, 15, 38–45.

Kuriya, B., Schneid, E.C., and Bell, C.M., 2008. Quality of pharmaceutical industry press releases based on original research. *PLoS One*, 3, 1–3. doi:10.1371/journal.pone.0002828.

Laaziri, K., Sutton, M., Ghadirian, P., Scott, A.S., Paradis, A.J., Tonin, P.N., and Foulkes, W.D., 2002. Is there a correlation between the structure of hair and breast cancer or BRCA1/2 mutations? *Physics in Medicine & Biology*, 47, 1623–1632.

Li, M., Chapman, S., Agho, K., and Eastman, C.J., 2008. Can even minimal news coverage influence consumer health-related behaviour? A case study of iodized salt sales, Australia. *Health Education Research*, 23, 543–548. doi:10.1093/her/cym028.

Light, D.W., 2014. New prescription drugs: A major health risk with few offsetting advantages. Available from: https://ethics.harvard.edu/blog/new-prescription-drugs-major-health-risk-few-offsetting-advantages [Accessed 12 October 2017].

Light, D.W., Lexchin, J., and Darrow, J.J., 2013. Institutional corruption of pharmaceuticals and the myth of safe and effective drugs. *Journal of Law, Medicine and Ethics*, 14(3), 590–610.

Lombrozo, T., 2015. What junk food can teach us about junk science. *NPR*. Available from: http://www.npr.org/sections/13.7/2015/06/08/412825282/what-junk-food-can-teach-us-about-junk-science [Accessed 9 September 2017].

Mak, I.W., Evaniew, N., and Ghert, M., 2014. Lost in translation: Animal models and clinical trials in cancer treatment. *American Journal of Translational Research*, 6, 114–118.

McCarthy, N., 2014. Americans visit their doctor 4 times a year. People in Japan visit 13 times a year. *Forbes*. Available from: https://www.forbes.com/sites/niallmccarthy/2014/09/04/

americans-visit-their-doctor-4-times-a-year-people-in-japan-visit-13-times-a-year-infographic/#2aed16e7e347 [Accessed 13 October 2017].

McCaw, B.A., McGlade, K.J., and McElnay, J.C., 2014. Online health information – what the newspapers tell their readers: A systematic content analysis. *BMC Public Health*, 14, 1316. doi:10.1186/1471-2458-14-1316.

Mitchell, L., 2015. Has the world gone coco? Eating chocolate can help you LOSE weight. *Daily Star* [online]. Available from: http://www.dailystar.co.uk/diet-fitness/433688/Chocolate-diet-how-to-lose-weight [Accessed 9 September 2017].

Moriarty, C.M., and Stryker, J.E., 2008. Prevention and screening efficacy messages in newspaper accounts of cancer. *Health Education Research*, 23, 487–498. doi:10.1093/her/cyl163.

Mosher, D., Ward, E., and Victory, J., 2017. Guardian leaves out a key potential conflict of interest in story on statin study. *HealthNewsReview.org*. Available from: https://www.healthnewsreview.org/review/guardian-leaves-out-a-key-potential-conflict-of-interest-in-story-on-statins-and-risk-of-heart-disease-death/. [Accessed 12 October 2017].

Most popular health and fitness magazines in the United States as of September 2016, by circulation (in thousands), 2016. Statista. Available from: https://www.statista.com/statistics/681631/most-popular-health-and-fitness-magazines-by-circulation/ [Accessed 20 October 2017].

Moynihan, R., Doust, J., and Henry, D., 2012. Preventing overdiagnosis: How to stop harming the healthy. *BMJ*, 344: e3502. doi:10.1136/bmj.e3502.

Murphy, M.W., Iqbal, S., Sanchez, C.A., and Quinlisk, M.P., 2010. Postdisaster health communication and information sources: The Iowa flood scenario. *Disaster Medicine and Public Health Preparedness*, 4, 129–134.

National Library of Medicine, n.d. Citations added to MEDLINE® by fiscal year, 2016. Available from: https://www.nlm.nih.gov/bsd/stats/cit_added.html [Accessed 13 October 2017].

Niederdeppe, J., and Frosch, D.L., 2009. News coverage and sales of products with trans fat: Effects before and after changes in federal labeling policy. *American Journal of Preventive Medicine*, 36, 395–401. doi:10.1016/j.amepre.2009.01.023.

Niederdeppe, J., Frosch, D.L., and Hornik, R.C., 2008. Cancer news coverage and information seeking. *Journal of Health Communication*, 13, 181–199.

Parente, L., Uyehara, C., Larsen, W., Whitcomb, B., and Farley, J., 2008. Long-term impact of the Women's Health Initiative on HRT. *Archives of Gynecology and Obstetrics*, 277, 219–224. doi:10.1007/s00404-007-0442-1.

Powell, J., and Clarke, A., 2006. Internet information-seeking in mental health: Population survey. *British Journal of Psychiatry*, 189, 273–277. doi:10.1192/bjp.bp.105.017319.

Rapaport, L., 2017. Menopause hormone therapy not linked to premature death. *Reuters*. Available from: https://www.reuters.com/article/us-health-menopause-hormones/menopause-hormone-therapy-not-linked-to-premature-death-idUSKCN1BN2LQ [Accessed 12 October, 2017].

Reynolds, T., 2001. News headlines feed on fear of cancer risk, experts say. *Journal of the National Cancer Institute*, 93, 9–11. doi:10.1093/jnci/93.1.9.

Schwartz, L.M., and Woloshin, S., 2002. News media coverage of screening mammography for women in their 40s and tamoxifen for primary prevention of breast cancer. *JAMA*, 287, 3136–3142.

Schwartz, L.M., Woloshin, S., Fowler Jr, F.J., and Welch, H.G., 2004. Enthusiasm for cancer screening in the United States. *JAMA*, 291, 71–78.

Schwitzer, G., n.d. Criterion #8: Does the story establish the availability of the treatment/test/product/procedure? *HealthNewsReview.org*. Available from: https://

www.healthnewsreview.org/about-us/review-criteria/criterion-8/ [Accessed 9 September 2017].

Sebastian, M., 2014. How four magazines increased their newsstand sales. *Advertising Age* [Online]. Available from: http://adage.com/article/media/magazines-increased-newsstand-sales/294514/ [Accessed 20 October 2017].

Silverman, B.G., and Kokia, E.S., 2009. Use of hormone replacement therapy, 1998–2007: Sustained impact of the Women's Health Initiative findings. *Annals of Pharmacotherapy*, 43, 251–258. doi:10.1345/aph.1L438.

Statement of principles of the Association of Health Care Journalists, n.d. Available from: https://healthjournalism.org/secondarypage-details.php?id=56 [Accessed 3 March 2018].

Statins cut the risk of heart disease death by 28% among men, study shows, 2017. *The Guardian* [Online]. Available from: https://www.theguardian.com/society/2017/sep/06/statins-cut-the-risk-of-heart-disease-death-by-28-among-men-study-shows [Accessed 12 October, 2017].

Stryker, J.E., 2002. Reporting medical information: Effects of press releases and newsworthiness on medical journal articles' visibility in the news media. *Preventive Medicine*, 35, 519–530. doi:10.1006/pmed.2002.1102.

Tai-Seale, M., McGuire, T.G., and Zhang, W., 2007. Time allocation in primary care office visits. *Health Services Research*, 42, 1871–1894. doi:10.1111/j.1475-6773.2006.00689.x.

The Times of India, 2015. Need a "sweeter" way to lose weight? Eat chocolates! *The Times of India* [online]. Available from: http://timesofindia.indiatimes.com/life-style/health-fitness/diet/Need-a-sweeter-way-to-lose-weight-Eat-chocolates/articleshow/46770172.cms [Accessed 9 September 2017].

Vader, A.M., Walters, S.T., Roudsari, B., and Nguyen, N., 2011. Where do college students get health information? Believability and use of health information sources. *Health Promotion Practice*, 12, 713–722. doi:10.1177/1524839910369995.

van den Bruel, A., 2015. The triumph of medicine: How overdiagnosis is turning healthy people into patients. *Family Practice*, 32, 127–128. doi:10.1093/fampra/cmv008.

van den Ende, C., Oordt-Speets, A.M., Vroling, H., and van Agt, H.M.E., 2017. Benefits and harms of breast cancer screening with mammography in women aged 40-49 years: A systematic review. *International Journal of Cancer*, 141, 1295–1306. doi:10.1002/ijc.30794.

Walsh-Childers, K., Braddock, J., Rabaza, C., and Schwitzer, G., 2016. One step forward, one step back: Changes in news coverage of medical interventions. *Health Communication*, 1–14. doi:10.1080/10410236.2016.1250706.

Welch, H.G., Prorok, P.C., O'Malley, A.J., and Kramer, B.S., 2016. Breast-cancer tumor size, overdiagnosis, and mammography screening effectiveness. *New England Journal of Medicine*, 375, 1438–1447. doi:10.1056/NEJMoa1600249.

Welch, H.G., Schwartz, L., and Woloshin, S., 2011. *Overdiagnosed: Making people sick in the pursuit of health*. Boston, MA: Beacon Press.

Woloshin, S., Schwartz, L.M., Casella, S.L., Kennedy, A.T., and Larson, R.J., 2009. Press releases by academic medical centers: Not so academic? *Annals of Internal Medicine*, 150, 613–618.

Yanovitzky, I., and Blitz, C.L., 2000. Effect of media coverage and physician advice on utilization of breast cancer screening by women 40 years and older. *Journal of Health Communication*, 5, 117–134. doi:10.1080/108107300406857.

Yudkin, J.S., and Montori, V.M., 2014. Too much medicine: The epidemic of pre-diabetes: The medicine and the politics. *BMJ*, 349, g4485. doi:10.1136/bmj.g4485.

PART V

Reporting science and the environment

9

REPORTING EMERGING AND CONTROVERSIAL SCIENCE

Shelley Thompson and Hilary Stepien

The social issue

Nanotechnology, medicine, biotechnology, and stem cell research, climate science, genome sequencing, astrobiology, forensic science, and so on. The impact of science and technology on society, the economy, and the environment cannot be overstated. Surveys in the US, UK, Europe, and Asia indicate that public interest and enthusiasm for science is quite high and that publics broadly support scientific development and government funding of science. The surveys further suggest publics see the potential for science and technology to improve quality of life and its economic importance (Castell et al., 2014). Mainstream news media (especially TV) continues to be the primary place in which citizens learn about science and technology, especially in the UK (Castell et al., 2014). And though US surveys show an increasing reliance on digital media for information about science, citizens seek out trusted mainstream news titles for that information (National Science Board, 2016). As such, it is important to ensure informed and rigorous reporting of these topics so as to enhance the quality of democratic debate about science and technology.

At the same time, science news is not exclusively the remit of specialised journalists assigned to science and technology beats. Scientists engage in research across a vast array of disciplines, which impact every patch in the newsroom and so science is potentially the remit of all journalists at one time or another in their career. Funding and regulation of science may arise as key issues for those on government and policy beats. Finance and economics journalists encounter science when covering news about jobs created by new scientific applications and new technology. Education journalists write about the need for education and training programmes at all levels to provide scientific solutions to significant social problems and challenges (e.g., climate change, an ageing population globally, food security, or access to clean water supplies). Court and crime journalists encounter forensic science and expert witnesses that rely on scientific evidence in their testimony. And of course, the latest developments and the risks and uncertainties associated with these new developments are regularly addressed by journalists assigned to science and technology. In all these cases, reporting on and dealing with the science in these news stories can be challenging, but especially so when the science is very new or potentially controversial.

Introduction

This chapter explores the research on science in news from the specialist pages and beyond and considers how science and technology, as well as the associated risks and uncertainties, are covered by journalists. It draws on the collective professional and research experience of the authors, specifically Dr Shelley Thompson's experience as a journalist in the US and a science journalism researcher in the UK, and Hilary Stepien's work in public affairs and strategic communication in Canada and her complementary research on health communication in the UK. Our combined experience and research perspectives from journalism and public affairs challenge, interrogate, and highlight how journalism and public relations, which also plays a role in the framing of science in news, communicates science in our respective professions. It also explores how and where journalists and PR professionals could work together to help citizens better navigate potentially controversial science and thus more meaningfully engage in democratic and informed debate in the public sphere.

The chapter explores some of the problems and pitfalls in the reporting of science and the role that sources play in both shaping the news about science and helping make sense of emerging and controversial science. It pays particular attention to how risk and uncertainty feature in science news and the implications for the ways in which risk is reported. The chapter uses emerging and controversial science case studies to illustrate some of the high-stakes consequences of science controversies and journalism's duty to report it responsibly (as with the vaccines case study), how the wider social and political context influences science and the reporting of it (as with the case study of biotechnology and stem cell research), and new trends in science that will likely become increasingly newsworthy but that to date have not been as robustly reported as we would expect (as with the case of nanotechnology).

The chapter begins by discussing themes from previous research on science journalism, including making a case for the importance of science journalism, the challenges and impact of professional norms of journalism (e.g., objectivity) when reporting science, what makes science newsworthy, and the sociological research on risk and uncertainty. We then discuss how to cover emerging and controversial science, which provides a foundation for the three case studies that follow. Finally, we identify some resources and tips to help you with reporting the science in stories you cover.

We hope readers will take away that:

- Journalists covering science and who encounter science in the course of covering other news can provide an audience for science and foster democratic debate about scientific issues.
- Journalists can also, and arguably should absolutely, correct misinformation and myths about science through appropriate fact-checking, rather than simply balancing truth claims by sources in the name of objectivity.
- Journalists should be aware of the proliferation of self-publication of "science" in the digital landscape, whereby individuals with claims to expertise in scientific fields may present opinion as fact. Despite certain flaws in the academic peer review process where dubious scientific claims have been published and reported on, a healthy journalistic scepticism is required when reporting science.

The research

News about science plays an important role in informing and engaging the public in discussion about science and scientific issues (Schafer, 2010), especially as it relates to emerging science where news reporting can draw attention to a topic and set the public agenda for debate (Friedman and Egolf, 2005; Gorss and Lewenstein, 2005; Boykoff and Boykoff, 2004). Despite the rise in use of social media and internet more generally, mainstream news media (TV in particular) remains the top way in which people learn about science in the UK (Castell et al., 2014) and the same appears to be true for Europe and Asia (National Science Board, 2016). For the US, the internet is the primary place for individuals to *seek out* information about science and they usually go to mainstream news organisations for that information (National Science Board, 2016). This tendency underlines the importance of mainstream news organisations, regardless of medium, to get the reporting of science right as the public relies on these sources in particular for reliable information.

The news audience for science is varied in terms of interest in science and relative expertise. The specialty pages for science are read by policy-makers, science enthusiasts, and individuals who are generally assumed to have a higher level of scientific literacy, but the broader news audience has a wider range of knowledge and expertise relative to science (Weigold, 2001; Bauer and Bucchi, 2007). These varying levels of scientific interest and expertise of the audience can pose significant challenges for journalists to cover the science in news; specifically, journalists need to calibrate their reporting to meet the needs of diverse audiences with a range of attitudes and predispositions to science. Even still, science journalism has been seen as translating, for lack of a better word, science for a lay audience and therefore attempting to make it simpler and more accessible (Lewenstein, 1992). The relative scientific knowledge and interest of the journalists covering news about science range from specialist journalists who may have a science degree in their background to general assignment journalists who may not. However, when science is reported by general assignment journalists and those on patches other than science, these journalists may interpret the science differently from a specialist journalist and introduce new voices and ideas to a scientific topic (Nisbet and Scheufele, 2009), which is arguably good for a democratic engagement with science and aligns with public understanding/attitudes/engagement with science campaigns and initiatives. This chapter sets aside the debate around the differences and the problems with notions of public understanding and engagement with science, as well as the measures of it through public attitude surveys as it would distract from its central focus and there is an existing robust literature that considers that (see, for example, Weigold, 2001; Schafer, 2009; Schafer, 2010).

Covering emerging and controversial science

As with any other topic, for science to be considered newsworthy it often needs to demonstrate a sense of newness, controversy, and/or human interest (see, for example, Priest 2001a; Weigold 2001; Lewenstein 2005a; Carvalho 2007; and Allan 2008). Routine science is generally not seen as newsworthy (Allan, 2002), and journalists' sense of the audience and what the audience wants to know plays an important part in determining what scientific topics to cover and how to cover them (Hughes, 2007). Drawing on interviews with British journalists, Hansen (1994: 115–116) identified a series of news values for science:

- relevance to the audience's daily life;
- weird and wacky (often human interest stories);
- scientific breakthrough;
- controversy;
- proximity; and
- social, political, and economic relevance.

The above, especially as it relates to "relevance to daily life", is why medical and health-related news are amongst the most common subjects for news reporting of science. Similarly, the more people who are impacted by the topic, the more likely it is to become news (Weigold, 2001). These news values, especially controversy and social, political, and economic relevance, are arguably why the chosen case studies were newsworthy or not as much, as in the case for nanotechnology.

Further, how journalists are introduced to relevant science for the news impacts how it is reported. As newsrooms have become smaller, science patches have been amongst those to be impacted by cuts; however, the demand for content in the news environment remains insatiable. Therefore, science journalism, like other "journalisms", has increasingly become desk-driven (Trumbo et al., 2001; Trench, 2009; Williams and Clifford, 2009) and originates from public relations (Bauer and Gregory, 2007), as research out of universities and institutions is communicated through press releases to news organisations globally. These press releases can lead to repackaged information from the research institutions and publishers, thereby leading to a "sameness" in the reporting (Allan, 2008; Trench, 2009). It also has an impact on story selection and story framing as journalists rely on their sources – including scientists – to help determine what scientific breakthroughs are significant, the meaning behind the science, and the relative risks associated with the science (Hansen, 1994). In some ways, journalists are particularly reliant on scientist sources when the science is new or controversial. Dunwoody (1999) points out, though, that the one-source story is a norm for science journalism, which can limit discussion and debate around a topic and is particularly problematic when dealing with controversial science. Therefore, it is incumbent on journalists to consider the potential range of sources that can be included in news about science, including NGOs, citizens, government officials, other scientists, industry analysts, and so on. Although, a note of caution, as the case study on vaccination will highlight, the motivations and biases of the sources included in a story are important to consider, which is true not only in covering science but also in covering other controversial news topics.

At the same time, professional norms of objectivity, balance, and fairness are also important in the reporting of science. In her research on news production habits of journalists covering human cloning, Priest (2001a) notes that where disputes emerge in scientific fields of study, "journalism strives to remain 'objective' by 'balancing' opposing points of view uncritically" (2001: 61). This has been especially problematic in the case of climate science, although the dispute was between a consensus within the scientific community of the anthropogenic causes of climate change and minority opinions and the norms of objectivity were, and sometimes still are, misapplied in seeking to balance unequal positions (see, for example, Boykoff and Boykoff, 2004; Antilla, 2005; Carvalho, 2007; Boykoff and Boykoff, 2007; Boykoff, 2007) (see also Prof. Robert Wyss' unpacking of this in the next chapter of this volume). Objectivity is also sometimes used in science stories as a shortcut for fact-checking (Miller and Riechert, 2000) whereby journalists include a limited range of viewpoints on a scientific story rather than checking the accuracy of claims made by individual sources.

Another important area of relevant academic research is the sociology of risk and notions of uncertainty. Uncertainty, in many ways, is inherently part of scientific research, and reporting that uncertainty poses challenges for journalists writing about science. As Zehr (1999) notes, scientists poke holes in previous work (in other words, create uncertainty) so as to identify where further investigation is required and then create new knowledge through their research (which in many ways could be seen as reducing uncertainty – at least as it relates directly to what the research was about). Uncertainty in science also arises when scientists write about their research as they use caveats and outline the limits of the application of findings. This is an important part of how scientists demonstrate their objectivity and authority, which is in some ways different from journalistic notions of objectivity and authority. So, these different approaches to objectivity – scientific and journalistic – are a challenge for how journalists and scientists communicate and therefore influence the final reporting of a topic. However, news about science often removes the caveats that scientists use to talk about their work (Stocking, 1999), which can make the science appear more certain than it is. Scientific uncertainty also occurs when researchers debate different theoretical positions or come from different scientific disciplines, and although the theoretical positions would not normally be seen as newsworthy it can mean that the scientific community appears divided or that the science is more controversial than it is. Therefore, familiarity with perspectives and theoretical underpinnings matter for a journalist's understanding of the science in the news, even if it's not something a journalist is likely to write about. As the vaccine case study will go on to show, while journalistic norms of objectivity and balance would suggest that juxtaposing experts on different sides of a debate is a good way to manage controversial science, it can sometimes make the science appear more uncertain than the scientific community might believe it to be, which is problematic (Dunwoody, 1999; Stocking, 1999).

Closely linked to the concept of uncertainty is that of risk. Risks are threats, hazards, and insecurities arising out of the development of modern society (Caplan, 2000); they are the things that might happen rather than something that has actually happened (Adam et al., 2000). They are not only associated with developments in science (Beck, 2009), but the focus here is on those that stem from science. As scholars point out, journalists play an important role in identifying risks for the wider public (Beck, 1999; Adam et al., 2000; Caplan, 2000; Beck, 2009), so it is important that the risks and uncertainties within science are adequately addressed in news reporting in order for a robust debate to take place about the risks associated with emerging and controversial science. As the nanotechnology case study discusses, the risks associated with science are not always robustly covered and can therefore make the science appear more certain and less risky than it may be. And although there are many reasons why the risk is not discussed in detail in the news, including that risk can be very complex and to report that simply (as journalism attempts to do for its audiences) is challenging, and journalists do not want to overhype risks either (Anderson et al., 2009).

CASE STUDY 1

Nanotechnology/ies

Nanotechnology, or "science of the very small", is an emerging science that works at the scale of one to 100 nanometres (a nanometre is one billionth of a metre). To put that into context, the paper on which a book is printed is roughly 100,000 nanometres wide. It is found in or has been used in nearly every industry and to make consumer products such as stain- and water-repellent clothing; stronger, lighter tennis rackets; and plastic wrap on meat that can detect and destroy contaminants, keeping our food fresher longer. There are some 1,600 nanotechnology-related consumer products marketed today and tens of billions of dollars of commercial and public investment annually (Rensselaer Lally School of Management and Technology, 2004; Sargent, 2008; Project on Emerging Nanotechnologies, 2015; National Nanotechnology Initiative, 2017). At the same time, there are risks and uncertainties associated with nanotechnology. These include the potential toxicity of nanoparticles for people, animals, and the planet; privacy concerns linked to ever smaller computer technology enabling surveillance equipment so small that we would be unaware of its presence; and the ethical questions surrounding the potential for extending life dramatically through repairing damaged cells repeatedly.

Nanotechnology, sometimes referred to as nanoscience, nanotechnologies, nanoscale technologies, etc., is an interdisciplinary field that draws on elements of chemistry, biology, physics, engineering, and computer science (Chakrabarty, 2008; Turner, 2008; Anderson et al., 2009b; National Nanotechnology Initiative, 2017), which means that identifying exactly what counts as nanotechnology can be difficult. That abstract quality to nanotechnology and its pervasiveness in a range of fields is part of what makes it challenging for journalists to write about. Though it is heralded as the next "Industrial Revolution", it has not been as widely published in news as we might expect as a result. There are a range of reasons for this, which we go on to discuss, but part of the challenge here is that nanotechnology goes by so many names and is impacting so many fields and facets of society, the economy, industries, etc. that it could be part of countless stories daily all over the world.

As discussed above, news is the primary place where citizens engage with science after formal education, but studies of public attitudes to science indicate that the public grasp of nanotechnology is very low. In the UK, according to the 2014 Public Attitudes to Science survey (Castell et al., 2014), 85 per cent of the public have either never heard of it or feel uninformed about it. So, citizens are limited in their ability to participate in informed discussion and debate about this emerging field and the potential regulation of it. In order to help democratic debate on these topics, when journalists write about nanotechnology (or other scientific fields for that matter) they can include the range of implications for new developments in nanotechnology, including the potential applications for new scientific findings. Cacciatore and colleagues (2011) note that relating nanotechnology to particular fields and applications (e.g. medicine, consumer products, the military, etc.) helps citizens make judgements about it. Although that may seem like an obvious point to make, a surprising number of news articles in Thompson's research (2012) did not mention how nanotechnology would be or could be used. By including the applications for scientific findings in news, journalists can not only draw interest to the topic, they can also make the science more meaningful and less abstract for their audiences.

In the main, nanotechnology has been positively portrayed in news reporting, arguably overly so. It tends to become news because of the positive and beneficial things it can now, and may in the future, do for individuals, businesses, society, and the planet, and as a result is often celebrated in news content. Reviewing news articles in *The New York Times* and *The Guardian* over a 30-year period, Thompson (2012) found evidence that journalists find stories about nanotechnology largely through desk-research, which has become the norm especially for science reporting (Trench, 2009). In many ways that makes sense as there is not a science-beat equivalent to the police station for a crime reporter. So, press releases from science publishers, universities, and research centres announcing breakthroughs in research and other such announcements are key to drawing journalists' attention to newsworthy stories about nanotechnology. That said, however, the means by which journalists learn about these newsworthy items can potentially lead to less critical questioning as announcements about new developments in nanotechnology naturally privilege the positive elements and can lead to cheerleading science, which is amongst the criticisms of science journalism in scholarship. Therefore, it is important that journalists remember to ask detailed questions about how the latest finding or the newest breakthrough might be used and what questions, concerns, risks, etc. remain or might arise as a result of these new findings/developments.

The latter is important to remember as there is little reporting of risks associated with nanotechnology, which is unusual given the news response to other emerging technologies and potentially controversial science (Satterfield et al., 2009). While nanotechnology holds much promise to bring a range of benefits to people and the planet, what makes it exciting (including that substances at the nanoscale have surprising properties) also makes it potentially risky (e.g., potential toxicity of nanoparticles in our bodies and the environment). Like with medical treatments for different illnesses, there may be serious side effects to new developments in nanotechnology (and not just in nanomedicine). While the positive and, arguably, celebratory nature of the reporting of nanotechnology so far may not seem problematic, it overall lacks the nuance and criticality that we might expect in journalism and could result in disproportionate negative responses if/when a potential problem arises (e.g., unforeseen side-effects of nanotechnology processes or products in the longer term) given the news' otherwise cheerleading science approach thus far. So, it is important for journalists to ask questions about potential side effects and unintended consequences of new developments.

Additionally, where the most commonly documented news values throughout the three decades were breakthroughs and scientific discovery, reporting of nanotechnology has not demonstrated critical questioning by journalists. This was especially true when considering the tone toward the science, which was primarily positive though we would expect it to be more balanced or measured toward the subject. Today, nanotechnology rarely appears in news except when there is a breakthrough (where reporting is almost universally celebrated) or a conflict, although the latter are rare except when a prominent person has commented on nanotechnology (e.g. Prince Charles in the early 2000s and more recently when high-profile entrepreneur Elon Musk suggested "nanotechnology" as a concept is meaningless given how pervasive it is). Regardless of whether it is seen as a single entity (as in nanotechnology) or not, as an enabling technology it is pervasive and so journalists across a range of beats in the newsroom knowingly and unknowingly encounter nanotechnology in their careers. So, awareness amongst journalists is an important first step to seeing nanotechnology in the news and potentially a more nuanced representation of nanotechnology so that citizens can engage in meaningful debates about it.

CASE STUDY 2

Vaccines

According to the World Health Organization (WHO, 2017b), a vaccine is "a biological preparation ... [that] typically contains an agent that resembles a disease-causing microorganism, and is often made from weakened or killed forms of the microbe, its toxins or one of its surface proteins" to protect against specific diseases and infections by stimulating the immune system (WHO, 2017a) to identify and "remember" a pathogen as foreign and to subsequently destroy it (WHO, 2017b). WHO (2017a) estimates that immunisation (typically delivered via vaccination) prevents the deaths of 2–3 million people annually. Globally, billions have benefitted from vaccination, with no other intervention saving more lives except the provision of clean drinking water (Plotkin, 2011). An incredibly cost-effective health intervention, immunisation is made available, via proven strategies, to even the most vulnerable and difficult-to-reach groups (WHO, 2017a).

Though vaccination has been proven to both control and eradicate deadly infectious diseases (WHO, 2017a), it has been subject to varying levels controversy since it was discovered in its modern form by Dr Edward Jenner in 1796 (National Health Service, 2016). Today, despite overwhelming mainstream recognition of the benefits, safety, and value of vaccines, they remain under attack by "sceptics, critics, and a movement set in motion by fraudulent scientists and fuelled by frustrated parents looking for answers to the autism conundrum" (Federman 2014: 417). In fact, Jang et al. (2017) refer to the link between autism and the combined MMR (measles, mumps, and rubella) vaccine in particular as one of the most controversial science issues of recent times. Arguably the media have played a key role in creating, or at least perpetuating, the long-standing controversy around the vaccine–autism link (Clarke, 2008), which has been almost universally rejected by experts in both science and medicine (Dixon and Clarke, 2013). As this case study will go on to discuss, the controversy has resulted in significant and wide-ranging consequences.

In February 1998, an article by Wakefield et al. in British medical journal *The Lancet*, one of the oldest and most prestigious medical journals internationally, implicated the MMR vaccine in the onset of autism. Jang et al. (2017) note that the article, which has since been retracted, was met with firm scepticism by experts in science and medicine; however, the suspected link attracted global media interest and many parents worldwide were frightened upon hearing the news. A subsequent decrease in vaccine uptake in countries resulted in countries like the US and UK, where rates dropped by up to 30 per cent in some areas (Petts and Niemeyer 2004 cited by Clarke, 2011). Two decades after Wakefield et al.'s (1998) infamous study was published the impact of the assertion that vaccines cause autism persists. In terms of public opinion, while 84 per cent of Britons say that the benefits of vaccines overshadow the risks (Castell et al., 2014), a recent study indicated that 29 per cent of American adults believe they cause autism (National Consumers League, 2014). Health behaviours also remain affected. While vaccination rates in the developing world are rising, they are on the decline in the developed world overall and in North America in particular (Krishna, 2017). Current rates of immunisation against measles in the US and Canada are 91 per cent and 84 per cent respectively, which is far below the 95 per cent required for "herd immunity" (Akumu 2015 cited by Krishna, 2017), which refers to the indirect protection against a particular disease provided to an entire population when a certain percentage of people been vaccinated (Andre et al., 2008). In the UK, it has taken almost 20 years for UK vaccination rates to recover post-controversy.

Moreover, vaccine-preventable diseases are now reappearing in developed countries where they were once essentially eradicated. For example, measles was declared eliminated in the US in 2000; however, 1,586 cases were reported between 2010 and 2017 (Centers for Disease Control [CDC], 2018). Unsurprisingly, most of these cases occurred in unvaccinated people. Meanwhile, measles cases are also increasing in the UK (rising sharply from 2000 to 2013, with 531 cases reported in England and Wales in 2016) and in European countries (Oxford Vaccine Group, 2017).

The above strongly indicates that vaccination rates continue to be an important issue (and therefore potentially an important news story) for public health both within a country and globally, especially given the gap in vaccination rates in developing countries due to access and infrastructure. Worldwide, vaccination rates have stagnated in recent years, with approximately 19.9 million infants still going without basic childhood vaccines (WHO, 2018). As Schwartz (2017) states, increasing public confidence in vaccines is an important challenge for public health institutions, which Boykoff and Boykoff (2004) suggest the news media (because of the social "relationship" between journalists and their audiences) are obliged to not only identify and provide information about important issues, but to highlight possible solutions to those that are problematic. Thus, journalists can and should arguably play an important role in this confidence-building process by ensuring that news coverage of vaccines is accurate (i.e., appropriately balanced and based in fact rather than opinion) and rigorous.

Since the publication of Wakefield's research, there has been considerable evidence discrediting a connection between autism and the MMR vaccine, including the ethics, conflicts of interest, and scope and size of the research. The study had included only 12 participants, which is too small a sample on which to draw such a definitive conclusion. More recent research looking at the association between vaccination and autism included data from 1.2 million children and concluded there is no such association (Taylor et al., 2014). Therefore, it is useful for journalists to have some understanding of good practice in scientific research, which can help with ethical and accurate reporting through critical questioning. Despite the criticism of Wakefield's study and repeated calls for retraction, it took *The Lancet* 12 years to retract the study by which point there was a crisis of confidence in vaccines exacerbated by significant global news coverage.

While some media coverage of the MMR controversy has been criticised and blamed for declines in vaccination rates and perceptions of vaccine safety, others (e.g., Dixon, 2002 cited by Lewis and Speers, 2003) contend that most journalists covered the story both fairly and responsibly. In addition to a lack of critical questioning about the extent and ethics of the research, perhaps most problematic in the reporting of the MMR controversy was the source strategies of journalists at the time. Scientists were the most oft-quoted sources in news, followed by parents (Lewis and Speers, 2003). Despite overwhelming consensus in the science and medical communities for vaccination, the news reporting disproportionately represented proponents of the link between MMR and autism. This includes the voice of parents in the news responding to the perceived safety of the vaccine for their children. This included questions to then Prime Minister Tony Blair who refused to answer whether his youngest son had received the MMR vaccine, citing his son's privacy (Lewis and Speers, 2003). Blair's refusal to answer was widely reported and did little to encourage public confidence in the MMR vaccine's safety. Ultimately while it seemed that most British parents were still opting for vaccination, those quoted in news reports were five times more likely to speak negatively about the vaccine as opposed to positively (Lewis and Speers, 2003). This imbalance of opinion in reports, or "false balance", as discussed previously, could have been avoided had there been an accurate representation of parental views and contributed to the impression that fewer and fewer parents were opting to vaccinate their children.

Journalists should be aware that falsely balanced presentations create an illusion of disagreement within scientific and medical opinion about the vaccine–autism link or another controversial issue, thus generating uncertainty where it doesn't exist and sometimes giving fringe groups unwarranted visibility (Clarke, 2008). Given today's media landscape, where debate and discussion about these issues increasingly take place online and news stories may emerge from that online debate, it is ever more important for journalists to fact check the scientific basis of truth claims like these. Otherwise, it may appear as an unintentional endorsement or at the very least lend credibility to truth claims grounded in or at least partially based on emotion rather than sufficient scientific evidence.

To appropriately balance controversial science stories like the vaccine-autism controversy, journalists should provide enough information to make clear when a claim has been almost unanimously rejected by the scientific and/or medical communities. This can be challenging when high-profile sources, including politicians and celebrities publicly express doubt about the safety of vaccines. However, giving undue attention to such claims over the overwhelming medical and scientific evidence to the contrary can have significant public health consequences. This is what Dixon et al. (2015) describe as the "weight of evidence", which can be more persuasive and accessible to the news audience if depicted in infographics and other visual storytelling techniques. For example, the WHO has created an animated infographic that explains current trends in global vaccinations and other infographics on the importance of vaccinations and the implications of reduced vaccination rates globally.

News reports on vaccines and other public health stories involving risk should also include guidance information for the audience (e.g., names, times, and locations of events, and the provision of guidance or "what to do" in a situation involving risk) that equips people with knowledge to make informed decisions. As Clarke argues, journalists can (and arguably should) do so because "as with political participation, media can serve as a resource through which people become aware of an issue, aware of strategies to address this issue, and potentially motivated to take action" (Clarke, 2011: 622).

When using online information to research stories about vaccinations, journalists must maintain a critical eye. Despite substantial scientific evidence disproving the link between vaccination and autism, there continues to be a proliferation of antivaccination claims not supported by scientific or medical evidence (Federman, 2014). Research has shown that the internet and social media, in particular, facilitate the spread of hearsay and scientific and medical misinformation (Wilson and Keelan, 2013 cited by Jang et al., 2017), which is problematic for a number of reasons including that people regularly use a range of online sources to inform personal decisions about vaccination (Brunson, 2013). Further, parents who go online for information about vaccines are also more likely to be hesitant to vaccinate their children (Kata, 2012). Where parents may also include online journalism as part of their research, journalists can play an important role in dispelling the misinformation about vaccines by clearly and accurately reporting that the link between vaccinations and autism has been disproved in the scientific and medical community.

Finally, journalists use the internet and social media debates as a means of checking public sentiment on important news stories. As Kata (2012) has found, social media and other online sources are used by the anti-vaccination community to spread misinformation about vaccines. Typical tactics include suppressing dissent, "skewing science" and attacking detractors. Studies such as Jang et al. (2017) suggest strong support for social media leading the mainstream media agenda around the vaccine–autism link. Although this conflict around vaccinations may appear newsworthy, journalists should consider the motivations and biases underpinning the claims made.

CASE STUDY 3

Agricultural and medical biotechnology

Biotechnology is a group of technologies – rather than a single technology as the name might suggest – that use "living cells and/or biological molecules to solve problems and make useful products" (Keener et al., 12). There are many applications for biotechnology, but here we focus on two that have been more controversial in news reporting – agricultural (especially genetically modified (GM) crops/food) and medical (especially stem cell research and "human cloning"). In the main, biotechnology, as with the other case studies, has had relatively good press overall where the benefits of biotechnology applications are well documented in the reporting. And although the risks are reported, the news tends to indicate that overall benefits outweigh the risks. The primarily positive tone of news reporting was especially true early on (see, for example, Marks et al., 2007; Nisbet and Lewenstein, 2002; Priest, 2001b), but there has been some crisis/controversy within news reporting of GM food and stem cell research that offer lessons to be learned for journalists.

Genetically modified foods (also referred to as genetically engineered foods, biotechnology-derived foods, transgenic foods) are foods which have had their genetic material (DNA) modified in some way that would otherwise not occur naturally. There is some resistance within the scientific community for the term "genetically modified food" as imprecise because all food can be described as modified through domestication and farming processes (e.g., selecting which crops to plant from the best seeds). The UK and European public have been and continue to be leery of GM foods (Castells et al., 2014). According to Castells and her colleagues' work in the UK Public Attitudes to Science Survey, GM foods continue to be a hot button issue amongst the public, and although study participants cited benefits (e.g., increased food production, increased plant disease resistance, and greater consistency in crop quality, taste, and nutrition) they continue to have concerns about health effects and the potential for longer-term risks associated with GM foods. As Bawa and Anilakumar (2013) note, public concern primarily focuses on "human and environmental safety, labelling and consumer choice, intellectual property rights, ethics, food security, poverty reduction, and environmental conservation" (2013: 1035). Therefore, there is a range of stories that journalists can do to investigate and address public concern about GM foods and help people make informed choices about GM foods and crops.

In reviewing a range of academic studies on safety, risks, and public concern about GM foods, Bawa and Anilakumar (2013) say GM foods potentially address some of the global challenges of the twenty-first century, but also acknowledge that there are a range of risks (known and unknown) associated with GM foods and crops. The potential benefits of GM foods and crops include improved food production to address global food shortages, developing crops that are disease and insect resistant, enhancing the nutrition of foods to combat malnutrition in the developing world, and so on. Further there has been a range of studies pointing to the potential for GM foods to ensure food supplies in the face of climate change impacts globally (see, for example, Hanjra and Qureshi, 2010; Lu et al., 2017; Qaim and Kouser, 2013).

There has been considerable academic research looking at the reporting of agricultural biotechnology, especially GM foods. Some have suggested that the reporting is more focused on the politics than the science of GM foods and highlighted risk over benefits (Hoban, 1995) or at least are broadly ambivalent to the technology (Marks et al., 2007). In other words, news reporting of agricultural biotechnology focuses on policy and political debate about GM foods and crops, rather than discusses the science behind it and providing citizens with evidence-based information on which to make informed judgements. The reporting has been sensationalised with headlines and references to "Frankenfoods" and similar science fiction themes (Augoustinos, 2010), which draws attention to the issues but does not engage in robust and critical questioning of the issues related to GM foods and crops. As with the vaccinations case study, the discussion is more emotionally driven than based in scientific evidence.

In many ways, the same can be said when considering medical applications for biotechnology as similar emotional arguments emerge in the reporting of stem cell research. Specifically, reporting of stem cell research has focused on the backlash from the pro-life community and some policy-makers' rejection of embryonic stem cell research on religious grounds. Stem cells are unspecialised cells that can develop into different kinds of cells in the body, thereby playing an important role in maintaining and repairing organs and tissue. There are two types of stem cells: embryonic stem cells (which can develop into any type of cell) and adult stem cells (which are more limited in their ability to develop into other cell types). Much of the controversy and public concern around stem cell research centres on embryonic stem cells because it raises questions of "sanctity of life" vs "quality of life", drawing out religious arguments particularly in the US (Allum et al., 2017). Even still, there is broad support for stem cell research in the US, Canada and Europe (Allum et al., 2017). As with nanotechnology, although most broadly support the science, UK citizens feel less informed about stem cell research (Castell et al., 2014), which is something journalists can address through reporting on research and applications for medical biotechnology such as the regeneration and repair of tissue to address a range of diseases.

Academic research looking at the reporting of stem cells has documented that by and large the reporting could be read as positive, framing it around scientific progress and economic development (Nisbet et al., 2003). As with other controversial science topics, biotechnology reporting is dominated by official sources, namely government officials, industry sources, and scientists, although journalists should look for opportunities to include a greater range of sources including citizen voices. Biotechnology is largely focused on scientific, industrial, and economic development. However, the more controversial elements surrounding stem cell research have also included religious interests and environmental groups. The news reporting in these cases focuses on the dramatic conflict between those for and against stem cell research and includes emotive language and images, especially from stem cell research opponents. The language used, often from pro-life interests, includes adjectives like "evil", "murderous", and "gruesome" to describe the research and likens it to "playing God", "Dr Frankenstein", "Brave New Worlds", and the Nazi Holocaust. Though these references add to the drama of the narratives, they are problematic for a range of reasons, including sensationalism and inaccurate analogies. The science fiction references, which are often used in news reporting of science and perhaps especially for controversial science, are likely included not only for the dramatic imagery it evokes but also to make the science relatable for the audience. However, in doing so it potentially blurs the boundary between scientific fact and science fiction.

Conclusion

This chapter has pointed out the important role that journalists play not only in society but also in the reporting of science. As we noted earlier in the chapter, journalists covering science and who encounter science while reporting other news (e.g., forensics in crime stories, the availability of new medical treatments in the NHS, new consumer products enabled by scientific and technological developments) can create an audience for science and foster democratic debate about it. Of course, for the debate to be robust, so too must the reporting be robust. It should highlight the risks and benefits of science and technology in ways that are meaningful for the audience, include a range of sources to help draw out key areas of debate though taking time to contextualise the highlighted perspectives and not as a replacement for appropriate fact-checking, and ensure that the reporting dispels myth and misinformation rather than contributes to it or perpetuates it.

References

Adam, B., Beck, U., and Loon, J.V. 2000. *The risk society and beyond critical issues for social theory*. London; Thousand Oaks, Calif.: SAGE.

Allan, S. 2002. *Media, risk and the environment*. In: Media, Risk and Science. Buckingham: Open University Press.

Allan, S. 2008. *Making science newsworthy: exploring the conventions of science journalism*. In: Holliman, R., Whitelegg, E., Scanlon, E., Smidt, S. and Thomas, J. (eds.) *Investigating*

Science Communication in the Information Age: Implications for Public Engagement and Popular Media. Oxford: Oxford University Press.

Allum, N., Allansdottir, A., Gaskell, G., Hampel, J., Jackson, J., Moldovan, A., Priest, S., Stares, S., and Stoneman, P. 2017. Religion and the public ethics of stem-cell research: attitudes in Europe, Canada and the United States. *PLoS ONE*, 12(4): e0176274. Available: https://doi.org/ 10.1371/journal.pone.0176274 [Accessed 4 January 2018].

Anderson, A., Petersen, A., Wilkinson, C., and Allan, S. 2009. *Nanotechnology, risk and communication.* Basingstoke: Palgrave Macmillan.

Andre, F.E., Booy, R., Bock, H.L., Clemens, J., Datta, S.K., John, T.J., Lee, B.W., Lolekha, S., Peltola, H., Ruff, T.A., Santosham, M., and Schmitt, H.J. 2008, Vaccination greatly reduces disease disability, death and inequity worldwide. *Bulletin of the World Health Organization*, 86(2), 140–146.

Antilla, L. 2005. Climate of scepticism: US newspaper coverage of the science of climate change. *Global Environmental Change-Human and Policy Dimensions*, 15(4), 338–352.

Augustinos, M., Crabb, S., and Shepherd, R. 2010. Genetically modified food in the news: media representations of the GM debate in the UK. *Public Understanding of Science*, 19(1), 98–114.

Bauer, M.W., and Bucchi, M. 2007. *Journalism, science and society: science communication between news and public relations.* London, Routledge.

Bauer, M.W., and Gregory, J. 2007. From journalism to corporate communication in post-war Britain. In: Bauer, M.W. and Bucchi, M. (eds.) *Journalism, Science and Society: Science Communication between News and Public Relations.* New York: Routledge.

Bawa, A.S., and Anilakumar, K.R. 2013. Genetically modified foods: safety, risks and public concerns—a review. *Journal of Food Science and Technology*, 50(6), 1035–1046.

Beck, U. 1999. From industrial society to risk society: Questions of survival, social structure and ecological enlightenment. In: *World Risk Society.* Cambridge: Polity Press.

Beck, U. 2009. *World at Risk.* Cambridge: Polity Press.

Boykoff, M.T. 2007. From convergence to contention: United States mass media representations of anthropogenic climate change science. *Transactions of the Institute of British Geographers*, 32(4), 477–489.

Boykoff, M.T., and Boykoff, J.M. 2004. Balance as bias: Global warming and the US prestige press. *Global Environmental Change*, 14(2), 125–136.

Boykoff, M.T., and Boykoff, J.M. 2007. Climate change and journalistic norms: A case-study of US mass-media coverage. *Geoforum*, 38(6), 1190–1204.

Brunson, E.K. 2013. The Impact of Social Networks on Parents' Vaccination Decisions. *Pediatrics*, 131(5), e1397–e1404.

Cacciatore, M.A., Scheufele, D.A., and Corley, E.A. 2009. From enabling technology to applications: The evolution of risk perceptions about nanotechnology. *Public Understanding of Science*, 20(3), 385–404.

Caplan, P. 2000. *Risk Revisited. Anthropology, culture, and society.* London; Sterling, Va.: Pluto Press.

Carvalho, A. 2007. Ideological cultures and media discourses on scientific knowledge: re-reading news on climate change. *Public Understanding of Science*, 16(2), 223–243.

Castell, S., Charlton, A., Clemence, M., Pettigrew, N., Pope, S., Quigley, A., Navin Shah, J., and Silman, T. 2014. *Public Attitudes to Science 2014* [online]. London: Ipsos MORI.

Centers for Disease Control and Prevention (CDC). 2018. Measles cases and outbreaks [online]. Atlanta. Available from: https://www.cdc.gov/measles/cases-outbreaks. html [Accessed 12 December 2018].

Chakrabarty, A. 2008. *Nanotechnology: an introduction.* New Delhi: Rajat Publications.

Clarke, C.E. 2008. A question of balance: The autism-vaccine controversy in the British and American elite press. *Science Communication*, 30(1), 77–107.

Clarke, C.E. 2011. A case of conflicting norms? Mobilizing and accountability information in newspaper coverage of the autism-vaccine controversy. *Public Understanding of Science*, 20(5), 609–626.

Dixon, G.N., and Clarke, C.E. 2012. Heightening uncertainty around certain science: Media coverage, false balance, and the autism-vaccine controversy. *Science Communication*, 35(3), 358–382.

Dixon, G.N., McKeever, B.W., Holton, A.E., Clarke, C., and Eosco, G. 2015. The power of a picture: Overcoming scientific misinformation by communicating weight of evidence information with visual exemplars. *Journal of Communication*, 65(4), 639–659.

Dunwoody, S. 1999. Scientists, Journalists, and the Meaning of Uncertainty. In: Friedman, S. M., Dunwoody, S. and Rogers, C. L. (eds.) *Communicating Uncertainty: Media coverage of New and Controversial Science*. Mahwah, NJ: Lawrence Erlbaum Assoc.

Federman, R.S. 2014. Understanding vaccines: A public imperative. *Yale Journal of Biology and Medicine*, 87(4), 417–422.

Friedman, S.M., and Egolf, B.P. 2005. Nanotechnology: risks and the media. *Technology and Society Magazine, IEEE*, 24, 5–11.

Gorss, J., and Lewenstein, B. 2005. The salience of small: Nanotechnology coverage in the American press, 1986–2004. Paper presented at the International Communication Association (ICA), New York.

Hanjra, M.A., and Qureshi, M.E. (2010). Global water crisis and future food security in an era of climate change. *Food Policy*, 35(5), 365e377.

Hansen, A. 1994. Journalistic practices and science reporting in the British press. *Public Understanding of Science*, 3(2), 111–134.

Hoban, T.J. 1995. The construction of food biotechnology as a social issue. In: D. Maurer and J. Sobal (eds.) *Eating Agendas: Food and Nutrition and Social Problems*. New York: Walter de Gruyter Inc.

Hughes, J. 2007. Insects or neutrons? Science news values in interwar Britain. In: Bauer, M. W. and Bucchi, M. (eds.) *Journalism, Science and Society: Science Communication between News and Public Relations*. New York: Routledge.

Jang, S.M., McKeever, B.W., McKeever, R. and Kim, J.K. 2017. From social media to mainstream news: The information flow of the vaccine-autism controversy in the US, Canada, and the UK. *Health Communication*. Available from: http://dx.doi.org/10.10 80/10410236.2017.1384433 [Accessed 17 October 2017].

Kata, A. 2012. Anti-vaccine activists, Web 2.0, and the postmodern paradigm – An overview of tactics and tropes used online by the anti-vaccination movement. *Vaccine*, 30(25), 3778–3789.

Kitzinger, J., Henderson, L., Smart, A., and Eldridge, J. 2003. Media coverage of the social and ethical implications of human genetic research. The Wellcome Trust.

Kitzinger, J., and Williams, C. 2005. Forecasting science futures: Legitimising hope and calming fears in the embryo stem cell debate. *Social Science and Medicine*, 61(3), 731–740.

Krishna, A. 2017. Poison or prevention? Understanding the linkages between vaccine-negative individuals' knowledge deficiency, motivations, and active communication behaviors. *Health Communication*. Available from: https://doi.org/10.1080/10410236. 2017.1331307 [Accessed 17 October 2017].

Lewenstein, B.V. 1992. The meaning of 'public understanding of science' in the United States after World War II. *Public Understanding of Science*, 1(1), 45–68.

Lewenstein, B.V. 2005. What counts as a "social and ethical issue" in nanotechnology? *International Journal for Philosophy of Chemistry*, 11(1), 5–18.

Lewis, J., and Speers, T. 2003. Misleading media reporting? The MMR story. *Nature Reviews Immunology*, 3, 913–918.

Listerman, T. 2010. Framing of science issues in opinion-leading news: international comparison of biotechnology issue coverage. *Public Understanding of Science*, 19(1), 5–15.

Liu, H., and Priest, S. 2009. Understanding public support for stem cell research: media communication, interpersonal communication and trust in key actors. *Public Understanding of Science*, 18(6), 704–718.

Lu, H., McComas., K.A, and Besley, J.C. 2017. Messages promoting genetic modification of crops in the context of climate change: evidence for psychological reactance. *Appetite*, 108, 104–116.

Marks, L.A., Kalaitzandonakes, N., Wilkins, L. and Zakharovam L. 2007. Mass media framing of biotechnology news. *Public Understanding of Science*, 16(2), 183–203.

Miller, M.M., and Riechert, B.P. 2000. Interest group strategies and journalistic norms: News media framing of environmental issues. In: Adam, B., Allan, S., and Carter, C. (eds.) *Environmental Risks and the Media*. London: Routledge.

National Consumers League, 2014. Survey: One third of American parents mistakenly link vaccines to autism [Press Release], April 2. Available at: http://www.nclnet. org/survey_one_third_of_american_parents_mistakenly_link_vaccines_to_autism [Accessed 30 December 2017].

National Health Service (NHS), 2016. The history of vaccination [online]. Available from: https://www.nhs.uk/Conditions/vaccinations/Pages/the-history-of-vaccination.aspx [Accessed 27 December 2017].

National Nanotechnology Initiative. 2017. What is nanotechnology? [Online]. Arlington, VA: National Nanotechnology Initiative. Available: https://www.nano. gov/nanotech-101/what [Accessed 4 January 2018].

National Science Board. 2016. Science and technology: public attitudes and understanding. In: *Science & Engineering Indicators 2016* [online]. Alexandria, VA: National Science Foundation.

Nisbet, M.C. and Lewenstein, B.V. 2002. Biotechnology and the American Media: The Policy Press and the Elite Press, 1970 to 1999. *Science Communication*, 23(4), 359–391.

Nisbet, M.C. and Scheufele, D.A. 2009. What's next for science communication? Promising directions and lingering distractions. *American Journal of Botany*, 96(10), 1767–1778.

Nisbet, M.C., Brossard, D., and Kroepsch, A. 2003. Framing science: The stem cell controversy in an age of press/politics. *Harvard International Journal of Press-Politics*, 8(2), 36–70.

Oxford Vaccine Group, 2017. Measles [online]. Available from: http://vk.ovg.ox.ac.uk/ measles [Accessed 4 January 2018].

Plotkin, S. 2011. Foreword. In: Bazin, H. *Vaccination: A History From Lady Montagu to Genetic Engineering*. Montrouge: John Libbey, 11–12.

Priest, S.H. 2001a. Cloning: A study in news production. *Public Understanding of Science*, 10(1), 59–69.

Priest, S.H. 2001b. *A Grain of Truth: The Media, the Public, and Biotechnology*. Plymouth: Rowman & Littlefield Publishers, Inc.

Project on Emerging Nanotechnologies. 2015. Consumer Products [Online]. Washington, D.C.: Pew Charitable Trusts. Available: http://www.nanotechproject.org/cpi/ [Accessed 15 December 2018].

Qaim, M., and Kouser, S. (2013). Genetically modified crops and food security. *PLoS One*, 8(6), e64879. Available: https://doi.org/10.1371/journal.pone.0064879 [Accessed 4 January 2018].

Rensselaer Lally School of Management and Technology. 2004. Nanotechnology sector report: Technology roadmap project. Troy, NY: Rensselaer Polytechnic Institute.

Salleh, A. 2008. The fourth estate and the fifth branch: the news media, GM risk, and democracy in Australia. *New Genetics and Society*, 27(3), 233–250.

Sandler, R., and Kay, W.D. 2006. The GMO-Nanotech (Dis)Analogy? Bulletin of Science, Technology & Society, 26(1), 57–62.

Sargent, J.F. 2008. Nanotechnology and U.S. Competitiveness: Issues and Options. Washington, D.C: Congressional Research Service.

Satterfield, T., Kandlikar, M., Beaudrie, C.E.H., Conti, J., and Herr Harthorn, B. 2009. Anticipating the perceived risk of nanotechnologies. *Nature Nanotechnology*, 4, 752–758.

Schafer, M.S. 2009. From public understanding to public engagement: An empirical assessment of changes in science coverage. *Science Communication*, 30(4), 475–505.

Schafer, M.S. 2010. Taking stock: A meta-analysis of studies on the media's coverage of science. *Public Understanding of Science*, [Online]. Available: https://journals.sagepub.com/doi/10.1177/0963662510387559 [Accessed 15 December 2018].

Schwartz, J.L. 2017. Vaccines and the Trump Administration—Reasons for Optimism Amid Uncertainty. *American Journal of Public Health*, 107(12), 1892–1893.

Stocking, S.H. 1999. How journalists deal with scientific uncertainty. In: Friedman, S. M., Dunwoody, S. and Rogers, C. L. (eds.) *Communicating Uncertainty: Media Coverage of New and Controversial Science*. Mahwah, NJ: Lawrence Erlbaum Assoc.

Taylor, L.E., Swerdfeger, A.L., and Eslick, G.D., 2014. Vaccines are not associated with autism: An evidence based meta-analysis of case-control and cohort studies. *Vaccine*, 32(19), 3623–3629.

Thompson, S., 2012. News about nanotechnology: a longitudinal framing analysis of newspaper reporting on nanotechnology. Thesis (PhD). Bournemouth University.

Trench, B. 2009. Science reporting in the electronic embrace of the internet. In: Holliman, R., Whitelegg, E., Scanlon, E., Smidt, S., and Thomas, J. (eds.) *Investigating Science Communication in the Information Age: Implications for public engagement and popular media*. Oxford: Oxford University Press.

Trumbo, C.W., Sprecker, K.J., Dumlao, R.J., Yun, G.W., and Duke, S. 2001. Use of E-mail and the Web by science writers. *Science Communication*, 22(4), 347–378.

Turner, A. 2008. *Nanotechnology: an introduction*. Chandigarh: Abhishek Publications.

Wakefield, A.J., Murch, S.H., Anthony, A., Linnell, J., Casson, D.M., Malik, M., Berelowitz. M., Dhillon, A.P., Thomson, M.A., Harvey, P., Valentine, A., Davies, S.E., and Walker-Smith, J.A., 1998. Retracted: Ileal-lymphoid-nodular hyperplasia, non-specific colitis, and pervasive developmental disorder in children. *The Lancet*, 351(9103), 637–641.

Weigold, M.F. 2001. Communicating science: A review of the literature. *Science Communication*, 23(2), 164–193.

Williams, A., and Clifford, S. 2009. Mapping the Field: Specialist science news journalism in the UK national media. The Risk, Science and the Media Research Group. Cardiff: Cardiff University School of Journalism, Media and Cultural Studies.

World Health Organization (WHO), 2017a. Immunization [online]. Geneva. Available from: http://www.who.int/topics/immunization/en/ [Accessed 27 December 2017].

World Health Organization (WHO), 2017b. Vaccines [online]. Geneva. Available from: http://www.who.int/topics/vaccines/en/ [Accessed 27 December 2017].

World Health Organization (WHO). 2018. Immunization coverage [online]. Geneva. Available from: https://www.who.int/news-room/fact-sheets/detail/immunization-coverage [Accessed 12 December 2018].

Zehr, S. C. 1999. Scientists' representations of uncertainty. In: Friedman, S. M., Dunwoody, S. and Rogers, C. L. (eds.) *Communicating Uncertainty: Media Coverage of New and Controversial Science*. Mahawah, NJ: Lawrence Erlbaum Assoc.

10

REPORTING CLIMATE CHANGE

Robert Wyss

The social issue

One of the biggest news stories of the twenty-first century, and for that matter the last decades of the twentieth century, is how the world's atmosphere is growing hotter. Scientists agree that rising industrial air emissions will heat the planet and cause drought, famine, violent storms, and other environmental calamities.

Those of us in journalism who cover the environment have struggled at times to fully understand and then to engage news consumers in the seriousness of climate change. Despite those obstacles, in most nations climate change is viewed as the most dangerous threat in the world, virtually tied with the Islamic State as a security threat, according to results by the Pew Research Center in 2017. Many fear that the consequences of climate change will be so debilitating that it could lead to mass destruction, warfare, and deaths. However, in the United States research has found that climate change ranked a low third as a security threat. One poll found that 77 per cent of respondents labelled attacks from the Islamic State as the most serious security threat, 71 per cent labelled cyberwarfare, and 56 per cent said global warming. Researchers blamed the lower numbers on a partisan divide in the US (Friedman, 2017), but it may also demonstrate that journalists need to hone their reporting on the issue.

Those of us in the US have documented how climate change has become politically divisive. President Donald Trump has called the issue a "hoax" (Jacobson, 2016) and in 2017 the president backed out of the terms of the 2015 Paris climate accord (Shear, 2017). While the science community is overwhelmingly convinced that humans are warming the planet, as journalists covering this issue we must be vigilant because a massive public relations campaign funded primarily by the fossil fuel industry has been underway designed to sow doubt about the science (Oreskes and Conway, 2010).

Environmental stories are rarely dramatic, and climate change is particularly slow-moving, difficult to portray, and a challenge in demonstrating how it affects individuals. A number of journalists have observed that no one ever broke a story announcing that climate change erupted today.

Scientists have struggled to get their message out at times. Many have long preferred the lab and their studies to a podium and an audience. They have developed a communication system that is precise and specific when talking to each other, but one that with its jargon and acronyms seems more like a foreign language to the press and public (Hartz and Chappell, 1998). That has resulted in misunderstandings, prompting stumbles in public policy dealing with climate change. That, in turn, caused an increasing number of scientists to work to improve their communications and their engagement with the public, the press and policymakers

Introduction

As an energy and environmental reporter in the 1980s and 1990s for a larger newspaper in the Northeastern United States, I rarely wrote about climate issues. I faced many of the challenges journalists still encounter today – the issue was difficult to localize, it was abstract and complex. Plus, scientists were struggling with communication. It was easy to set the issue aside.

That was changing by 2006 when as a journalism professor I wrote *Covering the Environment*, the seminal textbook that defined environmental journalism. By then the issue of climate change was being clearly identified as a major issue facing the world. Yet other issues, from biodiversity and species extinction to the threat of overpopulation, were also concerns.

In 2016 I began writing a new second edition of the textbook and by then there was no mistaking what was clearly not just the paramount environmental issue, but one that could compete with terrorism or any other global threat. It is now clear that unless an unforeseen and radical development occurs, the consequences of the globe's rising temperature will be dealt with not just by our generation, but future generations. Fortunately, journalists are far more adept today than they were in the past; some of the best journalism today has been addressing climate and its impacts. Consider just a few examples. *The Guardian* launched an ambitious editorial campaign in 2015 called "Keep it in the Ground" that urged financial institutions to divest from oil, natural gas, and coal companies (Randerson, 2015). A consortium including the Center for Public Integrity, Al Jazeera and *USAToday* produced a series called the Carbon War that focused on super polluters that wilfully spewed alarming amount of greenhouse gases into the atmosphere (Morris, 2016). The *Seattle Times* produced "Sea Change: The Pacific's Perilous Turn", featuring a stunning nine-minute video that documented how rising levels of carbon dioxide were imperiling the ocean and seafood that a billion people depend upon (Welch and Ringman, 2013).

Over the years I have led students to many of these stories. In the Florida Everglades we talked to scientists about how rising sea levels could one day consume this unique estuary. In Louisiana we met survivors of Hurricane Katrina and walked on new barrier islands that are being erected in the Gulf of Mexico to provide buffers for future storms.

In considering what is important in reporting about climate change, I have developed the following points to consider:

- Don't be intimidated by the science. Terms such as ocean acidification and carbon sink are nothing more than jargon used by scientists. One does not need an advanced degree in climatology or chemistry to understand the basics; although the issue will take time to understand.
- Finding the right expert is absolutely critical. It is also important to cultivate sources within the sciences that can provide valuable assistance. While the science is clear, the politics of the issue often clouds the truth.
- The important stories that will make individuals care about this issue take time to report. One does not need to go to Greenland where glaciers are melting to find a story; it might be there on the eroding coast of New Jersey or the absence of bees in an English cottage garden.

The research

The terms climate change and global warming are sometimes used interchangeably to describe a build-up in global temperature produced by human activity. Climate change can also mean global cooling and either increases or decreases in global temperature, which can be spawned by natural events or forces. Scientists agree that the earth's temperature has been rising dramatically and that human activity is the likely cause.

A network of scientists formed by the United Nations, the Intergovernmental Panel on Climate Change, has warned that global temperatures will rise between 2.5 and 10 degrees Fahrenheit in the future. In its 2013 Summary for Policymakers report, the IPCC was "unequivocal" in stating that the warming is occurring, noting that the observed changes since the 1950s are unprecedented in long-term global history (IPCC, 2013). Oceans have warmed, snow and ice have disappeared, and greenhouse gases have risen.

Early suggestions that these increases were part of a natural variability have been discarded for findings that a build-up of gases in the upper atmosphere are the cause. These gases, including water vapour, carbon dioxide, methane, ozone, and nitrous oxide, create what has been called the greenhouse effect, allowing the sun's radiant energy to warm the earth while slowing the escape of heat back into space. The IPCC said that the earth's surface has warmed more in each of the last three decades than any time since the 1850s and that the period between 1983 and 2012 was the warmest 30-year period in the last 1,400 years. The report provided detailed factual evidence to support ocean warming, ice sheet melting in Greenland, Antarctica and elsewhere, sea level rise, and increased levels of carbon dioxide and other greenhouse gases. The uptake of carbon dioxide into the upper atmosphere began around 1750 with the dawn of the Industrial Revolution. Skeptics have criticized models that forecast what was happening with the atmosphere and the IPCC addressed this issue head-on by stating those models have improved significantly and are accurate. "Human influence on the climate system is clear," the 2013 report stated (IPCC, 2013).

Internationally, the IPCC that was formed in 1989 has become the key source for information about the science of the climate. It issued its first report in 1990, and has continued to make reports periodically. The fifth report was issued in November 2014, the sixth was scheduled for acceptance and publication in April 2021 (IPCC, n.d.). About 1,300 scientists from nations around the world have spent years tracking the most recent research to determine what should go into a report. The reports do not feature policy recommendations, but many of the conclusions based on the science have often been stark in warning what the consequences could be without action to reduce greenhouse gases (C2ES, n.d.).

The political and public policy side of climate change has been far more complicated. The United Nations Framework Convention on Climate Change (UNFCCC), composed of nearly 200 nations including the United States, was created in 1992 as a means to negotiate international strategies on climate change. This led to what was called the Kyoto Protocol in 1997 that called on 37 of the world's industrialized nations to reduce their greenhouse gases. The US failed to endorse the agreement, and emissions continued to soar not only in the US but such developing industrial nations as China and India (West et al., 2003). Still, the nations kept meeting and finally what was billed as a monumental breakthrough occurred in December 2015 with the Paris Agreement. The representatives of the 196 nations participating, which included all major powers, agreed to limit global rises in temperature to no more than 3.6 degrees in Fahrenheit (2 degrees Celsius) in this century, or if they could, an even greater target of 2.6 degrees F (1.5 degrees C) was also established. The subsidiary organization of the UNFCCC that was the primary participant in Paris and continued to meet periodically to tweak the public policy issues involved in the Paris Agreement is called the Conference of the Parties (COP). Each time this conference meets in an international city the number designating each successive conference is added to the name. Paris has been called COP21 (UNFCCC, 2014).

Covering climate change

When several severe hurricanes struck the Caribbean and later the Gulf coast of the United States, many wondered if the cause was climate change. The answer was no. However, scientists explained that climate change likely had influenced the strength of the storms. In the days when the storms formed in the Atlantic the ocean temperature was warmer, because the planet has become warmer, and that exacerbated the storms (Fritz, 2017).

That example is a demonstration of how careful reporters must be in covering climate change. Getting the question right is important, finding the best sources has become critical. About 1,300 scientists work with the IPCC, which makes them a good starting point in looking for sources. Another one would be universities or research institutes. Public information officers at these institutions are paid to assist. Yet another option would be professional associations that represent virtually every scientific discipline. The organization may not have a staff, but it has officers who are usually very knowledgeable. Many have websites on the internet, including lists of organizations, officers, and members.

Questions about what public policy decisions will be made to accommodate climate clearly are the bailiwick of elected and appointed officials. In the US there are a range of governmental bodies responsible for managing climate change but their roles will vary depending upon who is president. For instance, the administration of President George W. Bush was passive in doing anything about climate change; Barack Obama embraced a campaign to reduce emissions and support the Paris accord, and President Trump opposed both the accord and encouraged greenhouse gas emissions. This can make consulting with government agencies problematic. For instance, the US Environmental Protection Agency under Trump eliminated most information about climate change from its internet site and often refused to allow its scientists to even talk about climate issues (Friedman, 2017). Prospects in other nations will vary depending upon the extent of its science and national infrastructure and political outlook. While EU nations have primarily aggressively embraced programs to reduce carbon-based air emissions, the experiences in the US demonstrate how rapidly political willpower can wilt.

The parties most often quoted or featured in news stories are the activists, and the range of activists and their positions is stark. Organizationally, they vary from small grassroots organizations up to international groups such as Greenpeace that can hire their own ships to transport protesters to distance places. Most, but not all, work towards carbon reduction programs. On the other side are companies and industrial groups, especially fossil fuel producers and their associates. Both sides can produce vibrant sound bites and great copy. Both can also be very biased. Clearly, simply reporting what each side said only creates further problems for the reader.

When the climate change debate began heating up in the 1980s many journalists would balance scientists who were concerned about the issue with a second faction who disputed that humans were having any impact on the atmosphere (Boykoff and Boykoff, 2004). As the research on greenhouse gases matured and the evidence became overwhelming it became obvious that giving equal time to climate deniers was the equivalent of talking to those who believed that the earth was flat.

A final suggestion is that journalists covering environmental issues must get out in the environment. It is difficult to report on the coal industry and its mountaintop removal operation without seeing it. Even if it is a local story, involving the examples given earlier of the New Jersey shore or the English cottage garden, even a good journalist will struggle without visiting the site. Years ago a colleague was reporting about an oil tanker that had run aground on the coast, spilling its cargo, and coating the shoreline and wildlife with black muck. Even though a deadline was looming, my colleague took the two hours to hike down to the scene and back, to absorb what he could, to make the story more detailed, more vivid, and, in this case, more terrifying.

CASE STUDY 1

Storms

At first it was called "disaster porn". That's the label an editor at the *New Orleans Times-Picayune* gave to a proposal by Mark Schleifstein. It was the early 1990s and Schleifstein, the newspaper's environmental writer, believed that New Orleans was in grave danger. For years engineers had built levees on the Mississippi River and elsewhere to protect the region from flooding and to keep shipping flowing. The flooding had stopped, but so had the sediment build-up that sustained South Louisiana's estuaries. Now New Orleans was actually below sea level and the once vibrant wetlands that had protected the city from an ocean assault were sinking into the salt water. Plus the levees were aging and engineers were worried about their reliability.

At first editors were not interested in his proposed series about the hazards New Orleans faced from a major hurricane. They were cynical, hence the disaster porn accusation. Schleifstein persisted and after several years he convinced the newspaper to produce the 2002 series "Washing Away" (Schleifstein and McQuaid, 2002). Written with colleague John McQuaid, it warned that it was only a matter of time before a major hurricane hit New Orleans, causing widespread flooding and likely killing thousands. Hundreds of thousands would be left homeless, and it could take months for the area to dry out. It would be impossible to evacuate everyone and many would likely seek shelter in the Superdome stadium in downtown New Orleans. The series said "Thousands will drown in homes or cars from the flooding, which most likely would come from a storm surge but might come from the collapse of a levee" (Schleifstein and McQuaid, 2002).

In the following years, no one disputed the stories but New Orleans did very little to prepare for the arrival of Hurricane Katrina in August 2005. Even in the days leading up to the storm Schleifstein was worried sick. Journalists have a responsibility to find a line between reporting the worst-case situation and not alarming people. Schleifstein in his coverage tried to be conservative while still warning of the grave consequences of a storm with winds of 100 miles an hour. Later, an editor told Schleifstein that the reporter looked as white as a sheet in the days before Katrina. At synagogue one of those days a friend indicated he was wavering on whether to leave. Schleifstein told him to get the hell out of town (Schleifstein, 2005).

It took days for the world to understand the full horror of the disaster. Up to 80 per cent of New Orleans was flooded, more than 100,000 structures destroyed and property damage was estimated at up to $100 billion (Johnson, 2006). The death toll for Louisiana was more than 1,500 (Hunter, 2006). But the greatest horror may have been the inability of local, state and federal officials to help the trapped and homeless of New Orleans. Tens of thousands of poor people were unable to leave the city, many trapped at the Superdome and the city's convention center. Dead bodies were left in open streets for days or trapped in fetid attics for weeks or months.

Schleifstein was a key reporter in the continuing coverage, even though the flooding destroyed his own home and forced the newspaper to evacuate New Orleans. "It was a frustrating experience and a number of times reporters were overcome by what they were reporting," he said. "I was one of them. It became clear to me that people were going to be dying from this storm. And as bad as it was, it was not as big a storm as we had feared. It could have been worse" (Schleifstein, 2005).

Schleifstein's experiences in forecasting what became Hurricane Katrina is an excellent blueprint for what many journalists are likely to experience in the future. As noted earlier, climate change does not cause hurricanes. But the weather conditions influenced by a hotter than normal planet can intensify storms, fires, droughts, and other events. Consider the three storms that struck the Caribbean and Southeastern United States in the summer and fall of 2017. Hurricane Harvey hit Texas and Louisiana while dropping a mind-boggling 19 trillion gallons of rain. Hurricane Irma was one of the strongest ever recorded in the Atlantic Ocean at winds of 180 miles per hour. Hurricane Maria with winds of 100 miles an hour and 30 inches of rain made a direct hit on Puerto Rico, virtually destroying the island's electric grid (Fritz, 2017). In addition, two of the world's biggest forest fires have occurred in recent years. The Richardson fire in Alberta, Canada began in May 2011 and continued until the following January. It destroyed an area the size of Delaware (Thompson, 2012). A massive brush fire in Australia in 2009 killed 173 and destroyed 2,000 homes (Williams, 2011). Droughts have also struck worldwide. One in California lasted from 2012 to 2016 (USGS, 2018). A second in Cape Town, South Africa by 2017 had left the city with only 10 per cent of its remaining water supply (Van Dam, 2017).

Increasingly journalists need to get ahead of the story, review local conditions, and assess the potential risks. In many communities around the world, governments are already embracing these tasks. Some coastal communities have been reviewing what they can expect from rising sea levels and bigger storms.

Inland areas are calculating the prospects of drought, fires, reduced agricultural production, and increased risk of insect infestations. New York City has developed a $20 billion plan (Russ, 2013). But journalists cannot count on governments, which traditionally are loath to address such long range, expensive issues. Instead one might need to do independent research among scientists, engineers, planners, and others to assess the risk and costs to society.

Unfortunately, as Schleifstein discovered, there is no guarantee that the stories will necessarily influence change. In the aftermath of Katrina, Schleifstein struggled to accept any praise for his work, including the stories that had forecast this disaster. "Yeah, we were right, but what does that mean?" said Schleifstein. "The part that everybody failed was getting the people out" (Martin, 2005). Others praised him, arguing that Scheifstein and McQuaid had likely saved thousands because of their reporting. "As bad as the preparedness and response to Katrina was, it seems to me likely it would have been far worse without the kick-in-the-butt this series provided," said Joseph Davis, an environmental reporter in Washington, DC (Davis, 2006).

CASE STUDY 2

Denial

Exxon scientists beginning in the 1980s were growing increasingly excited about new prospects for oil drilling. Ken Croasdale, a senior ice researcher for Exxon's Canadian subsidiary Imperial Oil, oversaw research between 1986 and 1992 on how global warming would clearly lower exploration and development costs in the Arctic. "The issue of CO2 emissions was certainly well known at the time in the late 1980s," Croasdale said.

Yet for years the company publicly maintained that there was significant doubt about that science. Lee Raymond, Exxon chief executive at the time of an annual meeting in 1999, said future climate "projections are based on completely unproven climate models, or more often, on sheer speculation" (Jerving et al., 2015).

It is not unusual for journalists to take sides if they are exposing corruption, ignorance, or malfeasance. But a basic journalistic tenet is to be fair and provide balance, especially on an ongoing public policy issue that could cost the world trillions of dollars to rectify. For years, journalists failed to understand that there was only one side on the issue of climate science. While journalists deserve some blame for failing to understand the issue, there is at least some evidence that a sophisticated public relations campaign was also underway designed to sway news coverage of the issue.

The mistakes by the press are now obvious. A study of *The New York Times, Los Angeles Times, Wall Street Journal,* and *Washington Post* between 1988 and 2002 found that 52.7 per cent of the stories during that period gave equal weight to critics and proponents of the scientific view that climate change was increasing because of human activity (Boykoff and Boykoff, 2004). Yet in the first IPCC report issued in 1990 scientists were firm in their assessment that humans were heating the atmosphere and that by 2100 temperatures could rise at least 3 degrees Celsius, or 5.4 Fahrenheit (Hougton, 1990).

The decline of the newspaper industry and an alarming ignorance of science by some journalists contributed to some of these misunderstandings. Yet the wilful insistence that balance was necessary lasted for years. For instance, *USA Today* has long insisted that any editorial on a controversial subject needed a response from a group with a counter viewpoint. That meant that in October 2014, when the newspaper wrote about the latest IPCC report, it felt compelled to invite the Heartland Institute to offer a competing opinion. Much of Heartland's funding comes from the fossil fuel industry and its viewpoints do not reflect established climate science (Eshelman, 2014).

It was not until recently that research has uncovered another, more insidious cause for why bad science continued to appear in news stories. Science historians Naomi Oreskes and Erik M. Conway (2010) documented in great detail how the fossil fuel industry had funded a campaign to support sceptics of climate science. In their book *Merchants of Doubt* (2010) they detailed the parallels in the public policy debate between tobacco smoking and climate change. The writers said that some of the same officials who had expressed doubt about cancer and tobacco were also engaged in expressing concerns about the science behind climate research (Oreskes and Conway, 2010).

The primary goal was to sow doubt, which allowed government officials to delay any meaningful action. David Miller and William Dinan (2015) in describing this strategy wrote that for contrarianism to be successful it "does not need to convince scientists, policy makers or even a majority of the public. It needs only to foster the conditions under which meaningful action on climate are seen as too difficult or too politically costly".

In failing to recognize the source of this campaign, journalists sacrificed accuracy for balance. Said Oreskes: "The obvious lesson for journalists is to know that this (type of campaign) exists, that it depends on appealing to journalistic virtues of balance and objectivity". Such a move, she said, "leads journalists into a swamp" (Eshelman, 2014).

In 2015 *InsideClimate News*, the *Los Angeles Times*, and others produced yet more evidence about the fossil fuel industries tactics. In a series of articles journalists showed that for years Exxon knew far more from its scientists than it was saying in public debates about climate change (Jerving et al., 2015). The oil company vigorously denied those assertions and it accused activist organizations of publishing deliberately misleading reports (ExxonMobil, 2017).

While journalists continue to give both sides to the increasingly contentious public policy arguments over climate change, most now are categorical in how they report the science. The BBC Trust, which oversees the BBC news organization, created a committee in 2010 to review the BBC's climate coverage. The committee reprimanded the BBC for giving too much coverage to climate sceptics (BBC, 2011). When then US presidential candidate Donald Trump was campaigning in 2016 and he said that climate change was a hoax created by the Chinese, US journalists were firm in labelling the remarks false (Jacobson, 2016). Scientists have also launched their own journalism reviews of climate stories and weighed in on their accuracy. One of these is Climate Feedback, comprised of about 100 scientists (Ward, 2016).

Perhaps the greatest failure here was not that the press provided unnecessary balance but that too many reporters did not have faith in their own reporting. It is far easier to fall back on a system that in theory upsets neither side by giving them equal access to presenting their viewpoints. But strong reporting should have uncovered the truth earlier – that the story only had one legitimate viewpoint. Giving space to a minority viewpoint also minimizes the threat of criticism about the accuracy of the reporting. It is the safe route. Yet in this situation avoiding the risk of complaints meant policymakers and the public were manipulated. It meant that a fundamental tenet of journalism – accuracy – had been lost. Reporting that is thorough, that touches all possible angles, is the only solution in such situations.

CASE STUDY 3

Agreement

When representatives of 196 nations convened in December 2015 for the United Nations Paris Summit it promised to be a media extravaganza. More than 6,000 reporters from around the world attended the two-week conference that world leaders agreed was crucial to the future of the planet. "Never have the stakes been so high", declared Francois Hollande, the host and French president at the time, "because this is about the future of the planet, the future of life" (Russell, 2015).

It concluded on Saturday December 12, 2015 by making history. As *The New York Times* reported, for the first time nearly every nation agreed to reduce greenhouse gas emissions. Thousands of delegates stood and cheered for history. Whether the accord succeeds, or like a similar agreement in Kyoto, Japan fails abysmally, remains to be seen (Davenport, 2015). President Donald Trump created the first major crevasse in the accord in June 2017 when he pulled the US out of the treaty (Shear, 2017).

While global news coverage of climate change often gets poor attention that did not happen in Paris. Thousands of reporters filed tens of thousands of stories and afterwards commentators analysed the news coverage and academic researchers busily counted stories and compared coverage of Paris with everything including past stories of terrorism.

Christine Russell, writing for the *Columbia Journalism Review*, was impressed by the high-quality writers that came from *The New York Times*, the *Financial Times*, *The Washington Post* and especially at *The Guardian*, which invested and produced more copy than anyone. The wire services were heavily staffed, live blogs conveyed events blow-by-blow, as did social media, especially at Twitter's #COP21 (for 21st Conference of the Parties) hashtag (Russell, 2015).

Stephane Mahe in *The Conversation* praised press coverage but said that there were distinctive differences depending on the political slant of the news organization. Examining UK publications, she found that the left-leaning *The Guardian* was enthusiastic, calling it the end of the fossil fuel era; the centrist *The Independent* labelled the agreement historic but offered a series of cautions; and the more politically right *The Telegraph* refrained from using the word historic while detailing what had happened.

"One of the strong messages of the news coverage was that investors and governments could now make choices based on a collective commitment to emissions reduction; something regarded as a very positive step", said Mahe (2015).

An academic report from the University of Colorado found that there had actually been more coverage of the 2009 climate conference in Copenhagen than in Paris. Max Boykoff, who helped direct that study, said that climate sceptics were very active in 2009 and that might have been why overall climate coverage was higher in 2009. Said Boykoff: "A lot of coverage can be a lot of noise in the system. You need to look at the quality of coverage, beyond the counts of stories done" (Pashley, 2016).

Brookings Institution published one of the most instructive analyses, based on work from Brown University researchers. They did a content analysis of the Paris coverage by four US publications, the *Los Angeles Times*, *The New York Times*, *USA Today*, and *Wall Street Journal*. Coverage was robust; the newspapers published 424 articles during the conference. Still, authors Timmons Roberts and Sonya Gurwit expressed some reservations. They wrote: "Not all of that coverage was instructive, and many key issues in the negotiations were scarcely mentioned. Citizens informed by the US print media gained only a partial understanding of the issues at the core of the climate change negotiations" (Roberts and Gurwit, 2015).

Because of the complexity of some issues, some stories focused on key leaders such as US President Barack Obama or how any agreement would affect a key country such as China or India. The researchers argued that as a result several major issues were rarely addressed, such as how less developed nations would fare under the agreement. One conundrum for journalists is that often news consumers have only a limited interest in arcane details, making it less likely they would even absorb a news report on every detail under negotiation.

The researchers also compared the coverage to the terrorist attack that had occurred a month earlier in Paris. Coverage of the two events was about the same in *The New York Times* and *Los Angeles Times*, but the climate coverage fell significantly in the comparison with *USA Today* and *The Wall Street Journal* (Pashley, 2016).

Despite the criticisms, the Paris coverage was a milestone, never before had a once misunderstood and often-ignored science story received such prominent attention by a global press corps. The accolades were so high, the coverage so widespread and sweeping, that it seems inconceivable that journalism can fail to recognize the story as it progresses in the future.

Conclusion

Journalism has sometimes been called the first draft of history. If so, early climate change coverage has had its share of omissions and mistakes. Yet as this analysis found, over time journalism has overcome many of the early blunders and in recent years has thrived in climate coverage. Earlier we considered three basic reporting goals on this issue. In light of what we have covered since then, consider:

- Don't be intimidated by the science. Understanding it is the first step, translating it so that it is understandable to readers or viewers is second, and making it relevant is an important and vitally important third measure.
- Finding the right scientists is absolutely critical. Journalists hurt their credibility for too many years both with the science community and the public by not understanding the science. What is important now is to keep pace with research which will show either how dire the world's future will be, or how and if science can find solutions to solve that future.
- The important stories that will make individuals care about this issue take time to report. The story is complex and it is global. But it can be broken down into pieces and made local. It is just a matter of taking the time and using a fair degree of ingenuity.

References

BBC praised for science coverage. (2011). *BBC*, [online]. Available at http://www.bbc. com/news/entertainment-arts-14218989 [Accessed 19 Sept. 2017].

Boykoff, M. and Boykoff, J. (2004). Balance as bias: Global warming and the U.S. prestige press. *Global Environmental Change, 14*(2), pp. 125–136.

C2ES (Center for Climate and Energy Solutions). (n.d.). IPCC fifth assessment report. Available at https://www.c2es.org/content/ipcc-fifth-assessment-report/ [Accessed 31 Oct. 2017].

Davenport, C. (2015). Nations approve landmark climate accord in Paris. *The New York Times*, [online]. Available at https://www.nytimes.com/2015/12/13/world/europe/ climate-change-accord-paris.html?_r=0 [Accessed 12 Dec. 2017].

Davis, J. (2006). Hurricane Katrina and Mark Schleifstein.

Eshelman, R. (2014). The danger of fair and balanced. *Columbia Journalism Review*, [online]. Available at http://archives.cjr.org/essay/the_danger_of_fair_and_balance. php [Accessed 7 Sept. 2016].

ExxonMobil. (2017). Understanding the #Exxonknew controversy. Available at http://cdn.exxonmobil.com/page-not-found?item=%2fcurrent-issues%2fclimate-policy%2fclimate-perspectives%2funderstanding-the-exxonknew-controversy& user=extranet\Anonymous&site=website [Accessed 21 Nov. 2017].

Friedman, L. (2017). Climate change and ISIS are seen in poll as world's greatest threats. *New York Times*, 2 Aug., p.A6.

Fritz, A. (2017). Harvey. Irma. Maria. Why is this hurricane season so bad? *Washington Post*, [online]. Available at https://www.washingtonpost.com/news/capital-weather-gang/wp/2017/09/23/harvey-irma-maria-why-is-this-hurricane-season-so-bad/ ?utm_term=.6dd878763a17 [Accessed 31 Oct. 2017].

Hartz, J. and Chappell, R. (1998). *Worlds apart: How the distance between science and journalism threatens America's future.* Nashville, TN: First Amendment Center.

Hougton, J.T., Jenkins, G.J. and Ephramus, J.J., eds., (1990). Climate Change, the IPCC scientific assessment. Cambridge, UK: Cambridge University Press.

Hunter, M. (2006). Deaths of evacuees push toll to 1,577: Out-of-state victims mostly elderly, infirm. *Times Picayune*, May 19.

IPCC (Intergovernmental Panel on Climate Change). (2013). Summary for Policymakers. In T. Stocker, D. Qin, G-K Plattner, M. Tignor, S. Allen, J. Boschung, A. Nauels, Y. Xia, M Bex and P. Midgley, eds., *Climate Change 2013, the Physical Science Basis, Contribution of the Working Group 1 to the Fifth Assessment Report of the Intergovernmental Panel on Climate Change.* Cambridge, UK and New York, NY: Cambridge University Press.

IPCC (Intergovernmental Panel on Climate Change). (n.d.). Provisional schedule for the working group 1 contribution to the IPCC Sixth Assessment Report. [online]. Available at https://wg1.ipcc.ch/AR5/AR5.html [Accessed 31 Oct. 2017].

Jacobson, L (2016). Yes, Donald Trump did call climate change a hoax. *Politifact*, [online]. Available at http://www.politifact.com/truth-o-meter/statements/2016/jun/03/ hillary-clinton/yes-donald-trump-did-call-climate-change-chinese-h/ [Accessed 16 Feb. 2016].

Jerving, S, Jennings, K., Hirsch, M., and Rust, S. (2015). What Exxon knew about the Earth's melting arctic. *Los Angeles Times*, [online]. Available at http://graphics. latimes.com/exxon-arctic/ [Accessed 6 Dec. 2016].

Johnson, D. (2006). *Service assessment: Hurricane Katrina August 23–31, 2005.* Silver Spring, MD: National Oceanic and Atmospheric Administration.

Mahe, S. (2015). How the media spun the Paris climate agreement. *The Conversation*, [online]. Available at https://theconversation.com/how-the-media-spun-the-paris-climate-agreement-52331 [Accessed 12 Dec. 2017].

Martin, A. (2005). Paper keeps head above water. *Irish Times*. Available at http://web.lexis.nexis.com [Accessed 10 Nov. 2005].

Miller, D. and Dinan, W. (2015). Resisting meaningful action on climate change. In Hanson, A. and Cox, R., eds., *The Routledge Handbook of Environment and Communication*. London: Routledge, Taylor & Francis, pp. 86–96.

Morris, J. (2016). 'Get someone up here. We're all dying.' Oil refineries don't just pollute. They also kill and main workers and threaten the public. Center for Public Integrity. In Carbon Wars, Center for Public Integrity, weather.com, Al Jazeera English, publicintegrity.org, USA Today network, [online]. Available at https://www.publicintegrity.org/2016/12/13/20523/get-someone-here-we-re-all-dying [Accessed 28 Nov. 2017].

Oreskes, N. and Conway, E. (2010). *Merchants of Doubt*. London: Bloomsbury Press.

Pashley, A. (2016). Why did Paris climate summit get less press coverage than Copenhagen? *Climate Home News*, [online]. Available at http://www.climatechangenews.com/2016/03/07/why-did-paris-climate-summit-get-less-press-coverage-than-copenhagen/ [Accessed 12 Dec. 2017].

Randerson, J. (2015). Controversial newspaper campaign takes on climate 'fatalism.' *SEJournal*, 25(2/3), pp. 8, 20–21.

Roberts, T. and Gurwit, S. (2015). The Paris climate talks according to U.S. print media: Plenty of heat but not so much light. Brookings, [online]. Available at https://www.brookings.edu/blog/planetpolicy/2015/12/18/the-paris-climate-talks-according-to-u-s-print-media-plenty-of-heat-but-not-so-much-light/ [Accessed 12 Dec. 2017].

Russ, H. (2013). New York lays out $20 billion plan to adapt to climate change. *Reuters*, [online]. Available at https://www.reuters.com/article/us-climate-newyork-plan/new-york-lays-out-20-billion-plan-to-adapt-to-climate-change-idUSBRE95A10120130612 [Accessed 12 Dec. 2017].

Russell, C. (2015). At the Paris climate talks, media coverage takes a turn. *Columbia Journalism Review*, [online]. Available at https://www.cjr.org/analysis/paris_climate_talks_kick_off_on_somber_note.php [Accessed 12 Dec. 2017].

Schleifstein, M. (2005). Hurricane Katrina.

Schleifstein, M. and McQuaid, J. (2002). The big one. *New Orleans Times-Picayune*, [online]. Available at http://www.nola.com/environment/index.ssf/2002/06/the_big_one.html [Accessed 11 Oct. 2005].

Shear, M. (2017). Trump will withdraw U.S. from Paris climate agreement. *The New York Times*, [online]. Available at https://www.nytimes.com/2017/06/01/climate/trump-paris-climate-agreement.html [Accessed 12 Dec. 2017].

Thompson, J. (2012). Circle of life rebuilding a year after Richardson wildfire. *Fort McMurray Today*, [online]. Available at http://www.fortmcmurraytoday.com/2012/08/30/circle-of-life-rebuilding-a-year-after-richardson-wildfire [Accessed 12 Dec. 2017].

UNFCCC (United Nations Framework Convention on Climate Change). (2014). Background on the UNFCCC. The international response to climate change. [online]. Available at http://unfccc.int/essential_background/items/6031.php [Accessed 31 Oct. 2017].

USGS (United States Geological Survey). (2018). California drought. Available at https://ca.water.usgs.gov/california-drought/index.html [Accessed 13 December 2018].

Van Dam, D. (2017) Cape Town contends with the worst drought in over a century. *CNN*, [online]. Available at http://www.cnn.com/2017/05/31/africa/cape-town-drought/index.html [Accessed 12 Dec. 2017].

Ward, B. (2016). Scientists critique media reports on climate. *SEJournal*, 26(2), p. 8.

Welch, C. and Ringman, S. (2013). Sea change, the Pacific's perilous turn. [video]. Available at https://www.seattletimes.com/video/2650204511001/sea-change-the-pacifics-perilous-turn/ [Accessed 12 Dec. 2017].

West, B., Sandman, P. and Greenberg, M. (2003). *The reporter's environmental handbook*, 3rd ed. New Brunswick, NJ: Rutgers University Press.

Williams, L. (2011). The worst brushfires in Australia's history. *Australian Graphic*, [online]. Available at http://www.australiangeographic.com.au/topics/science-environment/2011/11/the-worst-bushfires-in-australias-history/ [Accessed 12 Dec. 2017].

11

REPORTING DISASTERS IN THE DIGITAL AGE

Amanda Gearing

The social issue

Natural disasters are events caused by natural forces such as extreme weather events or seismic events. Extreme weather events include severe storms, droughts, floods, wildfires, tornados, and cyclones. Seismic events include earthquakes, tsunamis, volcanoes, and landslides. Natural disasters have a high level of newsworthiness because of their impact and potential impact on large numbers of people. More than 500 million people were affected by natural disasters in 2016 and almost 9,000 people died in 342 natural disasters around the globe (Guha-Sapir et al., 2017). The death toll in 2016 was the second lowest toll since 2006 and much lower than the toll in the Haiti earthquake that resulted in 222,570 deaths in 2010.

Journalists, via their news outlets, have a duty to provide timely warnings and advice from experts about what preparations citizens can make to reduce the risk of death and property loss. During a natural disaster, reporters may provide live coverage from scenes of disaster and interview eyewitnesses. Once the event is over, journalists report on the immediate impact of the event on society – including deaths, injuries, missing people, property damage, infrastructure damage, power outages and blocked roads, and the projected cost of repair to infrastructure. In the immediate aftermath of the event, coverage may focus on funerals, accounts of heroic rescues or feats of personal survival and endurance, causes of the disaster and evaluations of the response of emergency services to those in need. In the weeks and months after the event, attention will turn to recovery, rebuilding, rewarding human courage and sacrifice, and planning for improved resilience of communities and infrastructure in future.

Reporting on natural disasters is emotionally exhausting and often physically challenging. When a disaster is imminent, reporters are despatched to various locations that are predicted to bear the brunt of a severe weather event. Reporting for the 24/7 news cycle means reporters may need to work very long hours in danger zones with little sleep and sparse living conditions, for extended periods of time. Strong relationships with news contacts must be developed before the disaster because emergency services news sources are frequently very busy with life-saving tasks during disasters and may be unable to respond to individual interview requests from reporters.

Natural disasters and the official or media responses to them frequently become social issues because particular types of disaster can disproportionately affect specific groups of people such as farmers, rural populations and poor people (Sakai et al., 2017; Naqvi and Rehm, 2014). Additionally, wealthy people have more agency to choose to live in locations that are less exposed to natural disasters, and poor people who are affected by disasters are less able to move to escape the risk of future disasters (Gearing, 2017).

Disaster reporting can be very fast-paced and exciting but it can also be dangerous and emotionally confronting. The writing of disaster stories – often under tight deadlines and in difficult circumstances – requires careful attention to detail and a dedication to accuracy and balance. Reporters should resist any temptation to sensationalism, cliché, and the use of superlatives. Avoiding clichés in disaster reporting can be difficult because formulaic disaster reporting produced under pressure can easily lapse into hyperbole, exaggeration and sensation. Care should be taken to calmly consider the words and phrases used, to ensure they are accurate whilst avoiding exaggeration or causing undue panic.

Research is showing that the recovery of survivors can take many years after a disaster and long-form multimedia journalism – typically reports of 1,000–20,000 words with audio and images – is an emerging field in disaster reporting (Henley, 2013). This chapter will present case studies of how to report on three of the most common types of natural disaster: droughts, fires, and floods.

Introduction

My first job as a reporter was in Outback Australia where the climate was predominantly drought, punctuated by fires or good seasons punctuated by dramatic floods. I have reported on droughts, fires, and floods since the early 1980s when graziers were forced to shoot their breeding herds rather than watch them starve to death. In the 1990s, the introduction of seasonal climate forecasting in Queensland, Australia enabled farmers and graziers for the first time to react to forecast seasons, thereby reducing their risk in poor seasons and capitalising on good seasons (Stone, 1992).

As scientists have come to better understand the global climate influence of the Pacific Ocean El Nino-Southern Oscillation, the use of seasonal forecasting has spread around the world (Hewitt, Stone, and Tait, 2017). The worst drought in 100 years in Australia, in 2002, was forecast but despite this prior warning, the drought affected agriculture severely and jeopardised the water supplies of towns and cities (Horridge, Madden, and Wittwer, 2005). Fierce and deadly wildfires swept through rural districts. Then, in a dramatic reversal of climate patterns, record floods in 2011 covered 75 per cent of the landmass of the state of Queensland – an area seven times the size of Great Britain (Chanson, 2011). Entire populations of towns were airlifted to safety by helicopter for the first time (ABC Radio News, 2010).

In early 2011, a sudden and deadly inland tsunami swept across south-east Queensland roaring down river systems of the Lockyer Valley and killing 23 people, sweeping away houses and leaving a trail of destruction (Walker and Gearing, 2011). For the first time in my career, social media suddenly became a powerful tool of connection linking reporters directly with community members and communicating with a global audience. A Facebook page sprang into being in response to a missing person. Within 48 hours it had 43,000 readers – far surpassing the circulation of the local newspaper. The community crowd-sourced news and information and shared it, faster than any media outlet could provide it. People locally and overseas who inquired about relatives inside the disaster zone received direct confirmation of their survival and safety. This local disaster suddenly became world news, reaching a global audience as people with mobile phones uploaded video footage to the internet, and news outlets produced audio and video coverage that seemed to defy belief.

There are three take-home messages from this chapter:

- Prepare for the unexpected.
- Learn how to interview traumatised people.
- Learn to use social media tools for reporting on disasters.

The research

Natural disasters have high newsworthiness because they embody several news values including impact, timeliness, prominence, proximity, currency, and human interest (Schlesinger, 1987). Covering natural disaster warnings accurately and in a timely manner is very important for the safety of individuals and communities (Earth Journalism Network, 2016). Reporting during both natural disaster emergencies and in the immediate aftermath is a significant responsibility of media outlets. Audiences look to the media to convey warnings, to keep them updated and to report on community recovery. For unusual disasters, audiences expect the media to investigate the causes, possibly over months or years and to report on changes to public policy that will lead to improved forecasting and resilience in future. The digital tools that are now available to report breaking news, make this a challenging and interesting area of practice for journalists. The collaboration of reporters across national boundaries has untapped the potential to reframe natural disasters as a global problem that could be mitigated with collective effort (Gearing, 2016).

Natural disasters coverage can be complicated by social, economic and political considerations. For example, coverage of increasing numbers of natural disasters around the globe has led to "compassion fatigue" in which audiences are exhausted and become unresponsive to appeals for funds after hearing, reading, and seeing many reports about overwhelming numbers of people suffering and dying (Collins, 2010; Moeller, 1999). Large-scale disasters in the third world have led to mass human starvation, mass migration, and have created "climate refugees" who leave their homeland seeking shelter and food in adjacent countries, that frequently lack capacity to cope with a mass influx of people (Maharatna, 2014). Some locations that have not previously been seriously affected by climatic extremes are now experiencing impacts from severe weather events. Droughts are causing mass migrations of populations because growing seasons have shortened, thereby reducing yields and causing mass starvation (Johnston, 2017). The increased intensity and extent of wildfires in many countries including Africa, Canada, and the United States are generating costly and deadly mega-fires that defy firefighting efforts to control them (Williams et al., 2011). The media's role is vital to community safety: relaying timely warnings, advising of safety precautions, evacuation orders and reporting on the impacts.

The effects of climate change in many parts of the world are becoming increasingly serious and resulting in more intense and more frequent extreme weather events. However, no single severe weather event is evidence of climate change. The effects of climate change are expected to increase the frequency and intensity of extreme weather events and therefore their impact on people and ecosystems (Letcher, 2009; Torabi, Dedekorkut-Howes and Howes, 2018; Gearing, 2004).

Disaster reporting has traditionally been formulaic – a dispassionate numeric account of death, injury, property damage at a particular time and location. The inverted pyramid death, injury, damage lead is very common. Many reporters still adopt this "narrowly conceived, geo-politically informed and essentially amoral journalistic outlook" (Cottle, 2013). However, this "calculus of death" approach is being replaced by a style of reporting in which the journalist infuses their reports with emotion and contextual details that produce a more authentic and morally responsible account of what has happened. These reports may include narrative accounts from those who have "felt, seen and survived" (Cottle, 2013). Care must be taken, however, to maintain a distinction between simply witnessing an event and the moral responsibility of "bearing witness" to human suffering on behalf of the public (Cottle, 2013). Bearing witness is a confronting and arduous task that honours courage, sacrifice, and resilience. However, reporters who take on the challenge do so to craft narratives that engage audiences and explain the plight of distant people (Cottle, 2013). Reporters play an important role as professional witnesses who act in an ethical framework "to care and to act" on behalf of the public (Zelizer, 2007; Tait, 2011).

Disaster reporting has been revolutionised by the advent of digital technologies that enable members of the public to publish words, photographs, and videos online more immediately than is possible for traditional media outlets (Bowman and Willis, 2003). The technical development of a video camera function being added to mobile phones has enabled members of the public on the scene of unexpected events to record them as they occur and to upload footage almost instantaneously to the internet. Onlookers with mobile phones have therefore become eyewitness recorders of events ranging from the personally significant to the globally significant. While bloggers may be primarily focused on their microlocal area, if the events that happen are of state, national, or global significance, the content can quickly attain a global audience via social media platforms. Early examples of global news blogs include the attack on the World Trade Centre in New York on September 11 in 2001; the wars in Afghanistan and Iraq; the Boxing Day tsunami in 2004 near Sumatra; and the London Bombings in July 2005 (Bruns, 2006). By 2009, it was common for first reports of disasters to come not from traditional media outlets but from local residents using social networks (Shirky, 2009).

Reporters who are exposed to repeated events involving human suffering, violence, and death are affected by their exposure and require self-care and support from their media organisation (Ochberg, 1996). The Dart Centre for Journalism and Trauma produces self-care resources to prepare journalists for their role of bearing witness on behalf of the public (Hight and Smyth, 2001; Brayne, 2007). Please also reference chapters 3 and 15 in this volume for more information on how to protect yourself when covering sensitive topics.

Covering disasters

Reporting on a disaster comprehensively requires quick and thorough information-gathering and verification. Typical leads in natural disaster stories will include the number of people who have died or who are injured, and the extent of damage to houses and infrastructure. Key sources for this information in the past have been police, fire, and ambulance authorities and they remain important sources; however, the advent of social media platforms enables those reporters who are well connected to their communities to contact news sources directly and possibly well ahead of emergency services. For example, in the 2011 Queensland flash flood disaster I was able to report on deaths and missing people on the actual day of the disaster because next of kin had recovered and identified their relatives who had died. Authorities were not able to find or identify some of the flood victims for several days and in some cases, several weeks. Three bodies were never recovered (Walker and Gearing, 2011). In situations where a reporter has exclusive information about deaths, extreme care must be taken to ensure that the information is correct, and that next-of-kin are the informants or have been informed before publication.

Journalists typically rush towards disaster zones as residents are fleeing from them. The journalists quickly determine the "worst-affected" areas and search for witnesses and next of kin. Unfortunately, most reporters are ill-prepared for interviewing next-of-kin in situations that the industry terms "death knocks" and defines as intrusive (Duncan and Newton, 2010).

In practice, there are situations where bereaved family and friends welcome the opportunity to inform the public via the media of the circumstances of a sudden death. Relatives may also want to speak about the special qualities of the deceased person and provide photographs of the person. It is not until a young reporter has taken on this role that they discover that "most approaches are met with approval from the family, who are often glad of the opportunity to talk about their loved one and let the community know what has happened" (Duncan and Newton, 2010).

Personal safety

Despite the urgency of reaching a disaster zone quickly, journalists must prioritise their personal safety, equipping themselves with supplies of food, water, medication, first aid kit, and sunscreen, as well as relevant accreditation and personal protective equipment (PPE). Fire departments will usually require reporters to undertake fire training sessions before the fire season begins. Successful completion will qualify them for media accreditation to cover wild-fires. This accreditation will then become a condition of professional entry to an active fire ground if it is safe to do so. Fire departments will usually require media crews to wear PPE compliant with the relevant standards, including smoke masks or respirators, fire resistant clothing, boots, helmet, gloves, and eyewear. Anyone found in a fire ground without accreditation or correct PPE may be evicted from the fire ground area. PPE for floods and flood clean-up grounds may include waterproof boots to protect from floodwaters carrying sewage, hazardous indus-trial chemicals, pesticides, and flammable liquids.

Reporters should also be aware of potential dangers from obscured physical hazards such as fallen power lines, snakes, and other wildlife. PPE may include protective headwear, gloves, buoyancy vest, long-sleeved shirt, and trousers.

Sources

Contacts should be made and maintained well before any disaster emergency, with official sources such as the Bureau of Meteorology, local and regional police, fire and ambulance services and helicopter rescue service and coastguards. Local government contacts including mayors and councillors and local members of parliament who are likely to be kept well informed by emergency services. School headmasters, medical superintendents of hospitals, and managers of aged care homes are also likely to be kept updated on warnings and recovery efforts. Transport authorities are useful for updates on damage and delays to road and rail services and disruption to air travel. It is often useful to have direct phone numbers for operational personnel in emergency services such as fire investiga-tors, scenes of crime officers, firefighters, ambulance officers, communications room staff, helicopter rescue pilots and crewmen, coastguard rescuers, and fire spotter plane crews.

Social media platforms have become essential tools for crowd-sourcing information from communities. Purpose-built Facebook community groups can be established ready for use if any type of disaster occurs. These groups can enable reporters or media outlets to receive timely and exclusive information, photos and video from eyewitnesses. Contributors and commenters expect and are entitled to be contacted before publication. Although some Facebook pages are available for public viewing, the contents are not public property. Commenters are therefore entitled to request retraction and deletion if their content is published without consent. Publication of online content should also be curated to ensure comments are not hurtful or insensitive to disaster victims. Purpose-built secret Facebook groups can also be created to establish private ongoing connection with disaster victims while maintaining exclusivity of the information. A major benefit of a Facebook group is that even if people are displaced by the disaster or subsequently move house, the reporter can easily maintain contact with them despite changes to their contact details.

Social media platforms, especially Facebook and YouTube were vital sources of information in the immediate aftermath of the disaster. Next-of-kin were posting photos of family members in the hope that they were found (Walker and Gearing, 2011; Gearing and Thomas, 2011). Over the following days and weeks, Facebook contacts provided photographs and video footage and information even if people had been displaced by the disaster to other districts or even overseas. In 2014, a secret Facebook group was created to gather evidence of the need for a public inquiry into the onset of the Grantham flood. Screenshots of aerial helicopter vision were posted to the group and members of the group were able to quickly provide names and contact details of people in the photographs. This method was much faster and easier than traditional on-ground investigation.

One of the first state authorities to experiment with providing news direct to the public via social media platforms was the Queensland Police Service (QPS). Media and Public Affairs Branch executive director Kym Charlton had begun an experimental QPS Facebook account in May 2010. During the following eight months the readership grew steadily to more than 7,000 users (Charlton, 2011: ii). However, as the summer storm season approached the number of users more than doubled in two weeks. Spikes in user numbers occurred immediately prior to Cyclone Tasha and flooding of the coastal city of Rockhampton (Charlton, 2011: iii). However, these rises paled in comparison with the significant spike in user numbers as news of the dramatic flash flooding in Toowoomba broke just after midday on 10 January 2011. QPS Facebook user numbers soared that day to almost 18,000 (Charlton, 2011: iii).

Striking as the growth in user numbers had been, the growth was to be eclipsed by far by the growth in user numbers during the Ipswich and Brisbane floods and Cyclone Yasi. At the height of the Cyclone Yasi emergency in early February 2011, the site had more than 170,000 followers (Charlton, 2011: iv). As the flood peak headed towards the state capital over the following days, Twitter followers shared warnings and information. Axel Bruns et al. (2012) found a spike of Twitter traffic of more than 600 tweets on the hashtag "qldfloods" on the evening of 10 January in response to the Toowoomba Central Business District flooding. Tweets on #qldflood increased in frequency over the following day as the flood approached Brisbane, peaking at 1,100 tweets per hour.

The risk of power supply cuts means natural disaster emergency contact lists should be kept as hard copies — as well as digital files — so that the contact details are portable, accessible, waterproof, and independent of batteries and power supplies. Sealable, waterproof, and airtight bags are useful for protecting reference lists and mobile phones. It is also useful to be familiar with local and regional online amateur weather and climate communities. These groups can often provide detailed local knowledge of vulnerable areas such as flash flood hotspots and can update you on the possible on-ground impacts if there is a severe weather event forecast. Reporters should make careful preparations in advance to ensure you can file your copy, audio, and video even if terrestrial communications systems are damaged or destroyed. Reliable communications are vital for reporting and for maintaining personal safety in fast-changing disaster zones. Reporters should ensure they have accurate situational awareness and that they are updated on changing conditions frequently.

Situational awareness of existing hotspots for particular risks in the geographic areas that your media outlet covers, such as roads and bridges that are vulnerable to flooding, is useful.

Ideally, you should be aware of the locations and after hours contact numbers of critical infrastructure such as power substations, water supply pumping stations and sewerage works ahead of time so that if services are cut, you have that information to hand.

Interviewing traumatised news sources

Many disasters will leave people traumatised in some way. Reporters need to assess, ahead of time, their attitude towards interviewing traumatised people. My ethical position on approaching traumatised news sources is to be guided by the maxim used in medical ethics: "first, do no harm". This duty to not cause harm to people who have already been harmed is balanced with my duty to gather information and to bear witness to events. My aim therefore, is to avoid causing harm and preferably to leave some positive legacy of my involvement as a reporter. This may include facilitating for people to speak about their experiences, obtaining and sharing information that may reduce future risk, or bringing deficiencies in warning systems or infrastructure to public attention for action by authorities.

In my experience, survivors of disasters are frequently willing to speak to reporters within hours or days of being bereaved in a disaster (Gearing, 2013). Of course, there will be other people who are not willing to speak to the media and intrusion is unethical in these circumstances. Reporters who simply provide the opportunity for survivors to speak if they wish, without applying any pressure are not only more ethical as journalists, but are also more likely to secure an interview, than a reporter who hounds news sources who are unwilling to speak to them. A long-term view is the best approach since there will be future opportunities when a relative may be willing to speak. For example, the person preparing to deliver a eulogy for a funeral is emotionally prepared to speak publicly and will be equipped and possibly willing to provide information to a reporter who is respectful and patient with bereaved relatives.

In my reporting of the 2011 disaster, I recorded my interviews and discovered during the transcriptions that people who were narrating their experiences were waylaid when I interrupted them with questions. I found also that the interviewees were not easily able to pick up their narrative but changed track and did not return to their original line of thought. I determined to try to minimise my interruptions. For subsequent interviews, I assured the interviewees that I would not interrupt them, after asking the simple question, "what happened?". I discovered that the interviewees were able to narrate a comprehensive account of their experiences on the day of the flood (Gearing, 2012a). I also noticed that people who observed deaths omitted details about how the deaths occurred and seemed to jump-cut to the next section of their account. During their narrative, I made eye contact and listened carefully. I did not break eye contact in order to make notes or write follow-up questions. At the end of their narrative – that may have taken an hour to 90 minutes – I asked the questions I had committed to memory. I found the interviewees were able and willing to provide compelling details, for example in moments when they believed they were dying (Gearing, 2017).

An unexpected but significant result of my prototype interview method was that the interviewees gave very positive feedback about the benefit of this approach for them. Several of the interviewees said their experience of the interview was healing for them and no one gave feedback that they had been distressed by the interview or that they felt over-exposed and therefore wanted me to exclude information they had provided.

Searching the research literature, I discovered that trauma counsellors use a similar interview method with survivors. The counsellor's role is to listen to their client's narrative and avoid providing advice, passing judgement or making suggestions. Tedeschi and Calhoun (2004) found that the counsellor's role of "listening – without necessarily trying to solve – tends to allow patients to process trauma into growth". Several survivors described positive personal or emotional outcomes of the disaster – post-traumatic growth – such as feeling more grateful for their life and their family and resolving to focus on the important intangibles of life instead of the pursuit of material possessions and wealth.

Why talk to reporters?

Understanding the reasons why traumatised survivors choose to speak to the media provides reporters with a useful knowledge-base to perform their role.

Knowing the possible motivations of interviewees can empower reporters to bear witness to events, rather than avoiding contact with survivors because of a misplaced fear that the reporter's request for an interview might be perceived as unwelcome. Of course, not everyone approached will want to be interviewed at the time or place they are asked. However, for those who do wish to speak to the media, it is the responsibility of reporters to be available to listen at a time and place suitable to the news source.

I was surprised that the high load of trauma that the flood survivors had experienced had not deterred them from wanting to speak to a reporter. I conducted a practice-led research study to explore the reasons why 120 of the 125 traumatised survivors and rescuers I interviewed were willing to speak to a reporter. Their willingness seemed to contradict a common belief that bereaved people would not want to speak to the media. I asked the 33 interviewees who had a near-death experience on the day of the flood why they agreed to be interviewed. Their reasons were all different but they fell into six categories of reasons, which are summarised at the end of this section.

Interestingly, the most frequently cited reason given by interviewees for speaking to a reporter was that *they believed their participation would contribute to their personal recovery.* For example, Grantham resident John Mahon, who had clung to his gutter in the torrent before being airlifted to safety by helicopter, said that talking about his ordeal had helped him to recover:

> I think talking to people and telling my story helps me a lot. You relive it again but it helps me get over it. Talking to reporters and other people has helped me get through it.

Murphy's Creek resident Sue Patterson commented on the therapeutic effect of talking about the event for her:

> I think it's very beneficial to be able to talk it out. I think that as you talk it helps you sift through things in your own mind. It's very healing.

Grantham resident Marie Van Straten, who was in her Grantham house when it was ripped from its footings and swept two kilometres across farm paddocks, said she wanted something positive to come from her ordeal that would help others:

> You can help people more when you've been through something like that but if you withdraw into yourself and don't talk about it, you don't help yourself and you don't help anybody else either. I'm really happy to be able to do this.

The second most frequent response was that the *interviewees wanted the public to know what had happened.* Several participants said that despite the substantial newspaper, radio and television coverage of the disaster, there had not been enough detail given so that audiences could understand the complexity of what happened, and how severely it had affected people in the various small townships and rural districts. In the town of Helidon, Jean Warr, who along with Lloyd Warr, had scrambled to the roof of their house to escape fast-flowing treacherous flood water said she felt a responsibility to let people know what had happened:

> If people don't tell people what happened, the next time it happens there will be just the same awful consequences. We will be in the position again where too many people will die for stupid reasons.

Craig Ritchie from Spring Bluff spoke of the importance of keeping the public informed *so that community support could be provided to victims*:

> It really helps with public donations. It really just shows people that we are all vulnerable. We'll all pitch in and help each other. It's extremely important to get that news out there.

Six of my research participants decided to speak because *they felt authorities needed to understand the disaster and to make changes to reduce future risk*. Grantham resident Gilbert Kilah who had clung to a telegraph pole in the torrent for an hour and a half, spoke because he realised the flood could have been much more dangerous if all six creeks that affect the town had been in flood on the same day, instead of only two. He wanted authorities to be aware of the risk:

> There are lessons to be learned from all this. It had the potential with rain falling in a wider catchment area to be five or six feet deeper in Grantham. If all the creeks had flowed at the same time and at the same rate, I wouldn't be sitting here talking to you. Simple as that.

Helidon teenager, Angela Emmerson, 19, took part in an interview in the hope *that other people could learn from her experience*:

> If someone else can learn just one lesson from what I've told you, then that might save someone's life. It was horrible for me. Yes, I survived though. If I can save someone else's life from them hearing this, then that's great.

Four of the interviewees said their reason for being willing to be interviewed was their *sense of duty to make sure warning systems and disaster responses are improved* in future. Murphy's Creek resident Nelly Gitsham, who was rescued by her neighbour after risking her life to save a horse, said her hope was that state authorities would improve warning systems.

> I've got no problem with talking because if my story is out there then maybe the state can look back and say "there's a person who didn't get warning,

like everyone in Murphy's Creek and all the poor people in Grantham who lost their lives. Maybe they should do something else about it.

Grantham resident Matthew Keep spoke about his ordeal *to highlight system failures* that resulted in the deaths of his mother, mother-in-law, and his two-year-old daughter, Jessica, at Grantham (Gearing, 2012b).

> There has to be a level of accountability for local governments to adhere to frameworks that are determined at a state level. To say that they will get it right for the future holds little comfort for my family; they should have had it right to start with. This was one of the biggest floods to take place in Queensland's history and yet no-one knew about it.

Two of the interviewees agreed to be interviewed because *they thought an interview with a reporter would be more helpful than speaking to a psychologist.* They found the interview cathartic. Grantham resident Danny McGuire whose wife and two children perished in the flood said he was uncomfortable paying a counsellor to listen to him:

> It's better talking to you than to a psychologist because I can talk to someone without paying them to listen to me.

A Postman's Ridge resident Rod Alford expressed a similar view:

> I find it more relaxing talk to you than the highly educated professionals. They tend to be more financially focused – they are watching their clock and say "time's up" – would you like to make another appointment? And I think "you bastards – you're caring and sharing for two hours – but only because you're being paid.

Interestingly, only two of the interviewees said the timing of my interview request was their reason for engaging with a media interview. Murphy's Creek resident Susan Mouflih said her *ability to talk about the disaster increased over time.* When she was asked for an interview within a week of the flood she spoke to a reporter but could not say more than "My brother saved my life". When I interviewed her several months after the flood she was able to give detailed information about what happened and her thoughts as she was submerged and lost hope of surviving.

To summarise, the reasons given for agreeing to be interviewed were personal recovery; public understanding of what happened; lessons need to be learned; a sense of duty to make sure warning systems and disaster responses are improved in future; financial disinterest of reporters in listening to survivor stories; and, enough time has elapsed for victims to be able to speak (Gearing, 2012b: 55).

Catharsis

Longform journalism – of up to 20,000 words – about a natural disaster can provide a sense of catharsis for survivors, forming a lasting record that acknowledges the experience and the effect of the event upon individuals and communities. One unexpected outcome of my long-form journalism about the flood was that several interviewees experienced a sense of catharsis when they read about the disaster. The flood survivors were able to identify with other people who had similar experiences and to realise they were not alone in their struggles to recover. Readers and listeners also said they understood how the event had occurred and the effects on people better through the written or spoken word. Some flood survivors used the book I published in 2012, to help their family and friends to understand what happened:

> We must commend you on the book and your detailed accounts of the events of January 2011. This book will be on our shelf (once all the family have read it) for future generations of our family to read and realise what was endured by so many last year. Many friends have bought your book and now have a more informed account of those few days. Sometimes it is hard for us to relate these things to people and now through your book they understand.

Several interviewees commented that once their relatives and friends read the book, the survivors felt they were better understood. For some couples in which one partner was in the flood and the other was away at the time of the impact, understanding was improved and relationships were rebuilt based on a shared understanding of the scope and severity of the disaster.

Five years on

Five years after the disaster I returned to the disaster zone to update and revise my book. I interviewed 30 survivors and rescuers and discovered that many people were worse off after five years than they had been in the year immediately after the disaster. My revised book was published in 2017 (Gearing, 2017). The follow-up interviews revealed serious shortcomings in recovery and rebuilding policies and severe problems for individuals and families who were still affected by physical and psychological conditions such as unemployment and delayed or failed insurance claims that prevented them being satisfactorily re-housed.

Some individuals and families recovered relatively quickly from the disaster. These people typically had not been traumatised and had not been injured or lost possessions. They were able to return to work, and their insurance was paid promptly for their house to be repaired. Recovery for those who had been bereaved was a lot slower and more difficult, especially for those who had also lost their home and possessions.

Those who were injured so that they could not return to work had not yet recovered emotionally or materially from the disaster. Many people had been diagnosed with PTSD, anxiety, depression, or other psychiatric conditions. Families whose insurance did not pay their claim adequately or at all were left trapped in houses in the flood zone and with valuations that were likely to remain depressed for many years. The reduction in land value meant they could not afford to sell and move to a location above the flood zone.

CASE STUDY 1

Drought

Drought is a challenging natural disaster to cover because these events are newsworthy for what is *not* happening rather than what is happening. Rainfall figures and weather records are slow to emerge but the effects of the drought will usually be obvious long before the statistics are available that will prove, only in retrospect, the severity of the event. Coverage during the drought can be achieved, however, by illustrating the effects of the drought on people, crops, domestic animals, water supplies, native animals, and feral animals, long before statistics prove the severity of the drought (Gearing, 2006, 2005). For example, crops may be failing and having to be ploughed back into paddocks because the crops are not economic to harvest; stock may be turned off because of a lack of fodder reducing prices and, therefore, farm incomes; farmers may be having to leave their farm and find work elsewhere to support their family (Gearing, 2007). Social effects may include a spike in children leaving boarding schools because their parents can't afford school fees, or a spike in farmer suicides or relationship breakdowns. Native and feral animals may be forced to migrate to more settled areas and damage or destroy crops and pastures. News coverage may usefully explain why produce prices in supermarkets are higher than normal, or the reason for a need for government assistance to support farm families.

Drought reporting can be emotionally confronting for reporters because they are exposed to their news sources' personal distress; these sources are likely to be under financial pressure, physically exhausted, and emotionally vulnerable. Positive stories do occur and coverage of farmers who diversify their operation into hospitality or other fields can bring some relief from the negative tone of drought stories. The uptake of scientific advances by farmers who, for example, reduce soil compaction by using controlled traffic GPS systems on their tractors and adjust their fertiliser rates and sowing dates and planting rates to minimise risk and maximise crop yields, can provide upbeat stories in an otherwise dismal season.

The effect on urban communities of a drought usually lags well behind the effect on rural communities. Supermarket prices of fruit and vegetables may jump, or water restrictions may be introduced. Urban water supplies can become matters of political debate if water resources are shared between states or countries (Shakdom, 2015).

CASE STUDY 2

Fire

Reporting on wildfires is dangerous and hot work. On a day when fires are likely to be very dangerous, news editors will predictably want photographs of flames on a fire front. Unsurprisingly, preparation is the key to both survival in the field and to coming home with great stories and photographs. One of the most memorable fires I reported on was a wildfire in the wine-growing region of south-east Queensland that was so hot that the ground was left carpeted in white ash and the branches of trees were burnt off, leaving black pointed tree trunks studding the landscape. Two residents who returned to pick over the ashes in all that remained of their home rescued a few fire-proof items and spoke about how they had survived. One reader was so moved by the story that she sized up the woman in the photo as being of a similar size to herself, went to her wardrobe, took out some clothes and sent them addressed to the woman care of the local post office. This and other acts of generosity in response to stories of tragedy are timely reminders that when disaster strikes there are people who respond with kindness and extraordinary generosity.

Reporting on fires will ideally begin well before the fire season with updates and assessments of the coming fire season to alert residents and property owners how to prepare for the risk of wildfires. Although lightning is sometimes the cause of wildfires, human activity is far more often the cause of large dangerous wildfires (Chas-Amil, Touza, and García-Martínez, 2013). The most vulnerable locations are where forested areas are interspersed with urban developments – the wildland–urban interface. Studies have shown that the incidence of wildfires is twice as high where there is a rural-urban interface. than in forested areas with no settlements (Chas-Amil, Touza, and García-Martínez, 2013). Some authorities are adapting their responses to wildfires based on experiences in other parts of the world. For example, in the USA, fire agencies have routinely ordered evacuations of populations and fought fires with professional firefighters. In contrast, Australia's approach has been to give residents the choice in all but the most catastrophic fire weather forecasts, either to "prepare, stay and defend" their property or to "leave early". The Australia approach has been found to be effective in engaging residents in being self-sufficient to fight fires and well prepared to defend their property (Stephens et al., 2009).

Once the fire season arrives, satellite monitors become indispensable tools for monitoring the emergence of fires and their speed and direction. Satellite technology is now capable of monitoring current fires around the globe using the MODIS Fire Rapid Response System (Justice et al., 2002). Wildfires flare in weather conditions that have the combination of high heat, low humidity and strong wind. Caution should be exercised with attributing liability for lighting a wildfire. Fires may ignite without any human intervention: for example, by lightning strikes, by a piece of glass that focuses sunshine onto dry undergrowth, by electrical wires arcing, or by sparks flying from a sawmill pit's 24/7 fire.

One of the most hazardous fire conditions occurs when a narrow fire front that has burned predictably in one direction, is struck by a wind change that blows the flanks of the fire into an extensive and potentially uncontrollable fire front. Journalists and their managers must be aware of the timing and direction of forecast wind changes so they avoid being trapped by a fire front. Learning how to use a compass, especially in unfamiliar territory is a potentially lifesaving skill.

CASE STUDY 3

Flood

Predicted climate change effects in Britain and Europe include more frequent and severe flood events. Current estimates are that five million people and two million homes are at risk of flooding each year in England and Wales (Crichton, 2005). This figure has arisen partially because flood insurance premiums were kept artificially low by an insurance guarantee, which resulted in many houses being built in flood-risk areas (Crichton, 2005). The cost of insurance premiums and who will pay for the increasing cost of flood repairs is likely to become a political issue and a topic of intense public debate. In Scotland, building restrictions are tighter. Local governments are reluctant to allow building in areas with a flood risk that exceeds a one-in-200 year interval (Crichton, 2005). Any repeat of major floods such as the 1953 storm surge that raised sea levels in Britain by up to three metres, would have resulted in costly consequences that may overwhelm the capacity of insurers to pay (Crichton, 2005).

My experience reporting on the 2011 floods impressed upon me the long-term consequences for those people who were affected. Research studies are beginning to validate the relatively high incidence of post-traumatic stress disorder many years after a flood event. In China, for example, 10 per cent of flood survivors interviewed 17 years after the flood had post-traumatic stress disorder (Dai et al., 2017). Risk factors identified in the study included exposure to three flood-related stressors, and a low level of social support. The researchers recommended early and effective psychological intervention for flood survivors (Dai et al., 2017).

Conclusion

Reporting on natural disasters is a solemn responsibility for journalists. Accuracy, timeliness, and objectivity are important goals, despite the often chaotic circumstances under which disaster reporting is carried out. Readers and viewers need timely and accurate forecasts, reports and analysis in the aftermath of events that for some people will be life-changing. Journalists reporting on a disaster must prepare thoroughly for their task well before there is an emergency.

Compelling stories of courage and survival, of rescues and tragedies, can be obtained by reporters who are willing to give their time to patiently and conscientiously listen to survivors who are willing to speak to them. Reporters who can set aside the feelings of urgency projected by news desks and chiefs of staff will be deservedly rewarded as they bear witness to some of the highs and lows of human experience.

Reporters who prepare for disaster reporting by experimenting with social media platforms to gather and hold exclusive information will lay a firm foundation for trust between them and their news contacts. Social media groups can be established according to geographic locations or in subject groupings, thereby allowing reporters to receive information directly from trusted sources who have situational awareness during a disaster and who are trusted experts in relevant fields.

References

ABC Radio News. 2010. "Residents airlifted from flood zone". *ABC Queensland*.

Bowman, Shayne and Chris Willis. 2003. "We media: How audiences are shaping the future of news and information". Virginia: The Media Center at the American Press Institute.

Brayne, Mark. (ed.) 2007. *Trauma and journalism: A guide for journalists, editors & managers*. New York: Dart Centre for journalism and trauma.

Bruns, Axel. 2006. "The practice of news blogging". In *Uses of blogs*. Axel Bruns and Joanne Jacobs (eds). New York: Peter Lang, 11–22.

Bruns, Axel, Jean Burgess, Kate Crawford, and Frances Shaw. 2012. *#qldfloods and QPSMedia: Crisis communication on twitter in the 2011 south east Queensland floods*. ARC Centre of Excellence for Creative Industries and Innovation, Queensland University of Technology, Brisbane QLD Australia.

Chanson, Hubert. 2011. *The 2010–2011 floods in Queensland (Australia): Photographic observations, comments and personal experience*. Brisbane: School of Civil Engineering, The University of Queensland.

Charlton, Kym. 2011. *Disaster management and social media – a case study*. Brisbane: Media and Public Affairs Branch, Queensland Police Service. Accessed February 22, 2012. URL: https://www.police.qld.gov.au/corporatedocs/reportsPublications/other/Documents/QPSSocialMediaCaseStudy.pdf.

Chas-Amil, M.L., J. Touza, and E. García-Martínez. 2013. "Forest fires in the wildland–urban interface: A spatial analysis of forest fragmentation and human impacts". *Applied Geography*, 43: 127–137.

Collins, Donald A. 2010. "Heading for a world apocalypse?" *Journal of Social, Political, and Economic Studies*, 35 (2): 242–254.

Cottle, Simon. 2013. *Journalists witnessing disaster: From the calculus of death to the injunction to care. Journalism Studies*, 14 (2): 232–248.

Crichton, David. 2005. *Flood risk and insurance ion England and Wales: Are there lessons to be learned from Scotland?* London: Benfield Hazard Research Centre.

Dai, W.J., A.C. Kaminga, H.Z. Tan, J.R. Wang, Z.W. Lai, X. Wu, and A.Z. Liu. 2017. "Long-term psychological outcomes of flood survivors of hard-hit areas of the 1998 Dongting Lake flood in China: Prevalence and risk factors". *PLOS ONE*, 12 (2): e0171557.

Duncan, Sallyanne and Jackie Newton. 2010. "How do you feel?" *Journalism Practice*, 4 (4): 439–453.

Earth Journalism Network. 2016. "Reporting on disasters". In *Earth Journalism Network*: Internews. Accessed 14 December 2018. URL: https://earthjournalism.net/resources/reporting-on-disasters.

Gearing, Amanda. 2004. "Greenhouse risks spark wide review of policies". *The Courier-Mail*. 11 September 2004.

Gearing, Amanda. 2005. "Welcome to the valley of death". *The Courier-Mail*. 2 June 2005.

Gearing, Amanda. 2006. "Teens have never seen a good season". *The Courier-Mail*. 24 February 2006.

Gearing, Amanda. 2007. "Dams are dry, no time to cry". *The Courier-Mail*. 5 May 2007.

Gearing, Amanda. 2012a. *Amanda Gearing Queensland flood collection 2011-2012*. Brisbane: Queensland State Library

Gearing, Amanda. 2012b. "Lessons from media reporting of natural disasters: A case study of the 2011 flash floods in Toowoomba and the Lockyer Valley". M A Research, School of Journalism, Queensland University of Technology.

Gearing, Amanda. 2013. "Why disaster survivors speak to reporters". *Australian Journalism Review*, 35 (1): 71–81.

Gearing, Amanda. 2016. "Global investigative journalism in the network society". PhD, Department of Media, Entertainment and Creative Arts, Queensland University of Technology.

Gearing, Amanda. 2017. *The Torrent: A true story of heroism and survival*. Brisbane: University of Queensland Press.

Gearing, Amanda and Hedley Thomas. 2011. "The seconds that separated life and death". *The Australian, 12 January*..

Guha-Sapir, Debarati, Philippe Hoyois, Pasacline Wallemacq and Regina Below. 2017. *Annual disaster statistical review 2016: The numbers and trends, UN Office for the Coordination of Humanitarian Affairs*. New York: Centre for Research on the Epidemiology of Disasters.

Henley, Jon. 2013. "Firestorm", edited by Katharine Viner, Lee Glendining, Madhvi Pankhania, Francesca Panettas, Jonathan Richards, and Mustafa Khalil. Australia: *The Guardian*.

Hewitt, C., R. Stone, and A. Tait. 2017. "Improving the use of climate information in decision-making". *Nature Climate Change*, 7 (9): 614–616.

Hight, J. and F. Smyth. 2001. "Tragedies & journalists: A 40-page guide to help journalists, photojournalists and editors report on violence while protecting both victims and themselves". *Dart Centre for Journalism and Trauma*. Accessed 5 May 2011. URL: https://dartcenter.org/content/tragedies-journalists-6.

Horridge, M., J. Madden, and G. Wittwer. 2005. "The impact of the 2002–2003 drought on Australia". *Journal of Policy Modeling*, 27 (3): 285–308.

Johnston, Ian. 2017. "Hundreds of thousands face starvation and death in Africa in the growing crisis no one is talking about". *The Independent*. 24 December.

Justice, C.O., L. Giglio, S. Korontzi, J. Owens, J.T. Morisette, D. Roy, J. Descloitres, S. Alleaume, F. Petitcolin, and Y. Kaufman. 2002. "The MODIS fire products". *Remote Sensing of Environment*, 83 (1): 244–262.

Letcher, T.M. 2009. *Climate change: Observed impacts on planet earth*. First ed. Amsterdam; Boston: Elsevier.

Maharatna, Arup. 2014. "Food scarcity and migration: An overview". *Social Research: An International Quarterly*, 81 (2): 277–298.

Moeller, Susan D. 1999. *Compassion fatigue: How the media sell disease, famine, war, and death*. London; New York: Routledge.

Naqvi, Ali Asjad and Miriam Rehm. 2014. "A multi-agent model of a low income economy: simulating the distributional effects of natural disasters". *Journal of Economic Interaction and Coordination*, 9 (2): 275–309.

Ochberg, Frank. 1996. "A primer on covering victims". *Nieman Reports*, 50 (3): 21–27.

Sakai, Y., J.P. Estudillo, N. Fuwa, Y. Higuchi and Y. Sawada. 2017. "Do natural disasters affect the poor disproportionately? Price change and welfare impact in the aftermath of typhoon Milenyo in the rural Philippines". *World Development*, 94: 16–26.

Schlesinger, Philip. 1987. *Putting "reality" together*. Second ed. London: Methuen.

Shakdom, Catherine. 2015. "ISIS vying for control of water". *The Guardian*. 17 June.

Shirky, C. 2009. "How cellphones, Twitter, Facebook can make history". In *Speech recorded at TED@State, US State Department, June 2009, Washington DC*.

Stephens, Scott L., Mark A. Adams, John Handmer, Faith R. Kearns, Bob Leicester, Justin Leonard, and Max A. Moritz. 2009. "Urban–wildland fires: how California and other regions of the US can learn from Australia". *Environmental Research Letters* 4 (1): 014010.

Stone, R. 1992. "SOI phase relationships with rainfall in eastern Australia". *International Journal of Climatology*, 12: 625–636.

Tait, Sue. 2011. "Bearing witness, journalism and moral responsibility". *Media, Culture & Society*, 33(8): 1220–123.

Tedeschi, Richard G. and Lawrence Calhoun. 2004. "Posttraumatic growth: A new perspective on psychotraumatology". *Psychiatric Times*, 21 (4): 58–60.

Torabi, Elnaz, Aysin Dedekorkut-Howes, and Michael Howes. 2018. "Adapting or maladapting: Building resilience to climate-related disasters in coastal cities". *Cities*, 72: 295–309.

Walker, James and Amanda Gearing. 2011. "Eight dead, 70 missing as flash floods strike Queensland". *The Australian*. 11 January 2011.

Williams, Jerry, Dorothy Albright, Anja A. Hoffmann, Andrey Eritsov, Peter F. Moore, Jose Carlos Mendes De Morais, Michael Leonard, Jesus San Miguel-Ayanz, Gavriil Xanthopoulos, and Pieter van Lierop. 2011. "Findings and implications from a coarse-scale global assessment of recent selected mega-fires". *5th International wildland fire conference*.

Zelizer, Barbie. 2007. "On 'having been there': 'Eyewitnessing' as a journalistic key word". *Critical Studies in Media Communication*, 24 (5): 408–428.

PART VI

Reporting cultural, ethnic and geographical difference

12

REPORTING "OTHER" CULTURES

Alexandra Wake

The social issue

The traditional language of the Wurundjeri people is Woi-wurrung. "Wumen Bagung Ngang-gak ba Boorndap" translates as "Come Gather, Listen and Respect" (Noske Turner, 2017). Despite attempts by news organisations to employ more culturally, linguistically, and socially diverse reporters, most journalists in advanced liberal democracies continue to represent a group narrowly defined by class and culture (Ewart and Beard, 2017). They tend to be highly educated city dwellers from the middle classes who have had little, if any, exposure to, or understanding of, the various cultural communities which are featured in the news. For a range of reasons (including time and format constraints, the convenience of visual stereotypes, and ingrained newsroom attitudes about particular communities), news reports can perpetuate damaging stereotypes about race, class, and gender as journalists inadvertently "other" certain individuals or groups of people, usually from cultures outside their own experience. To "other" a group or a person is simply to report as if "our" world is known and accepted, and "theirs" is different and strange (Gregory, 2004). When we create ill-informed, damaging, or inflammatory reports featuring stereotypical images in this way, we can reinforce inaccurate perceptions, add conflict to communities, and make bad situations worse.

While some media institutions are becoming more aware of cultural diversity and positively addressing it with successful recruitment policies (ABC, 2013), the stereotypical white Anglo Saxon, middle-aged male journalist employed by those institutions has not necessarily taken this structural change into his heart, mind, and practice (see, for example, the Media Diversity Australia response to radio presenter Red Symons' interview with Beverley Wang) (Lo, 2017). And yet the ABC is decades ahead of Australia's largest newspaper organisation, Fairfax, whose diversity policy is still limited to the gender issue (*Fairfax Media diversity and inclusion guideline*, 2017).

Importantly, we fail as journalists because, in creating our stories we can end up with biased reporting that does not give the wider community the opportunity to reach informed conclusions. The key issue in changing the negative impact our reporting can have on communities and people is to acknowledge our role in framing these views and to reflect on our news-seeking and news-gathering practices. Journalists who want to report credibly about people from cultural groups and diverse communities outside their own experience are required, in the parlance of the time, to "check your privilege" and question the assumptions that underlie their understandings.

Introduction

My formative years were a cliché of stereotypes. In the country town where I grew up (and started as a cadet journalist) I remember the white kids, the Aboriginal kids, a boy called Farook, one Greek family, and a Chinese one. The Chinese daughter worked hard and became a doctor, the Greek girls got married and started successful businesses, the Muslim boy left town, and almost all of the Aboriginal kids simply disappeared to the edges of my life. It wasn't until much later, when I moved away and began to meet and interview people who had vastly different backgrounds to me, that I began to understand that where and how I had been raised had framed the way I viewed the world, and therefore how I framed it in my reporting. In other words, I could not see that despite the best efforts of my parents to give me a world view, the way I saw the world was narrow, privileged, and filled with often hurtful stereotypes based on where I grew up, my gender, and my education.

Fast forward to 2017 and my children are amused when I say I did not go to school with anyone called Mohammed. We now live in a suburb with a big Lebanese community; my son had five Mohammeds in his primary school class. For him, birthday parties which only offer Halal food are normal, women wearing headscarves are just part of the crowd, and knowing how to distinguish one Aisha from another is no more difficult from telling the two Emilys apart. While we both now have an insight into Muslim people from a particular part of the world, it does not mean we have a full or complete understanding of every one of the Muslim faith. My son has never met a woman who has been forced to wear a burka (because her husband insists) and he has yet to be dressed down by a highly educated Muslim feminist who believes covering her hair gives her the freedom to be judged on her words, not her appearance.

After 30 years of reporting and training journalists I know of very few fortunate enough to have been exposed to all the people and variations in communities that they are likely to encounter as part of their reporting practice. Only a select few will have the luxury of being able to become a specialist in one culture. Even those who do know a good mixture of people – and might have in their smartphone contact lists the names Oscar, Linh (Vietnamese), Tainui (Maori), Jandamarra (Australian Indigenous) or Minoos (Sudanese) – need some guidelines to enhance their reporting practice, even if they come from one of those diverse communities.

I have chosen to write about reporting on people and issues from different cultures, because frankly many in the media avoid doing it for fear of getting it wrong. To avoid an issue is only to make it worse. I want journalists to do a better job than I initially did in my reporting, and for that to happen they need to have knowledge and skills. I'll outline some best practice guidelines, and draw upon news reports where it's all gone terribly wrong, or right. This chapter does not seek to cover all the world's cultures, but to give some useful tips for journalists encountering new cultural groups. In doing so, it acknowledges that groups are never homogenous. A feisty head-scarfed Pakistani woman who would make a progressive French feminist blush can be representative of Muslim communities. But this chapter is underpinned by the belief that journalists are likely to do a far better job of reporting when they stop to reflect on what they are unintentionally bringing to their reporting and, in doing so, avoid perpetuating stereotyped beliefs and values.

Who are from cultures outside our own? Why do we need to consider them in our reporting? It's not just people who live in other countries, people from "other" cultures are our neighbours, our friends, and our workmates, or those who live unseen among us, perhaps in outlying suburbs or even "hiding" in plain sight among "us" in jobs we overlook, such as cleaners, cab drivers, and ticket sellers. News reports about people from other cultures − or excluding people from other cultures − can have a profound impact on how those people feel, and also how people from these communities are ultimately treated. It can cause great chagrin if you call someone from Tibet, Chinese. Similarly, the Rohingya are often passionate that their homeland is in Myanmar rather than Bangladesh. When you consider that even the issue of where someone is from can be deeply traumatising, you begin to understand the importance of journalists getting it "right".

I do not wish to suggest that I have all the answers. Learning about people from other cultures is a constant journey. It was just a few weeks ago someone of Chinese descent asked me why we call the children's game "Chinese whispers" when she'd only ever heard it called "telegraph". Such a little thing in our language that can cause hurt. We need to stop, think about it, and change our language.

The research

The way journalists report upon various cultural groups and cultural diversity in general has a long history of academic enquiry, without much positive change. In 2008, McCallum and Posetti reviewed four decades of academic work in Australia and found that "journalists by and large resist the accusation that their reporting perpetuates individual and systemic racism, and research findings seem to have had little impact on the nature of news researching journalism and diversity in Australia" (2008: 121). They also note Cottle's earlier (2000: 10) examination of the UK system found: "… media representations of 'race' are a product of social and discursive processes mediated through established cultural forms; they are not a foregone conclusion and they most certainly are not beyond challenge or change" (McCallum and Posetti 2008: 121).

This chapter acknowledges that, despite a political environment in many countries that seeks to encourage clashes between groups, change can, and is, occurring slowly. Government and interested groups invest in workshops to improve knowledge of targeted cultural groups, and produce guides and training packages to help reporters, with varying degrees of effectiveness (Ewart and Beard, 2017). Evidence that journalism is changing is that you, right now, are reading this chapter. Stephen Ward (2010) points to the growing number of what he calls cosmopolitan journalists who have a global news ethic, who think beyond parochial news values to the global picture. These are a new type of journalist, ready with the skills and cross-cultural competencies to produce stories that can unite people and nations.

But despite all the goodwill in the world, and professional training, news reporters can still fall back on a range of biases that frame their stories. Even careful journalists will, at times, come under criticism for failing to be sensitive enough to issues within a cultural community, or conversely be labelled "politically correct left-leaning" journalists by strident conservative critics. It's not a job for the faint hearted.

This chapter hopes to give some help to reporters who want to create richer, more nuanced stories of our communities, ensuring that all cultural groups are included, particularly those who are often overlooked. In doing so, this work acknowledges that framing (Entman, 2010) can help to change the way audiences view communities simply by the way journalists cover the issues.

As part of the fallout from the attacks in the United States on 11 September 2001 (9/11) there has been a real change in the way many journalists report on issues of people from other cultures (Gregory, 2004; Hage, 2002). Since then journalists have paid more attention to the framing of people from one place, religion, or culture as "good" or "bad" with educators and newsrooms increasingly concerned about how their reports may exacerbate tensions in society and within communities. The idea of "othering" initially gained traction in the work of Edward Said (1978), where he argued in *Orientalism* that Western scholars had entrenched thinking about the world which presented the East within a specific frame. A quarter of a century later he clarified his words, to say: "There is, after all, a profound difference between the will to understand for purposes of coexistence and enlargement of horizons, and the will to dominate for the purposes of control" (Said, 2003). His work, and that of post-colonial writer Frantz Fanon (Fanon et al., 2008), have been particularly influential on those who seek to see journalists alter the news frame, and work in a constructive manner with cultural communities in a post-colonial frame. It is now acknowledged that journalism can be used as a tool to counter the alterity (otherness) of people from cultures under-represented in the world's news organisations.

If journalists want to sustain relationships with their communities so they can create better stories, they need to be culturally competent professionals. There are four general steps taken to cultural proficiency (*Building Culturally Competent Organizations,* 2017): cultural awareness, cultural knowledge, cultural sensitivity, and cultural competency. To be culturally aware, it is important to first understand what is our own "normal". By acknowledging what we think is "normal" we can see that others may see normal in another way. We need to think about our own culture and its mores because we listen and think about people's stories though our own cultural filters, those we have the most experience of. Unless we recognise this, we cannot understand the impact our view of "normal" has on our reporting and how, in turn, that hobbles our ability to accurately report issues of concern to "others".

The second step to becoming a culturally competent journalist is to gain cultural knowledge. This means both recognising and resisting stereotypes and researching a culture and its community's history to understand its current behaviour and position. In so doing you acknowledge that as a journalist you will be seen as having power over those you include in your stories. Acquiring cultural knowledge also requires understanding that people from different cultural backgrounds react in different ways to journalists, and may not have the language to explain what is going on.

Being culturally sensitive requires journalists to develop a strong sense of empathy, demonstrated by working positively with interviewees. Sympathy is not generally helpful, unlike empathy. Taking time to build trust with those you interview is even more important in communities that have had bad interactions with the media. Respecting those you interview and acknowledging the inherent dignity of all people, regardless of their circumstances, are core to cultural sensitivity. That said, it is important to maintain professionalism along with a humanistic approach.

You will know you are on your way to being a culturally competent journalist when you can interview people in a way that leaves both you and them feeling valued and heard. Your work with those within the community – and those within your news organisations – should result in the presentation of stories about those communities that make them feel appropriately represented. You will know you have made it when you are seen as a role model for others who wish to address inequality, prejudice, and cultural blindness.

Producing good journalism about and for various cultural communities takes more skills than just cultural competence and cultural humility. It also requires a journalist to work with managers and editors, often in a highly stressful, time-poor situation. One of the biggest contributors to stereotypical reporting is auto-pilot, when journalists simply fall back onto visual and verbal tropes to meet a deadline.

We know that good journalism takes time. For that reason many journalists are referring to the work of Daniel Kahneman (2011) who extols the advantages of slow brain thinking – which is logical, calculating, conscious, and thoughtful – as opposed to fast brain work, which is automatic, emotional, stereotypical, and subconscious. When journalists are constantly doing fast brain work, it is impossible to see stories that are right in front of us, if they require us to think more deeply, to go beyond stereotypes and other lazy heuristic habits.

Journalists are also increasingly aware of their personal biases. The #BlackDeaths campaign in the United States put a spotlight on the cognitive biases of the wider population. Journalists Tonya Mosley and Jenée Desmond-Harris (2014), working for Stanford University, created a training tool for journalists called "Bias Breakthrough: how to deepen reporting on race, identity and inequality". They draw upon the work of psychologists and academics to awaken journalists to a range of cognitive biases that can affect unbiased reporting. They point to some of the most common forms of cognitive biases that help us determine what we believe and what we don't. They include:

Confirmation Bias

The tendency to interpret new evidence as confirmation of one's existing beliefs or theories. For instance, a journalist who is doing research may primarily search for information that would confirm his or her beliefs. [NB: Confirmation bias also means we simply don't accept as true evidence that does not support our pre-held position on/understanding of an issue.]

Availability Heuristic

Judging the probability of events by the ease in which instances could be brought to mind. If someone sees a number of news reports about homes being auctioned after being repossessed by banks, then people believe the likelihood of this happening is much greater.

Halo Effect

The halo effect is a type of cognitive bias by which overall impressions of a person influence how we think and feel about him/her – she's beautiful, so she must also be truthful.

Anchoring Bias

The tendency to rely heavily on the first piece of information offered when making decisions. For example, your parents raised you to believe, like them, that 16 is the minimum age for dating. But your child believes he/she should date at 14, like many classmates. The anchoring effect leads you to believe that 16 is the earliest age dating should be allowed.

Consensus Effect

This effect overestimates the extent to which our opinions, beliefs, preferences, and values are normal and typical of others. You assume because you believe something, others do too.

(adapted from Mosley and Desmond-Harris, 2014)

Covering other cultures

Trying to be a culturally competent reporter can be extremely difficult in a busy newsroom. One way to counter the bone-crushing busyness of daily news practice is to deliberately use quieter times, such as weekends, to research, work on, and publish your stories on communities you want to support, particularly those who find themselves repeatedly victims of poor reporting. It could be wise to deliberately plan your story for a Saturday or Sunday when there is traditionally a larger audience for your work. You may find it's less of a battle with your editor to get a constructive piece of journalism run on the weekend. Don't forget you will still need to pitch it, and talk it up, but on the weekend there is sometimes less to compete with. If this isn't true at your news organisation, find the day, the time, and people who may promote your story.

Before an interview

It is important to #checkyourpriviledge before starting any story in a cross cultural context. Journalists coming across stories from other cultures not only need to reflect before pitching on why it's their story to tell, and how they can tell it in a way that avoids "rescuing" or belittling the culture concerned. We all have a backstory that makes us the people that we are. It might have been the reason that propelled you to become a journalist in the first place, but sometimes even a desire to help other people can blinker you to see stories only in the way you want to, with confirmation bias.

It's hard, for instance, to break the habit of portraying people as needing rescuing from people like "us". Try taking a moment to ask:

- Do I have a personal view on the matter?
- Can I manage my own feelings on this issue?
- Is this story or issue really about a particular group of people or a wider problem?
- What's the value of using, or ignoring, offensive voices?
- Are there multiple sides to this issue?
- Do all the sides to the story require equal space?

One of the biggest mistakes we often make is thinking that people from one cultural or ethnic group are all the same. People from different cultural groups – and sometimes within cultural groups – often have different ways of looking at the same event. In Australia, for example, Australia Day has long been recognised as the day the country was "discovered" by Captain James Cook and claimed for the British Empire. Aboriginal people, however, consider the day as the beginning of the invasion of Australia. They point out many earlier explorers and, more significantly, their own long association with the land.

We also need to be aware that there is always diversity and a variety of opinions within any group. Just as not all Christians are the same, those who follow Islam are vastly different. Context is everything, and without that context terrible tragedies can occur. For example, in 2010, a US pastor, Terry Jones, announced he would burn 200 Qur'ans. This action garnered international news headlines with few noting he had a mere 50 members in his small congregation (Najafizada & Nordland, 2011). Nonetheless the attention the media threw on his threat lead to global protests, including reports of more than 12 deaths.

Remember, when finding people to talk to, or feature in your work, portray people as human beings, without any undue emphasis on religion or ethnic background. If the religious element is important to the story then mention it, but make sure you do not lapse into stereotypes. And remember to observe respectful cultural behaviour while conducting interviews: should you cover your hair, shake the interviewee's hand, sit cross-legged, or only use your right hand when eating food in their presence? All of these questions can generally be answered with a quick Google search.

Do not just settle for the easiest spokesman or woman. There is a tendency among journalists to return to the same reliable person in the contact book for stories, instead of reaching out to different members of a culture or community to get a range of viewpoints. There will almost always be a number of experts in the same area. When engaging with a cultural community think about who has the right to speak, but also about whose voice in that community is not being heard. You may need to do some research to find out. If someone says they're the spokesperson for a group, you could ask if they were elected, or if it is an inherited role (like a Sheikh). Including how many people are in the group or community will give your story strength. The safest way is to ask the person how they should be identified in your report. They may want to be called "one of the group of 50", but elevating someone to a spokesperson may be a step too far. If they are speaking on behalf of a group, name the group or community and identify how they came to be in that position.

As Western journalists, we are used to insisting on passing police lines and getting into places that no one else can access. While in most situations this is applauded by our news bosses, when dealing with traditional cultures it may be more appropriate to seek permission to visit and to film what might be a private or sensitive event. Just as we would not walk naked through Notre Dame Cathedral, you wouldn't walk "on country" in parts of regional Australia without asking the local people, who could see the area as a sacred site. There are cultural groups around the world from Native Americans to Aboriginal Australians who do not want to be filmed at all. Almost everyone now knows that images of the Prophet Mohammed cause offence to devout Muslims, but in outback Australia even a rock can have a sacred significance and taking a photograph of it can be considered insulting. Sometimes it is in the public interest to go into an area or take images without permission, but making that decision should be well considered.

Starting an interview

First impressions count, particularly if you want to develop trust with those you are interviewing. For that reason it's important to get greetings right. You might think that shaking hands is a good way to start, however this tradition first started as a way of men demonstrating they were not holding weapons and while it's a popular greeting it's not universal. Don't forget, it wasn't that long ago that women did not shake hands with men, and handshaking still isn't accepted between genders, or even among all people in Australia. Best practice is to follow the example of the locals. If they hold out their hand, shake it, but don't offer first. If someone bows, bow back. And if a Maori wants to press their nose and forehead to yours, enjoy the cultural experience. Don't read too much into a lack of eye contact. What you may consider as demonstrating openness and honesty is considered rude in many cultures around the world. It may not even be a cultural issue. The person you are interviewing may think it's disrespectful to look you in the eye, or even just be too nervous to do it. Never forget that some people regardless of their cultural background are simply socially anxious, or have low self-esteem.

We all know about getting names right, but it's also important to ensure that you call people what they want to be called. It can be highly political, and part of the story. People from Tibet, for example, want to be called Tibetan, but the Chinese government will be annoyed if you do. Many First Nations people detest being called the names used by those who settled on their shores. Australia's Torres Strait Islanders don't want to be grouped with the South Sea Islanders who were brought to Australia as slaves. Check with your source, and if there is little agreement about what they wish to be called, it could become an important part of the story.

Always ask, is there someone else who might want to talk. You may assume that everyone relevant has gathered together. However, there are reasons that men or the women gather in different places. Remember some cultures do not allow men and women to be alone together. In some traditional Aboriginal communities, it might be an avoidance between a mother and son-in-law. In some Muslim cultures, it might be between unrelated adults of different genders. If in doubt about what is acceptable, ask in preparing for the interview.

Remember the best interviewee may not have arrived yet. Promptness can also be a cultural issue. There is a reason that people joke about "island time" or "desert time": many cultures simply do not have the same relationship to the 24-hour clock that working journalists must have. Realistically, in some communities, a story is going to take longer. Don't fall into the trap of thinking that lateness is being deliberately obstructive, it could just their way of dealing with time understood in that context.

After finding the right people to interview, don't rush in with your questions. The key to a good interview is listening. However, listening requires more than not talking. It requires journalists to truly consider a different perspective, to avoid just confirming our own preconceived views. Aboriginal Australians say "I hear you", but they are also saying, "I see you", and in doing so are acknowledging and respecting our words, our humanity, and our spirituality. It's far more than taking dictation. You may find you need to change your normal way of interviewing. While Australian journalists are well known for being among the bluntest interviewers in the world, this style of confrontational interview will fail in some communities. Rephrasing a question to be less confrontational, and more explanatory, could yield far better results.

Again, resist judging people because of their accent or grammar. A good journalist will test for understanding by asking questions or repeating back to the interviewee has said. You could say something like "I understood that you have no memories before your time in the refugee camp. Is that correct?". Although it's a slower process, this will ensure there is understanding on both sides.

Using a translator can be useful, but it's not without issues. There have been instances, even in formal court settings, where those fulfilling the role of translator had kinship relationships that interfered with their work (Goldflam, 1997). If someone speaks for ten minutes and the translation takes one minute, then there could be a problem.

Subtitles are sometimes used for people with strong accents on television, but this can be seen as insulting. Conversely, not using subtitles might make it difficult for a wider audience to understand the interviewee and thus cement an attitude that people from different backgrounds are just too difficult to deal with. Each news organisation will have a different policy of dealing with this issue, but ensuring that you only use well-articulated sound bites of interviewees, and using scripting well, could avoid or at least lessen these issues.

How you frame a story

How you set up a story, from the first image and the first sentence, sets the tone. Sacrificing important background and context for narrative and brevity can upset people. Sometimes your editor will say something along the lines of "use some visual shorthand", such as men praying inside a Mosque or Aboriginal people playing a didgeridoo or "just use the pictures of the bodies". But these images may be inappropriate for the story, and using them may reinforce sexism, racism, and cause great harm. For example, shots of an ISIS flag instead of a beautiful image of the words from the Qur'an will quickly change the meaning of a story to those who know the difference.

Behaviour based on personal or cultural relationships can sometimes be misconstrued. Don't assume, for example, that something you regard as "corruption" isn't in fact just an obligatory kinship tie. In some traditional cultures, in particular, there are often very important kinship ties that dictate how people interact, the privileges they have, and the obligations they must satisfy. When reporting on some Pacific Islander cultures, and some Middle Eastern groups, power and influence within communities is complex. The only way to fathom how this complex social system works is to directly ask those you are interviewing, although be prepared for a complex, or even deflected, answer.

We can make assumptions on the basis of gender about what people should or shouldn't do. That's not the role of a journalist. Our role is to report on what we find before us, leaving our assumptions aside. A really good example of gendered "assumptions" surrounds women who cover themselves. Many people in advanced liberal democracies are often extremely critical of women who choose (as distinct from being forced) to cover their hair. This denies the views of women in Muslim cultures who believe that covering themselves allows them to be judged only on their words and actions, not on their looks.

Similarly, if someone says "this story is only for women" (or only for men) then our job as ethical journalists is to respect that view, unless there is a pressing public interest issue that overrides the need to respect the culture. In traditional Australian Aboriginal cultures, for example, there are stories, dances and rituals that are associated only with men, or only with women. It would be disrespectful to film these and put them to air without permission of the traditional owners of the land.

Your reporting will be more accurate and insightful if you observe cultural idiosyncrasies. That said, do not assume that in being conscious of differences in beliefs around gender you should stop covering difficult stories. Gender violence in many ethnic communities often comes with strong ideology and rhetoric to inappropriately justify it. It can and should be in the public's interest to bring these issues to light, particularly sexual, ethnic, and gender violence and torture, including rapes of all kinds against children, women, and men.

Before a story is published

Every story needs pictures, and you'll get pressure from some newsroom editors to "use the best" first. But consider if the "best" truly represents the story you are telling. A scuffle among five people shouldn't be the focus if the crowd of 5,000 were peaceful marchers. Some good questions to ask yourself may be: What is the role of the photographer images in telling this story? Does it enhance the story? Could it (or the angle) be seen as racist? Can the photograph or images add depth to the story or provide a different, more empathetic perspective to the story?

Take a deep breath and think before you use an image of a dead person, in any circumstance. The news media can take an image and transmit it around the world in what seems like seconds. It may be an image of a poor refugee child with no name to you, but to someone in a refugee camp watching cable news or scrolling through Facebook, it may be their grandchild, niece or nephew. Showing images of dead people can cause distress, but particularly to some Australian Indigenous communities or even among refugee communities where family members are sometimes separated in distressing circumstances.

Always ensure that you are not putting someone in danger by publishing where they are located or who they are with. There have been examples where journalists, and those that they report upon, have been systematically targeted as result of their work. The deliberate tracking and killing of photographer Marie Colvin in Syria is a good example of this. If in doubt, check with the person you interview. If you can't, think carefully about using the image or identifying the location.

Before publishing, do a quick check that you have not caused offence, or that someone in the production process has not changed a fact or a name, or the cropping of an image that may cause an issue for the subjects of your story.

It is always valuable to ensure that people who are not used to dealing with the media are clearly told how and where their stories will be published, so they can be forewarned of what may occur and who might see it, even on a flickering TV set on the other side of the world. Be fair and avoid creating unrealistic expectations. People may think you are in a position to make their situation better. It is important not to offer false hope while explaining that you can give them an opportunity for their voice to be heard.

After a story is published

Consider whether you need to do another story. With some communities, it can be important to do several positive stories to balance the negative ones. Many communities believe they are only ever featured in the news media when there is a conflict or a negative issue. As decent journalists, we should seek to find the many positive stories across a broad range of topics and issues, and rely, for instance, on the stereotypical "great sportsperson" angle.

CASE STUDY 1

The "Apex" gang

Australia has become home to refugees from many parts of the world. Over the early 2000s there have been a series of stories where refugees from a number of African countries have been cast as the perpetrators or victims of violent crime in the outskirts of Melbourne. At various times, claims have been made that these groups of boys and men are more dangerous than other refugee groups. Dubbed the "Apex gang", the group is reportedly made up of Sudanese, Somali, and some Pacific Islanders and is held responsible for a range of criminal activities: from home invasions to people-smuggling with the most public event a so-called "riot" through streets during an annual parade.

Media reports often include lines like this: "African youths causing a crime wave in Victoria are the product of eroded family units, trauma and an Australian society which does not sanction corporal punishment as a means of keeping them in line" (Morton, 2016), and media outlets have linked youths from the "Apex gang" to violent crimes ("Teen arrested following Melbourne car chase reportedly member of notorious Apex gang", 2016). Most stories on Australia's Sudanese youths rely upon police and political statements which repeatedly talk about worsening violence and problems with integration. Many of these stories have been told using single photo and short (or CCTV) video clips that add to a feeling of fear of young people. However, some members of the so-called gang claim media reports of their "Apex gang's" activities are overblown and the focus on them by police is racist (Morris, 2016).

Tips from this case study:

- Consider the frame of the story – is it about crime or a link between poverty and gang recruitment?
- Ask yourself, do the images you have add depth to the story or provide a different, more empathetic perspective?
- Do not just rely on police statements, talk to criminologists for context.
- Ask is it really a gang? Or are police using language that is shorthand for them?
- Be specific with descriptors of those involved (avoid "African").
- Consider using the voices of youth and community leaders.
- Consider if the ethnicity of the person is actually part of the story.
- Be careful not to identify (or show in pictures) innocent bystanders.
- Check and recheck witnesses' statements, and ensure they are not mistaken.
- Check the statistics. Try comparing the facts to wider crime statistics.
- Ensure you do not cast all people from the ethnic group into the same mould.

CASE STUDY 2

The dog meat markets

Nothing divides a newsroom more quickly than a discussion of what animals can be eaten by humans. If you've been raised in a Western nation, it takes a lot of deep thinking about one's own cultural perspective to respectfully cover a story about keeping/hunting, slaughtering, and eating whales, dogs, monkeys, or insects. Each year, stories of China's dog meat markets appear in the media. In fact, dog and cat meat is consumed in many Asian and African countries. How those stories about China's habits are covered by reporters can range from stories simply about different eating habits, through to reports rich in hysterical stereotypical references to cultures defined by cruelty.

This case study has been included to demonstrate the importance of covering controversial stories that have a strong public interest, but with a warning to journalists to consider how their stories are framed, and to what end.

In raising the issue of cruelty to animals, it is important to ensure that generalisations about all people from one culture are avoided and that animal welfare spokespeople are quoted only on the specific cases. The consumption of dog meat does not necessarily indicate any more cruelty to animals than any other meat, but in reporting such cases it is easy to include the most graphic of descriptions of animal cruelty, as has been the case in a number of tabloid reports (Pleasance, 2017). Knowing where the line is between telling a story and considering both cultural context and audience sensitivities is important. Sourcing information from experts, authorities, or academics about humane methods of slaughtering animals would be useful for readers of this story.

Tips from this case study:

- Do not shy away from a story of cruel treatment of animals (or people), but think about how the story is framed.
- If it's an issue of animal cruelty, then state clearly the laws around the issue.
- Avoid labelling people from one cultural group as cruel; it is the act that is cruel.
- Consider if your objection to the practice is based on your own culture's view or something else.

CASE STUDY 3

"All Asian Mall"

In this story a television current affairs program claimed a shopping centre in Sydney was being overtaken by Asian retailers (McCormack, 2012). The story featured a cameo from Pauline Hanson, the leader of Pauline Hanson's One Nation party, known to have made racist statements about Asian people. The program used inflammatory language and visuals which were found by the Australian Communications and Media Authority (ACMA) to generate feelings of threat from people of Asian ethnic origins and language as it implied that Australians of Asian ethnic origins did not belong in Australia. The television program apologised for the story, including the racial slurs and inaccuracies.

Tips from this case study:

- Consider your talent carefully. There may be a perceived benefit (social media shares and hits) for the media organization in using controversial talent, but this may be outweighed by the station's need to maintain a level of credibility.
- Check your facts. While the changing demographics of suburbs is interesting and potentially newsworthy, in this instance the reporter failed

> to check the most basic fact on the number and proportion of shops owned by Asian retailers.
> * Do not use racist statements.
> * If you are asked by your editor to do such a story, perhaps suggest an angle celebrating the acceptance and cultural richness typified by the shopping centre.

Conclusion

Poor journalism comes from a combination of factors: cultural norms, journalistic decision making, what's happening in the world, and the efforts of elites to manage the news. While reporters can influence some of these practices, it is important to be upfront and remind ourselves that we cannot change it all.

Despite attempts by news organisations to employ more culturally, linguistically, and socially diverse reporters, most journalists in advanced liberal democracies continue to represent a group narrowly defined by class and culture, even as this widens journalists of any cultural background need to be aware of otherness and exercise and reflect empathy, understanding, and tolerance in their reporting.

It is important in our work with minority, marginalised, and indigenous communities to ensure that we avoid the "us vs. them" paradigm and biases, and create stories that provide context and understanding of the "them", often for difficult social issues.

As journalists we have the ability to create depth and moments of reflection around a story when depicting one event which is negative and is associated with a particular group. One of the benefits of living in an advanced liberal democracy and having some autonomy within newsrooms is that journalists can make news choices for the public good, and feed factual information into the social media debates that they mediate.

While today's journalists generally have an appreciation of power: who has it, how they hold it, and how they use it, they have less awareness of how their reporting impacts on communities and individuals in different cultural communities. Understanding power and using it wisely is vital for journalists who want to be excel in their work.

The author would like to acknowledge the professional editing by Rilke Muir, and feedback from colleagues, Dr Nasya Bahfen, Olivi Guntarik, Sonja Heydeman, and Gordon Farrer.

References

Australian Broadcasting Corporation (ABC). 2013. *Australian Broadcasting Corporation equity and diversity annual report 2012–13: Equal employment opportunity report to the Minister for Communications.* Sydney, ABC.

Building Culturally Competent Organizations. 2017. Center for Community Health and Development, Kansas. Available online at: http://ctb.ku.edu/en/table-of-contents/culture/cultural-competence/culturally-competent-organizations/main (Accessed 12 December 2018).

Cottle, S. 2000. "Introduction: media research and ethnic minorities: mapping the field". In S. Cottle (ed.), *Ethnic minorities and the media*. Open University Press: Buckingham.

Entman, R.M. 2010. "Media framing biases and political power: Explaining slant in news of Campaign 2008". *Journalism*, vol. 11, no. 4, pp. 389–408.

Ewart, J. and Beard, J. 2017. "Poor relations: Australian news media representations of ethnic minorities, implications and Responses". in J. Budarick and G–S Han (eds), *Minorities and media*. UK: Palgrave Macmillan, 165–191.

Fairfax Media diversity and inclusion guideline, 2017, Fairfax Media.

Fanon, F, Markmann, C.L., Sardar, Z, and Bhabha, H.K. 2008. *Black skin, white masks*. London: Pluto Press.

Goldflam, R. 1997. "Silence in court! Problems and prospects in Aboriginal legal interpreting". *Australian Journal of Law and Society*, vol. 13, pp. 17–53.

Gregory, D. 2004. *The colonial present: Afghanistan, Palestine, Iraq*. Blackwell Pub.: Malden, MA.

Hage, G. 2002. "Multiculturalism and white paranoia in Australia". *Journal of International Migration and Integration*, vol. 3, no. 3–4, p. 20.

Kahneman, D. 2011. *Thinking, fast and slow*, First edition. Farrar, Straus and Giroux: New York.

Lo, I. 2017. *About Red Symons*, Media Diversity Australia. Available online at https://www.mediadiversityaustralia.org/news/ (Accessed 28 February 2018).

McCallum, K. and Posetti, J. 2008. "Researching journalism and diversity Australia: history and policy". In F. Papandrea and M. Armstrong (eds), *Communications Policy & Research Forum*. Network Insight Pty Ltd.: Sydney, 109–29.

McCormack, B. 2012. *All Asian Mall*, Channel Nine, 9nine.com, Available online at https://www.youtube.com/watch?v=FEj7Bc3yAWQ (Accessed 12 December 2018).

Morris, M. 2016. "Melbourne brawl blown out of proportion, says Apex gang member", *ABC News*, 17 March.

Morton, R. 2016. "'Failure to fit in' feeding African-linked crime surge", *The Australian*, 26 July.

Mosley, T. and Desmond-Harris, J. 2014. "Bias breakthrough: How to deepen reporting on race, identity and inequality", presentation, Stanford University, California.

Najafizada, E. and Nordland, R. 2011. "Afghans kill 12 in protest over Koran-burning", *The New York Times*, April 2.

Noske Turner, J. (ed.) 2017. *Wumen Bagung: Communication for development and social change bulletin*, 3 vols., RMIT University: Melbourne.

Pleasance, C. 2017. "Horrific moment a dog is BOILED ALIVE and Chinese villagers rip out its fur in clumps before incredibly it gets up and runs away". *Daily Mail*, 3 January.

Said, E. 1978. *Orientalism*. Pantheon: New York.

Said, E. 2003. "Orientalism 25 years later: Worldly humanism v. the empire-builders". *Counter Punch*, 5 August.

"Teen arrested following Melbourne car chase reportedly member of notorious Apex gang". 2016. *9 News*, 16 November.

Ward, S. J. A. 2008. A theory of patriotism for journalism. In S. J. A. Ward and H. Wasserman (eds.), *Media Ethics Beyond Borders*. Johannesburg, Heinemann: 42–58.

Ward, S.J.A. and Wasserman, H. 2010. "Towards an open ethics: implications of new media platforms for global ethics discourse", *Journal of Mass Media Ethics*, vol. 25, no. 4, p. 15.

13

REPORTING INTERNATIONAL MIGRATION

Jeremaiah M. Opiniano

The social issue

Talents, workers in search of greener pastures, and people forced to flee their homes are among those who make up today's large-scale global migrations. Migrants living in countries apart from their own number to over 257 million. This demographic phenomenon also has its attendant socio-economic gains and costs, affecting families, communities, economic sectors, governments, and countries. Journalism – from news items to Pulitzer Prize-winning narrative stories – has long been reporting about migrants from their countries of origin and from their communities of temporary and permanent settlement. It is thus the mission of journalists to illustrate how migrants/foreigners/immigrants live their lives in two worlds. This is while journalists present evidence on how migrants contributed or posed problems to their new and old societies. Journalists will be oriented in this chapter on how to weave their way into seeking various sources, especially overseas migrants, so as to present a balanced picture of modern-day international human mobility.

Reporting about migration issues may have to employ zooming in and zooming out – from the family to a migrant's origin and destination country and back – since these are the levels where the positive and negative consequences of international migration occur. Reporters may also have to use a combination of field observations, interviews with various stakeholders (especially overseas migrants), computer-assisted reporting, and data analysis, some historical research and the getting of views from origin and host countries. Ethical issues that may face journalists here include being overly biased for the host country and not listening to various views from migrant groups, or hate speech in the guise of sensational or even investigative reporting. Journalists may even have to tread sensitive diplomatic discussions when reporting on delicate migration issues being handled bilaterally.

These methods and ethical concerns are suggested in the light of negative, sensational, and (some) hate-oriented reportage about migrants.

Introduction

A coffee shop in Barcelona, Spain may just be an ordinary watering hole for foreigners. But just stay there. Listen to the chatter of people walking by. Find voices resembling your race's diction, then language. Subtly eavesdrop to their discussion. And when you finally find a compatriot willing to sip coffee with you on a weekday afternoon, dip in and start a conversation (*Kamusta ka,* "how are you?" in Filipino).

Who would think there is a story in that *Bracafe* outlet at Ronda Sant Antoni in Barcelona's Paloma district? After the *camarero* (waiter) gave Filipino bystander Rodrigo his order, the storytelling began. This former *camarero* is jobless and is getting unemployment insurance. But that monthly amount or *paro* (covering 18 months) is not enough, and Rodrigo is hunting for a job. He is prohibited to work part-time while receiving *paro*.

His tale has the backdrop of how a host country is reeling from its own debt crisis that, like the United States, started off from a mortgage crisis. One of five workers in Spain was unemployed that year (2012). Job cuts reached some 130,000. Many local and foreign unemployed workers were on *paro*. Queues at the *Oficina de Empleo* (job centre) are getting longer. Under all those scenes, Rodrigo just wanted to have his Bracafe cup – just for a while.

But this 2012 story (Opiniano, 2012) was about how do Filipino workers and permanent settlers in Spain find ways to help each other out (*bayanihan*, in Filipino) amid this economic madness. A Filipino male passed by Rodrigo's table at Bracafe and shared a pamphlet about some job openings in *hostelerias* (restaurants).

There are more of these stories from migrants on the street. Grab them and share to the world.

This chapter is about migration journalism. Whether foreigners working or living in other countries are called *migrants, immigrants, foreigners, third-country nationals, expats,* or *aliens,* they are covered. Refugees and asylum seekers are also covered, even if the circumstances of their movement differ from economic migrants, family migrants, or marriage migrants.

This chapter is brought about by the author's experience as a journalist writing about migrants for a Philippine non-profit news service. What complements this journalistic enterprise is the author's involvement in social science research on international migration and development. Both writing experiences span over ten years, even before Facebook started.

Migration has never waned as an emotionally charged issue in host countries (i.e., countries that receive migrants), as well as in home countries where family members endure separate lives while rearing their families. American President Donald Trump wants stricter borders, the "illegal" migrants out, and the numbers of incoming refugees capped significantly (Trump, 2016). Australian citizens are complaining their country is getting more and more migrants in the last decade and wants a reduction of migrant inflows (Smith, 2017). European countries are struggling to handle the influx of refugees from Syria (European

Commission, 2017). Some Middle East countries have recent episodes of economic slowdown, due to low oil prices, and this impacts prevailing economic and immigration policies of countries (Kemp, 2016). How should a journalist, be it the local journalist, the ethnic reporter, or the journalist in the migrant's home country, handle all this madness?

Reading this chapter, it is hoped that journalists covering migration and international migrants will take away the following:

- An understanding of the global context of international migration and development issues, thus widening the recognition of migration's complexities by journalists.
- Knowledge of the actors in the migrant sector, both directly and indirectly affected by migration.
- Familiarity with the personal and (un)published sources of information on migration issues, these being products of verification.

The research: migration and development

Let us first discuss two types of migration, which the discipline of geography defines as "the act or process of moving from one place to another with the intent of staying at the destination permanently or for a relatively long period of time (Clark, 2003: 260). We have internal migration which is movement within a country. Contrast that to international migration which is movement from one country to another.

The latest data from 2017 shows that there are now 257.7 million international migrants, up from the 173 million in 2000. Refugees number to 25.9 million as of 2016 (United Nations Department of Economic and Social Affairs, 2017). (Take note that internal migration is obviously bigger in number, though global estimates are not available.)

The United Nations' Department of Economic and Social Affairs (2017) gives us a rundown of the geography of international migration, as of 2017:

- Some 61 per cent of all international migrants live in Asia (80 million) and Europe (78 million).
- Two-thirds (67 per cent) of international migrants live in just 20 destination countries.
- Some 157 million migrants worldwide come from middle-income origin countries. And of the 257.7 million international migrants, some 41 per cent of them (105.6 million) were born in Asia.
- The United States hosts the most number of international migrants at 49.8 million, nearly a fifth of global migrant stock. Saudi Arabia, Germany (12.2 million each), and the Russian Federation (11.7 million) follow suit.
- India is the largest origin country of migrants (17 million) followed by Mexico (13 million), the Russian Federation (11 million), and China (10 million).

- Turkey is the biggest destination country for refugees, hosting some 3.1 million of them (nearly doubled from the 1.6 million in 2015).
- More than half (53 per cent) of refugees come from only three countries: Syria (3.8 million), Afghanistan (2.5 million), and Somalia (1.1 million).
- Females made up slightly less than half of all international migrants in 2015 (49 per cent).
- The mean age of international migrants worldwide is 39 years old (United Nations 2017).

The total number of international migrants, however, only makes up 3.4 per cent of the global human population (2017: 7.55 billion people) (United Nations Department of Economic and Social Affairs, 2017) Some take note of this ratio to emphasize that there are not many movers worldwide, and that more resources are needed to move to another country (De Haas, 2010). The refugee movements are a different case, with refugees from Syria running for their lives.

Remittances are a major motivation for international movers. Data from the International Monetary Fund and the World Bank show that there are US$536.665 billion in "personal remittances" in 2016 (Ratha et al., 2016), referring to incomes migrants remit or send back to their home countries. And since the World Bank, in a 2003 report (*Global Development Finance*), had noticed the exponential rise of remittance flows, remittances were seen to be a major source of development finance to developing countries. Since the turn of the new millennium, remittance incomes are higher than official development aid and capital flows (Kapur, 2004). Economists observe that remittance flows continue their uptick or rise even if the home countries of migrants have economic crises (Ratha, 2013).

Showing here the numbers of migrants and the incomes they remitted provides the basic information of what scholars call the "migration-and-development nexus" (or links). But this phrase is where the issues come into play – at every level (micro to macro in either origin or destination). Journalists should note that migration is a phenomenon that has "gainers" and "losers". The gaining and the losing happen on both sides of the border, and occur even at the level of households. These positive and negative *consequences* of migration are also multi-faceted: economy, social welfare, family dynamics, peace and order/security, employment, politics, and many other aspects (Taylor et al., 1996a, 1996b; De Haas, 2010). Two tables below provide snapshots; though, they are not complete, extensive summaries of the consequences of migration on origin and destination countries (Tables 13.1 and 13.2).

Reporters in either the origin or host countries naturally capture the proximate consequences of migration in their immediate societies. So if locals of a host country protest growing immigration numbers and flows, the host country's news outfits will report these developments and capture host-country contexts to such a protest. News organisations in origin countries will naturally report about compatriots abroad. Nevertheless, a global understanding of the migration

TABLE 13.1 Consequences of international migration to *origin* countries

Impacts–origin country	Consequences	
	Positive	Negative
Economic	Remittances sent home, benefiting households and indirectly communities and the entire country	A home country economy's dependence on remittance incomes, then not diversifying income sources locally and overseas
	Brain gain: Current and return migrants bringing new skills to benefit origin community/country	Brain drain: Loss of origin-country workers, especially skilled workers – affecting a home country's competitiveness
	Less pressure on economic resources, especially for migrant households	Allegations of migrants "taking away" local jobs from natural-born citizens
	Some poverty reduction	Income inequality
Social	Reduced population density	Family-rearing issues given the absence of a parent or both parents
	Remittances financing human development needs (e.g., education, health)	Households' dependency on remittance incomes, seeming to promote laziness
	Increased social expectations, by current and returning migrants, for improvements at home (e.g. governance, public services)	Possible conflicts between non-migrants and migrants on supposed practices and norms in local origin communities
Political	Migrants abroad an electoral partner for home country politicians; migrants as source of home country politicians' legitimacy	Dependency on remittances putting socio-economic reforms at home in abeyance
	Home country policy-making and public services do not forget compatriots working or living abroad	Home government's public services feel the burden of reaching out to a globally dispersed compatriot population
	Escape from civil and political unrest	Depopulation of origin areas affected by war and conflict

Adopted from: a) Jackson 2015; b) Taylor et. al 1996a, 1996b; c) De Haas 2010.

phenomenon and its issues will help sharpen journalists' understanding of the contexts for human mobility and the many experiences that migrants can share. This situation forces the journalist to understand the other country – like the origin country/ies – and its/their contexts given this immigration-related discussion. Online research is a companion when going to a migrant's origin or destination country is not possible.

TABLE 13.2 Consequences of international migration to *host* countries

Impacts host country	*Consequences*	
	Positive	*Negative*
Economic	Contributions to host countries' domestic production	Migrants allegedly drain host government's resources
	Migrants taking up menial jobs that locals said to disregard	Over-dependency on migrant labour in some industries/sectors
	"Cheap" skilled labour for host countries	Not much of migrants' incomes are spent in the host country
	Labour "surplus" from abroad fills up host country's labour shortages, skills gaps	More people increase pressures to have migrants covered by public services (e.g., health)
	Training acquired abroad is applied in the host country, at no cost to said country	Language issues facing migrants may impact on their employment, social integration
	Work, business productivity in some industries with the help of migrants	Alleged work-related abuses of migrant workers by employers
	Migrants' contributions to taxation and pension systems in host countries	Complaints from nationals: migrants also have to be covered by social security
	Migrants form enterprises in host countries	Entrepreneurial migrants not necessarily paying taxes
Social	Multi-ethnic societies help promote understanding and tolerance of cultures	Aspects of local cultural identity seem to be "lost" given migrant influx
	Migrants can encourage the learning of new languages	Difficulty of some migrants to integrate in host societies gives them negative perceptions from locals
	Positive views of migrants' contributions to the host country/community	Racism and xenophobia
	Migrants filling population shortages in host countries' rural areas	Language barriers of migrants turning off locals
Political	Origin-host country diplomatic relations cite migrants' positive contributions	Illegal immigration and refugee/asylum entry
	Local politicians find migrants an electoral ally, a sector needing political representation	Calls for immigration control dividing people's, politicians' views of migrants
	Host country policy-making takes migrants' needs into account, not just locals	Migrants as alleged instigators of criminality and (on the extreme) civil unrest and extremism

Adopted from: a) Jackson 2015; b) Taylor et. al 1996a, 1996b; c) De Haas 2010; d) Organisation for Economic Cooperation and Development 2018.

Covering migration: stakeholders and reporting approaches

The primary actors in this storyline are migrants, refugees, and asylum seekers. Migrants are all over the place in a host country: restaurants, convenience stories, hotels, and homes. They can be successful migrants abroad (e.g., with gainful incomes, naturalized citizens, entrepreneurs) as well as vulnerable ones (e.g., female domestic workers abused by employers, male construction workers trafficked to working in plantations). Migrant families, whether being petitioned to join the migrant breadwinner abroad or staying in the origin country, are the extensions of overseas migrants.

Of interest are the intermediaries that/who can broker the migration of a foreigner. Labour migrants pass through recruitment agencies in either origin or host countries, or both. Some of them pay recruitment fees as required by their work contracts. These agencies may have to have licenses (either in origin or destination countries, or both) to operate as legitimate recruiters, not as fly-by-night or fraudulent intermediaries. Some permanent settlers seek the help of immigration consultants and consulting firms, which educate would-be migrants on the host country's requirements, visa processing services, and the concomitant fees. Some of these consultants may also have to have licenses or authorities from regulatory bodies in either origin or host countries.

However, the murky universe of intermediaries also includes informal agents. They can be traffickers, linked to alleged illegal activities. Others can be legitimate naturalized citizens of host countries who informally broker for migrant workers, for a fee.

Persisting to this day are mail-order bride arrangements for prospective marriage migrants (Cudowska, 2016). The Internet and social media have also been venues for migrant recruitment, what with multinational companies on the lookout for global talents. And as of late, extremist groups have civilian "agents" in foreign countries and recruit either prospective members of the extremists groups or wives for individual (suspected) terrorists (Bennhold, 2015).

Ensuring orderly, safe emigration (origin country) and assimilation or integration (destination country) becomes a mandate for another relevant stakeholder: government. Destination countries vary in immigration policies, which may change depending on a country's prevailing economic and demographic circumstances or on who sits in power (e.g. Donald Trump, USA; Angela Merkel, Germany; Justin Trudeau, Canada). These destination countries also implement domestic policies that cover nationals and foreign workers (e.g. work and employment, entrepreneurship, social services, education, etc.). Developed countries also institute integration programs to benefit early arrivals, young migrants and refugees.

Given that international migration involves at least two countries, and outcomes impact many sending and receiving countries, governments have been talking to each other. Their dialogues are facilitated by multilateral organisations, led by the International Organization for Migration (or IOM, recently made part of the United Nations System) and the International Labour Organisation (ILO). Since 2006, annual global dialogues on migration and development have been held. Particular reference here is the yearly Global Forum on Migration and Development (GFMD), a non-binding discussion by governments and civil society groups (including migrants) to put forward relevant migration issues. After a series of GFMD editions, the UN will organise a High-Level Dialogue (HLD) on Migration and Development in New York (2006 and 2013). As issues are discussed, these global meetings produce bilateral or multilateral projects related to migration. The high-level dialogues are occasions to put migration-related actions by states close to the UN General Assembly.

On 19 September 2016, heads of state talked about migration and refugees for the first time (i.e., at the UN General Assembly). Thus, after years of GFMDs and HLDs, the outcome here was the adoption of a major policy agenda: the New York Declaration for Refugees and Migrants. This declaration is said to be a "comprehensive approach to human mobility and enhanced cooperation at the global level". The declaration also dove-tailed with the current 2030 Agenda for Sustainable Development in which migration is target 10.7 in the said agenda, also called the sustainable development goals (SDGs) (International Organization for Migration, 2017).

Thus, international migration got enacted into the UN policy-making formalities after decades-long advocacy work and worldwide discussions. The outcome is the *Global Compact of Safe, Regular and Orderly Migration* (or the "Global Compact"), which is an intergovernmental agreement that will cover all dimensions of international migration, under the ambit of the United Nations System. As the consultation processes for this Global Compact began in April 2017, UN member states hope to formally adopt the Global Compact in 2018 (United Nations, 2017).

Civil society groups and migrant organisations (the latter especially in host countries) have also been major sources of information for journalists. Many times these organisations defend the rights of migrants, or of particular nations to which migrant organizations are represented. Migrant organisations are also organized according to various purposes: providing social welfare assistance to compatriots; raising charitable donations for their origin countries; bonding as part of a neighbourhood or geographic community in the host country; promoting migrant entrepreneurship in the host country; and many more.

Migrant organisations, especially if registered as non-profits in the host country, may be categorised as part of "civil society". Though, these organisations differ from what are called development-oriented non-government organisations (NGOs) focusing on migration and refugees issues. These groups do various functions like many other NGOs: policy advocacy, research and data-banking, direct social services, entrepreneurship development, community organising, networking, information and awareness raising, among others. Both migrant organisations and migrant NGOs are publicly or privately funded by all sorts of donors —national/federal or local governments, private companies, international development organisations, individuals, etc.

Academics and analysts from think tanks are an underutilised source of information for journalists. Many universities worldwide, especially in host countries, are studying the international migration phenomenon. These universities also do scholarly and policy research on migration, depending on the preferred topic of academics or the migration-oriented research centre. Given the academic freedom universities enjoy, academics may provide contextual and broader insights on certain international migration issues. Think tanks, for their part, are research organisations directly dealing with policy-makers but are not necessarily aligned to any university. Among the renowned research centres on migration is the Sussex Centre for Migration Research of the University of Sussex (United Kingdom), the Migration Policy Institute or MPI (United States), the Migration Policy Centre or MPC (Belgium) and the International Centre for Migration Policy Development or ICMPD (Austria).

Thus, when dealing with these sources, journalists may have to try their best to hear as many voices and perspectives as possible. Doing so can be done while journalists are aware of the various (conflicting) agendas of policy-makers, recruiters, civil society groups, businesspeople, or even migrants themselves. Whenever possible, getting the perspectives of both the host country and the origin country will help journalists provide a broader picture of the migration issue at hand and elude possible ethical issues (e.g., biased, one-sided reporting given allegiance to either home or host country).

So how will news organisations and their journalists make sense of these various local-to-global voices in the migration "beat?" Daily journalists housed in beats may have migration-related issues as one of the stories to be covered, but not as the main beat. Migration may also be traditionally lodged in beats such as labour, immigration, and foreign affairs ministries or departments. In this case, expect these journalists to have government officials and their official releases as immediate (even "trusted") sources. It is thus incumbent upon this journalist to find time searching for backgrounders offline and online as substance to the official government statements. If time permits within a day (especially if the news organisations require more than two sources), calling usual analyst-sources like a civil society leader or a migration academic/researcher can provide comment.

Explanatory or investigative journalists have the benefit of time to interview many sources, especially migrants and their families in proximate geographic communities (be it in the origin or in the destination country). Unless the news group is well endowed, editors may not allow their reporters to gather information in the destination country. Yet since the project is an explanatory report or investigative story (or perhaps a narrative journalism piece), forward planning is necessary. Map out the issue and its sub-issues. Identify the sources of information and the stakeholders to interview. Use the internet to the hilt by getting backgrounders and, more importantly, statistics.

The next section lists reporting tools and what can be done to harness these in order to package compelling, insightful migration stories.

Covering migration: reporting methods

Interviews

Whether a migration story is assigned to the reporter in advance (e.g. two days) or suddenly by editors, reporters have no choice but to prepare for interviews. Thanks to search engines, looking for backgrounders and previous stories becomes easy. So is conducting a background check on the sources: a government official, a recruitment agency owner, a civil society leader, or perhaps an individual overseas migrant.

If interviews are brief owing to deadline pressures, the reporter may have to ask the sources precise but challenging questions. However, if interviews with sources have the luxury of time (say 30 minutes to an hour, or more), approaches can be through the following:

a) *Government officials, recruitment officials, and civil society groups.* Much background work on the issue prior to the interview, and listing your questions, allows for crisp questions. Take note that these stakeholders are *deeply involved* in the migrant sector.

b) *Analysts and academics.* These sources may offer deeper analyses on a migration issue, even if their involvement in the issue's dynamics and developments is distant. Thus, the reporter can freely ask about the positive and negative repercussions of an issue being covered since analysts/academics-cum-researchers are trained to be objective in analysing phenomena. If some of their answers have a stand, act like a devil's advocate. If the reporter can also search online the research that the analyst or academic has written, this will give the journalist insights on the perspectives and leanings of the analyst or academic.

c) *Locals in the host country or in the origin country alleged to conspire in duping (would-be) migrants.* The approach to interviewing these sources is like how crime reporters deal with allegations against suspects.

d) *Allegations that migrants in the host country have perpetrated some crime.* For host-country reporters, such sources can easily fuel hatred between migrants and locals, with the latter a primary target audience of news organisations in the host country. A way to interview these migrants and refugees is to exercise tolerance and objectivity.

e) *Migrants and their families.* Perhaps nobody is nearer to feeling migration issues than overseas migrants and their households. If the migrant or migrant family is a case study for a "zoom in, zoom out" type of a story, cognitive interviews will be helpful. The objective of cognitive interviews is to capture previous stories by making the person remember moments or anecdotes in relation to the story. The reporter can feel empathetic toward migrants and their families yet s/he knows how to step back and assert the journalistic stance. And if journalists always exercise doubt in relation to "official" sources, the same can be exercised with regard to migrants and their families.

As mentioned earlier, migrants form organisations in the host country. But these organisations also have splits and internal differences – "non-newsy" backgrounds – of which journalists may still want to take note, especially if a migration issue affecting a specific ethnic community may divide this identified community.

The challenge in conducting interviews is how journalists will capture many voices so as to allow readers to understand various perspectives about migration. Overcoming this challenge especially applies to stories that cite only single sources (e.g., politicians' rhetoric about immigration) but with limited or nil views from other sources.

Internet research

In the pre-Facebook era, journalists used the internet to search for documents, laws, administrative issuances from government agencies, research papers, previous news releases, and statistics. These are still being searched through this day, though it may depend on the level of access to these documents. If inaccessible online, nothing beats going to sources to ask for these documents. Social media though opened up wider opportunities to access information. Social media can provide journalists story tips (from text posts to videos and images) or even analyses, as well as link reporters to possible sources.

Migration policies

The reporter may have to understand the overall policy landscape of international migration in the country where the news group is found. For example, host countries like Australia and New Zealand have points systems for temporary migrants wishing to become permanent migrants. However, while Singapore allows permanent residency, that country's migration regime does not allow for naturalisation of foreigners. Meanwhile, some origin countries may have more advanced programs and policies (e.g., the Philippines) or are still developing their policy frameworks and programs (e.g., Kosovo). One also has to note the existence of state or local-level policies and programs on foreigners that may differ from national-level policies. Examples can be found in the region of Umbria in Italy and the city of Dublin in Ireland (Lethbridge, 2016).

The policy landscape expectedly involves many government agencies with differing (and perhaps some overlapping) mandates when dealing with foreigners. If the journalist is dedicated to the migration beat, national and even local laws on foreigners/migrants/migrant workers must be understood. These regulations may even change quickly (not necessarily through legislation) in host countries. These changes may be because of economic developments that may impact on migrant intake (host country) or labour export (origin country), or because of public sentiment unto foreigners in host countries.

Statistics

One of the internet's benefits is the abundance of data, including statistics. Government agencies in migrants' home and host countries regularly or occasionally release migration-related statistics. Some data is even unpublished, and journalists access such information through their contacts. But what is of interest is the period of coverage of the dataset. Remittances data are released monthly in the Philippines, for example. Migration flows and stocks are annual releases.

Statistics can be used to see trends and eventually unearth stories beyond official pronouncements. The dedicated migration journalist here can employ the trick of economists: compile *time series* or *multi-year* data on a certain variable. Excel will be the journalist's best friend here, especially since government and multilateral agencies – in the era of open data, data visualisation and data journalism – publish multiple-year statistics online. The major data usually shared online are migrant flows, net migration numbers, number of refugees and asylum seekers, remittance inflows and outflows (especially for developing and developed countries, respectively), number of temporary migrant visas issues, number of permanent residency permits issued, number of naturalised citizens, among others.

- Search the main portals where the migration statistics are to be found in a country, as well as the portals of intergovernmental and multilateral agencies.
- Be regularly on guard when these data are released. If the archives of such data are available, download these.
- Data of various years covering a variable can then be put together to develop your own database. You are lucky if the data producers (e.g., multilateral organisations) have produced these databases for you. If not, your own panel database of certain migration variables will be the envy of even government agencies and academics.
- This database thus becomes your armour to generate stories. The data here are used as leads to develop your story, that which interviews, field reporting and observations can beef up. Your news organization can even use the database you have developed as a "news product" to be sold or subscribed to.
- If you are a journalist from an origin country of migrants, you can develop databases about your migrants in major destination countries. These data then become assets for your specialised stories on migrant compatriots in these countries.

Multilateral organisations have made available various statistics on international migration. These include the United Nations Population Division (under the Department of Economic and Social Affairs), The World Bank, International Organization for Migration (IOM), International Labour Organisation (ILO), Organisation for Economic Cooperation and Development (OECD), the regional development banks, and the national statistics offices of origin and destination countries. The "big data" era has also allowed for more accessible development data, like migration.

Then again, statistics on migration challenge the journalist to think critically: What do the numbers mean? What is the impact of the rising numbers of migrants on Canadian society, or on remittance inflows to the health of the Nigerian economy, or the continued exodus of nurses on the Indian health system?

Migration research

An underutilised source of information for journalists is research on migration, whether academic or policy research. Not only do academics produce research; civil society groups, government agencies, intergovernmental organisations, and the UN agencies have their own studies on migration. The launch of policy research is through press conferences and media releases. Meanwhile, there are also international academic journals on migration (e.g. *International Migration, Journal of Ethnic and Migration Studies*).

Treat migration research as *one of the sources* for your stories on migration. Let research-triggered stories on a migration issue spur debate and discussion; if your story on a migration study allows you to conduct interviews and to analyse data (like your database), let these sources illuminate research findings. If you are from an origin country and the ILO released a study in relation to global migrant workers, angle the story with the implications of research findings on migrant workers in your country. Insightful, balanced stories you produce on migration research findings may even make the reporter an analyst, especially since journalists have their own way of analysing phenomena (a nice complement to how researchers analyse the same phenomena).

Observation

But one of the best reporting tools for migration journalists is observation. This is a favourite tool of narrative journalists who are immersed into the universe of their sources (especially migrants and their families). This tool humanizes the facts gathered for a story and, if used effectively, can lead to engaging, compelling stories – from personality profiles to feature articles to full-blown narrative stories. Editors seeking for such observatory details in stories always ask journalists "where is the colour from your story?"

CASE STUDY 1

Best practice on multiple-source reporting about an under-explored migration issue

The long wait for young unaccompanied migrants in Italy by Giacomo Zandonini (an Italian freelance journalist)

link to English-translated story here: https://openmigration.org/en/analyses/the-long-wait-of-young-unaccompanied-migrants-in-italy/

The story is an example of how a relevant migration issue was explained by data, by views from varied stakeholders, and by voices from ordinary migrants in Italy. The freelance journalist was able to explain discrepancies in numbers of unaccompanied migrant minors given ground realities facing these minors. The views from a diverse set of stakeholders also helped illuminate the issue. Stakeholders, especially ordinary migrants, were even able to reveal geographic areas where other unaccompanied migrant minors may have passed but are unaccounted in Italian government estimates.

The piece won third place (print category) in the 2017 Migration Media Awards, handed out by the International Centre for Migration Policy Development (ICMPD) and European Union-funded partner organisations.

CASE STUDY 2

Powerful narrative journalism on a migration issue

Enrique's Journey: A six-part Times series *Los Angeles Times* by veteran reporter Sonia Nazario

Nazario won the 2003 Pulitzer Prize in feature writing for her six-part series on the danger-filled journey of a Honduran boy to find and get reunited with his mother in the United States. Thanks to resources given by the *Times,* Nazario and a photographer joined the journey. Nazario had numerous observations on her main character, Enrique, throughout the entire journey.

- The six-part series can be found here (reprinted by the Pulitzer website with permission from the *Los Angeles Times*): http://www.pulitzer.org/winners/sonia-nazario
- Reporting methods for the said project can be found here: http://beta.latimes.com/nation/immigration/la-fg-enriques-journey-chapter-six-notes-story.html

The story is an example of how newsroom-provided resources can produce good migration journalism. Being a Mexican also helped Nazario understand the context of such a typical migration story (i.e., the underground emigration of Latin Americans to the United States).

CASE STUDY 3

A legitimate story of a host country's welfare loophole fanned by seemingly anti-migrant, sensationalist language

Benefits Boulevard: Gypsies' gaudy mansions built in Romania ... with your money by Sue Reid (21 May 2011)

link to story here: http://www.dailymail.co.uk/news/article-1389282/Benefits-boulevard-Built-Romania--YOUR-money.html

This story by the *Daily Express* exposed an alleged loophole of the British welfare system. Here, Romanian migrants (referred to here by a derogatory synonym, gypsy) were able to access welfare benefits of the UK by becoming self-employed migrants. They become self-employed migrants by selling the street news publication *The Big Issue*. Started by a few, this approach has enabled some Romanians to not only receive welfare benefits for the homeless, but to send remittances to a hometown named Tandarei (a town with 12,000 inhabitants, located some 100 miles east of the Romanian capital Bucharest). Families receiving these remittance incomes from the UK are able to build concrete houses (reportedly worth £500,000) and buy some British-registered vehicles like BMWs and Land Rovers. The investigation reported that this scheme led Romanians to recruit townmates and issue bogus documents (birth certificates, photos of children, Home Office residency documents, and job references) so as to receive national insurance numbers, tax credits, income support, child benefits, and housing handouts. British authorities apprehended some of these Romanians who benefited from this "scheme". Reportedly, the leaders of this scheme are from a group called the Radu clan.

The *Daily Express* reported on this story repeatedly for several years. Reporting was done in both the UK and in Tandarei. It seemed that reporters and the newspapers did a good job uncovering this scheme by Romanian migrants. The Sue Reid story even had the benefit of having balanced sources, including Romanians who benefited from the scheme. The story is strong enough to speak for itself.

Unfortunately, an apolitical reader can obviously notice the language of the story as anti-migrant:

- Romanian migrants here were consistently called "gypsies".
- Words in the headline fan an anti-migrant tone. In print, the main head "You pay for Roma gypsy palaces" directly tells British readers of how these Romanian migrants allegedly duped the UK's welfare system cleverly. The subhead "Another reason to quit EU" is an opinionated statement. No text in the article talked about the impact of EU membership on the United Kingdom welfare system. In the online version, the headline "Benefits Boulevard: Gypsies' gaudy mansions built in Romania ...

with YOUR money" only sensationalises a supposedly legitimate story, tagging Romanians as "criminal".

- The Sue Reid story had these words and phrases that may be read as taking a malicious tone against these Romanian migrants:
    - "Romanians are gleefully exploiting our generosity"
    - "Gangs" and "gangmasters" (the latter referring to the leaders of this scheme to bring Romanians to the UK as *The Big Issue* vendors)
    - "Scam", with reference to the methods Romanians employed to go to the UK as *The Big Issue* sellers (though, a paragraph in Reid's story stated: "They are doing nothing illegal". What was illegal in the scheme was the issuance of bogus documents that led to the claiming of welfare benefits)
    - The final paragraph of the story is but an opinionated take against these Romanians: "Such a view perfectly describes the Roma gypsy people who blatantly use (*The Big Issue*) magazine to milk our welfare state, deprive the real homeless and have spawned a huge criminal industry".

Concern over present-day migration journalism

Migration analysts, journalists, and academics have expressed concern over current trends on migration journalism. Essentially, studies and analyses on migration journalism covered three major observations: a) much negative reportage and media framing on migrants, affecting public opinion; b) hateful language in migration news stories; and c) limited resources to gather and write complex migration issues with context, and leading to missing out aspects of the migration phenomenon that are not necessarily about usual themes like migrant criminality, irregular migration, or visible number of refugee movements (White, 2015; Allen et al., 2017).

The IOM gave special attention to media and migration in the *World Migration Report 2018*. Chapter 8 of the said report (Allen et al., 2017) revisited studies worldwide on how migrants are reported by the media, how do the news public (including policy-makers) view migrants given the reportage, and how journalists report about overseas migrants and refugees. The authors of the chapter note the political sensitivities of migration issues within countries which the news media may have helped fan into anti-immigration public sentiments and political rhetoric. Earlier studies, especially those of the International Centre for Migration Policy Development and the Ethical Journalism Network (White, 2015), confirm these observations (Allen et al., 2017). These observations were products of not just content analyses of stories in migrants' destination *and* origin countries (e.g., McAuliffe et al., 2015; Berry et al., 2016; White, 2015) but also interviews with journalists and some overseas migrants (e.g. Gemi et al., 2013).

On the aspect of published stories, there seems to be "unfavourable" news coverage of migrants especially in destination countries with high levels of human development. The unfavourable coverage was said to be twice more than "favourable" stories (McAuliffe et al., 2015). This trend on the tone of migration reportage can also be seen in individual destination countries of migrants (White, 2015). A related trend is negative words being used in stories: hate speech, stereotyping, and social exclusion (White, 2015). The hate speech in migration stories, especially in destination countries, then fuels politically charged views against foreigners. Though negativity is a usual story theme in journalism, whatever issue is being reported.

This is not to say, however, that migration stories are all negative. There have also been positive stories, including stories laced with "empathy" (especially during the height of the refugee crisis in Europe). Nevertheless, some observe that not many issues on international migration are covered. What still prevails are usual stories on migrants, linked to their alleged criminal activities or alleged abuses in their stay and residency in host countries. There is still a search for more stories linking issues in both migrants' destination and origin countries, as well as a more holistic approach to reporting about migration issues (White, 2015). The concerns over the "negativity" prevailing in migration journalism have led EJN to produce a guide in migration reporting (*see Appendices section*). This is because migration reportage, especially of a negative nature, provides outcomes like what usual journalistic stories do: influences public opinion, impacts policy-making, and builds either positive or negative perceptions about an affected stakeholder (Berry et al., 2016; Gerard, 2016; White, 2015).

What may have brought these observations in the reportage about over-seas migrants? Some studies noted the prevailing constraints facing journalists, particularly those in mainstream news media, when they were asked to give their views about migration journalism. For one, migration is a "newsy" topic – of high news value – especially when "something sensational and worth report-ing happens" (Gemi, Ulasiuk, and Triandafyllidou, 2013: 278). But even while there are some "human interest" stories being published, migration seems not a frequently reported news topic. And when the stories come out, the news public's association with migration news stories is about problem, conflict, or difficulties (Gemi et al., 2013).

Journalists and their news organisations are also affected by their economic conditions. The internet and social media have dwindled the usual advertising revenues of traditional news organisations (print, broadcast). Editors of news organisations also operate within a social context; not surprisingly, these editors' gatekeeping of migration stories also considers the prevailing political condi-tions in an individual country and the information tastes of audiences. There are also usual issues in the daily news beat, like trusting human sources (espe-cially migrants); (in)accessibility of information, data, and human sources; fre-quent deadline pressures; and limited resources to conduct enterprise reporting. Some journalists even admit that not many newsrooms have dedicated migration reporters, as well as a deeply nuanced understanding of migration issues (Gemi et al., 2013; White, 2015).

It is noteworthy, though, that similar issues can be seen in other social issues that journalists report, like environmental issues (e.g., climate change), agriculture, or the illicit drug trade.

Recommendations for better migration journalism (Ethical Journalism Network 2017)

1. *Ethical context*. Application of ethical principles, avoidance of crude stereotyping, development of good newsroom practice and engagement with the audience.
   - Accuracy
   - Independence
   - Impartiality
   - Humanity
   - Accountability

2. *Newsroom practices*. Editorial and organisational responses such as:
   - Having specialist reporters on migration
   - Providing detailed information and backgrounders on migrants and the positive and negative consequences of migration
   - Avoiding political bias and challenging "deceptive" facts
   - Respecting sources; granting anonymity to sources who are vulnerable and most at risk
   - Establishing feedback systems for stories on migration and on migrants
   - Reviewing newsroom policies to accommodate newsroom diversity among editors and reporters
   - Providing training to journalists on migration issues, migration law, etc.
   - Monitoring migration reportage frequently
   - Managing online comments about migrant reportage

3. *Media engagement and connection with migrants*. This will be through multi-sourced reportage, capturing the views and voices of stakeholders (including migrants) while posturing editorial independence.

4. *Challenge hate speech*. This can be done through a five-point test (*see Appendices*):
   - The position of the speaker
   - The reach of the speech
   - The objectives of the speech
   - The content of the speech
   - The status of the speaker.

5. *Demanding access to information*. This concerns pressing for transparency by institutions, especially government, when it comes to migration issues.

Conclusion

This chapter provided insights on migration journalism. Contents here may provide helpful resources and basic contexts to individual journalists (both affiliated with news organizations and freelancers) and news organizations (commercial and non-profit) when reporting about international migration. One should note that general contexts on international migration and development, and on migrants and refugees, take into account cultural nuances, migration regimes, and laws/regulations in both origin and host countries, particular patterns of migration flows (between a migration corridor, within a continent or between-and-among continents), and development conditions of particular origin and destination countries.

An understanding of the global content of migration-and-development issues was presented in the early part of this chapter. Presented here is an enumeration of the positive and negative consequences of migration on both origin and destination countries. While there is common knowledge and some empirical evidence on these consequences of migration, they remain under-reported. Empirical studies on these consequences may be helpful. For example, OECD (2018) recently released a study on the economic contributions of migrants to ten developing nations that are *destination* countries of migrants. A look at these ten countries (found in Asia, South America, and Africa) studied showed that migrants contributed an average of 7 per cent to the gross domestic product of these destination countries. This empirical finding brought about by research may help journalists in some destinations to do further reporting and have a broader understanding of migrants' contributions to host societies.

Knowledge of actors in the migration sector was then outlined. This portion can be linked to another segment of this chapter: Concern over present-day migration journalism. Sources enumerated here provide certain pieces of information, whether they are distant analysts or directly involved actors like migrant workers or refugees who just moved to Germany from Syria via boat rides. The challenges stem from the political and socio-economic environment where migrants are found and where journalists report about migration, as well as the level of knowledge of newsrooms about migration and development issues. There are visible concerns surrounding imbalanced reportage about migration issues, or the exercise of fairness regardless of one's nationality, or even letting the facts about a migration speak for themselves so as to present (hopefully) insightful analyses to news audiences. Journalists may easily fall prey to sensationalistic, simplified presentations of migration issues (Jacomella, 2010; Greenslade, 2015).

Finally, enumerated also are the types of sources (data, government records, people trail) for migration stories. Human sources enumerated here give readers an understanding on the nature and biases of these sources (also in OFW Journalism Consortium, 2003). Statistics on migration are a frequently used piece of information. Nevertheless, journalists may have to verify such dataset(s). Academia and published studies on migration are used less in migration stories; while exercising editorial independence, journalists can use findings from studies (e.g., scholarly journals, published reports by NGOs and multilateral organisations) to illuminate and verify real-life migration issues. Another under-utilised reporting tool is observation. Reporters skilled in narrative journalism, like Sonia Nazario of *The Los Angeles Times*, have the potential to powerfully present migration phenomena as legitimate policy issues, not just as mere tear-jerking tales.

Migration is a beat where a journalist's take on issues will be tested. This disposition by the journalist is not just influenced by usual editorial posturing. The nationality of the journalist is a factor. That demographic profile is the most proximate lens for a journalist to look at migration issues – as affecting her or his country, be it an origin or a destination country of migrants. Migration journalism unfortunately becomes an "us versus them" type of reportage, even in today's multi-cultural world.

The challenge for migration journalists, regardless of nationality or ethnic origin, is to exercise editorial independence, fairness, enterprise reporting, and balance. These elements of journalism (Kovach and Rosenstiel, 2007) remain the same regardless of the topic of reportage. For origin countries, how can journalism capture the views from the destination country and understand the contexts that country is in? For countries hosting migrants, how can journalism promote tolerance of and openness to diverging views while presenting incisive information that may even lead to editorial trust from both locals and migrants?

The journalist's obligations to the truth, to the discipline of verification, to independence from factions and from the halls of power, and to the presentation of realities with proportionality and comprehensiveness are among the hallmarks of good journalistic practice (Kovach and Rosenstiel, 2007). Actually, another hallmark is loyalty to citizens; in the case of migration, there is a "divided" loyalty between migrants and locals. So for reporting complex issues like migration, that loyalty to citizens means presenting varied voices and presenting a representative picture (Kovach and Rosenstiel, 2007) of the gains and costs of a demographic phenomenon – international migration – that has long been impacting people's lives.

References

Allen, W., Blinder, S., and McNeil, R., 2017. Media Reporting of Migrants and Migration. In: *World Migration Report 2018* [online]. Geneva, Switzerland: International Organisation for Migration, pp.190–207. Available from: https://publications.iom. int/system/files/pdf/wmr_2018_en.pdf [Accessed 28 Jan. 2018].

Bennhold, K., 2015. Jihad and girl power: How ISIS lured 3 London girls. *New York Times* [online]. Available from: https://www.nytimes.com/2015/08/18/world/europe/jihad-and-girl-power-how-isis-lured-3-london-teenagers.html [Accessed 24 Jan. 2018].

Berry, M., Garcia-Blanco, I., and Moore, K., 2016. UK press is the most aggressive in reporting on Europe's "migrant" crisis. *The Conversation* [online]. Available from: http://theconversation.com/uk-press-is-the-most-aggressive-in-reporting-on-europes-migrant-crisis-56083 [Accessed on 9 Sep. 2017].

Clark, A., 2003. *Dictionary of geography*. London, United Kingdom: Penguin Books.

Cudowska, M., 2016. Mail-order brides and marriage migration: A comparative study of the problems in the US, Great Britain and Ireland. *Miscellanea Historici-Juridica*, XV (1), 351–370.

De Haas, H., 2010. Migration and development: A theoretical perspective. *International Migration Review*, 44 (1), 1–38.

European Commission, 2017. The EU and the migration crisis. [online]. Available from: https://publications.europa.eu/en/publication-detail/-/publication/e9465e4f-b2e4-11e7-837e-01aa75ed71a1/language-en [Accessed on 20 Dec. 2017].

Gemi, E., Ulasiuk, I., and Triandafyllidou, A., 2013. Migrants and media newsmaking practices. *Journalism Practice*, 7 (3), 266–281.

Gerard, L. (2016). The press and immigration: Reporting the news or fanning the flames of hatred? [online]. Available from: http://www.sub-scribe.co.uk/2016/09/the-press-and-immigration-reporting.html [Accessed on 20 Dec. 2017].

Greenslade, R., 2015. Where media fails on the reporting of migrants and refugees. *The Guardian* [online]. Available from: www.theguardian.com/media/greenslade/2015/dec/17/where-media-fails-on-the-reporting-of-migrants-and-refugees [Accessed 9 Sep. 2017].

International Centre for Migration Policy Development (ICMPD), 2017. *How does the media on both sides of the Mediterranean report on migration?* [online]. Vienna, Austria: Author. Available from: https://www.icmpd.org/fileadmin/2017/Media_Migration_17_country_chapters.pdf [Accessed 9 Sep. 2017].

International Organization for Migration, 2017. Global Compact for Migration [online]. Available from: http://www.iom.int/global-compact-migration [Accessed 17 Dec. 2017].

Jacomella, G., 2010. Media and migrations: *Press narrative and country politics in three European countries*. Reuters Institute Fellowship Paper [online], University of Oxford-Reuters Institute for the Study of Journalism. Oxford, United Kingdom: Reuters Institute for the Study of Journalism. Available from: https://reutersinstitute.politics.ox.ac.uk/sites/default/files/research/files/Media%2520and%2520migrations%2520Press%2520narrative%2520and%2520country%2520politics%2520in%2520three%2520European%2520countries.pdf [Accessed 14 Sep. 2017].

Jackson, A., 2015. Migration. *Geography AS Notes* [online]. Available from: https://geographyas.info/population/migration/ [Accessed 9 Sep. 2017].

Kapur, D., 2004. *Remittances: The new development mantra?*. G-24 Discussion Paper Series no. 29 [online]. New York, USA and Geneva, Switzerland: United Nations Conference on Trade and Development, pp.1-32. Available from: http://unctad.org/en/Docs/gdsmdpbg2420045_en.pdf [Accessed 9 Sep. 2017].

Kemp, J., 2016. Gulf migrant workers will be biggest victims of oil shock. *Reuters* [online]. Available from: https://www.reuters.com/article/us-gulf-economy-migrants-kemp/gulf-migrant-workers-will-be-biggest-victims-of-oil-shock-kemp-idUSKCN0WS06Y [Accessed on 20 Dec. 2017].

Kovach, B. and Rosentiel, T., 2007. *The elements of journalism: What newspeople should know and the public should expect*. New York, USA: Three Rivers Press.

Lethbridge, J., 2016. *Migration and local authorities — Impact on jobs and working conditions*. Report commissioned to Public Services International – Research Unit (PSIRU) by the Council of European Municipalities and Regions (CEMR) and the European Public Service Union (EPSU). London, United Kingdom: University of Greenwich Business School.

McAuliffe, M., Weeks, W., and Khoser, K., 2015. *Media and migration: Comparative analysis of print and online media reporting on migrants and migration in selected countries (Phase II)*. Occasional Paper Series no. 17/2015 [online]. Belconnen, Australia Capital Territory: Australia Department of Immigration and Border Protection, pp. 1-43. Available from: http://www.border.gov.au/ReportsandPublications/Documents/research/mcauliffe-weeks-koser.pdf [Accessed 16 Sep. 2017].

Nazario, S., 2004. *Enrique's journey*. Pulitzer.org [online]. Available from: http://www.pulitzer.org/winners/sonia-nazario [Accessed 9 Sep. 2017].

Opiniano, J., 2012. Amid euro crisis, Pinoy "bayanihan" brews in Spanish café. *OFW Journalism Consortium (published in ABS-CBN News Online)* [online]. Available from: http://news.abs-cbn.com/global-filipino/01/01/12/amid-euro-crisis-pinoy-bayanihan-brews-spanish-caf%C3%A9 [Accessed 9 Sep. 2017].

Organisation for Economic Cooperation and Development, 2018. *How immigrants contribute to developing countries' economies*. Paris, France: Author.

Overseas Filipino Workers Journalism Consortium, 2003. *Philippine migration journalism: A practical handbook*. Quezon City, Philippines: Institute on Church and Social Issues (ICSI).

Ratha, D., 2013. *The impact of remittances on economic growth and poverty reduction*. Migration Policy Institute Policy Brief no. 8 [online]. Washington, D.C., USA: Migration Policy Institute, pp. 1–11. Available from: https://www.migrationpolicy.org/pubs/Remittances-PovertyReduction.pdf [Accessed 9 Sep. 2017].

Ratha, D., Eigen-Zucchi, C., Plaza, S., and Ratha, D., 2016. *Migration and Remittances Factbook 2016*. Washington, D.C.: The World Bank.

Reid, S., 2011. Benefits Boulevard: Gypsies' gaudy mansions built in Romania. with YOUR money. *Daily Express* [online]. Available from: http://www.dailymail.co.uk/news/article-1389282/Benefits-boulevard-Built-Romania--YOUR-money.html [Accessed 9 Sep. 2017].

Smith, D., 2017. Australia is full to bursting and must rethink immigration. *The Australian* [online]. Available from: https://www.theaustralian.com.au/opinion/australia-is-full-to-bursting-and-must-rethink-immigration/news-story/1611f29517fe65530b55d96737b1fe99 [Accessed on 20 Dec. 2017].

Taylor, J.E., Arango, J., Hugo, G., Kouaouci, A., Massey, D., and Pellegrino, A., 1996a. International migration and national development. *Population Index*, 62 (2), 181–212.

Taylor, J.E., Arango, J., Hugo, G., Kouaouci, A., Massey, D., and Pellegrino, A., 1996b. International migration and community development. *Population Index*, 62 (3), 397–418

Trump, D., 2016. Immigration reform that will make America great again. Available from: https://assets.donaldjtrump.com/Immigration-Reform-Trump.pdf [Accessed 20 Dec. 2017].

United Nations, 2017. Compact for migration. Available from: http://refugeesmigrants.un.org/migration-compact [Accessed 17 Dec. 2017].

United Nations Department of Economic and Social Affairs, 2017. *International migration report 2017*. New York, USA: Author.

White, A., ed., 2015. *Moving stories: International review of how media cover migration*. London, United Kingdom: Ethical Journalism Network.

World Bank, 2003. *Global development finance 2003*. Washington, D.C., USA: Author.

Zandonini, G., 2017. The long wait of young unaccompanied migrants in Italy. *OpenMigration.org* [online]. Available from: http://openmigration.org/en/analyses/the-long-wait-of-young-unaccompanied-migrants-in-italy/ [Accessed 9 Sep. 2017].

CONCLUSION

Further hints and tips

Ann Luce

Ethical Reporting of Sensitive Topics in Journalism has taken you through a wide variety of sensitive topics from sexual abuse and suicide to gang violence and migration, all topics that require careful reporting, attention to detail and respect for the sources with which we engage. This book has not been a volume about ethics *per se*, but you have read about the ethical practice journalists must employ when writing about difficult, complicated, and challenging social issues, issues that you more than likely will face in your journalism career. We each hope that the message is clear: journalists must report on sensitive topics accurately, ethically, and responsibly.

There are many academic books about journalism: how to become a specialist journalist, how to be an ethical journalist, understanding the culture of news, how to write well, how to conduct interviews, how to write for online, broadcast journalism, radio journalism, the purpose of journalism, the history of journalism. And the list goes on and on.

What won't be found "out there" is a book like this. One that takes you through those tricky topics that journalists need to cover. The stories that deal with vulnerable sources, many of who may be grief-stricken, in shock, pain, and the victims of violence. Or the complex and controversial stories that affect our lives on a macro level: health, science, environment, cultural, and ethnic and geographical difference. We journalists, who now teach journalism to thousands of students around the world, came together to share with you our best guidance, advice and direction on how these types of stories should be covered. We have each been in the position aspiring journalists are now: we have each experienced the pressure to meet deadlines, and the pressure to get the story first; we have all had editors that have pushed for ethical codes of practice to be just stretched that little bit farther; we have all questioned our personal morals and beliefs in relation to "the job", at one time or another. And we have all made mistakes, and we have all learned from those mistakes.

The contributors to this volume share what we have learned, so that journalists can be better prepared when faced with these types of stories. In the preceding chapters, we have provided information that should be applied to your own stories, whatever the stage of your career. In this concluding chapter, we want to share some final thoughts, a few more hints and tips. We hope you will find them useful.

Part I: Ethics, responsibility and self care

Ethical reporting

Prof. Chris Frost

- If something leaves you uncomfortable, then it is probably unethical.
- Be wary of gifts and freebies – is it reasonable to sample something in order to review it? What would you say if you had to pay full price?
- Good journalism requires boldness: challenge authority, especially if editors demand unethical behaviour.
- Journalists need to stand up for ethics standards.
- Does one really need to promise that source confidentiality? Would it better to find a way to show the credibility of the source?
- Don't be afraid to take advice, but also don't be afraid to argue against it if you believe it is unethical.
- Take care to think through the situation before doing anything in breach of a journalism code.
- Think the situation through carefully and, if in doubt, consider calling the NUJ or IPSO hotline to discuss the issues.

Self-care and wellbeing

Dr Lyn Barnes

- **It's good to talk.**
  Talk to a colleague. Find a mentor or a colleague; even if it is a virtual friend. Young journalists are being encouraged to discuss their feelings openly as a way of processing the unpleasant side of their work (Duncan and Newton, 2010), and to deal with what Rentschler (2010) has described as "the emotional burdens of their work lives" (2010; 448). Unlike police, who now have compulsory counselling especially if they work in child abuse for a concentrated period of time, journalists do not. But it demonstrates that cultures can change.
- **Encourage in-house training** (such as discussion and support in newsrooms). Regular in-house training sessions could provide an opportunity to distribute information within newsrooms and also highlight where to get appropriate help for stress, anxiety, or depression. News organisations

need to be more pro-active in providing help for journalists. Hopper and Huxford's study (2015) concluded that there is a need for specific training for journalists who deal with emotionally charged situations.

- It seems that although journalists are learning the language necessary to cover mental health in the community, they don't always use it on themselves (Jones, 2014). It is time to discuss it in the workplace.
- **Don't be a bystander**
  Be alert to the discomfort levels of colleagues and do something about it! A lack of intervention is called bystander apathy or bystander effect (Darley and Latané, 1968). This social psychological phenomenon prevents others from stepping in to assist someone who may be distressed or being bullied. Bystander apathy or effect suggests that other journalists might deliberately choose not to intervene when they observe irrational or out-of-character behaviour, often by not comprehending the effects of secondary stress or believing it is up to management to step in if necessary.

  Check out the **Dart website** for tips to protect your mental health **www.dartcenter.org** Because of the traditional lack of support in newsrooms, the Dart Center supports the argument that journalists need to take responsibility for looking after themselves.

The Dart Center for Journalism and Trauma, based at the Columbia University Graduate School of Journalism in New York, was set up to foster informed, innovative and ethical news reporting on violence, conflict, and tragedy. Established in 1999, Dart is now a resource base for journalism educators, graduates, working journalists, and media managers.

Part II: Reporting sensitive topics

Reporting child sexual abuse

Dr Amanda Gearing

- Give victims of abuse the agency to speak or not speak to the media. Never pressure a victim into giving an interview they do not want to give.
- Once you have a story, give the individual time to consider the personal ramifications regarding media coverage. Be willing to drop the story if an individual changes their mind about publication.
- Check all facts and details carefully and rely on primary documentary evidence whenever possible, such as letters, statements, or photographs.
- Do not identify victims of child sexual abuse by name in a story unless they sign a statement that they are willing to be publicly named.

- Do not identify an alleged perpetrator of abuse by name unless you have incontrovertible evidence, and they have been given a right of reply, or they have been found guilty or pleaded guilty in a court.
- Tell your manager about any potential legal issues and ensure your story is thoroughly checked for legal issues before publication.

Reporting suicide

Dr Ann Luce

- Do not use the phrase "committed suicide". Try "died-by-suicide", "killed themselves", "took their own life". The phrase "committed suicide" is steeped in historical concepts of criminality. It is not a crime to take your own life (in most Western countries).
- Be sure to provide accurate and clear information in a sidebar (or pull-out box) that accompanies a story on where people can seek help, e.g. Samaritans (UK/Ireland), Lifeline/Veteran's Crisis Line/The Trevor Project (USA), Lifeline/Kids Helpline/Beyond Blue (Australia), Lifeline/Suicide Crisis Hotline (New Zealand).
- Do not explicitly describe the method used in the suicide. Detailed description and/or discussion of the method should be avoided as this will increase the likelihood that a vulnerable person will copy the method used. For example, in the case of an overdose, *Do not* detail the brand/name, nature, quantity, or combination of drugs taken, or how they were obtained.
- Do not use sensationalised headlines. There may be an editorial diktat to try and attract more readers with bold headlines, but avoid stating the method and the location of the suicide. If not writing the headline, be sure to check it, or work with your copy-editor or sub-editor, before it goes to print. Many careful stories on suicide have become unhelpful and detrimental due to a poorly phrased headline.
- Think twice before interviewing family and friends bereaved by suicide – would you want to be interviewed in the hours following the suicide of a loved one? Take extreme care and caution when interviewing someone bereaved by suicide – they could be in a crisis situation themselves. (This is not like interviewing someone who has lost a loved one in a car accident, or to a murder.) People bereaved by suicide are at an increased risk of suicide or self-harm while dealing with grief. Respect for privacy should take precedence. That said, those bereaved by suicide can serve as useful sources when writing a story about educating communities about suicide, but these should be volunteers, rather than door-stepped.
- Be careful when using photographs, video footage, digital media links, or social media in suicide reporting. Explicit permission should be obtained from family members, as publication of these items can cause great distress

and further propagate a crisis for the bereaved. Do not publish material linked to the location of the suicide. Do not publish suicide notes, final text messages, social media posts and emails from the deceased individual.

- Download, read and reference the World Health Organisation Guidelines for Reporting on Suicide: http://www.who.int/mental_health/suicide-prevention/resource_booklet_2017/en/
- For more guidance on reporting suicide, check out Mindframe, Australia's National Media Initiative for reporting suicide responsibly: http://www.mindframe-media.info/home/resource-downloads/media-resources

Part III: Reporting violence

Reporting mass shootings

Glynn Greensmith

This open letter to all US media outlets was published after the worst (at time of writing) mass shooting in US history, in Las Vegas (1 October 2017). It is signed by 149 experts on mass shootings, this author included, and details four simple steps related to best practices when reporting crimes of this type.

By changing the script, we can save lives. That is the power of ethical journalism.

October 2, 2017

Dear Members of the Media,

We are scholars, professors, and law enforcement professionals who have collectively studied mass shooters, school shooters, workplace shooters, active shooters, mass murderers, terrorists, and other perpetrators of crime.

We strongly urge you to take a principled stand in your future coverage of mass killers that could potentially save lives:

1. Don't name the perpetrator.
2. Don't use photos or likenesses of the perpetrator.
3. Stop using the names, photos, or likenesses of past perpetrators.
4. Report everything else about these crimes in as much detail as desired.

We agree – and believe you will as well – that the particular sequence of letters that make up offenders' names, and the particular configuration of bones, cartilage, and flesh that make up offenders' faces are among the least newsworthy details about them. That information itself tells us nothing, and has no inherent value. However, by reporting everything else about these crimes in as much detail as desired, you can continue to fulfill your responsibility to the public.

As scholars, professors, and law enforcement professionals, we do not agree on everything. Some of us believe that by denying mass shooters fame, we would deter some future fame-seekers from attacking. Some of us believe that by no longer creating de facto celebrities out of killers, we would reduce contagion and copycat effects. Some of us believe that by no longer rewarding the deadliest offenders with the most personal attention, we would reduce the competition among them to maximize victim fatalities.

However, all of us agree that it is important to stop giving fame-seeking mass shooters the personal attention they want. This sentiment has already been echoed by many members of the United States government, the law enforcement community, and the media itself.

We recognize that there are exceptional cases, such as during the search for an escaped suspect, when the publication of that individual's name and image may be temporarily necessary. However, we believe that in the vast majority of cases, the media can easily adhere to the guidelines stated above.

There is already precedent for this approach: the media typically does not broadcast fans who run on the field during professional sporting events, does not publish the names of sexual assault victims, and does not publish the names of underage mass shooters who attack in Canada, where such information is already kept confidential.

We hope that as members of the media, you are ready to take a stand, adopt the measures listed above, and encourage your colleagues to do the same. The costs would be minimal, and the benefit is that you could literally save lives.

Reporting urban violence and gangs

Dr Mathew Charles

- Do not judge those who have perpetrated violence or committed murder and other serious crimes. Remain as objective as possible and do not let one's own prejudices show. Treat contributors who have committed violent acts in the same way as you treat other interviewees. This does not mean that awkward or difficult question should not be asked, but think about tone and tenor when one does so. Most importantly, listen.
- Never pay for an interview or for information.
- Do not patronise victims or survivors and their relatives.
- Take every possible measure to protect your sources and be careful with guarantees of anonymity.
- Do not pretend to be a friend. Be honest about the purpose of your work and do not take sides with rival factions.
- Do not provide information on factions to their rivals.
- Do not promise that one's work will not be seen in the country one is working in. People can often be scared to contribute for fear of repercussion. It can be tempting to tell them that the work is for publication in another country, and that it will not be seen or read in the local context, but never forget the affordances and reach of the internet.
- Do not overplay the potential impact of one's journalism.

- Be prepared before visiting hostile environments and conduct thorough risk assessments. If one is a freelancer, use the Reporters Without Borders safety booklet for advice (available here: https://rsf.org/sites/default/files/2015-rsf-safety-guide-for-journalists.pdf).
- Take steps to protect oneself, both physically and digitally. Refer to The Intercept's guidance on digital surveillance, available here: https://medium.com/theintercept/surveillance-self-defense-for-journalists-ce627e332db6.

Part IV: Reporting health

Reporting critical health journalism

Dr John Lister

- There are a wide variety of free-to-access internet resources available that can provide guidance for journalists new to the health beat or those wishing to hone their skills, with resources, and online courses. One website combines a number of these, including links to the Project HeaRT materials and is free to use for registered users (www.europeanhealthjournalism.com.).
- The 2014 e-book First Do No Harm (Lister 2014) is not free but offers guidance from a number of health journalists and a wealth of live online links to additional material and potential sources.
- For journalists covering medical topics and new drugs and research, a free primer on epidemiology is available to download from the World Health Organisation.
- healthnewsreview.org has a simple ten-point checklist of questions to ask about new medical treatments.
- A resource identifying flawed research can be found at retractionwatch.com.
- For more guidance on reporting health policy issues and a better understanding of the government's role in healthcare, begin by checking out the Top Ten Questions for Health Policy Journalists, available here: http://www.europeanhealthjournalism.com/pdf/ten-points.pdf

Part V: Reporting science and the environment

Reporting controversial science

Dr Shelley Thompson and Hilary Stepien

- Journalists can play an important role in correcting errors, and dispelling myths and misinformation about science in other media (e.g., social media). This could be a useful opportunity to identify news stories for publication or as part of news on the broader topic.

- The World Federation of Science Journalists (WFSJ is a not-for-profit NGO that represents science journalists' associations and encourages informed and critical coverage of science and stories in related fields. It promotes best practice in science journalism and supports journalists via education, training, and mentorship (among other methods). (available here: http://www.wfsj.org).
- The Royal Statistical Society provides journalists with a number of helpful resources, including free online (self-guided) courses to help you improve your work on stories involving science and statistics (https://www.statslife.org.uk/resources/for-journalists).
- Science for Journalists (http://www.statslife.org.uk/rss-resources/science/story_html5.html?lms=1) teaches learners essentials about science (how it works and is communicated) and how to write about it better (where health and science stories begin, finding appropriate experts, questions to ask).
- Journalist's Resource is a website published by the Shorenstein Centre on Media, Politics and Public Policy at Harvard University. It curates the latest academic research on a number of topics, including science, relevant to journalists. The centre believes that peer-reviewed research can help reporters better navigate controversial topics and competing truth claims. (https://journalistsresource.org/studies/society/public-health)
- The Social Research Association (the professional membership body for social researchers) identifies a number of the main fact-checking organisations and websites at: http://the-sra.org.uk/sra_resources/fact-checking/. Several of the resources listed are specific to science.
- The Science Media Centre is a charity that describes itself as an independent press office to provide news media with information and resources to cover science and scientific issues, including fact sheets, briefings, access to experts, and analyses of new research studies to help journalists with the meaning and implications of the latest developments in science. (http://www.sciencemediacentre.org)

Reporting climate change

Robert Wyss

- One of the best guides on reporting on climate change has been prepared by the Society of Environmental Journalists and can be found here: http://www.sej.org/initiatives/climate-change/overview.
- Climate change has become an issue worthy of daily stories. News organizations that specialize in daily coverage include: Climate Central, ClimateDesk, ClimateWire, and Daily Climate.

- The individual most closely tied to the issue is former US Vice President Al Gore, who authored Earth in the Balance in 1992, helped create the documentary An Inconvenient Truth in 2006 and with the IPCC won the Nobel Peace Prize in 2007.
- Art and culture have discovered climate change. Noteworthy fiction: *Bone Clocks* by David Mitchell; *Flight Behavior* by Barbara Kingsolver; *The Sea and the Summer* by George Turner; and *The Year of the Flood* by Margaret Atwood.
- Noteworthy (but not always good) films on climate change: Interstellar, 2014; Snowpiercer, 2013; The Day After Tomorrow, 2004; and Waterworld, 1995.
- Inspiring longform journalism in varying media about climate change would include: Every Other Breath by the *Charleston Post & Gazette*; Meltdown, Terror at the Top of the World, *InsideClimate News* and *Vice*; and Our Rising Oceans, *Vice*.
- The United Nations Framework Convention on Climate Changes monitors and schedules future meetings of the world's public policy-makers. The IPCC schedules future meetings and reports of the world's climate scientists.

Reporting disasters in the digital age

Dr Amanda Gearing

- Establish emergency contacts in each location one may cover.
- Keep digital and hard copy contact phone numbers and email addresses including after hour numbers for key stakeholders:
  - Bureau of meteorology
  - Police; fire; ambulance; helicopter/coastguard rescue services
  - Mayor; members of parliament
  - Schools; hospitals; aged care homes
  - Transport authorities – road, rail and air
- For emergency services, keep direct contact numbers for operational personnel including police officers, firefighters, ambulance officers, communications room staff, helicopter rescue crews, fire spotter plane crews.
- Ensure one has a portable phone charger for times when there is no access to electricity.
- Be familiar with the online amateur weather and climate communities. These groups can often provide detailed local knowledge of vulnerable areas and updates on the possible on-ground impact of a forecast severe weather event.
- Be aware of existing hotspots for particular risks in the geographic areas that a media outlet covers: for example, critical infrastructure, highways and rail bridges that are vulnerable to flooding.

Part VI: Reporting cultural, ethnic, and geographic difference

Reporting international migration

Dr Jeremaiah M. Opiniano

- The Ethical Journalism Network (EJN) has provided a set of resources for migration journalists worldwide on doing responsible, fair, ethical migration journalism: https://ethicaljournalismnetwork.org/
    - The Five-point Guide for Migration Reporting
    - The Five-point Test for Hate-Speech
    - Moving Stories: International Review of How Media Cover Migration lists recommendations for better migration journalism and useful links for journalists.
- Other resources listed below may be of good use for journalists, especially when it comes to understanding migration policy:
    - "Eight practical tips for migration coverage," from the purview of a government source involved in migration – see https://europeanjournalists.org/blog/2016/11/28/8-practical-tips-for-migration-coverage/
- "Covering immigrants and immigration: Tips from experts" by Columbia University's Dart Center for Journalism and Trauma, https://dartcenter.org/content/covering-immigrants-immigration-tips-from-experts
    - "Reporting on refugees: Tips on covering the crisis" also by the Dart Center (https://dartcenter.org/resources/reporting-refugees-tips-covering-crisis)
- Global Migration Data Analysis Centre (GMDAC) by the International Organisation for Migration (https://gmdac.iom.int/)
- United Nations Global Migration Database (https://esa.un.org/unmigration/) and the Migration Data Portal (https://migrationdataportal.org/about)
- Global Forum on Migration and Development or GFMD (www.gfmd.org)

INDEX

Note: Page numbers in italics indicate figures. Page numbers in bold indicate tables.